WEST'S LAW OF

WEST'S LAW OF

DILAPIDATIONS

NINTH EDITION

BY

PF SMITH, BCL, MA,

Lecturer in law,
University of Reading

Visiting Lecturer
College of Estate Management

With a Foreword by

PW Huntsman, BSc, FRICS

Principal, College of Estate Management

1988

THE ESTATES GAZETTE LIMITED
151, WARDOUR STREET · LONDON · W1V 4BN

NINTH EDITION 1988

ISBN 0 7282 0115 1

Printed in Great Britain at The Bath Press, Avon

FOREWORD

The principles and practice of dilapidations have come into sharp focus in recent years. Disputes are arising more frequently at the end of leases on commercial property.

Landlords are now much more determined to ensure that tenants fulfil their covenants to maintain their buildings to an acceptable standard. Tenants, on the other hand, hold the view that they need only carry out the minimum repairs and maintenance throughout the period of their lease. Conflict therefore frequently surfaces at the end of the lease when the landlord and tenant cannot agree whether the repairing covenants have been property fulfilled within the terms of the lease.

Case law is the basis of much of the law of dilapidations. The author of this book has gone to considerable lengths to explain the logic behind recent case law so that lawyers and surveyors, involved in advising either landlord or tenant, can judge whether the decisions in these cases might apply to similar cases with which they are involved.

This book is topical, pragmatic and right up to date and is therefore, I believe, an essential source of reference for all those professional people who have the task of advising the owners and tenants of commercial residential and agricultural buildings.

P. W. Huntsman, BSc, FRICS,   December 1987
College of Estate Management,
Whiteknights,
Reading RG6 2AW

PREFACE TO THE NINTH EDITION

This book concentrates on the law relating to property dis-repair as it applies to landlords, tenants and property owners generally, in the commercial, private residential, and agricultural sectors. Though in name the Ninth Edition of the Law of Dilapidations, the book has been completely re-written, and is offered as a new text, though its structure is based on that of the last Edition.

The law has undergone some major changes in recent years, particularly in the residential sector, where the Landlord and Tenant Act 1987 has conferred on flat tenants some important new rights, which are discussed in Chapter 9. At the date of going to press, no commencement orders for this Act had been made; but the text is written as though the relevant provisions were in force.

Many, but by no means all, of the most important recent reported cases have been decided on the meaning and scope of repair, inherent defects liability, damages, tenants' remedies against landlords, and forfeiture. It is hoped that the text reflects the significant impact of these important decisions.

The whole emphasis of the book is on the commercial, private residential and agricultural sectors. Consequently, there is little material in the text on housing and public health law. There is no material on negligence liability in surveying and building, as this is adequately covered elsewhere; as are the practical aspects of surveying, in a text written by Mr Malcolm Hollis and recently published by the Estates Gazette.

I am very grateful to Sweet & Maxwell Ltd for permission to cite, in various parts of the text, passages from Woodfall's *Law of Landlord and Tenant*, and from *Precedents for the Conveyancer*. I am likewise very grateful to Sweet & Maxwell Ltd and the authors, to cite from Bernstein and Reynolds, *Handbook of Rent Review* in Chapter 15. I acknowledge with grateful thanks any other permissions given, which have been acknowledged in various parts of the text of this book.

I am very grateful to Mr P. W. Huntsman, BSc FRICS, Principal of the College of Estate Management, for contributing the Foreword to this book and for his consistent general help and encouragement during the time this book was written.

My grateful thanks are due to Mr S. Burman, FRICS CAAV, for reading through a draft of the Chapter on Agricultural Dilapidations and for his comments, though responsibility for the contents remains solely mine.

I was substantially assisted, during the final preparation of the manuscript, by Miss J. Spooner, LLB, Barrister. She prepared the Tables, the List of References and, with me, the Index, checked through the whole manuscript and read the proofs with me. I am most grateful for the helpful way she approached the work involved.

Last, but by no means least, I should like to express my very great thanks to Mr George Kirton, of the Estates Gazette, for his patient handling of the whole production process from start to finish.

The law as stated in the text is as it stood on August 31, 1987, when the manuscript went to press.

P. F. Smith,   November 1987
Reading

CONTENTS

STANDARD REFERENCES

ADKIN, *Landlord and Tenant,* The Estates Gazette Ltd, London, 18th Edn, Walton & Essayan, 1982.

ALDRIDGE, T, *Boundaries, Walls and Fences,* Oyez Longman, London, 6th Edn, 1986.

ANSTEY, J, *Trouble with the Neighbours,* Calus, College of Estate Management, Reading, 1983.

BERNSTEIN and REYNOLDS, *Handbook of Rent Review,* Sweet and Maxwell, London, 1980 (Loose Leaf).

EVANS, David Lloyd, *The Law of Landlord and Tenant,* Butterworths, London, 2nd Edn, PF Smith, 1985.

FARRAND, JT and ARDEN, A, *Rent Acts and Regulations,* Sweet and Maxwell, London, 2nd Edn, 1981.

FOX-ANDREWS, James, *Business Tenancies,* The Estates Gazette Ltd, London, 4th Edn, 1987.

Halsbury's Laws of England, Volume 27, Butterworths, London, 4th Edn, 1981.

HOLLIS, Malcolm, *Surveying for Dilapidations,* The Estates Gazette Ltd, London, 1988.

Muir Watt: Agricultural Holdings, 13th Edition, J. MUIR WATT, Sweet and Maxwell, London, 1987.

POWELL-SMITH, *Boundaries and Fences,* Butterworths, London, 2nd Edn, 1975.

Precedents for the Conveyancer, (2 Volumes), Sweet and Maxwell, London, 1970, (Loose Leaf).

RODGERS, *Agricultural Tenancies, Law and Practice,* Butterworths, London, 1985.

ROSS, Malcolm, *Negligence in Surveying and Building,* The Estates Gazette Ltd, London, 1986.

ROSS, Murray J, *Drafting and Negotiating Commercial Leases,* Butterworths, London, 2nd Edn, 1984.

WILLIAMS, DW, *A Casebook on Repairs,* The Estates Gazette, London, 1987.

WILLIAMS, RG, *Agricultural Valuations – A Practical Guide,* The Estates Gazette Ltd, London, 1985.

WOLSTENHOLME, EP and CHERRY, BL, *Conveyancing Statutes,* Oyez Publishing Limited, London, 13th Edn, JT Farrand, 1972.

WOODFALL, *Landlord and Tenant,* (3 Volumes), Sweet and Maxwell, London, 28th Edn, 1978, (Loose Leaf).

YATES and HAWKINS, *Landlord and Tenant Law,* Sweet and Maxwell, London, 2nd Edn, 1986.

TABLE OF CASES CITED

C

D

E

I

M

xxii   *Table of Cases Cited*

U

W

Y

TABLE OF STATUTORY PROVISIONS

Note—Bold face = provision either quoted in full or in part or fully summarised at page referred to.

11 ....21, 43, 52, 54, 55, 60, 102, 111, 123, 232, 233,
                                              234, 235, 236, 237, 239, 240, 245, 246, 248
11(1)(a) **233–234**
11(1)(b) **234**, 237
11(1)(c) **234**, 237
11(2) **236**
11(2)(a) **238**
11(2)(b) **238**
11(2)(c) **238**
11(3) **238**
11(4) 120, 237, **238**
11(5) 237, **238–239**
11(6) 62, 63, 239, 241, 314
12(1) 231, 239
12(2) 231, 239
13 ....**239**
13(1) **232**
13(2)(a) **233**
13(2)(b) **233**
13(2)(c) **233**
14(4) **232**
14(5) **232**
16(b) **233**
17 ....**197**
17(1) **197**, 198
17(2) **198**
19(1) **209**
19(2) **209**
19(3) **210**
20(2) **209**
20(4) **209**
20(5) **209**, 210
20(5)(a) **210**
20(5)(b) **210**
20(5)(c) **209**
20(5)(g) **210**
20(9) **209**, 210
20B(1) **211**
20B(2) **211**
21 ....**210**
28 ....**210**
29 ....**209**
32 ....**193**
32(2) **232**, 248
Schedule **211–212**, 223
Landlord and Tenant Act 1987 ....2, 7, 45, 200
s 13(5) **218**
21(1) **200**
21(2) **200**
21(3) **201**
21(4) **201**
21(5) **201**

Chapter 1
INTRODUCTION

The aim of this Chapter is to provide a general review of the main aims, objects and contents of this book. The title of the book owes much to the fact that there was a time when dilapidations formed a separate subject for study in some branches of the landed professions. That is no longer the case.

Nonetheless, the title has been retained to emphasise the common element underlying the legal principles which this book is an attempt to cover. That element is simply the legal consequences of property disrepair.

These consequences weigh heavily and with great potential cost on all landowners, but for the most part the present treatment of the legal implications of property disrepair is confined to various aspects of the law of landlord and tenant. In this area, the relevant principles of law apply with equal force to the commercial, residential and agricultural sectors, but this is not invariably the case. In the commercial sector the parties to a lease are in general left to their own negotiating devices by the courts. If unexpectedly a commercial tenant finds that as a result of a so-called "clear lease" (from the landlord's viewpoint), he has to pay a very large and unexpected bill for repairs at the end of his lease, then often as not the attitude of the courts will be, save in very exceptional circumstances, to hold the tenant liable no matter how harsh the result. For example in a recent case[1] the tenants of commercial premises holding (as respects the relevant part) a lease by assignment of something over eight and a half years found themselves—much to their discomfort—being held liable to pay for a new roof to the industrial unit in question at a cost of over £80,000, when the value of the whole building as repaired was about £140,000. Similarly, a landlord who

---

[1] *Elite Investments Ltd v. TI Bainbridge Silencers Ltd* (1986) 280 EG 1001.

1

had covenanted to (in effect) guarantee the structural soundness of the (new) demised building, a restaurant and motel
complex, must have been somewhat surprised to find himself
liable to pay for the whole cost of extensive structural work
to the demised premises (including the foundations) when
they required very extensive remedial work due to their original defective design.[2] No doubt drafting may take care of
some of these problems but not all of them can be solved
in advance.

The landlord cannot as a general rule[3] be made impliedly
liable for repairs of any description. If he expressly undertakes
responsibility for repairs, as in the case of a multi-occupied
building such as a block of residential flats, he will no doubt
extract service charges from the tenants, as to common-law
and statutory controls on which, see Chapter 9.

The harsh common law rule of no implied liability on landlords to carry out repairs or to see to it that the premises
are reasonably fit or suitable for occupation by the tenant
is notably modified by Parliament. In the case of short leases
of "dwelling-houses" (houses and flats) ie terms of less than
seven years, Parliament has imposed on the landlord, in the
form of statute-implied covenants, certain repairing liabilities
which cannot be contacted out of in the lease or tenancy
(to repair the structure and exterior of the house or flat concerned).[4] Legislation has also intervened as regards the incidence of liability for repairs where a long residential tenant
has security of tenure under Part I of the *Landlord and Tenant
Act 1954*, in the case of extended leases under the *Leasehold
Reform Act 1967*, and also in some other instances, all of
which are discussed in Chapter 11. That Chapter also deals
with the powers of local authorities under Part VI of the *Housing Act 1985* to compel repairs to unfit housing or housing
seriously out of repair.

In the case of commercial leases Parliament has protected
business tenants' occupation under Part II of the *Landlord*

---

[2] *Smedley* v. *Chumley & Hawke Ltd* (1982) 261 EG 775, CA.

[3] See Chapter 3 of this book.

[4] *Landlord and Tenant Act* 1985 ss 11–16. These provisions apply also to prescribed installations (such as radiators) within the confines of the "dwelling-house" concerned: see Chapter
11.

and Tenant Act 1954: this has some impact on liability for repairs and this too is dealt with in Chapter 11.

The interpretation of commercial (and residential) express covenants to repair, whether by the landlord or the tenant, is a matter which occupies much space in the law reports and increasingly so in recent years as the cost of repairs escalates and the unwillingness of either landlord or tenant to pay for them seems to increase. These matters are discussed especially in Chapters 4 to 6 and they are of first-rate importance. Moreover, since there are many variants of repairing covenants, no-one can predict precisely what the result will be of a dispute on liability to repair, as already indicated. This is not merely because of narrow disputes about wording in a covenant: the courts have tended to adopt a broad view, holding that in interpreting repairing covenants, all relevant factors are to be taken into account such as the age of the building, the wording of the covenant, and the contemplation of the parties at the time of the entering into of the lease, just to name a few points to be taken up later in this book.[5]

Where a lease is silent as to responsibility for repairs then the relevant principles depend on whether the premises are commercial, residential or agricultural. In the case of leases of commercial premises, the harsh rule is—generally—that the landlord is under no implied duties to repair or to keep fit for use for any particular purpose of the tenant: see Chapter 3. In the case of residential lettings the same rule applies unless either the lease falls within a narrow series of common-law exceptions (see Chapter 3) or is covered by one of two sets of statutory regimes, one of which has just been mentioned (see Chapters 3 and 11).

In the case of agricultural tenancies, very specialised rules apply, and these are dealt with in Chapter 13 which is an attempt to digest them.

In connection with the question of implied obligations against landlords or owners to repair, it is worthy of note that in relation to a licence to occupy a brand-new industrial unit it was recently held[6] that the freeholder of the unit concerned was under an implied obligation to see to it that

[5] See eg *Brew Bros* v. *Snax (Ross) Ltd* [1970] 1 QB 612, CA.
[6] *Wettern Electric Ltd* v. *Welsh Development Agency* [1983] 2 All ER 629.

it was suitable for the purpose for which it was licensed. Since
this was not so—serious structural defects appeared soon after
the licensees moved into the unit rendering it dangerous so
that the licensees left and claimed damages for their losses—
the freeholders were obliged to pay the licensees damages
for breach of an implied warranty. This was to the effect
that the premises were of sound construction and reasonably
suitable for their required purpose. In the absence of express
warranties as to fitness (see Chapter 4) or express covenant,
this result could not generally be arrived at in the case of
leases at common law, and it is a sign of the times that ordinary
contractual rules have invaded commercial licences but not
leases. There are presumably limits to this new principle, as
yet ill-defined, but in another decision it was held that the
licensee of a 100-year old oven used to store and sell antiques
had no implied warranty of fitness and so could not—given
that the owner was under no express covenants—complain
about water penetration into the oven.[7] It may be that the
difference between these two cases is that, as with leases, it
is more readily assumed that new premises will be soundly
built whereas this cannot be taken for granted with old premises.

   The enforcement of repairing covenants both by landlords
and tenants has given rise to much very significant and lengthy
legislation and many important cases. In the case of landlords
of commercial premises, forfeiture for tenants' breaches of
covenant to repair is a method of terminating a business lease
which entails a number of complications,[8] for example: the
process of serving a preliminary warning notice under section
146(1) of the *Law of Property Act* 1925 and with that notice
an accompanying Schedule of Dilapidations.[9] The tenant may,
moreover, delay proceedings by invoking the *Leasehold Property (Repairs) Act* 1938, which was designed to prevent
oppressive forfeitures. He may eventually obtain relief from
forfeiture. If before the forfeiture action is heard the tenant

---

[7] *Morris-Thomas* v. *Petticoat Lane Rentals* (1986) *Times* 18 June.
[8] One of its advantages in the case of business tenancies is that forfeiture if successful precludes the tenant from gaining security of tenure under Part II of the *Landlord and Tenant Act* 1954 (s 24(2)) unless the tenant is granted relief from forfeiture: *Meadows* v. *Clerical, Medical and General Life Assurance Society* [1981] Ch 70.
[9] See further M. Hollis, *Surveying for Dilapidations*, Estates Gazette 1988.

carries out all the works of repair specified in the Schedule of Dilapidations then no forfeiture can be enforced and the tenant will be entitled to remain in possession[10]—even if his past record regarding repairs and maintenance of the premises has been bad. The tenant may in a forfeiture action (or on a separate action of his) claim relief from forfeiture under section 146(2) of the *Law of Property Act* 1925, which he will, as appears from Chapter 11, in principle obtain if he is able and willing to do the repairing work required of him. If there is no possibility of relief (and hence re-instatement) for the tenant, sub-tenants and mortgagees are entitled to ask the court for an order vesting the tenant's (forfeited) interest in their respective favour—in the form of a new lease under section 146(4) of the *Law of Property Act* 1925.[11]

The landlord may decide to wait until the lease ends and claim damages from the tenant for breaches of his repairing covenants, and in this case too there are complications, discussed in Chapter 7, first, because of the limit on the maximum amount of damages recoverable imposed on landlords by section 18(1) of the *Landlord and Tenant Act* 1927. The second main complication for landlords claiming damages is that the *Leasehold Property (Repairs) Act* 1938 may apply, requiring the whole forfeiture notice procedure to be gone through so that the tenant may claim the 1938 Act. There are ways round this problem and these are discussed in Chapter 7.

The statutory ceiling in the *Landlord and Tenant Act* 1927 does not apply where it is the tenant claiming damages from the landlord, whether for breaches of an express covenant to repair or a statute-implied obligation to repair. Those rules, which have been much developed in very recent years, are discussed in Chapter 9, which also discusses other remedies available to tenants to enforce their landlord's repairing covenants, such as the right to deduction or set-off (a sort of limited

---

[10] He will not of course be bound to undertake works of renewal of the whole or substantially the whole premises and if these are required in the Schedule it will to that extent be of no effect: on repairs and renewals, see Chapter 6.

[11] The landlord is under an obligation to notify mortgagees and underlessees of whose existence he knows of pending forfeiture proceedings, by serving copies of his writ claiming forfeiture on them—see SI 1986/1187 and SI 1986/1189 amending RSC Ord 6 and CCR 1981 Ord 6 respectively from 1 October 1986. See Chapter 8.

self help as where the tenant carries out the repairs in question
and sets off the cost of the work from rent arrears or future
liability for rent). The tenant may in a proper case obtain
an order for specific performance of his landlord's repairing
covenants, as will be seen from Chapter 9; curiously this
remedy is not available to enable landlords to compel their
tenants to execute repairs. This latter anomaly, dating back
to a single case in 1810,[12] appears to lack justification as
specific performance is fully available to tenants.

Also discussed in Chapter 9 are statutory and common law
controls on service charges, as where the landlord of a multi-
occupied block of flats reserves the common user parts and
means of access from the demises to the tenants and is under
a liability to repair and maintain the structure, exterior and
reserved parts of the building and charges the cost of the
work to tenants in the form of service charges.

Recently in some cases such as high-class multi-occupied
blocks of residential flats, tenants have succeeded in asking
the court to appoint a receiver and manager of the building
where the landlord has been particularly neglectful of his
repairing and maintenance responsibilities. These problems
were highlighted when a committee set up in 1984 (the Nugee
Committee) produced a report.[13] That report recommended
a number of changes especially: (1) a more regulated system
for appointing receivers and managers. (2) The creation of
housing assessors where management breaks down—these
would be county court officials sitting in a judicial capacity
to deal with disputes. (3) A better system to deal with service
charges—such as a requirement to hold the funds in a trust
account. (At present there is no uniform or adequate system
for dealing with these moneys: if they are specifically set aside
by some person such as a supervisor and held in a specially
created separate bank account which receives all future sums
then a trust may be inferred in favour of the tenants whose
money fed the account.[14]) (4) Reform of the present rules
which inhibit the alteration by agreement of defective leases.

[12] *Hill* v. *Barclay* (1810) 16 Ves Jun 402.
[13] The Report is summarised by Hawkins [1986] Conv 12. It is available from the DOE.
Annexed to The Nugee Report is the *James Report* from the RICS.
[14] See *Re Chelsea Cloisters Ltd* (*In Liquidation*) (1980) 41 P & CR 98.

Many though not all of these recommendations were adopted by the government and enacted in the *Landlord and Tenant Act* 1987. This important provision is fully discussed in Chapter 9. The main outlines of the Act relevant for present purposes are:

(a) There are provisions enabling tenants to apply to the court for the compulsory purchase of the landlord's reversionary interest where the landlord has seriously neglected his repairing obligations or where a court-appointed manager has been appointed for at least three years.

(b) The Act empowers the court on application by one or more flat tenants to appoint a manager where the landlord is in serious and persistant breach of his repairing obligations.

(c) New provisions are made for service charges and consultation with tenants' associations.

(d) The court is empowered to vary the terms of any long lease of a flat where it fails to make satisfactory provision for repairing obligations.

The insurance of demised premises against fire and other insurable events is relevant to the present topic in so far as if the premises are destroyed by fire the landlord may be under covenant to rebuild them and the tenant may require the insurance moneys to be applied to that purpose, and these matters are outlined in Chapter 10.

The repair and maintenance of party walls dividing two neighbouring properties is a subject of some antiquity and the relevance to this topic is obvious. One set of rules regulating the rights of adjoining party wall owners applies to most of England and Wales and another set, in a private Act[15] applies to Inner London. The subject is discussed in Chapter 12.

A matter of obvious relevance is the impact of disrepair on third parties, as where a passer-by on the highway, for example, is personally injured by the defective condition of premises abutting the highway. Or where some visitor to the premises is personally injured by a defect on the premises. These questions, which give rise to liabilities in tort (negligence

---

[15] *The London Building Act (Amendment) Act* 1939 as amended by Building Regulations 1985 SI 1985/1936 and SI 1987/798.

and nuisance) and contract (occupier's liability) are dealt with in Chapter 14 of this book.

In Chapter 15 there are discussed some topics which all relate in some way to dilapidations but do not fit easily into any single place. The first of these is the extent, if any, to which a freeholder or leaseholder may be put under an obligation to fence his land for the benefit of a neighbouring owner. In fact, the general principle is that no obligation to fence may be imposed in the absence of express contract on a freeholder, though there are a number of slightly ill-defined exceptions to this rule. In the case of leaseholders an obligation to keep up fences may validly be incorporated into the landlord's or tenant's covenant to repair and the burden of that obligation will run with the land in the same way as any other real covenant. The second topic in Chapter 15 is an outline of compensation for tenant's improvements, and the third topic is the question of the impact of disrepair on rent reviews. The fourth topic is tenants' break clauses.

There is a safety net where there is in occupation of land or premises an occupier of uncertain status, or where there is a tenant on a short periodic term, for example, with no express repairing obligations. This safety net is the tort of waste. It prevents the occupier or tenant from doing wilful or deliberate injury to the land or premises—among other things. It is discussed in Chapter 2. However, waste is not a mere historical survival—though many of the older cases and principles are certainly explicable on the basis—as a very recent case served to remind all concerned.[16]

To sum up: the main thrust of this work is the various questions arising out of express, implied and statute-imposed repairing obligations in relation to commercial, residential and agricultural leases. Many of the principles applicable are common to all three types of lease or tenancy. Where there are differences, these are dealt with separately, as with Chapter 11 (this deals with statutory incidence of repairs) and Chapter 13 (agricultural dilapidations, where there are specialised rules of some complexity on dilapidations).

---

[16] *Mancetter Developments Ltd* v. *Garmanson Ltd* [1986] 1 EGLR 240; [1986] 1 All ER 449, CA (the status of the occupier was not certain and it was under no repairing obligations, which is why waste became relevant).

Some but not all of the problems which have to be faced up to might at least be scaled down if not eliminated by suitable drafting, as a leading work in the subject constantly points out.[17] An example might be afforded by problems arising out of inherent defects. At the same time, even though the law in the area of property disrepair is apparently somewhat complex, there is still some stability underlying it. Two initial illustrations may be given.

In the first place, many of the rules of interpreting covenants are simply applications of general common law principles to the specific area of landlord and tenant and the same might be said of rules governing the assessment of landlords' and tenants' damages. Secondly, while the question of liability for extensive remedial work is a vexed and much—some might think over—litigated one, the fact that it is still possible to initiate a discussion of the matter by reference to two comparatively old cases[18] is, to that extent, an illustration of the underlying continuity of the subject.

[17] Ross, *Drafting and Negotiating Commercial Leases.*
[18] *Lister v. Lane and Nesham* [1893] 2 QB 212, CA; *Lurcott v. Wakely and Wheeler* [1911] 1 KB 905, CA, fully discussed in Chapter 6.

Chapter 2
WASTE[1]

I. DEFINITION OF WASTE

Waste may be defined as any act or omission which causes a lasting alteration to the land or premises affected to the prejudice of the owner or landlord. Waste is a tort and independent as a source of liability from any contractual relationship express or implied, between the parties, so that an obligation not to commit waste is not excluded by an express or implied covenant in the lease dealing with the same subject-matter.[2] While in the present context waste may be thought of as fairly marginal, an action in waste may be brought at the landlord's option even if he could sue in respect of the damage under the covenants in the lease, if any. For example, in the case of a short periodic tenancy from year to year or for some other period, the landlord may prefer to bring an action in waste in respect of injury to the premises or alterations in their character of a damaging nature as an alternative to suing on the implied covenant in the tenancy to use the premises in a tenant-like manner.[3] Waste may also be the sole means of redress against some person without a tenancy who is in occupation of the land or premises, such as a licensee or other person in occupation of land without any express or implied obligations to repair.

This was strikingly shown in *Mancetter Developments Ltd v. Garmanson Ltd*[4] where an occupier of uncertain status removed tenants' fixtures, which it had purchased from the previous tenants, and was held liable in voluntary waste to the owner of the freehold because in removing the fixtures, the occupier had left holes in the walls of the building to which the fixtures had been attached; as a result the building

---

[1] See generally Wilkinson "Liability for Waste" (1986) 136 New Law J 675.
[2] *Marker v. Kenrick* (1853) 13 CB 188; *Defries v. Milne* [1913] 1 Ch 98, CA.
[3] Woodfall 1–1577.
[4] [1986] 1 EGLR 240; [1986] 1 All ER 449, CA.

was no longer waterproof. The Court of Appeal held the occupier (a company in liquidation) liable to pay for the cost of in-filling the holes left in the building by the removal of the fixtures. Because the second defendant controlled the company, it being at his instance that the removal of the fixtures was carried out, he was also held personally liable in damages to the plaintiff owners. (The original tenants could not have been sued for installing the fixtures.)

It will be evident that in this case the original tenant was entitled to install the fixtures and also that he and any successors would be also entitled to remove them, but not in such a way as to injure the premises; if injury was caused, then any damage to the premises must be made good. As Dillon LJ said: "the liability to make good the damage, or to repair the injury the premises may sustain by the act of removal of tenants' fixtures must, so far as it is a liability at common law and not under a contract, be the liability of the person who removes the fixtures and not of the person, if different, who installed the fixtures and left them there."[5]

It is a condition precedent to liability in waste that occupation other than as a trespasser must be shown to exist. Occupation as a contractual licensee suffices for this purpose.[6] It has been seen that if some act gives rise to an action both for breach of an express or implied covenant (say, to use the premises in a tenant-like manner) and also constitutes waste, the landlord may elect under which head, contractual or tortious, he will claim, but he cannot recover damages under both heads at once.[7]

For present purposes there are, in the landlord and tenant or owner and licensee relationship, two relevant kinds of waste, voluntary and permissive, and each of these is now considered.

A. *Voluntary Waste*

Voluntary waste may be defined as the deliberate carrying out of some act which tends to destroy or injure the land

[5] [1986] 1 EGLR 240, at p. 242.
[6] *Mancetter Developments Ltd* v. *Garmanson Ltd supra.*
[7] *Marsden* v. *E Heyes Ltd* [1927] 2 KB 1, CA; *Mancetter Developments Ltd* v. *Garmanson Ltd supra.*

or premises or landlords' fixtures thereon. The following actions have been held to amount to voluntary waste: pulling down a building—even where the building was replaced by other buildings;[8] the conversion of pasture land into arable land.[9] Also the removal of tenants' fixtures built into the structure of the building which left it open to the elements without making good the injury thereby caused and if tenants' fixtures are removed by the tenant or by some other person authorised by the tenant, while this is in itself perfectly proper, if any injury is caused to the structure of the relevant building or premises by the removal, then the damage must be made good by the person responsible.[10]

It has been held further that the destruction of a building is an act of voluntary waste, but this is not so where the destruction results from the use of the building in an apparently ordinary and reasonable manner for the purpose for which it was let, as where a tenant (who was not under any express obligation in relation to such user) overloaded the floor of a warehouse, causing it to collapse: no waste was committed.[11]

However, unauthorised alterations (even if there is no covenant in the lease) may amount to voluntary waste but if the alterations add to the value of the premises, different considerations may apply, dealt with in section II of the present Chapter.

Finally, the destruction of the premises by accidental fire, by tempest or by Act of God, is not waste of any kind.[12]

B. *Permissive Waste*

The basis of permissive waste is negligence and omission and it is constituted by such things as allowing buildings to fall down due to total neglect to repair or maintain them.[13] Neglect to carry out repairs is, as one would expect, a matter to be covered generally by some form of express covenant

---

[8] *Cole v. Green* (1672) 1 Lev 309.
[9] Example given in *Halsbury* Vol 27 para 279.
[10] *Mancetter Developments Ltd v. Garmanson Ltd* [1986] 1 EGLR 240, CA.
[11] *Manchester Bonded Warehouse Ltd v. Carr* (1880) 5 CPD 507. For an express provision see *Precendents for the Conveyancer* Vol 1 p. 2823.
[12] *Woodfall* 1–1517.
[13] 2 Co Inst 145.

on the part of either landlord or tenant. Accordingly, as mentioned earlier, in the case of a tenant from year to year, an
alternative action for neglect to maintain may be framed under
an implied covenant.[14] Therefore, little need be said on
permissive waste, for any possible liability under that head
would add nothing to that imposed contractually—see as to
this Chapter 3.

In the event of the premises being occupied by a contractual
licensee rather than a tenant (so that there could be no liability
under implied covenant) then it might be thought that the
licensee should be under a duty not to commit permissive
waste, but there is no directly applicable authority either for
or against liability being imposed in such a case. Presumably,
if a contractual licensee committed acts of wanton destruction
on the premises as opposed to merely neglecting them, he
could be liable either in trespass or voluntary waste.

II. AMELIORATING WASTE

Any unauthorised change in the nature or character of the
premises is waste—though presumably in a long lease one
would expect to find prohibitions if desired, in some form,
against structural alterations—see Chapter 5. If this is not
so, then, in relation to waste, it has been held that if the
alterations to the land or premises improve them and add
to their value, the court will not interfere and there is ameliorating waste. For example no remedy was granted to a landlord
where his tenant (of agricultural land) converted part of it
into a market garden, improving the value of the land.[15]
It would appear from this case that if the landlord in any
event expressly sanctions a change in the nature of the
premises, he cannot later bring any action in waste.

The alleged act of waste may not improve the value of
the premises. Even then the courts may decline to interfere.
This will be so if the court rules that the acts which might
technically constitute waste, are too trivial to be enforced,
an example being where the tenant put in easily removable
partitions in rooms on the premises.[16]

[14] *Marsden* v. *E Heyes Ltd* [1927] 2 KB 1, CA.
[15] *Meux* v. *Cobley* [1892] 2 Ch 253.
[16] *Grand Canal Co* v. *McNamee* (1891) 29 LR IR 131 (Ir CA).

It is not necessarily a defence to an action in waste that the acts of the tenant or other occupier have improved the rental value of the land. In *West Ham Charity Board* v. *East London Waterworks Co*[17] the landlord leased meadow land on a long lease to the tenants, who were supposed to use the land as a reservoir. In fact, they used the land for other purposes and eventually sub-let it. The sub-tenant began dumping waste material on the land which raised its level and increased its rental value. This "improvement" was held to afford no defence to the tenant and sub-tenant who were both held liable in voluntary waste. Buckley J held that the test was whether, as a question of fact and degree, there had been such an alteration to the thing demised as to constitute waste. In this case on the facts there was found to be waste.

In deciding whether a tenant's alterations to the premises amount to voluntary or ameliorating waste the court has regard to the matters just set out plus the user, if any, permitted or intended for the demised premises at the outset of the lease, where the effect of alterations is to completely change the character of the premises. So in *Marsden* v. *E Heyes Ltd*[18] tenants under a yearly tenancy caused a dwelling-house and shop to be rebuilt as a large shop. The tenancy did not contain any express covenant against the making of alterations. The tenants then assigned the tenancy. They, as original tenants, were held guilty of voluntary waste, by having completely altered the character of the premises originally let to them. It was also held in this case that the court may grant a remedy in waste for any substantial alteration in the character of the demised premises, even if their value is increased by the alteration, because, held Bankes LJ, the tenant "must deliver up premises of the same character as those which were demised to him: for example, a tenant who takes a dwelling-house cannot yield up a store-house or stable or cow-house."[19]

III. EXTENT OF LIABILITY FOR WASTE

In a long lease one would expect the question of repairs and maintenance to be regulated by express covenants and

[17] [1900] 1 Ch 624.
[18] [1927] 2 KB 1, CA.
[19] *Ibid* at p. 6.

in the case of periodic tenancies, as explained in Chapter 3, there are limited implied obligations on the part of tenants. If waste is for some reason resorted to as a ground of action by the landlord then there are various kinds of periodic tenant who are, and some who are not liable for permissive waste though in principle liability for voluntary waste is general.

A tenant for years is liable both for voluntary and for permissive waste.[20] It is doubtful whether his liability for permissive waste imposes anything on him beyond the duty implied by law into his tenancy to use the premises in a tenant-like manner (see Chapter 3). A tenant from year to year and for any other period such as for a month, is liable for voluntary waste but not (it seems) for permissive waste.[21] In the case of voluntary waste it appears that the liability of a periodic tenant may extend to cases where the tenant holds over after the termination of the tenancy.[22] Finally, a weekly tenant has been held to be liable for voluntary but not for permissive waste (but in view of his implied duty to use the premises in a tenant-like manner this seems of little importance).[23]

A tenant at will is not liable either for voluntary or permissive waste as such.[24] Voluntary waste operates to terminate a tenancy at will and thereafter the ex-tenant is liable to the landlord in trespass. The reason for this non-liability of a tenant at will is because of the uncertain duration of his interest. The reason for non-liability of certain periodic tenants in permissive waste is that they are under a contractual implied duty to use the premises in a tenant-like manner (see Chapter 3).

IV. RELATIONSHIP BETWEEN WASTE AND COVENANTS IN THE LEASE

It has been suggested earlier that the liability of a tenant holding under a term certain will almost certainly be governed by the express terms of the lease and so any remedial action

---

[20] *Yellowly* v. *Gower* (1855) 11 Ex D 274 at p. 294 (Parke B).
[21] *Torriano* v. *Young* (1833) 6 C & P 8.
[22] *Burchell* v. *Hornsby* (1808) 1 Camp 360.
[23] *Warren* v. *Keen* [1954] 1 QB 15, CA.
[24] *Countess of Shrewsbury's Case* (1600) 5 Coke 13a: *Harnett* v. *Maitland* (1847) 16 M & W 257.

by the landlord would be expected to be taken under the
leasehold covenants, if sufficiently comprehensive. If not and
if the tenant's implied covenants are also insufficient, or if
the occupier is not a tenant, then waste may well come into
play. In any event, the remedies for waste are cumulative with
those for tenants' breaches of covenant and so the landlord
may if he so wishes elect to sue in waste (ie in tort) or on
the covenants (ie in contract).[25]

As for those cases where there are no express covenants
of any kind, then, as was seen above, the relationship between
liability for waste and liability under implied covenants is
more difficult. As is apparent from Chapter 3, there is an
implied duty on any periodic tenant to use the premises in
a tenant-like manner and to deliver them up at the end of
the tenancy in the same state of repair as when the tenant
took them, fair wear and tear excepted.[26] This obligation
is very limited in scope and does not oblige the tenant to
carry out substantial, lasting or structural repairs, such as
replacing the main roof or timbers. What it is aimed at is
protecting the landlord from deliberate damage to the
premises by the tenant, so that if he breaks doors and windows
he must replace them.[27] As a result of these considerations
one would not expect the landlord to sue in permissive waste
even in those cases where the law allows him to, for the matter
will be sufficiently covered by the tenant's implied covenant.
Voluntary waste is a different matter and this is sufficiently
covered in earlier parts of the present Chapter.

V. REMEDIES FOR WASTE

The liability of a tenant or other occupier for waste may
be enforced either by an injunction or by damages. Damages
may be awarded to cover all past losses to the landlord occasioned by the acts of waste and then an injuction might be
awarded to restrain further acts of waste.

As to injunctions, no injunction will in principle be awarded
unless substantial injury to the landlord's reversion by the

[25] *Kinlyside* v. *Thornton* (1776) 2 W Bl 1111.
[26] *Warren* v. *Keen* [1954] 1 QB 15, CA.
[27] See *Ferguson* v. *Anon* (1797) 2 Esp 590.

alleged act of waste is proved by the landlord: trivial acts of waste will not be restrained.[28]

In any case full particulars of the alleged dilapidations must be given. If a claim succeeds, it seems that the person responsible for the damage may be ordered to put it right—even if some new materials may have to be added to the injured building or structure. In *Mancetter Developments Ltd* v. *Garmanson Ltd*[29] where, as was seen, the removal of the tenants' fixtures by the occupier from the landlord's industrial premises damaged the structure of the building in question by leaving holes in the external walls so that the building ceased to be wind and weatherproof, the occupier and a director of the occupier were held liable to pay for the cost of in-filling the holes. This was so even though the work partly involved replacing sheets of cladding and lining which had holes in them. "To make good that damage by filling in the holes . . . is part of the condition attached by law," said Dillon LJ, "to the defendant's right to remove the fixtures."[30]

Liability for waste is founded in tort and the measure of damages is the amount of injury to the landlord's reversion, ie the depreciation in the sale value of his interest in the premises.[31] This may differ from the cost of reinstatement but, as was seen, if the structure of the landlord's land or premises has been injured by an act of the tenant in not curing the injury when he ought to have done, then the tenant (or other person responsible) may be ordered as was seen above, to carry out sufficient works of reinstatement to the premises.

[28] *Doherty* v. *Allman* (1878) 3 App Cas 709, HL: *Grand Canal Co* v. *McNamee* (1891) 29 LR IR 131 (Ir CA).
[29] (1986) 1 EGLR 240, CA.
[30] *Ibid* at p. 242.
[31] *Whitham* v. *Kershaw* (1886) 16 QBD 613, CA.

Chapter 3
IMPLIED OBLIGATIONS OF LANDLORD AND TENANT TO REPAIR

I. INTRODUCTION

In this Chapter the question considered is whether, and if so, to what extent, the law is prepared to imply into a lease or tenancy, obligations to repair on the part of either the landlord or of the tenant. There is also considered the extent to which the law is prepared to imply warranties on the landlord's part that the demised premises are fit for habitation.

It will be seen that the common law is in principle very reluctant to imply any obligations to repair against landlords and is similarly reluctant to imply any warranties by landlords that the demised premises are fit for human habitation, but many exceptions to this principle exist even at common law. At common law, for example, a limited implied warranty as to fitness exists (as will be seen) while statute has imposed such warranties in the case of small houses let at a low rent and has also imposed duties on builders of buildings who then let them to see that the tenant and others are safe from injuries arising from a defective state in the demised premises. This rule is dealt with in Chapter 11 but in this Chapter there are set out the common law rules and main exceptions to them as well as the limited implied duty as to fitness in relation to furnished dwellings.

If the lease contains an express covenant dealing with the same matter as the common law then that covenant will displace the common law implied rule completely, however limited its scope.[1] In the case of any warranty or obligation imposed on the landlord by statute these cannot be contracted out of by the parties.[2]

---

[1] *Miller* v. *Emcer Products Ltd* [1956] Ch 304, CA.
[2] See also Chapter 11 of this book for statute-implied obligations to repair.

As a general rule one would not expect the parties to a long lease of residential premises and quite probably, though there is no hard and fast line, in the case of most leases of whatever duration of commercial premises, to leave the incidence of liability to carry out repairs to be settled merely by implication. Therefore the questions which arise as to the scope of implied covenants to repair and of implied warranties as to fitness for habitation (or suitability for the purposes for which the premises were let) are chiefly relevant to short periodic lettings of dwelling-houses and flats. In so far as any lease or tenancy fails to provide for the incidence of liability for repairs, the implied obligations will automatically arise however, and in any case, depending on the circumstances, statute-implied duties are relevant and must be borne in mind.

II. IMPLIED OBLIGATIONS OF LANDLORD TO REPAIR

In this section there are dealt with three areas where the question arises how far the landlord, where there is no express obligation imposed on him in the lease or tenancy in question, can be under any implied obligation to repair, first, in relation to land, buildings or unfurnished houses; secondly, in relation to offices and unfurnished flats and thirdly, in the case of furnished lettings whether houses or flats.

A. *Land, Buildings or Unfurnished Houses*

The common law rule concerning any implied obligations of the landlord of land, buildings or unfurnished houses is simplicity itself. Subject to statutory exceptions in the case of dwellings let at a low rent (see section III below) and also in the case of dwelling-houses and flats let on short tenancies,[3] the rule is that the landlord is under no implied duty to the tenant of land, buildings or unfurnished houses to put such premises into repair at the commencement of the lease.[4] Nor is the landlord of such premises under any implied duty to keep them in repair at any time during the lease.[5] As a logical consequence it was held that the landlord is under

[3] See Chapter 11 of this book.
[4] *Hart* v. *Windsor* (1844) 12 M & W 68; *Duke of Westminster* v. *Guild* (1983) 267 EG 762, CA.
[5] *Gott* v. *Gandy* (1853) 3 E & B 845; *Duke of Westminster* v. *Guild, supra.*

no similar implied obligation that the house shall last throughout the term of the lease.[6]

This harsh rule—which as will be seen in section III below
has been reduced in scope by a large number of exceptions—
does mean that, for example, in relation to repairing work
outside the scope of any expressly imposed or statute-implied
duties, such as interior repairs, the fact that the landlord may
reserve himself the right without more, in the lease or tenancy,
to enter and carry out repairs will not of itself impose any
liability on him to repair.[7] The responsibility here will simply
fall on the tenant. The rule means also that if, again, there
is no liability imposed expressly in the lease on the landlord
and the premises are such that not one of the exceptions to
the no-implied obligations rule applies, the mere fact that,
as in *Sleafer* v. *Lambeth Metropolitan Borough Council*[8]
the landlord had in fact expected to carry out repairs from
time to time will not oblige him to carry out the particular
repair in question in the absence of an express or statutorily
implied covenant.

A further consequence of the common law no-implied obligations rule is that where part of the demised premises is
retained in the control of the landlord, he is not by the fact
that these parts are not demised to any particular tenants,
obliged to carry out repairs to any non-demised part of the
premises. In *Colebeck* v. *Girdlers Co*[9] therefore, where two
houses let by the same landlord to different tenants were
divided by a party wall which neither tenant was under express
covenant to repair it was held that the plaintiff tenant could
bring no action against the landlord where the wall bulged
due to its lack of repair. In such a case, however, special
rules of mutual support will apply, discussed in Chapter 12.

The severity of the common law rule is illustrated further
by the fact that if the tenant covenants to repair the demised
premises with the exception of fair wear and tear, or with
fire damage excepted, and the excepted event materialises,
this does not mean that the landlord is impliedly bound to

[6] *Arden* v. *Pullen* (1842) 10 M & W 321.
[7] *Sleafer* v. *Lambeth Metropolitan Borough Council* [1960] 1 QB 43, CA.
[8] *Supra.* But see now *Landlord and Tenant Act* 1985 s 11.
[9] (1876) 1 QBD 234.

carry out the required repairs himself.[10] Indeed all that happens is that the tenant is under a continuing liability to pay rent.[11] Only an express convenant will cast an obligation to repair on the landlord in this case.[12]

Not surprisingly, the harsh common law rule has been modified in some particular instances by statute-implied obligations to repair (see Chapter 11) and also in certain other cases dealt with in section III below. However, at the risk of repetition it must be stressed that if none of these exceptions applies and if the landlord is under no express obligations to repair, the common law rule of no liability to carry out any repairs whatever remains and will apply.

B. _Offices and Unfurnished Flats_
General

The subject-matter and general conditions of a letting of offices and unfurnished flats differ in some ways from those applicable to the letting of an unfurnished house. In the latter instance the tenant has exclusive possession, in principle, of the whole premises including all parts of the structure and exterior. If the tenant has a lease of a flat—purpose-built or after conversion—or of an office in a larger block, different considerations apply. There should, for example, be precise clauses in the lease which define exactly what is meant, for the purpose of the incidence of liability for repairs, by structure and exterior; and then what part of either is demised to the tenant and what part, if any, is retained by the landlord under his control. The cases give some guidance on the general meaning of structure and exterior in the case of flats but no more: all the same it is usual to expect the landlord to undertake liability to repair the structure and exterior of a block of flats or offices and to recover his costs of doing so in the form of service charges from the tenants.

If the terms of the lease refer to 'all that' building, without further qualification, and the building is in single occupation, then it is generally assumed that general words of demise

[10] _Weigall_ v. _Waters_ (1795) 6 TR 488.
[11] _Matthey_ v. _Curling_ [1922] 2 AC 180.
[12] _Woodfall_ 1–1455.

mean just that, with the result that the roof will form part of the demised premises.[13]

If the premises are in multi-occupation, be they offices or blocks of flats, then the lease should ideally specify what parts of the structure and exterior are demised to the tenant and what are reserved by the landlord. If this is not done then the question is one of fact and degree.

In *Campden Hill Towers* v. *Gardner*[14] (concerned with service charges payable by the lessees of a series of flats in the building) it was held that as a matter of construction, the "exterior" of a particular flat included the outside walls of that flat, the outer walls of horizontal divisions between the flat in question and those above and below it, and the structural framework which directly supported the floors, ceilings and walls of the flat in question. In *Douglas-Scott* v. *Scorgie*[15] in relation to a lease of a top-floor flat in a block of flats, where the lease did not expressly demise the roof to the top-floor tenant, it was held on a preliminary issue, on the facts, that the roof was capable of forming part of the structure and exterior of that particular flat.

Position if Landlord demises only Certain Parts of Premises

At all events, in the case of leases of a block of flats or of a number of offices in the same larger building, it is often the case that the landlord will not demise certain parts of the main building to any tenant and will retain control of certain parts of it. What these parts are, if any, will depend on the precise terms of each lease: they may well include the approaches to the premises, common staircases, lifts, rubbish chutes (if any), possibly the basement, gutters, rainwater pipes and gullies and drains, ie facilities expected to be used by or of benefit generally to all the tenants in the building.

It has been held that where the landlord retains in his control steps or a staircase used by all the tenants as a common means of access he must—even if he has not covenanted to do this expressly—take reasonable care to keep the steps or staircase

---

[13] *Straudley Investments Ltd* v. *Barpress Ltd* (1987) 282 EG 1124, CA.
[14] [1977] QB 823; (1976) 242 EG 375, CA.
[15] (1984) 269 EG 1164, CA.

reasonably safe.[16] This is a duty imposed in tort and it refers only to the means of access as it exists at the start of the lease: the landlord is not impliedly bound, therefore, to provide his tenants with an improved means of access, say, a handrail, where none existed at the start of the lease.[17]

If the landlord expressly retains control of something ancillary to the demised premises, such as the roof or guttering, he is likewise under an implied duty in tort, which is totally independent of any contractual duty, to keep these in repair, if their maintenance in proper repair is necessary for the protection of the demised premises or the safe enjoyment of them by the tenant. If the landlord maintains a tank or other artificial thing he is similarly under a duty of care to his tenants to see that no damage is caused to them or to the parts of the premises let to them: reasonable care only is required.[18] Where therefore a rain-gutter in the roof, in the landlords' control, became to their knowledge, stopped up, the landlords' failure to do anything to remedy the disrepair caused them to be liable for the losses occasioned to their tenants.[19]

There are limits on these duties however. In *Duke of Westminster* v. *Guild*[20] the landlord of commercial premises was in the lease in question, under no express obligation to repair any part of the demised premises. All repairing obligations in relation thereto fell expressly on the tenant. A drain serving only the demised premises ran under the tenant's premises, then under the landlord's adjoining premises and thence into a public sewer.[21] The landlord's part of the drain had been blocked for years; damage resulted from the fact that water was not draining off the tenant's land but on the contrary was escaping onto it: by agreement the tenant carried out remedial work by building a new drain and claimed to set off the cost against his admitted rent arrears and failed to do so. It was held that there could be no implied obligation on the landlord to repair the drain. The escaping water had

[16] *Dunster* v. *Hollis* [1918] 2 KB 795.

[17] *Woodfall* 1–1469.

[18] *Woodfall* 1–1469.

[19] *Hargroves Aronson & Co* v. *Hartopp* [1905] 1 KB 472; also *Cockburn* v. *Smith* [1924] 2 KB 119.

[20] (1983) 267 EG 762: [1984] 3 All ER 144, CA.

[21] The tenants were held entitled to the implied grant of an easement of drainage over the landlord's land.

been on the tenant's part of the land. The fact that part of the drain passed under the landlord's own land was regarded as making no difference whatever—all the more so because the lease in this case contained a complete scheme for repairs and also because the tenants had a right to enter the landlord's land to carry out the works as part of that scheme, though they were not under any obligation to repair the landlord's part of the drain.

The implied duty on the landlord to keep in good repair parts of the premises he reserves from the demise was held to depend on the fact that the lack of repair on the landlord's part of the premises had caused an escape of a dangerous, noxious or unwelcome substance from the landlord's land. In the case under consideration, the real complaint of the tenant was that the lack of repair of the part of the drain running under the landlord's part of the land prevented the tenant from discharging water from his land onto the landlord's land. The remedy for that problem lay, as mentioned earlier, in the law of easements.

Implied Obligation of Landlord to Repair Common User Parts

Where there are lettings of blocks of flats, and the landlord retains possession and control of the common parts of the premises, there is implied into the tenancies an obligation to keep in repair those retained parts, on the part of the landlord. In *Liverpool City Council* v. *Irwin*[22] there were council lettings of some 70 flats in a tower block and the landlords retained possession and control over a common staircase, lifts and rubbish chutes. Due in part to vandalisation, the lifts failed, the stairs were not properly lit and the rubbish chutes became blocked. The landlords were under no express obligation to repair these parts of the premises. The House of Lords implied rights in the nature of easements into the tenancies in favour of the tenants regarding these common user parts, and implied a contractual obligation with regard to these easements. This was that the landlords must take reasonable care in the particular circumstances of the case, to maintain the

---

[22] [1977] AC 239, HL. This duty is not excluded by an express management scheme: *Gordon* v. *Selico Co Ltd* (1986) 278 EG 53.

common parts in a state of reasonable repair and efficiency. However, the standard imposed was not absolute: account would be taken, it was held, of the fact that reasonable conduct by the tenants, in relation to their own responsibilities, would be required. In the circumstances of the case it was held that it was not shown that the council had failed to comply with the requirement to take reasonable care to maintain the common parts and the tenants' case failed in regard to the common user parts. (Their case with regard to flooding lavatory cisterns succeeded but this was due to the application of statute-implied duties to repair, see Chapter 11.)

Even where there might otherwise be an implied contractual duty to repair, it will be displaced by any form of express covenant dealing with the same matter. In *Duke of Westminster* v. *Guild*[23] where, as indicated, the lease contained a perfectly workable scheme for repairing obligations, the tenants being under an express obligation to repair and maintain the drain in so far as it formed part of the premises demised to them, with an ancillary implied right of access to the landlord's premises, it was held, partly because of the existence of this scheme, that no obligation could be implied against the landlords to repair the part of the drain running under their own land adjoining the demised premises.

In any event, the principles discussed above in relation to implied obligations on landlords to keep the common user parts retained by him in repair, are special exceptions to the general rule, which is that at common law the landlord is under no duty to do any repairs at all, in the absence of an express or statute-implied covenant. According to Slade LJ in *Duke of Westminster* v. *Guild* the special exceptions are confined to "... a type of landlord-tenant situation which gives rise to special considerations, such as the case of a high-rise building in multiple occupation, where the essential means of access to the unit are retained in the landlord's occupation."[24]

Lastly, the duty of the landlord discussed above, to take reasonable care to see to it that parts of the premises retained

---

[23] (1983) 267 EG 762; [1984] 3 All ER 144, CA.
[24] (1983) 267 EG 762 at p. 766.

by him, which are ancillary to the demised premises, are kept in repair, where this is necessary to protect the demised premises is not an absolute duty. For example, the landlord is not liable thereunder for fortuitous happenings, such as a box-gutter being gnawed by a rat, leading to an escape of water damaging the tenant's goods.[25] Likewise, landlords who made satisfactory arrangements for the periodical inspection of pipes retained by them, were held not liable, negligence not being proved, to their tenants where a pipe became choked, overflowed, and caused damage to the tenant's stock.[26]

C. *Furnished Houses*

In the case of lettings of a furnished house, a furnished flat or of furnished apartments, the landlord impliedly undertakes that at the date of commencement of the tenancy, the premises will be fit for occupation. This implied condition is dealt with in section III of this Chapter since it is an implied undertaking that the premises will be, at the relevant date, reasonably fit for human habitation.

D. *Statute-Implied Repairing Obligations*

These are imposed by sections 11 to 16 of the *Landlord and Tenant Act* 1985 in the case of the structure and exterior of dwelling-houses and flats held on short leases and the matter is discussed in Chapter 11.

III. WARRANTIES OF FITNESS

A. *General Position*

The rule is stated as follows by a leading text:

"In general, there is no implied covenant by the lessor of an *unfurnished* house or flat or of land, that it is or shall be reasonably fit for habitation, occupation or cultivation,

---

[25] *Carstairs* v. *Taylor* (1871) LR 6 Ex 217.
[26] *Kiddle* v. *City Business Properties Ltd* [1942] 1 KB 269.

or for any other purpose for which it is let. No covenant is implied that the lessor will do any repairs whatever."[27]

The link between the general rule as to repairs and as to warranties as to fitness will readily be appreciated. In fact, the common law rule is of extreme severity. The landlord is not liable, at common law, for any defects which may exist in the premises, and which render them dangerous or unfit for occupation, whether these exist at the commencement of the lease or tenancy or arise during it. The landlord is not at common law liable for personal injuries caused to the tenant nor to any member of the tenant's family, by such defects, and this applies even if the landlord was fully aware of the existence of the defect. To take some examples, it was held in *Sutton* v. *Temple*[28] that in a lease of land for grazing there was no implied warranty that the land was fit for that particular purpose—in fact it was poisoned by heaps of refuse paint. Where, as in *Bottomley* v. *Bannister*[29] for example, a firm of builders sold a house on an estate they owned, and prior to completion X and his wife moved into the house, and where a gas boiler and burner in this house were in fact in a dangerous state, so that the fumes from them killed both X and his wife, it was held that since the boiler and burner were fixtures and thus part of the land, the builders were not liable. This particular decision and others for that matter have been overturned by statute—as will be seen below. It was mentioned purely to show to what extreme lengths the common law no-liability rule was taken. The same common law rule means that the landlord—unless he is also the builder (see below) is to this day under no liability at all for personal injuries caused by dangerous defects in the demised premises to the tenant nor to any members of the tenant's family nor to his customers or guests.[30] However, as will be seen, the tenant and other persons who are themselves strangers to the lease may have rights and remedies under the *Defective Premises Act* 1972; in addition, the common law rule itself

---

[27] *Woodfall* 1–1465, approved in *Duke of Westminster* v. *Guild, supra*.
[28] (1843) 12 M & W 52. Also *Manchester Bonded Warehouse Co* v. *Carr* (1880) 5 CPD 507.
[29] [1932] 1 KB 458, CA; also *Travers* v. *Gloucester Corporation* [1947] KB 71.
[30] See *Cavalier* v. *Pope* [1906] AC 428, HL; *Lane* v. *Cox* [1897] 1 QB 415, CA.

is severely abrogated or at least side-stepped by the statute-implied obligations as to fitness and repair.

If, however, the landlord is also the builder of the house, then it has been held in *Rimmer* v. *Liverpool City Council*[31] that the landlord will—assuming he was responsible for putting in the defects—be liable for personal injuries to the tenant and to all persons who might reasonably be expected to be affected by the design or construction of the premises. The duty is that the landlord must see to it that these persons are reasonably safe from personal injury due to such defects. The duty is not avoided merely by the fact that the person to whom it is owed knows of the danger unless it would be reasonable for him to remove or avoid it. In *Rimmer's* case therefore, where the landlord, a local authority, designed and built the flat where the tenant lived, it was held liable in negligence for damages for the personal injuries caused to the tenant from his putting his hand through a defectively designed glass panel. The panel, apparently a standard installation, was built into an internal wall in the flat—so the tenant could not really be expected to remove it or avoid it by quitting the flat.

Incidentally, the tenant in *Rimmer* did not have any cause of action under section 1 of the *Defective Premises Act* 1972 because the time-limit on actions thereunder is six years from the date of completion of the building (and this period had elapsed) and apparently the tenant had no cause of action under section 4 of that Act (Chapter 11) in that no neglect to repair the panel was shown on the landlord's part.

It was said earlier that there are many exceptions to the common law no-liability rule: but, though it is kept in close confinement, where none of the exceptions to it applies, then the common law rule will govern the matter.

Finally, it is worth noting that in the case of a contractual licensee of business premises, the position may be different at common law from the general rule of no liability. In *Wettern Electric Ltd* v. *Welsh Development Agency*[32] a factory unit was licensed for one year to manufacturers. The unit was brand-new. Soon after the licensees entered the unit, serious

---

[31] (1984) 269 EG 319; [1985] QB 1, CA.
[32] [1983] QB 796.

structural defects appeared and the licensees in due course
moved out of the unit before the expiry of their licence. They
successfully claimed damages for loss of production and under
other heads, on the basis that the licensors were in breach
of an implied warranty that the unit was of sound construction
and reasonably suitable to the purposes of the licensees. However, the principle is not unlimited and may depend on the
fact that the unit was brand-new, for in *Morris-Thomas* v.
Petticoat Lane Rentals Ltd[33] no implied warranty of fitness
for a licensee's purposes was inferred where the subject-matter
of the licence was a 100-year old oven used for storage purposes by the licensee. So while in the case of a business tenancy,
none of this would have applied and any warranties of fitness
would have only been available to the occupiers if expressly
given by the owners, in the case of a contractual licence of
business premises ordinary contractual principles apply as to
implied warranties (including fitness and suitability), at least
in the case of newly-built commercial or possibly residential
premises which exhibit structural design faults.

Now attention is given to the exceptions other than those
just stated, namely:
—*Defective Premises Act* 1972
—Houses in the course of erection
—Small Houses let at low rents
—Furnished Houses
As to the difficult and nowadays lengthy matters of negligence liability in building and negligence liability on local
authorities where (for example) they negligently exercise statutory powers of approval of plans and so on, these lie outside
the scope of this book and are fully dealt with in a text to
which reference should be made.[34]

B. *Defective Premises Act 1972*

If the landlord is the occupier of premises adjoining or
excepted from the demise (such as the common user parts
of the building) then his liability, if any, as occupier is governed by the *Occupiers Liability Act* 1957 (see Chapter 14).
The *Defective Premises Act* 1972 (section 4 of which is dealt

---

[33] (1986) *Times* 18 June.
[34] Ross, *Negligence in Surveying & Building*, Estates Gazette, 1986 esp Chapters 4 and 6.

with in Chapter 11) governs the liability in tort of the landlord for defects in the premises themselves.

Section 1

Section 1(1) of the *Defective Premises Act* 1972 provides that a person taking on work for or in connection with the provision of a dwelling (whether the dwelling is provided by the erection or by the conversion or enlargement of a building) owes a duty to two classes of person, and in particular to the tenant of a dwelling, to see that the work which he takes on is done in a workmanlike, or, as the case may be, professional manner, with proper materials and so that as regards that work the dwelling will be fit for habitation when completed. The two classes of person are:

(a) any person to whose order the dwelling is provided; and

(b) every person acquiring an interest (legal or equitable) in the dwelling—such as a tenant under a legal or equitable lease.

In *Alexander* v. *Mercouris*[35] section 1(1) was widely interpeted and it was held that the duty imposed by the words "taking on work" was a duty which arose when the contract to do the work was entered into, or, at the latest, when the work was commenced. However, it was held to be a duty required to be performed while the work was being carried out. It was further indicated that the reference in section 1(1) of the 1972 Act to the dwelling being "fit for habitation when completed" indicated the intended consequence of the proper performance of the duty and provided a measure of the standard of the requisite work and materials. What this means is that it is not, in principle, a requirement of the Act that the plaintiff should wait to take action until such time, if any, as the work is completed—he may act while the work is being carried out. At the same time the action in the *Alexander* case failed since the relevant work was begun prior to 1st January 1974, the date of the coming into force of the 1972 Act.

---

[35] [1979] 3 All ER 305, CA.

Section 6(3) of the 1972 Act nullifies any term of a contract which purports to exclude or restrict the operation of the above rules.

Under section 1(5) of the 1972 Act, any cause of action for a breach of the duty imposed by section 1(1) of the Act is deemed, for the purposes of the *Limitation Act* 1980, to have accrued at the time when the dwelling was completed. If, by section 1(5), after completion, a person who has done work for or in connection with the provision of a dwelling does further work to rectify the work he has already done, any cause of action with respect to the further work is deemed, for the purposes of limitation, to have accrued at the time when the further work is finished. Therefore, in the case of the 1972 Act, time begins to run from a different date from which time runs in the case of actions relating to structural damage caused by defectively-built foundations, for example, for in this latter case time is, in principle, deemed to run from the date when the state of the building first became such that it was a present or imminent danger to the health or safety of its occupiers.[36] This could be a lot later than the date when the work of building or, as the case may be, of rectification, is completed.

Lastly, it should be noted that section 1 of the 1972 Act is expressly subject to section 2 of the 1972 Act, which provides that all dwellings covered by an "approved scheme" are wholly excluded from section 1. The relevant scheme is run by the National House-Building Council[37] and the effect of section 2 is to limit the scope of section 1 very much indeed. Section 1 will however be relevant to, for example, alterations or conversions to dwellings carried out on or after 1st January 1974.

Section 3

Section 3(1) of the Defective Premises Act 1972 provides as follows:

"Where work of construction, repair, maintenance or demolition or any other work is done on or in relation to

---

[36] *Anns* v. *London Borough of Merton* [1978] AC 728, HL; see further Ross, *loc cit*, Chapters 5 and 6. See also *Latent Damage Act* 1986 s 14.

[37] See SI 1973 No 1843 and Ross *loc cit* pp. 100 and 147 for further details.

premises, any duty of care owed, because of the doing of the work, to persons who might reasonably be expected to be affected by defects in the state of the premises created by the doing of the work shall not be abated by the subsequent disposal of the premises by the person who owed the duty."

In the case in particular of a tenancy either commencing or being entered into prior to 1st January 1974, by section 3(2)(a), the above rule does not apply.

The effect of section 3(1) is to abolish the common-law immunity of a landlord/builder who—as outlined earlier—having built a dwelling-house or flat, then proceeded to let it.

However, while beneficial to tenants in itself, section 3 of the 1972 Act does not exist in isolation and it runs in parallel to certain common law liabilities, for example, those imposed on a landlord/builder and for breaches of statutory duty and for dangerous defects in a house or flat (discussed in Chapter 11).

C. *Houses in the Course of Erection*

It has been held at common law that, in the absence of express contrary agreement, a builder who sells or lets a house being erected but which is not completely finished by him, is under an implied duty to see that, when the house is completed, it will be fit for human habitation. This is because it is taken that the contract itself involves an express obligation to finish the house.[38]

D. *Small Houses let at Low Rents*

In the case of a tenancy of any length of a house for human habitation entered into on or after 6th July 1957 at an annual rent of £80 in London and £52 elsewhere, there are implied by section 8(1) of the *Landlord and Tenant Act 1985*[39] two obligations on the landlord.

---

[38] See *Perry* v. *Sharon Development Co* [1937] 4 All ER 390.

[39] This replaces the *Housing Act* 1957 ss 4 and 6. The 1985 Act came into force on 1st April 1986 (s40(2)).

Statutory Obligations

The first, by section 8(1)(a), is a condition that the house is fit for human habitation at the commencement of the tenancy. The second, by section 8(1)(b), is an undertaking that the house[40] will be kept by the landlord fit for human habitation during the tenancy.[41] These statute-implied obligations cannot be contracted out of (s 8(1)). It is to be noted that the landlord or a person authorised by him in writing has, by section 8(2) of the 1985 Act, a right, on 24 hours' written notice to the tenant or occupier, at reasonable times of the day, to enter the premises in question for the purpose of viewing their state and condition.

However, there is one express exclusion of the above obligations. By section 8(5) of the 1985 Act, where the house is let for a term of three years or more on terms that the tenant put the premises into a condition reasonably fit for human habitation then, subject to one exception, the statute-implied obligations of the landlord in relation to fitness for habitation do not apply. The exception from section 8(5) is that these obligations will apply if the lease is determinable at the option of either party before the expiration of three years.

In considering whether the 1985 Act obligations apply, regard is to be had to the annual rent levels paid by the tenant, whether inclusive of rates or not.[42]

Guidelines as to Fitness

Section 10 of the 1985 Act gives statutory guidelines as to fitness. It provides that in determining for the purposes of the statute-implied obligations whether a house is unfit for human habitation, regard is to be had to its condition in respect of the following matters: repair, stability, freedom from damp, internal arrangement, natural lighting, ventilation, water supply, drainage and sanitary conveniences, facilities for preparation and cooking of food and for the disposal of waste water. However there is a substantial limit on the landlord's statute-implied obligations: even if it is found that

---

[40] Defined in s 8(6) to include part of a house, any yard, garden, outhouses and appurtenances.
[41] For the rent limits see *Landlord and Tenant Act* 1985 s 8(4): in the case of tenancies granted on/after 6th July 1957 they are £80 pa in London and £52 pa elsewhere.
[42] *Rousou v. Photi* [1940] 2 KB 379.

the condition of the house is such that it is defective under the above statutory list in one or more respects, section 10 provides that for the purposes of the Act the duty of the landlord is broken if and only if the house is so far defective in one or more of the matters listed that it is not reasonably suitable for occupation in that condition. Therefore the tenant cannot necessarily say that because a defect listed in section 10 actually exists on the premises, therefore, *ipso facto* the landlord is in breach of his statutory duty.

Scope of Provisions

For reasons to be explained these particular provisions are not of much modern significance. Out of an excess of caution, some brief points on the scope of these provisions may be made. In the first place, the standard imposed on the landlord by section 8 of the 1985 Act is a much lower one than that required by a covenant to keep in good tenantable repair. It is that required to keep the house decently fit for human beings to live in.[43] Therefore the condition of the house—assuming it is out of repair in some way—must be such that by the ordinary user of it or of the part out of repair, damage or injury may naturally be caused to the tenant—as in *Summers* v. *Salford Corporation*,[44] for example, where one of the two sash-cords in a window of a house broke, jamming the window; later the other sash-cord on this window broke and the tenant was injured as a result. The landlord was held liable in damages for her personal injuries. The jamming of the window caused by the defect was such that the window could not, without danger to the tenant, be used; its condition impaired the ventilation of the room, interfered with its ordinary user and was such that the house was not in all respects fit for human habitation.

It might be thought superficially, that any covenant to repair by the tenant was invalidated by section 8(1) of the 1985 Act but this is not so. If the tenant is under an express covenant to repair, section 8(1) will not totally invalidate this covenant: what happens is that repairs to the house which are over

---

[43] *Jones* v. *Geen* [1925] 1 KB 659, CA.
[44] [1943] AC 283, HL.

and above those required by the lower obligation on the land-lord fall on the tanant.[45] A further limit on the obligations imposed by section 8 is that they only apply to the part of the house (where relevant) let to the tenant and not, therefore, to any common user parts retained by the landlord, though he is subject to common law implied duties to repair (as respects these, see above).

A very important limitation on the landlord's statute-implied obligations—assuming the house is unfit within the Act—is that of the doctrine of notice. Under this the landlord is not in breach of covenant unless and until he has actual notice (in principle from the tenant) of the existence of the defect in the house, and a reasonable time to execute the repairs has thereafter elapsed, and this applies whether the defect is patent or latent. Notice from a third party to the landlord of the defect, such as from local authority in a repair notice under the *Housing Act* 1985, is apparently sufficient notice for the purpose of triggering liability.[46]

A final judicial limitation on the above duties is that the landlord escapes liability if he is able to show that the house is not capable of being rendered fit for human habitation at reasonable expense.[47]

Assuming that the landlord is in breach of his statute-implied obligations and that he fails within a reasonable time after notice to do anything to put matters right, the tenant may apparently then quit without paying further rent and sue the landlord for damages, because the breach is of an implied condition in the tenancy: and damages both for personal injury and also for damage to the tenant's property are recoverable.[48] But this too is limited in scope for apparently the only person with any right of action is the tenant—so, if his visitors, guests or even family members are injured by defects then they themselves are without remedy under these provisions of the 1985 Act.[49]

---

[45] *Jones* v. *Geen, supra.*
[46] *McCarrick* v. *Liverpool Corporation* [1947] AC 219, HL; *O'Brien* v. *Robinson* [1973] AC 912, HL; *McGreal* v. *Wake* (1984) 269 EG 1254, CA.
[47] *Buswell* v. *Goodwin* [1971] 1 WLR 92, CA.
[48] *Woodfall* 1–1476.
[49] *Ryall* v. *Kidwell* [1914] 3 KB 35. A cause of action for third parties is given by *Defective Premises Act* 1972 s 4, discussed in Chapter 11.

The last thing to note is that the present topic has been inserted for the sake of completeness only. It is of very limited scope today. In *Quick* v. *Taff-Ely Borough Council*[50] Dillon LJ said that the rent levels provided for in the 1985 Act had not changed since 1963. In view of inflation, Dillon LJ noted, these provisions must nowadays have remarkably little application.

E. *Furnished Houses*

Where there is a letting of a furnished house or furnished flat there is an implied undertaking by the landlord that, at the commencement of the tenancy, the premises are in a fit state for habitation; and if this undertaking, which is a condition of the tenancy, if not fulfilled on the day the tenancy commences, the tenant may at once repudiate the tenancy, treat it as being at an end and quit.[51] The tenant is not bound to take this course of action however and he may, therefore, elect to take the tenancy, and sue for damages. If he elects to repudiate the tenancy, he is not under an obligation as a condition precedent to this to give the landlord an opportunity to do any necessary repairs to the house.[52]

Examples of breaches of the implied undertaking by the landlord have been held to include the following: substantially defective drains causing offensive smells in the house;[53] where a house was infested by bugs;[54] where the house in question was infected by measles;[55] or where a house had recently been occupied by a person suffering from pulmonary tuberculosis.[56]

It is no defence to liability that the landlord honestly believes that the house is habitable when let, if this is not in fact the case.[57]

There are substantial limits on the common law implied undertakings and where they apply, any further obligations on the landlord's part must be the subject-matter of an express

---

[50] (1985) 276 EG 452; [1985] 2 EGLR 50, CA.
[51] *Smith* v. *Marrable* (1843) 11 M & W 5.
[52] *Wilson* v. *Finch-Hatton* (1877) 2 Ex D 336.
[53] *Wilson* v. *Finch-Hatton, supra*.
[54] *Smith* v. *Marrable, supra*.
[55] *Bird* v. *Lord Greville* (1844) 1 C & E 317.
[56] *Collins* v. *Hopkins* [1923] 2 KB 617.
[57] *Charsley* v. *Jones* (1889) 53 JP 280.

covenant on his part. The implied undertaking in relation to furnished houses and flats does not extend beyond the state of the house at the commencement of the tenancy: the landlord is accordingly under no implied obligation that a furnished house or flat will continue to be fit for habitation during the term: if, therefore, subsequent to the start of the tenancy the premises become unfit, the tenant will not be able for that reason to repudiate the tenancy.[58]

The policy of this particular exception appears to be based on the fact, according to Kelly CB in *Wilson* v. *Finch-Hatton*,[59] that where a person takes a furnished house for a brief period of time, it is clear that he could expect to find it reasonably for habitation on the day he expected to enter. No doubt this is so but there is no limit to the length of the tenancy to which this implied undertaking may, in principle, apply.

IV. IMPLIED OBLIGATIONS OF TENANT

The implied obligations of a tenant who is not under an express covenant to repair depend on two sets of rules. The first set is to the effect that the tenant is—no matter what the length of the tenancy may be—bound not to commit voluntary waste. Certain tenants must not commit permissive waste. The whole topic of waste is discussed, in so far as it has any bearing on tenants, in Chapter 2.

The second set of rules are more ill-defined than the rules relating to waste and depend on implied covenant. A tenant holding under a term certain, as opposed to a periodic tenancy (say for a week or a month or a year), will almost certainly have whatever repairing obligations he may lawfully be subjected to, defined expressly in his lease. As a result, no doubt, the cases to be discussed are concerned with periodic tenants of various kinds.

In principle—and in theory this applies to all tenants fixed-term or periodic—it was held in *Marsden* v. *E Heyes Ltd*[60] that the tenant is, in the absence of express covenants on his part, subject to a continuing implied undertaking to use

---

[58] *Sarson* v. *Roberts* [1895] 2 QB 395.
[59] (1877) 2 Ex D 336 at p. 342.
[60] [1927] 2 KB 1, CA.

the demised premises in a proper and tenant-like manner and to deliver up possession of the premises to the landlord in the same condition as they were in at the commencement of the tenancy, fair wear and tear excepted. It would seem that this implied covenant will not be displaced by an express covenant to the same effect, such as a covenant to leave the premises in a certain state of repair.[61] However, it will be displaced by any express covenant on the tenant's part which is wider (or narrower) in scope.[62]

Despite the above, there is some uncertainty as to the exact scope of what is required of the tenant by this implied covenant. In the case of a weekly tenant and, it is thought, of any periodic tenant, whether for a month, a quarter or for a year or for years, the principle laid down by the leading decision, *Warren* v. *Keen*,[63] is this. The tenant is not, firstly, to commit voluntary waste—as to which see Chapter 2. The tenant must, secondly, repair damage to the premises caused, wilfully or negligently, by him, his family and his guests; the tenant must take proper care of the place—and, according to Denning LJ—must do those little jobs about the place which a reasonable tenant would do, such as chimney-cleaning, mending the electric light when it fuses, unstopping the sink when it is blocked by his waste. On the other hand it was accepted in *Warren* v. *Keen* that should the house fall out of repair owing to fair wear and tear, lapse of time or for any reason not caused by the tenant's action or negligence, then he will not be liable to repair the damage. As a result, in *Warren* v. *Keen* a weekly statutory tenant was held not liable to pay for repairs to certain damp and decaying walls of a house since the disrepair was caused merely by the lapse of time which had caused the walls to require re-pointing. Nor was the tenant liable to pay for repairs to decayed window-sills, which had fallen into that condition for want of external repainting at regular intervals.[64]

On further matter is probably of theoretical interest only. It appears to have been held in *Warren* v. *Keen* that a weekly

[61] *White* v. *Nicholson* (1842) 4 M & G 95.
[62] *Standen* v. *Christmas* (1847) 10 QB 135.
[63] [1954] 1 QB 15, CA.
[64] If the tenant deliberately injures the premises, he will be under a liability in voluntary waste, and will presumably have to pay the cost of remedial work: see Chapter 2.

tenant, at any rate (and it is thought all types of periodic tenant) is under no obligation to keep the premises wind and water tight—assuming that this adds anything to the work necessitated by the implied obligation just discussed. The expression "wind and water tight" was mentioned in a number of old and sometimes rather badly reported decisions;[65] and in *Warren* v. *Keen* Denning LJ considered the expression itself to be of doubtful value and said it should be avoided. While the rest of the Court of Appeal did not go that far, they evaded the issue by holding the work in question to fall outside the scope of any duty—if it existed—to keep the premises wind and water tight.

In other words the basic duty implied by law against periodic tenants is that they are to use the premises in a tenant-like manner, fair wear and tear (impliedly) excluded. This is based on the tenant having to rectify any disrepair which is the result of his or his family or guest's deliberate fault or their negligence.

Accordingly it was held in *Wycombe Area Health Authority* v. *Barnett*[66] that "tenant-like user" did not on the particular facts oblige the tenant to drain the water system and turn off the stop-cock on leaving the house in question for three nights in mid-winter. Nor was the tenant inevitably to be expected to lag water-pipes in the house to protect them against freezing or to keep the house heated as an alternative precaution. On the facts of this case the tenant escaped liability for damage caused to the house by a burst pipe because it was not reasonable to anticipate the pipe freezing during a short absence, given the temperature when the tenant left. It was said that the precautions which the tenant is obliged to take under the standard required by tenant-like user will depend on the circumstances, such as the severity of cold conditions in the house and the length of any contemplated absence. The case should be contrasted with *Mickel* v. *M'Coard*[67] where the tenant of a Scottish villa left it unoccupied for a whole month in mid-winter without having turned off the water or emptying the cisterns. Not surprisingly, she

---

[65] It was however referred to in *Wedd* v. *Porter* [1916] 2 KB 91, CA.
[66] (1982) 264 EG 619.
[67] 1913 SC 896.

was held liable for damage caused when the pipes burst, on the basis that she failed to use a reasonable degree of diligence to preserve the premises from injury—and she did not inform the landlord of her intended absence. These two cases show that the incidence of liability of the tenant, depending as it does on conduct, will vary with the particular facts and circumstances.

Chapter 4

EXPRESS OBLIGATIONS OF LANDLORD TO REPAIR

I. GENERAL RULES

Unless the landlord expressly covenants to put the demised premises into repair at the commencement of the lease or to keep them in repair during the lease, he is generally under no liability, except under certain statues in relation to particular classes of tenancy, to put the demised premises into repair nor to keep them in repair during the lease.[1] The landlord, as was seen in Chapter 3, may be under an implied obligation to put or to keep the premises in repair or in a state fit for human habitation, either under particular statutes or at common law[2] and he may also be under liabilities consequent on the *Defective Premises Act* 1972 (see Chapter 11) even though he has not covenanted expressly to do repairs. Moreover, other exceptions exist to the no-liability without express covenant rule.

Under the principles of waiver, the landlord may make himself liable for repairs which under the lease he is under no express liability to undertake, as in *Brikom Investments Ltd v. Carr.*[3] Here, the landlords of flats orally informed their sitting tenants that they, the landlords, would carry out certain roof repairs at their own cost, as part of an intended sale to the tenants of long leases in the premises—even though under the long leases later granted, the tenants covenanted to pay annual contributions towards the cost of structural repairs. The landlord's oral representations were made prior to the grant of the long leases. The landlords carried out the work and unsuccessfully tried to recover the cost from the tenants and their assigns. The landlords were held to have

---

[1] *Colebeck* v. *Girdlers Co* (1876) 1 QBD 234.
[2] For section 11 and following of the *Landlord and Tenant Act* 1985 (implied covenant to repair structure and exterior by landlords of dwellings), see Chapter 11.
[3] [1979] QB 467, CA.

waived their right (though it was written into the leases) to claim the cost of the roof repairs both from the original tenants and their assigns, in view of the oral representations that had been made before granting the leases. They had led the tenants to believe that their strict right to recovery of the cost of the repairs would not, in relation to the disputed work, in fact be enforced.

It also appears from this case that if the landlord orally undertakes to do certain repairs and the tenant is thereby induced to accept a lease, then, though the lease contains no express covenant by the landlord in relation to repairs, the landlord may be bound to execute the repairs in question on the basis of a collateral contract (see section II below). It is also possible that a landlord who induced a tenant to accept a lease on the basis of a promise himself to do repairs cast by the lease on the tenant could not, if the tenant took the lease in consequence, later make the tenant pay for the cost of the particular repairs in question, on the basis of promissory estoppel: such a promise, moreover, could be enforced against the landlord by third party assigns of the lease.

If the landlord leases only part of the premises to the tenant and retains possession and control over the other parts, he will, in the absence of express covenant, be under no obligation to repair the part demised merely because of his control over the other parts.[4] If, on the other hand, the landlord fails to keep in repair a part of the demised premises retained by him, such as the roof and guttering above a top-floor flat (the flat but not the roof being demised to the tenant) the landlord is, in principle, bound to take reasonable care to remedy any disrepair in the parts retained where these cause damage or injury to the tenant's own part of the premises.[5]

The fact that the tenant's covenant to repair may contain exclusions or limitations on the extent of his liability, such as "fair wear and tear excepted" or "damage by fire excepted" does not—in the absence of express covenant by the landlord—or of waiver, collateral contract or estoppel, oblige

---

[4] See *Colebeck* v. *Girdlers Co supra.*
[5] *Cockburn* v. *Smith* [1924] 2 KB 119, CA. See also Chapter 3.

the landlord to carry out repairs if the excepted events materialise.[6]

As to the position where the lease casts on the tenant an obligation to execute repairs but in practice it is the landlord who does them, it could presumably be argued that the landlord has impliedly undertaken the cost of paying for such repairs himself. Apparently, in the absence of any special circumstances such as estoppel or waiver, this argument will not succeed. In *London Hospital Board of Governors* v. *Jacobs*[7] where an argument of this kind was put up, the premises were a dwelling house held on a statutory tenancy under the *Rent Acts*. Since the start of the tenancy, despite the fact that thereunder it was the tenant who was under covenant to keep the premises in good tenantable repair, it was the landlords who since then had done substantially the whole of the relevant repairs. The landlords failed to have the rent put up on the basis that in fact liability for repairs had been varied.[8]

Two further general points may be mentioned here. First, it was seen in Chapter 3 that in the case of leases of individual flats in a block of flats, where the landlord retains control over the common user parts, he will in principle be under an implied obligation to repair these, even though he is not for some reason under express covenant to do so. On the other hand, it was held in *Gordon* v. *Selico Co Ltd*[9] that a very "cumbersome" (so described) management scheme for a block of flats, while it might not always suffice to give the lessees timely protection, was on the whole comprehensive, and it excluded therefore any further implied duty on the landlord's part to execute any repairs which fell within the scheme. In other words if the landlord fails to comply with his repairing and maintenance duties under schemes of management then the tenant's remedy will lie under the scheme, in damages for breach thereof, plus any other remedies available (such as specific performance) or even by means of the

---

[6] *Arden* v. *Pullen* (1842) 10 M & W 321; *Weigall* v. *Waters* (1795) 6 TR 488.
[7] [1956] 2 All ER 603, CA.
[8] Also *Sleafer* v. *Lambeth Borough Council* [1960] 1 QB 43, CA. In the case of a long lease of flats, landlords in this position could presumably invoke Part IV of the *Landlord and Tenant Act* 1987, see Chapters 5 and 9.
[9] (1985) 275 EG 899, varied on appeal (1986) 278 EG 53, CA.

appointment of a receiver in extreme cases (see Chapter 9).

The second point relates also to flats. Commonly, leases of flats in a block contain terms under which the landlord undertakes liability to execute structural and exterior repairs (which should be carefully defined in the lease itself) and then provides for contributions from each individual tenant upon presentation to the tenant of a surveyor's certificate stating the amount of his contribution, whereupon the tenant becomes liable to pay his share. Nonetheless, it was held in *Rapid Results College Ltd* v. *Angell*[10] that, on the question as to whether a particular item of work falls within the landlord's obligations (so that the tenant will have to make a contribution in due course) the certificate is not necessarily conclusive; the court will examine the lease so that where, as in that case, a lease referred to the "maintenance of the exterior" it was held that this, as a matter of construction, did not include the roof and parapet wall of the premises, which did not form part of the "exterior" of a second-floor office, despite a certificate stating the exact contrary.

II. EXPRESS WARRANTIES OF FITNESS

In principle, the terms of a lease are taken as a complete statement of the agreement between the parties as to the state of repair or fitness of the demised premises at the commencement of the term. If the lease is silent on the matter then, in principle, there can be no liability at common law on the landlord for disrepair to the premises at such commencement. This is because of the rules examined in Chapter 3, that the landlord gives no implied warranties (generally) as to the fitness or suitability of the premises at the commencement of the term. However, the landlord may be rendered liable for initial dilapidations if he has made oral or written statements, prior to the execution of the lease, as to the condition of the premises, offering the intending tenant some form of express warranty (ie almost a guarantee) as to the fitness or suitability of the premises. He may, for example, expressly represent to the tenant that the premises are fit for human habitation or that the drains and sanitation are in good

---

[10] (1986) 277 EG 856; [1986] 1 EGLR 53, CA; also *Concorde Graphics Ltd* v. *Andromeda Investments SA* (1983) 265 EG 386. See further Chapter 9.

order.[11] In principle, such statements by a landlord may be treated as both an express warranty and a condition: the tenant may, if the state of the premises is not as guaranteed, both claim damages and also repudiate the lease within a reasonable time of taking possession.[12]

The conditions for such collateral warranties to be enforceable are fairly strict and briefly are these. The relevant statement must precede the grant of the lease; it must be such that the tenant would have refused to complete and take possession if the representation had not been made and its truth were not the basis of the contract. An example of the operation of the rule is *De Lassalle* v. *Guildford*[13] where the plaintiff insisted on an assurance, which was given orally by the landlord, that the drains of the demised premises, a house, and the sanitary arrangements in question, were in good order, before the plaintiff finally handed over the counterpart to the lease and so completed the transaction. In fact the lease was silent on the matter. The drains were in fact in bad condition. It was held that the plaintiff was induced by the landlord's statement to take the lease and the latter was liable accordingly in damages for breach of an express warranty to the plaintiff.[14]

While there is a fairly strict standard of proof in these matters, it is easier to infer a warranty of the above kind where the person making the statement states a fact within, or presumed to be likely to be within, his knowledge (but of which the intending tenant is likely to be ignorant) where the statement is made with the intention that the intending tenant act on it, and he in fact does so.

The statement must not, in principle, contradict the terms of the lease.[15] If the lease deals with the matter in a given way, this is taken as conclusive unless the tenant is able to show that the representation supercedes the lease or a term in it, as where the landlord or his agent clearly indicates or represent to the tenant, with a view to inducing him to enter

---

[11] As in *De Lassalle* v. *Guildford* [1901] 2 KB 215, CA.
[12] *Bunn* v. *Harrison* (1886) 3 TLR 146, CA.
[13] [1901] 2 KB 215, CA.
[14] Another example is *Morgan* v. *Griffith* (1871) LR 6 Ex 70 (oral collateral agreement to put down rabbits).
[15] *Henderson* v. *Arthur* [1907] 1 KB 10.

into the lease, that he will not, whatever the lease may provide, enforce a particular covenant in it; or that the landlord will undertake liability for and pay for the cost of particular repairs despite the fact that liability for repairs generally is cast on the tenant by the lease.[16]

If the tenant is able to prove deceit on the part of the land-lord then damages and appropriate orders may be awarded on that basis—even though by definition no representation as to the condition of the demised premises at the date of the lease was made. Where a condition of dry rot in flats was deliberately covered up by a landlord's management com-pany, it was held that damages were not in themselves a suffi-cient remedy and an order to enforce the covenants in the lease concerning repairs was required.[17]

As a result of section 2 of the *Misrepresentation Act* 1967, a party who is the victim of an innocent misrepresentation which is a collateral warranty, is entitled to damages, if the maker of the statement would have been liable in damages for that statement had the misrepresentation been made fraudulently; but if the maker of the statement proves that he had reasonable ground to believe and did believe up to the date of the contract, that the statement was true, then the injured party has no right to damages. The reason for this provision is that prior to the passing of the 1967 Act, a false but innocent misrepresentation gave the injured party only the right to rescind the lease and this right had to be exercised promptly. Subject to the statutory defence, such party may, as a result of section 2, obtain damages.

Section 1 of the 1967 Act entitles a person, after he has executed a lease following an innocent misrepresentation, to rescind the lease nonetheless. Until the passing of the 1967 Act rescission of an executed lease in these circumstances was impossible.

By section 3 of the 1967 Act, any clause in the lease purport-ing to exclude or limit liability for misrepresentation may only be relied on to the extent that the court thinks it fair and reasonable.

---

[16] See *Brikom Investments Ltd* v. *Carr* [1979] QB 467, CA, discussed above.
[17] *Gordon* v. *Selico Co Ltd* (1986) 278 EG 53, CA.

III. DEPENDENT AND INDEPENDENT COVENANTS TO REPAIR

The tenant may be under some obligations to repair, but in the same lease the landlord may have covenanted to put the premises into repair[18] or he may have covenanted to supply the materials required for the tenant, who in turn may be under a covenant to repair. There are two possibilities at least. One is that the covenant to repair by the landlord is a separate and independent obligation from that of the tenant. In that case the landlord (or tenant) may enforce the other party's obligation to repair even though it may be the case that the plantiff is in breach of his *own* covenant. In *Cannock v. Jones*[19] for example, an agricultural tenant covenanted to do certain repairs such as to the windows, ditches, hedges, fixtures and so on, on the premises, these "being previously put in repair and kept in repair" by the landlord. The landlord's covenant was held to be independent of the tenant's own covenant to repair, being construed as absolute and unqualified.

The other possibility is that the tenant's obligation to repair will be construed as dependent on or conditional on the landlord first putting the premises into repair. In that case the tenant is not liable unless the landlord first complies with *his* covenant to repair.[20] Or the tenant's covenant to repair may depend on the landlord's first providing materials for the repairs in question—if this is treated as a condition precedent, then the tenant will be under no liability to repair unless and until the materials are provided.

The question of whether a tenant's covenant to repair is to be treated as dependent or independent of the landlord's own covenant to repair or to supply materials is vexed: it is one of intention and hence of construction of every lease. In *Westacott v. Hahn*[21] (where the Court of Appeal adopted this approach) the tenant of a farm covenanted that he would "from time to time during the term (being allowed all necessary materials for the purpose) . . ." repair the premises in ques-

---

[18] See *Henman* v. *Berliner* [1918] 2 KB 236.
[19] (1849) 3 Ex 223.
[20] *Howe* v. *Botwood* [1913] 2 KB 387.
[21] [1918] 1 KB 495, CA.

tion. It was held that the landlord had not covenanted to supply the necessary materials but that if these were not supplied, the tenant was not bound to carry out the repairs: it was a condition precedent of the tenant's liability that the landlord should first bear the cost of necessary materials. By contrast, in *Tucker* v. *Linger*[22] the tenant was under an obligation to keep certain buildings in repair and the landlord had undertaken to find materials for the repairs. The tenant failed to repair a dilapidated barn on the premises and was held to be in breach of his covenant despite the failure of the landlord to find the necessary materials. The two covenants were treated as independent. The case turns on the construction of the particular covenant in that case.

In the context of service charges payable by a tenant of a flat, a question arises whether, unless the tenant, or even all tenants pay them, the landlord is liable to execute repairs to the structure or exterior of the building. There is no hard and fast rule. For example, in *Yorkbrook Investments Ltd* v. *Batten*[23] it was held that prompt payment of tenants' service charges did not constitute a condition precedent to the liability of the landlords of a block of flats to provide services, under covenant in a different clause in the lease. The reason for this conclusion lies in policy: the landlords had remedies for they could sue for their money; they could forfeit or distrain, but a maintenance contribution was the total of a number of different items and the tenant could challenge individual items and pay for others. In other words the covenants were independent. By contrast, in *CIN Properties Ltd* v. *Barclays Bank PLC*[24] a clause in relation to service charges payable by tenants for exterior repair work provided that the landlords, who were liable to execute this work in return for service charges by the tenants, should not accept any tenders or contracts or commission any repairs without first submitting the plans for the tenants' approval. Very extensive external repair work to the premises was carried out but the condition about tenants' approval of tenders and so on was not first complied with by the landlords, whose claim to

[22] (1882) 21 Ch D 18.
[23] (1985) 276 EG 545; [1985] 2 EGLR 100, CA.
[24] (1985) 277 EG 973, [1986] 1 EGLR 59, CA.

recover £166,254 as the tenants' share of the cost, failed. The condition in question was held to be an unequivocal condition precedent to the tenants' obligation to pay service charges.

The question ultimately depends on the intention of the parties, the circumstances of the case, any statutory background and the consequences of a particular interpretation, so that where the landlord of an agricultural holding covenanted to do certain repairs, it was held that the tenant remained liable for rent even though the repairs were not, in breach of covenant, carried out.[25]

IV. POSITION WHERE LANDLORD IS UNDER AN EXPRESS COVENANT TO REPAIR

The landlord may undertake an express obligation to carry out repairs and, where this is so, the principles which apply to the interpretation of the tenant's covenant to repair apply equally to similar covenants by the landlord.[26] The interpretation of the tenant's covenant to repair is dealt with in Chapters 5 and 6 of this book. In what follows some specific points which apply to the landlord's covenant to repair are discussed. The position where the landlord is, by statute, under repairing obligations, is dealt with in Chapter 11. If the landlord commits a breach of his covenant to repair, and later the tenant assigns the residue of his term, the landlord remains liable in damages to the former tenant for those breaches notwithstanding the assignment.[27] If this case is followed,
landlords may face potentially very heavy liabilities for breaches by them of their repairing covenants, vis-à-vis former tenants who prove that they assigned the residue of the term at a reduced price due to the dilapidations. Moreover, overlapping damages claims by the former and current tenants could result if the disrepair continues after the lease has been assigned.

The present topics may be grouped under two heads: first, the meaning of structural repairs; secondly, some general principles of construction.

---

[25] *Burton* v. *Timmis* (1987) 281 EG 795; [1987] 1 EGLR 1, CA.
[26] *Torrens* v. *Walker* [1906] 2 Ch 166.
[27] *City & Metropolitan Properties Ltd* v. *Greycroft Ltd* (1987) 283 EG 199.

A. *Structural Repairs*

It may at once be noted that if the tenant undertakes responsibility for structural repairs, the following discussion applies
with equal force to the tenant's as to the landlord's obligation.
If the landlord undertakes responsibility for structural repairs
(say where there is a long lease of a block of flats or of commercial premises) the thing to discover is what is meant by "structural". The lease may itself define the term for the purposes
of the particular demise.

There is not much judicial authority in point. In *Granada
Theatres Ltd* v. *Freehold Investment (Leytonstone) Ltd*[28] it
was held that a landlord's responsibility for structural repairs
was for repairs which involved interference with, or alteration
to, the framework of the building in question. It was further
held (though this is rather a tautology) that structural repairs
meant repairs of, or to, a structure and that, accordingly,
the replacement of 350 to 500 slates out of a total of some
12,000 was a structural repair and within the landlord's
repairing covenant. It was also held that making good the
rendering and brickwork of the front elevation of the building
concerned were structural repairs of a substantial nature
within the landlord's covenant.

One would then expect that repairs to the roof, main outside
walls (and, in some cases, repairs to inside supporting or load-
bearing walls) and to the foundations of a building, to come
within the ambit of structural repairs. Or, in other words,
the term structural repairs includes any repairs to the essential
structure or fabric of the premises—even say to a skylight—as
opposed to the mere provision of equipment. Ordinary wooden-
frame windows have been held not to form part of the main
walls.[29] It may be otherwise if there are stone mullions
to the windows. However, for the purposes of section 11
of the *Landlord and Tenant Act* 1985 the landlord is liable
to keep in repair wooden-frame or other windows as part
of the exterior of the "dwelling-house"—see Chapter 11.

Repairs to fittings within the demised premises such as a

[28] [1959] Ch 592, CA; also *Blundell* v. *Obsdale* (1958) 171 EG 491; *Samuels* v. *Abbints Investments* (1963) 188 EG 689 (defective outside plumbing held within main structure of block and within landlord's covenant).
[29] *Holiday Fellowship* v. *Hereford* [1959] 1 WLR 211. The windows were accordingly held outside an exception in a lessee's covenant referring to the roofs and main walls.

kitchen sink or cooker would not, likewise, be structural.[30] However, in *Pearlman v. Harrow School Governors*[31] it was held that the installation of a central heating system, by affecting and being connected to the fabric of the house in question, amounted to a structural alteration to the house. In relation to windows it was held in *Boswell v. Crucible Steel Co of America*[32] that large unopenable plate-glass windows fixed in steel beadings were part of the structure of business premises and so not part of the tenant's liability to repair, which covered landlord's fixtures and the interior of the demised premises only. In *Green v. Eales*[33] a landlord's covenant to repair external parts of the demised premises was held to extend to a dividing wall which he failed to secure or support after the demolition of adjoining premises.[34]

Certainly decorative repairs cannot be regarded as structural because these will not interfere with the main structural framework or fabric of the demised premises.

B. *Construction of Landlord's Covenant to Repair*

General Principles

First, as with the tenant's covenant to repair, if the landlord covenants to keep premises in repair then he must, if they are out of repair, first put them into repair, to comply with his covenant.[35] Secondly, in no case is the landlord under a general covenant to repair, bound to give back to the tenant improved premises; but if, in the case of a lease of new premises, he has expressly guaranteed their structural soundness, he may well find himself liable to pay for very extensive rebuilding under what on its face is a heavy repairing covenant, unless the covenant is also drafted in such a way as to exclude liability for structural design faults. Attention is, therefore, turned to the principles as they apply first to old premises (and premises generally) and then to design faults in new premises.

---

[30] *Woodfall* 1–1460.
[31] [1979] 1 All ER 365, CA.
[32] [1925] 1 KB 119, CA.
[33] (1841) 2 QB 225.
[34] If a covenant refers to "outside parts" it has been stated that window repairs fall within it: *Woodfall* 1–1460.
[35] *Saner v. Bilton* (1878) 7 Ch D 815, CA.

Old Premises and General Approach

In the case of old premises a general covenant to repair
will not oblige the landlord to carry out work which will
substantially alter the original design of the premises and
which will improve them. In *Pembery* v. *Lamdin*[36] the landlord covenanted to keep the exterior of the demised premises
in good tenantable repair and condition. At the date of the
lease the premises were over 100 years old and were found
to be in a very damp state, as their external walls had never
been built with a damp-proof course. The damp which in
fact was present in the walls was ruinous to the tenant but
the landlord was held not liable to remedy it by putting in
what would be a new damp proof course. The landlord's
covenant was construed as relating to the existing premises
in their condition when demised: he was not bound to improve
on their original design.[37] Likewise, in *Wainwright* v. *Leeds
City Council*[38] the landlords, a local authority, were held
not obliged by the covenant implied by section 11 of the *Landlord and Tenant Act* 1985[39] to put into a back-to-back
house a new damp-proof course not there when the house
was built. The whole point of these two cases is that in each
of them the premises lacked, when built, a particular design
feature, a damp proof course, and the landlord's covenant
was, as was seen, construed as extending only to the premises
as originally built. On the other hand, in *Elmcroft Developments Ltd* v. *Tankersley-Sawyer*[40] three basement flats in
a larger block of flats had a damp proof course originally,
but it was defective. The result was water penetration, by
capillary action, into the walls of the three basement flats.
The landlords were under a general covenant to repair, the
costs of which work the tenants contributed to in service
charges. The landlords were held liable to insert a new damp
proof course, rather than simply being held liable to patch

[36] [1940] 2 All ER 434, CA.
[37] It would have been necessary to remove all the panelling and battening of the walls, to
asphalt the walls and then build in a new wall to hold the asphalt in position and build a
new concrete floor—in other words virtually to rebuild the premises as new.
[38] (1984) 270 EG 1289, CA; also *Mullaney* v. *Maybourne Grange (Croydon) Management
Co Ltd* (1986) 277 EG 1350.
[39] Which is to keep in repair the structure and exterior of the "dwelling-house" in question:
see Chapter 11.
[40] (1984) 270 EG 140, CA.

up the existing damp proof course, by means of silicone injection and other modern work. It is worth noting that on these facts the work did not involve reconstruction or renewal of the whole subject-matter of the demise.[41] If it had, the result would have been otherwise. Likewise in *Yorkbrook Investments Ltd* v. *Batten*,[42] landlords who covenanted to provide a good sufficient and constant supply of hot and cold water and an adequate supply of heating in the hot-water radiators, were held liable to replace or renew antiquated or unservicable equipment (ie to replace effectively broken-down equipment) although it must be pointed out that the covenant in the long leases concerned only excepted liability caused by matters beyond the control of the landlord and apparently they could, by taking prompt remedial action, have prevented the break-down which took place.

On more general principles, there is no doubt that in interpreting the landlord's express covenant to repair the court will, in the words of Sachs LJ in *Brew Bros* v. *Snax (Ross) Ltd*[43] "... look at the particular building, look at the state which it is in at the date of the lease ... look at the precise terms of the lease, and then come to a conclusion as to whether, on a fair interpretation of those terms in relation to that state, the requisite work can fairly be termed repair. However large the covenant it must not be looked at in vacuo."

Requirement of Condition of Disrepair

Whether in relation to a landlord's express or statute implied (under section 11 of the *Landlord and Tenant Act 1985*) covenant to repair, there must be a condition of disrepair to the physical condition of the item in question before the landlord can be obliged to carry out any repairs. In *Quick* v. *Taff-Ely Borough Council*[44] the tenant of a council house failed to obtain an order of specific performance against the landlord where the house in question suffered from severe

---

[41] See also *Stent* v. *Monmouth District Council* (1987) 282 EG 705; [1987] 1 EGLR 59.
[42] (1985) 276 EG 545; [1985] 2 EGLR 100, CA.
[43] [1970] 1 QB 612 at p 640, CA.
[44] (1985) 276 EG 452; [1985] 2 EGLR 50, CA.

condensation, caused by a lack of insulation around the concrete window lintels, sweating from the single-glazed metal-
frame windows and inadequate heating. The windows and
lintels were not themselves out of repair. The house was built
to conform to building regulations in force at the time. It
was held that the landlord could not be compelled to replace
the windows with warmer materials or to insulate the lintels.
Dillon LJ said that if, in the process of curing a state of disrepair, some design fault in the item out of repair was cured,
the landlord would have to carry out the work nonetheless
as the only practicable way of making good the damage. In
the *Quick* case there was no condition of disrepair shown
to exist and so at that stage the design fault was incurable.[45]
On the other hand, once a condition of disrepair is shown
to exist, then if the only sensible and practicable way of carrying out the remedial work is to replace the damaged item
rather than just to patch it up, the landlord will have to bear
the cost of replacement of the item and pay damages for consequential losses to the tenant. This was the position in *Stent
v. Monmouth District Council*[46] where a landlord under an
express covenant to repair the structure and exterior of the
dwelling concerned was held liable to pay for the replacement
of the front door which was damaged, letting in water, with
a front door of a different design, and also to pay damages
for the tenant's consequential losses. The position was similar
in this respect to that in *Elmcroft Developments Ltd* v. *Tankersley-Sawyer*,[47] where the landlords were held liable to
replace a defective damp proof course with a completely new
one (of presumably a different design). The only sensible way
of doing the repairs in both cases was the replacement of
the damaged item out of repair.

New Premises: Design Faults Liability

The landlord's liability for carrying out remedial work to
cure an inherent design defect in new premises is essentially
a question of interpreting his covenant to repair. It may
exclude all liability for design defects; or it may be a general

---

[45] The same rule applies to a tenant's general covenant to repair: *Post Office* v. *Aquarius
Properties Ltd* (1987) 281 EG 798; [1987] 1 EGLR 40, discussed in Chapter 6.
[46] (1987) 282 EG 705.
[47] (1984) 270 EG 140, CA.

covenant to repair in strong and unqualified terms. No general rule may therefore safely be laid down.

Inherent defects have been defined as defects existing but not visible at the commencement of the lease which result from (1) defective design or (2) defective supervision of the construction of the property or (3) defective workmanship or materials.[48]

A landlord's liability to remedy inherent defects has been spelt out of a strong covenant to repair. This was the position in *Smedley* v. *Chumley & Hawke Ltd*[49] where a restaurant was built as part of a motel complex by the landlords. They were under covenant to keep the main walls and roof of the demised premises in good structural repair and condition throughout the term and to promptly make good all defects due to faulty materials or workmanship in the construction of the premises. The building itself stood on a timber frame, standing on a concrete raft, supported by piles: one end of the raft sank into the ground, causing major structural damage to the whole building. The remedial work required was extensive, involving jacking up the building and raft, driving in additional support piles, building a new floor and other incidental work. The reason for the work was that the original foundations of the building were defectively-built. On the question of liability under the landlord's covenant (the tenant being liable to repair the structure and exterior of the demised premises) the Court of Appeal held that the cost of the structural repairs and the resulting losses caused to the tenants by their state of disrepair, must be borne by the landlords. They had undertaken responsibility, in this lease, for the structural condition of the walls and roof and for defects due to faulty materials or workmanship: the only way, it was held, to comply with their unqualified obligation was to replace the foundations. The Court of Appeal was much influenced by the fact that these were new not old premises and indicated that apparently the parties contemplated that, at the date of the grant of the lease, the walls and roof would be in good structural condition ie that the foundations would be sound.

---

[48] Murray J Ross, *Drafting and Negotiating Commercial Leases* Chapter 8 para 8–8.
[49] (1982) 261 EG 775, CA.

Conclusion

The words of the covenant of the landlords in the *Smedley*
case were very strong and it should not too readily be assumed
that in a different set of circumstances, with different words
and a different factual matrix, the result in that case would
automatically be repeated. Merely because the landlord of
newly-built premises has expressly undertaken liability for
structural or exterior repairs it will not necessarily follow
without more that he will be liable to replace the foundations
if defectively-built, at least not unless or until these defects
produce a state of disrepair within the landlord's covenant.[50]

Old Premises: Different Considerations

In the case of old premises very different considerations
might apply. Supposing that a building is near the end of
its useful life and is in danger of collapse as a result. It has
been held that a general covenant to repair by the landlord
will not oblige him to rebuild the premises as new. In *Torrens*
v. *Walker*[51] the landlord was under a general covenant to
repair the outside of a 200-year old house held by the tenants
on an 18-year lease and used by them as an hotel. The exterior
walls were demolished by the local authority due to their
dangerous condition and the open building was more or less
left standing and was totally unusable. The landlords were
held not liable to rebuild the walls: to have compelled them
to do so would have been to have required them to give back
to the tenant a totally different thing to that demised at the
outset of the lease. This result seems to accord with good
sense, for by the date of the commencement of the lease the
building was almost at the end of its effective life. Remedial
work to save the building would not have been repairing work
and the landlords did not undertake to rebuild the premises.

Conclusion

The *Smedley* and *Torrens* cases present extreme examples
of the limits of the relevant principles. In the former case

[50] See *Quick* v. *Taff-Ely Borough Council*, *supra* and *Post Office* v. *Aquarius Properties Ltd*, *supra*.
[51] [1906] 2 Ch 166.

the tenants secured from the landlord a virtual design guarantee of the soundness of the structure of the premises. In the latter case the building was at the virtual end of its effective life at the time of the demise, all that the landlords had undertaken to do was to repair an old and possibly inherently defective structure. As to cases falling between these two extremes, reference should be made to Chapter 6, which applies here, bearing in mind that ultimately the question is one of fact and degree.

V. DEPENDENCE OF LANDLORD'S OBLIGATION TO REPAIR ON NOTICE OF WANT OF REPAIR

General

The general rule is that in all cases, whether the landlord is under an express or implied covenant to repair (in the latter case irrespective of whether this is implied by statute or common law), he must have notice ie actual knowledge from the tenant or a third party of the want of repair, since it is only after a reasonable time from such notice has elapsed that the landlord's obligation to repair arises.[52] This rule applies to defects in the premises which existed prior to the granting of the lease which manifest themselves only during the currency of the lease.[53] It also extends to defects, latent or patent, which arise and manifest themselves during the currency of the lease; so if, as in *O'Brien* v. *Robinson*[54] a latent defect, of which the landlord has no advance warning, causes injury to the tenant, the landlord is not liable in damages to the tenant, so that where, as in that case, the ceiling of the bedroom in a dwelling-house fell in due to an unknown latent defect, the landlord was held not liable to the tenant for the injuries and damage sustained as no notice had been given to him (in advance) of the existence of the defect—even though, as the defect was latent, the tenant could not have notified the landlord.

[52] *McCarrick* v. *Liverpool Corporation* [1947] AC 219, HL; *O'Brien* v. *Robinson* [1973] AC 912, HL.
[53] *Uniproducts (Manchester) Ltd* v. *Rose Furnishers Ltd* [1956] 1 WLR 45 (where the doctrine of notice absolved the landlords from liability to repair a defect in the premises existing at the commencement of the lease).
[54] *Supra.*

Notice in the present context means giving the landlord knowledge of the existence of the defect, or at least sufficient information to put him on inquiry. In *O'Brien* v. *Robinson* the question was left open as to whether, if the landlord had had previous information from a source other than the tenant (say from his agent or rent-collector) of the existence of a particular defect, this would suffice to put the landlord on notice. In *McGreal* v. *Wake*[55] the point was settled. It was there held that a landlord on whom a local authority repair notice had been served was from that time liable for any consequences flowing to the tenant from the disrepair of the premises, being fixed as from the date of the repair notice, with knowledge of the want of repair.

The fact that the landlord may have a right to enter and execute repairs for which he is responsible, will not, of itself, fix him with notice, except in one instance. Under section 4 of the *Defective Premises Act* 1972, (see also Chapter 11) the landlord will be liable for breach of the duty imposed on him by that provision if he either knows (whether as the result of his being notified by the tenant or otherwise) or if he ought in all the circumstances to have known, of the relevant defect. This means that where the landlord is, for instance, under an obligation to repair imposed by section 11 of the *Landlord and Tenant Act* 1985, liability in tort under section 4 of the 1972 Act will arise as from notice to the landlord from the tenant or from notice to the landlord from a third party, or even from any knowledge which the landlord himself ought to have had.

Section 4 of the 1972 Act also imposes liability on the landlord if he has a right under the lease either expressly, impliedly or under statute, to enter and execute repairs.

Position once Notice is Given

Notice means the giving to the landlord of information about the existence of the defect such as would put a reasonable man on inquiry whether works of repair are required.[56] Once the landlord has notice then he has a reasonable time

---

[55] (1984) 269 EG 1254, CA. Also *Dinefwr Borough Council* v. *Jones* (1987) 284 EG 58 (notice to landlord from officer of housing and environmental health department sufficient).
[56] *O'Brien* v. *Robinson* [1973] AC 912, HL.

within which to comply with his obligations and only after this time runs out will he be in breach of covenant.[57] As to what amount of time is reasonable for this purpose, obviously there is no fixed rule though it may be suggested that a few weeks in principle should be a sufficient period of suspension to enable the landlord to organise the works—except in the case of urgent works where a very few days at most might be all the time allowable in the circumstances.[58]

Where the landlord retains the possession and control of part of the demised premises and that part falls into disrepair, and the landlord is under covenant to repair the part in question, then no notice is required from the tenant of the part of the premises so demised, of the want of repair. Hence, in *Melles & Co* v. *Holme*[59] a landlord who retained the roof of the demised premises was held liable to the tenant in damages when a gutter out of repair flooded the tenant's part of the premises, despite the landlord's regular inspections of the premises and though he had no notice of the want of repair from the tenant.

VI LANDLORD'S RIGHT OF ENTRY TO CARRY OUT REPAIRS

General Rule

If none of the exceptions mentioned below apply, and if there is no express reservation in the lease entitling the landlord to enter and execute repairs (possibly further allowing the landlord to charge the tenant with their cost) then the landlord, by the very fact that a lease grants the tenant exclusive possession, deprives himself of any right to enter the property to execute repairs. It makes no difference in this that the landlord may himself be liable to forfeiture under his own lease if the repairs are not executed, or that he enters with the permission of the sub-lessees (if any).[60] In such cases

---

[57] *McGreal* v. *Wake* (1984) 269 EG 1254, CA.

[58] See *Griffin* v. *Pillett* [1926] 1 KB 17. In *McGreal* v. *Wake supra*, it was held that a period of eight weeks from notice to the landlord (in the form of a local authority repair notice) was on the facts a reasonable time.

[59] [1918] 2 KB 100; also *Bishop* v. *Consolidated London Properties Ltd* (1933) 102 LJ KB 257.

[60] *Stocker* v. *Planet Building Society* (1879) 27 WR 877, CA. On unauthorised re-entry generally, cf in a quite different context *Ashton* v. *Sobelman* [1987] 1 All ER 755; (1987) 281 EG 303 (landlord cannot re-enter premises against tenant by arrangement with sub-tenants).

of unauthorised entry by the landlord the tenant is in principle entitled to seek an injunction.[61]

Exceptions

In the first place the lease may contain an express term entitling the landlord to enter, inspect, and to execute repairs and possibly also to charge the tenant with their cost, irrespective however of whether the repairs are landlords' or tenants' repairs.[62] Where this is not the case there are a number of further exceptions to the general rule.

Statute

Certain statutes contain provisions which expressly confer on the landlord and/or certain other persons the right to enter to inspect and to carry out repairs. The following are the chief provisions.

1. *Landlord and Tenant Act 1985 section 11(6).* Under this provision, a right of entry is given to the landlord or a person authorised by him in writing, at reasonable hours of the day, on giving 24 hours' written notice to the tenant or occupier, to enter the relevant premises to view their condition and state of repair. This by implication carries with it a right to enter and carry out any necessary repairs but the section does not expressly so provide. It is confined to dwelling-houses and flats to which the statute implies obligation in question applies, as to which see Chapter 11.

2. *Landlord and Tenant Act 1985 section 8(2).* This confers a similar right of entry on the landlord where he under a statute-implied duty to keep small dwellings in a state fit for human habitation. See further Chapter 3.

3. *Agricultural Holdings Act 1986 section 23.* This gives a right to the landlord or any other person authorised by him, at all reasonable times, to enter the holding for the purpose of viewing its state and also for the purpose of carrying out his responsibilities to manage the holding in accordance

---

[61] *Stocker* v. *Planet Building Society, supra; Regional Properties Ltd* v. *City of London Properties Ltd* (1980) 257 EG 65.

[62] See the Appendix to this book for a precedent (No V). Permission to reproduce this is gratefully acknowledged to Sweet & Maxwell Ltd.

with good estate management and providing or improving fixed equipment otherwise than in the fulfilling of those responsibilities.

4. *Rent Act 1977 section 148*.[63] This makes it a condition of a protected tenancy of a dwelling-house that the tenant will afford the landlord access to the dwelling-house and all reasonable facilities for executing therein any repairs he is entitled to execute. This condition is, by section 3(2) of the 1977 Act, automatically carried forward into any statutory tenancy arising on the termination of a previous protected tenancy. Section 3(2) of the 1977 Act in any case gives a right of entry identical to that under the previous protected tenancy, though strictly this conferral is totally unnecessary in view of section 148. But what section 148 and, by inference, section 3(2) of the 1977 Act do involve for a landlord, to his detriment, is that the landlord of any protected or statutory tenant will automatically be subjected to the liabilities imposed on him under section 4 of the *Defective Premises Act* 1972.[64]

Common Law

1. It is an implied condition of a weekly periodic tenancy that the landlord is to have the right to enter the premises to execute repairs.[65]

2. Even if the landlord in a given case fails expressly to reserve himself a right to enter, inspect and execute repairs, he will have an automatic implied licence from the tenant to enable him to enter, at a reasonable time, to execute the repairs in question.[66] A right of entry to do repairs (whether implied in the case of landlords' express covenants to do repairs, or conferred by statute such as section 11(6) of the *Landlord and Tenant Act* 1985) involves therefore an implied licence by the tenant allowing the landlord to enter the premises and occupy them for a reasonable time to do the

---

[63] Also *Rent (Agriculture) Act* 1976 Sched 5 para 8: in the case of agricultural tied houses it is a condition of the statutory tenancy that the tenant will afford the landlord access to the dwelling-house and all reasonable facilities for executing therein any repairs the landlord is entitled to execute.

[64] As to which see Chapter 11 of this book.

[65] *Mint* v. *Good* [1951] 1 KB 517, CA.

[66] *Granada Theatres* v. *Freehold Investment (Leytonstone)* [1959] 1 WLR 570, CA; *McGreal* v. *Wake* (1984) 269 EG 1254, CA.

repairs, but the right is limited to that which is strictly necessary in order to do the work. It does not involve a further obligation by the tenant to give the landlord exclusive occupation unless this is necessary to enable the repairs to be done, as where the disrepair is so serious that occupation of the whole premises is the only reasonable way in which the landlord can carry out the work. This would be so where the premises were destroyed by fire or the floors had collapsed and the walls bulged rendering the premises unusable.[67]

A landlord under an express covenant to repair (or where the covenant is implied or statute-implied) is not liable to execute any repairs unless he first has notice from the tenant or a third party of the want of repair as was seen above. After that however, and once a reasonable time has then elapsed to enable the landlord to comply with his covenant, he must enter and do the repairs for which he is liable within a reasonable time after notice; and as was said above, what is a reasonable time for this purpose really is a question of fact and degree. In this, if the landlord attempts within a reasonable time to do the work but is prevented from doing so by the tenant's refusing him access to the premises, the tenant, for so long as he persists in his refusal, will be unable to claim damages as the landlord will not be in breach of covenant.[68]

VII. OTHER MATTERS

For a discussion of the liability of the landlord to rebuild the premises in the event of fire see Chapter 10. As to tenants' remedies against landlords for their breaches of repairing covenant, see Chapter 9.

---

[67] *McGreal* v. *Wake* (1984) 269 EG 1254, CA; also *Saner* v. *Bilton* (1878) 7 Ch D 815.
[68] *Granada Theatres* v. *Frehold Investment* (*Leytonstone*) *supra.* On damages see further Chapters 7 and 9.

Chapter 5

EXPRESS OBLIGATIONS OF
TENANT TO REPAIR

I. INTRODUCTION

A. *Outline of General Principles*

Most leases of any significant length will contain a covenant by the tenant to keep the demised premises in repair during the lease and to deliver them up in repair at the end of the lease, and this may be linked to a covenant to repair after notice.[1] However there are limits on the power of landlords to take covenants to repair from tenants. In the first place, no covenant to repair may be taken from the tenant to the extent that it would impose obligations to repair any part of the structure or exterior of a dwelling-house to which section 11 of the *Landlord and Tenant Act* 1985 applies.[2] Secondly, it will be seen that, in principle, a general covenant to repair cannot extend to works which will require the renewal or replacement of the whole, or in substance the whole, of the demised premises. This is discussed in Chapter 6 of this book.

On the relationship between the tenant's express covenant to repair and other liabilities of his with regard to the maintenance of the demised premises, even where the tenant is under an express (ie contractual) obligation to repair this will not displace any tortious liability he may be under. The point becomes very relevant in one situation. If the covenant to repair has ceased to be enforceable, then the landlord's remedies against the tenant for damage to the premises lie in tort. This was the position in *Associated Deliveries Ltd* v. *Harrison*[3] where the landlords had served a writ claiming forfeiture for breaches of the tenant's covenant to repair and the

---

[1] *Woodfall* 1–1420. The length of the notice is normally three months. See further below.
[2] See further Chapter 11.
[3] (1984) 272 EG 321, CA.

premises then, after service of the writ, suffered further serious
damage due to vandalisation. It was held that since the effect
of the service of the writ was notionally to re-enter the
premises, this put the covenants in the lease to an end. That
being so, no damages could be claimed for alleged breaches
of the tenant's repairing covenant in relation to the damage
from vandalisation, this occurring after service of the writ,
for at that date the covenant to repair ceased to operate. The
landlord's remedy lay in tort, viz damages for wrongful occupation of the land after service of the writ. Such a claim,
to be enforceable, must be pleaded in addition to any claim
the landlord may have against the tenant for mesne profits.
Other questions arising out of forfeiture and damages claims
by landlords for breaches of a tenant's covenant to repair
will be discussed in Chapters 7 and 8.

Continuing Liability of Original Tenant after Assignment of Lease

Because the tenant's covenant to repair is a contractual
obligation, while it will always be enforceable in principle
between the original parties to the lease, if the original landlord (or his assign by deed of the reversion) wishes to enforce
the covenant against the tenant or his assigns, he must comply
with certain requirements.[4] The person to whom the landlord will look for performance of the repairing covenant is
presumably the present tenant; if however there is a breach
and the lease has been assigned, and damages cannot be paid
by the present tenant, the landlord has the right to have
recourse where appropriate against the original tenant who,
despite assigning the lease, remains liable in contract throughout the whole term granted by the lease. This means that
the landlord, if he fails to obtain performance from the present
tenant/assignee, may seek damages from the original tenant
and any sureties of his, even if he has obtained possession
from the assignee, unless he has released the original tenant.

The fact that, once the original tenant assigns his interest,
he is no longer in possession of the premises and so cannot

---

[4] See *passim* Woodfall Chapter 11; *Adkin* Chapter X; *Evans* Chapter 5; *Yates and Hawkins*
Chapter 7.

perform the covenant to repair is immaterial: he is supposed to be protected because he can look to the assignee for performance of the repairing covenants.[5] However, if the first assignee later assigns to another, his liability for breaches of covenant comes to an end, unless he has covenanted with the landlord to observe the covenants for the residue of the term.

Where the original landlord assigns the reversion expectant on the lease, it has been held that, first, the assignee of the reversion may enforce all breaches of the tenant's covenant to repair, and this whether the breaches took place before or after the assignment date, assuming there is a continuing breach at that date.[6] In other words, damages for breach of the tenant's covenant to repair may be assessed for pre and post assignment periods and awarded to the assignee of the reversion. The original landlord drops totally out of the picture. In the second place it has been held that if the lease has been assigned as well as the reversion, and the assignee of the lease is in breach of covenant, but cannot compensate the assignee of the reversion, the latter may enforce the covenant against the original tenant, who is liable throughout the term to him for breaches of covenant by the current tenant.[7]

The original landlord may insist on a surety or sureties guaranteeing the due performance by the tenant (or any assign of the lease) of their obligations. If the tenant defaults and cannot pay damages (say by reason of his insolvency) the landlord should then be able to look to the sureties for damages. If the landlord assigns the reversion by deed, provided the covenant of suretyship relates to real covenants, such as to pay rent or to repair, the assignee of the reversion will be able to enforce the covenant of suretyship automatically: no separate assignment of the benefit of it to him will be required.[8]

The next matter to consider is what sort of language one might expect to find in standard-form tenants' covenants to repair.

[5] *Thames Manufacturing Co v. Perrotts (Nichol & Peyton)* (1984) 271 EG 284.
[6] *Re King* [1963] Ch 459, CA, applying *Law of Property Act* 1925 s 141.
[7] *Arlesford Trading Co Ltd v. Servansingh* [1971] 1 WLR 1080, CA (rent arrears).
[8] *Kumar v. Dunning* (1987) 283 EG 59, CA.

B. *Examples of Precedents of Tenant's Covenant to Repair*

The following are given as examples of the standard-form covenants to repair commonly imposed on tenants of leases of varying duration.

Long Lease

"At all times during the said term when and as often as need shall require well and substantially to cleanse repair support and uphold and from time to time when necessary rebuild to the satisfaction of the Landlord all present and future buildings forming part of the demised premises and all fixtures additions and improvements which may at any time be fastened or affixed to or erected or placed upon the demised premises..."[9]

This onerous form of covenant is to be construed on the same principles as would apply to construing a similar covenant by a landlord; that said, the scope of this form of covenant is considered in detail in Chapter 6. As will be seen, such a covenant as this is apt to require all but extensive rebuilding work to be carried out by the tenant not the landlord. Clearly, such a covenant would not be found in a short lease; in the case of a lease of residential flats or offices, while much depends on the exact circumstances, the landlord may, as was pointed out in Chapter 4, undertake extensive liabilities to repair and maintain the structure and exterior of the premises in return for contributions in the form of service charges from tenants. Lastly, in this, difficulties arise with general covenants to repair in relation to inherent design faults in the premises especially in the case of new or relatively new premises. These are discussed in Chapter 6.

It will be appreciated that lighter obligations would be expected to be imposed on tenants of short terms.

Short Leases

An example of the sort of covenant which might be found in the case of residential premises is this.

[9] The source for this and for all the following extracts is *Precedents for the Conveyancer* Vol 1, 5–3 Cl 14(b) and (7); 5–5 Cl 2(3); 5–31 Cl 5(a); and 5–31 Cl 5(b). Permission for the reproduction of these extracts is gratefully acknowledged to Sweet & Maxwell Ltd.

"At all times during the said term to keep the interior [exterior if required] of the demised premises including all fixtures and fittings therein in a good and tenantable state of repair and condition and the windows whole and clean and in the last year thereof (whether determined by effluxion of time or in any other way) to redecorate the whole of such interior [exterior if required] ..."

It will be appreciated that difficulties of interpretation may arise as to what is the "interior" or "exterior" of the demised premises for the purpose of the above covenant. Reference should be made first to Chapter 4 where some aspects of this are dealt with and also to Chapter 11. As to the meaning of "good tenantable repair" or similar terms, reference may be made to Chapter 6.

Another example of a tenant's covenant to repair on a short or medium term business lease is as follows:

"At all times during the said term when and as often as need shall require well and substantially to cleanse repair support uphold and keep in good and substantial repair and condition the inside of the demised premises [and certain defined parts of the exterior of the demised premises] ..."

In these cases and others no doubt, the above covenants by the tenant may be accompanied by a further covenant to deliver up the demised premises in good repair, perhaps along the following lines:

"At the expiration or sooner determination of the said term quietly to yield up unto the Landlord the premises in such state of repair and condition as shall in all respects be consistent with a full and due performance by the Tenant of the covenants on the part of the Tenant."

Inherent Defects

The problem of inherent defects is discussed in Chapter 6. It may be worth noting that clauses have been designed which limit or exclude the liability of the tenant to carry out remedial work necessitated by inherent defects, along the following lines.

"Provided that the Tenant shall not be liable ... for remedying any defect in the land or buildings which shall (or might) give rise to a claim by the Landlord or Tenant against any third party in relation to the surveying design or construction of the demised premises..." Provision would then be made for the reference of any disputes to arbitration.[10]

It will be seen from Chapter 6 that if remedial work is classified as repair not renewal then the fact that it is required to remedy an inherent defect is of itself no defence.

For extracts from a covenant to paint and decorate, see below. As regards lettings of residential premises on weekly or other periodic tenancies, the obligations of the landlord will in principle be regulated by statute (see Chapter 11), and this means that those of the tenant will be very limited.

There is a measure of protection for the landlord under waste even if no covenants or obligations are taken from the tenant (see Chapter 2). The only express covenant usual in these cases is one which ensures that the tenant keeps the premises clean and in good condition (damage by fair wear and tear and fire excepted) and that he returns the premises to the landlord in the same condition as they were in at the commencement of the tenancy, fair wear and tear and accidents by fire or acts of God excepted. The meaning of fair wear and tear is discussed later in this Chapter.

C. *Power to Vary Repairing Covenants in Long Leases of Flats*

Part IV of the *Landlord and Tenant Act* 1987[11] enables any party to a long lease of a flat[12] to apply to the county court for an order varying the terms of the lease (s 35(1)). A variation order may be applied for where the lease fails to make satisfactory provision for the repair or maintenance of:

(1) the flat in question
(2) the building containing the flat, or
(3) any land or building let to the tenant under the lease or in respect of which rights are conferred on the tenant under it (s 35(2)(a)).

Further grounds for a variation order application are that the lease fails to make satisfactory provision for:

[10] *Precedents for the Conveyancer*, 5–66, with due acknowledgement, see note 9.
[11] In force on a day to be appointed (s 62(2)).
[12] Defined as a lease granted for a term certain exceeding 21 years (s 59(3)(a)).

(1) the provision or maintenance of any services reasonably necessary to ensure that the occupiers of the flat enjoy a reasonable standard of accommodation—examples might include porterage and attendance (s 35(2)(d);

(2) the repair or maintenance of installations, whether in the flat concerned or not, provided that the installations are necessary to ensure that flat occupiers enjoy a reasonable standard of accommodation (s 35(1)(c)).[13]

It is certainly not possible to predict precisely in what cases variation orders will be made, given that the terms of Part IV of the 1987 Act are general, not is it possible to predict how many applications will be made. However, there may be long leases of flats where the covenants to repair and maintain the structure and exterior, or those relating to the common parts or installations both in the flats themselves and in the main block (providing heat and hot water or central refrigeration for example) fail to draw up the exact boundaries between the responsibilities of the landlord and the tenant. There may be cases also where there are discovered, after the granting of long leases of the flats concerned, inherent defects in the main building. If the liability for rectifying these as between landlord and tenant is not clearly delineated in the leases themselves, Part IV of the 1987 Act would presumably allow the court on the application of either the landlord or one or more of the tenants to make a variation order.[14]

The provisions of Part IV are limited to long leases of flats. It remains to be seen whether at some future date they might be extended to enable variations to be made in relation to other classes of lease or tenancy in the residential or commercial sector.[15]

---

[13] "Reasonable standard of accommodation" for the purposes of s 35(1)(c) and (d) is not defined but s 35(3) provides that relevant factors may include: (a) factors relating to the safety and security of the flat and its occupiers and of any common parts in the building; (b) other factors relating to the condition of any such common parts.

[14] See further Chapter 9 of this book, where Part IV is discussed in relation to variation of service charges provisions. In so far as that discussion relates to the making and terms of variation orders, and the effect on third parties, it applies to repairing covenants also.

[15] In the case of agricultural holdings, the maintenance, repair and insurance provisions of a tenancy may be varied by an arbitrator on application by landlord or tenant following a request by the other party to bring the provisions of a written agreement into conformity with the 1973 model clauses, where the parties cannot agree on variations: *Agricultural Holdings Act* 1986 s 8, discussed in Chapter 13.

D. *Reform*

In 1975 the Law Commission produced a report on repairing obligations.[16] It has not been enacted. The chances are that, at least in the near future it will not be.[17] One matter which has been exposed by developments in interpreting covenants to repair is at once deserving of mention. The Law Commission note that some inherent defects may have to be rectified under a general covenant to repair. They believe that, nevertheless, there is a chance of neither side being held liable for a particular item of work.[18] Rent will still be payable in such a case. The Law Commission suggest overcoming this particular problem by giving the tenant the opportunity to end the lease or to renegotiate its terms, if a substantial, inherent defect is found.[19]

With regard to multi-occupied buildings containing flats, a working group of the Law Commission has produced a report advocating the adoption of commonhold tenure.[20] This new tenure would apply to freehold land, only, and to new buildings, with provision for enabling existing buildings to be converted into commonhold premises. The principle behind commonholds is that the management of the building would be vested in a commonhold association, of which all unit holders in the building would be members. A reserve fund for management costs would have to be maintained.

The idea no doubt is to promote the efficient management of blocks of flats in particular. Commonhold would be limited to areas of compulsory registration of title. It would be optional not compulsory.

The Report is at the time this book went to press, with the main Law Commission, but it cannot be predicted whether and if so, on what time-scale, its radical proposals will be implemented. If they are implemented, then over time long leasehold tenure of residential flats might die out or at least be much reduced in significance.

[16] Law Com No 67.
[17] Acknowledged by the Law Commission in Law Com No 162 (Landlord and Tenant: Reform of the Law 1987), para 1.6.
[18] As happened in *Post Office* v. *Aquarius Properties Ltd* (1987) 281 EG 798, CA, discussed in Chapter 6.
[19] Law Com No 162 (1987) para 4. 70.
[20] Law Com No 179 (1987)—a good summary is given in 137 (1987) New Law J 699 and 715.

II. CONSTRUCTION OF COVENANTS TO REPAIR

Introduction

Tenants' covenants to repair are not completely standard-form, as the extent of the obligation imposed by them will vary with all the circumstances.[21] Nonetheless, as was seen, there are certain well-known types of standard-form tenants' repairing covenants, those found commonly in long leases being onerous and extensive, while those found in short leases are generally far narrower in scope. Accordingly, when the courts are faced with the problem of interpreting a particular covenant to repair, they have adopted a position of compromise. On the one hand it has been said by Fletcher Moulton LJ in *Lurcott* v. *Wakely and Wheeler*[22] that the words of the covenant must be given their proper legal signification as applied to the subject-matter to which the covenant refers. In other words, each covenant to repair must be construed according to the actual words used, having regard to the factual matrix of the case, the age of the building in question (where relevant) and the intention or expectation of the tenant at the date of commencement of the lease. However, the "actual words used" does not necessarily mean that blindly literal meanings will always be adopted since it is the good sense of the agreement which must be ascertained.[23] Moreover, there is some difficulty in directly applying one case on a particular form of words directly to another case, where the words used in the particular covenant may be different. Hence it has been stated that the court is not necessarily looking for the strict literal meaning of the covenant, but also it appears that decisions on the meaning of terms like "repair", "renew", and so on, give valuable but by no means conclusive guidance to subsequent cases if the circumstances of the second case do not fairly allow of the same construction being put on the words.

"It appears to be still less useful to take a number of terms

---

[21] A fact judicially recognised eg in *Post Office* v. *Aquarius Properties Ltd* (1987) 281 EG 798, CA. "Clear words are needed to impose a contractual obligation on the tenant to remedy the defects in the original construction, at least at a time before these have caused any damage" (Slade LJ *ibid* at p. 804).

[22] [1911] 1KB 905, at p. 915, CA.

[23] *White* v. *Nicholson* (1842) 4 Man & G 95, at p. 98.

which may be found in different leases, and so impute to all of them a special meaning attached by authority to one of them."[24]

To take two examples, first, it has been held that a reference in a lease to premises as they "now" are, was taken to mean the date when the relevant tenant took possession even though this might be later than that when the covenant was first entered into.[25] Secondly, a covenant to put premises into repair "forthwith" is taken to allow the tenant a reasonable time after his entry into possession to carry out the relevant repairs.[26]

Modern Approach

The modern approach to the interpretation of a tenant's covenant to repair was summed up as follows by Sachs LJ in *Brew Bros* v. *Snax (Ross) Ltd.*[27]

"... The correct approach is to look at the particular building, to look at the state which it is in at the date of the lease, and then come to a conclusion as to whether, on a fair interpretation of those terms in relation to that state, the work can be fairly termed repair. However large the covenant, it must not be looked at in vacuo."

A tenant's covenant to repair is not a covenant to rebuild the whole premises (unless such additional words clearly appear), and that which requires repair must be in a condition worse than it was at some earlier time.[28] In *Post Office* v. *Aquarius Properties Ltd*[29] it was held that where a structural design defect had been present since the construction of the demised building and no damage to the premises had so far occurred, the tenant under a general covenant to repair would not expect to have to cure the defect. Very clear words would be needed to require the tenant to execute that work. The result was that neither landlord nor tenant was liable to cure the inherent defect in the building concerned.

---

[24] *Calthorpe* v. *McOscar* [1924] 1KB 716 at pp. 731–732 (Atkin LJ).

[25] *White* v. *Nicholson, supra.*

[26] *Doe d Pittman* v. *Sutton* (1841) 9 C & P 706.

[27] [1970] 1 QB 612, CA, adopted in *Smedley* v. *Chumley & Hawke Ltd* (1982) 261 EG 775, CA.

[28] *Quick* v. *Taff-Ely Borough Council* [1985] 1 QB 809; [1985] 2 EGLR 50; (1985) 276 EG 452.

[29] (1987) 281 EG 798, CA.

In most leases of commercial and high-class residential property, at any rate, one would expect to find two main types of repairing covenant, first, a general covenant to repair, secondly, a covenant to paint and decorate. Most of the problems come in interpreting the scope and meaning of the general covenant to repair. The matter is discussed in Chapter 6. In particular, there are two problems which are there dealt with, first, how far "repair" includes by necessity an obligation to renew part or all of the demised premises; secondly, as to the standard of repair which must be complied with.

In the rest of this Chapter there are discussed various problems: the meaning of putting, keeping and leaving in repair; the covenant to repair after notice; the meaning of "fair wear and tear excepted"; the covenant to paint and decorate; liability to repair additional buildings and fixtures; and covenants of various kinds against alterations to the premises.

III. MEANING OF PUT, KEEP AND LEAVE IN REPAIR

It is possible that in a general covenant to repair the tenant will undertake one or all of the following obligations, namely: to put, keep and leave the demised premises in repair. Each of these is considered separately, though a specific covenant to put into repair by the tenant would be unusual, since it is implied by a covenant to keep in repair that the tenant will first put the premises into repair, if they are out of repair.

A. *To Put in Repair*

A specific covenant to put in repair is, for the reason just advanced, not commonly imposed except in the case of a letting of dilapidated premises where the intention is that the tenant will pay for repairs to the premises. The covenant may itself specify a particular standard of repair into which the premises are required to be put; if not the standard is that required to put the premises into such a state as they will be fit for the particular purpose for which they were let.[30] If, therefore, the premises are intended for residential occupation, they must be put into such a state that they may be

---

[30] *Belcher* v. *M'Intosh* (1839) 2 M & R 186.

used with reasonable comfort by the class of tenants likely to occupy them. Certainly, if the premises are dilapidated at the commencement of the lease, the state of the premises at this time is not the standard governing the required repairs. Thus, in an old case,[31] it was assumed that, where the tenant covenanted to deliver up the premises in good substantial repair, he had first put them into a tenantable state. On the other hand, it has been stated that the condition of the premises at the commencement of the lease provides a useful indication but no more, of the standard of repair contemplated by the parties.[32] Therefore an inventory or schedule of the condition of the premises, drawn up by the parties or their agents at the start of the lease will be a useful yardstick to measure the standard of repairs, though with the passage of time, it will gradually "date".

B. *To Keep in Repair*

An obligation on the part of the tenant to keep the demised premises in repair, a very common form of obligation indeed, requires of necessity that if the premises are out of repair, the tenant will first put them into repair: in other words the tenant is not able to claim that because the premises are in a bad state of repair at the commencement of the lease, he is bound only to keep them in that state.[33] Therefore, if the premises are not first put into repair, or, if they are, are not thereafter kept in repair at all times during the term, the tenant will be in breach of covenant. In other words, a covenant to keep in repair means first remedying any initial disrepair and then keeping the premises in repair. A covenant to keep in repair necessarily involves a further covenant to deliver up in repair at the end of the term.

This principle is limited to cases where the property in question is, in fact, proved to be in a state of disrepair. If the premises are not, at the start of the lease, out of repair, then the tenant cannot under a general covenant to repair be com-

---

[31] *Brown* v. *Trumper* (1858) 26 Beav 11.
[32] *Woodfall* 1–1434.
[33] *Proudfoot* v. *Hart* (1890) 25 QBD 42, CA.

pelled to carry out remedial work of a structural nature to cure a design fault in the premises.[34]

C. *To Leave in Repair*

Landlords may, despite what was said above, impose a separate obligation on the tenant to leave the premises in repair, with the result that an action may be brought at the end of the lease for breach of the tenant's covenant to repair if at that stage the premises are out of repair, and this even though a separate action may have been brought during the term for breach of the covenant to keep the premises in repair.[35] If the only repairing covenant in the lease is to deliver up the premises in good repair, then no action can be brought during the term for disrepair and the landlord must wait until the end of the lease before doing so.

Where a claim is made at the end of the lease for damages for breach of a repairing covenant, the condition of the premises will be decided on as at the date when the term is ended. In the context of forfeiture, this is the date of actual or notional re-entry (by writ). As a result, where serious damage was caused to the premises after issue of the writ, that damage could not form part of any claim based on the tenant's covenant.[36]

Consequently, the remedy of the landlord will lie in tort, for any disrepair or damage to the premises after the date of service of a writ claiming forfeiture. Unless such a claim is specifically pleaded the landlord runs the risk that post-writ damage will go uncompensated and merely to make a claim for mesne profits without more will not apparently suffice for the purpose of claiming for dilapidations. This is a potential loophole in the law for landlords, as there is a twilight period between the date of notional re-entry by writ and that of actual re-possession following a court order.

IV. COVENANT TO REPAIR AFTER NOTICE

A lease may contain a general covenant to repair and also

---

[34] *Post Office* v. *Aquarius Properties Ltd* (1987) 281 EG 798, CA. The covenant there did not expressly require rebuilding.

[35] *Ebbetts* v. *Conquest* (1900) 16 TLR 320.

[36] *Associated Deliveries Ltd* v. *Harrison* (1984) 272 EG 321, CA.

a covenant to repair after notice. The following is an example of the latter:

"To Mr CD,

Sir,—You are hereby required [forthwith or within three calendar months from the service of this notice upon you] to put into good tenantable repair, order and condition the [messuage] and premises, with the appurtenaces, situate at _____ pursuant to the covenants contained in a lease dated etc... and particularly to do all and singular the amendments and repairs specified in the Schedule hereinafter written."[37]

If the landlord serves a notice on the tenant under a covenant to repair after notice, he may, at any time within the period given to the tenant to repair in the notice, also serve on the tenant a statutory notice under section 146 of the *Law of Property Act* 1925 in respect of the general covenant to repair.[38] However, if the notice to repair relates to the general covenant to repair, the landlord waives any right to forfeit for breaches of the latter covenant until such time as the period given for repair in the notice expires, in that the landlord is in effect declaring that, if the premises are repaired within the three month period (or whatever period is chosen), he will be satisfied.[39] Once the three month period is up, the landlord's right to forfeit for breaches of the general covenant to repair automatically revives if the tenant is still in breach of it.[40]

Section 146(1) of the *Law of Property Act* 1925 (considered in detail in Chapter 11) prevents the landlord enforcing a forfeiture unless he has first served a suitable statutory notice on the tenant. As a result of this, the repair after notice procedure is mainly relevant to claims by the landlord for damages. To these, the *Leasehold Property (Repairs) Act* 1938 may apply so that, to be able to enforce a claim for damages for disrepair after notice to repair, certain formalities set out in

---

[37] Woodfall 1–2602. Permission to reproduce extracts from this precedent (it is *not suitable where the Leasehold Property (Repairs) Act 1938 applies*) is gratefully acknowledged to Sweet & Maxwell Ltd.

[38] *Cove* v. *Smith* (1886) 2 TLR 778.

[39] *Doe d Morecroft* v. *Meux* (1825) 4 B & C 606.

[40] *Penton* v. *Barnett* [1898] 1QB 276, CA.

Chapter 11 must be followed by the landlord: if he fails to do so, he will lose his claim to damages.

V. FAIR WEAR AND TEAR EXCEPTED

Introduction and General Rules

In the case of any lease, but more particularly a short lease, say for three years or less, the tenant's covenant to repair, such as it is, may be qualified by an exception for fair wear and tear. The object of this is to lighten the burden of the covenant to repair on the tenant. It is not precisely clear to what matters the exception will extend, but it appears that it is designed to prevent the tenant being held liable for, first, the results of the normal action of time and the elements on the demised premises and secondly, the results of normal and reasonable user by the tenant of the demised premises for the purpose for which they were let. The exception will not avoid liability for disrepair caused by abnormal or extraordinary events, such as lightning, flood or earthquake, fire or other accident or destruction by a catastrophe foreseen by neither party; and it was held not to excuse the tenant of a warehouse from liability for damage caused by the collapse of a floor due to overloading.[41] The exception was held in *Terrell* v. *Murray*[42] to excuse the tenant, who had covenanted to deliver up the premises, a house, in as good a state as they were in at the commencement of his (short) lease, reasonable wear and tear excepted, from having to repaint the exterior, to re-point the brickwork and to replace part of the kitchen floor affected by dry rot. All these things had occurred through the passage of time. If, moreover, the effect of wind and weather is greater on the premises, having regard to their character, than if the premises had been sound, the tenant is not, where fair wear and tear is excepted, bound so to repair as to meet the extra effect of the dilapidations so caused.[43] Therefore, apart from the case of consequential loss, considered below, a fair wear and tear exception may be very significant as a means of lightening the burden on the tenant of premises under a short lease.

[41] *Manchester Bonded Warehouse Co* v. *Carr* (1880) 5 CPD 507.
[42] (1901) 17 TLR 570.
[43] *Miller* v. *Burt* (1918) 63 SJ 117.

Exclusions from Fair Wear and Tear Exception

As to what the exception does not cover, in the first place it has been noted that if the tenant puts the demised premises to an abnormal degree of user not contemplated by the lease, then he cannot excuse himself from liability under a fair wear and tear exception. Secondly, it was held in *Gutteridge* v. *Munyard*[44] that the tenant is bound, despite a fair wear and tear exception, to take care that the premises do not suffer more than the operation of time and nature would effect, and is bound, where he is under covenant to repair (eg to keep the interior and possibly the exterior in good tenantable repair), to see to it that the premises are left by him in as nearly as possible the same condition as when let.

In relation to a fair wear and tear exception, it might be supposed that it applied both to direct and consequential damage. For example, if a hole developed in the main roof of the premises because a slate or tile fell off the roof due to old age, and there is penetration of water and consequential damage to the interior of the premises, the original disrepair and the consequential damage might both be covered by a fair wear and tear exception.[45]

In fact, direct damage only is covered by the exception. The principle regarding consequential losses stated by Talbot J in *Haskell* v. *Marlow*[46] as follows. The onus of proving that a disrepair lies within the fair wear and tear exception falls on the tenant. The exception must be construed as limited to what is directly due to wear and tear, and reasonable conduct on the tenant's part is assumed. Therefore if a defect originally proceeded from reasonable wear and tear, this will not exempt the tenant from his obligation to keep in good repair and condition everything it is possible to trace ultimately to that defect. Hence, the tenant will be bound to do such repairs as may ultimately be required to prevent the consequences flowing originally from wear and tear from producing others which wear and tear would not directly produce.

[44] (1834) 1 M & R 334, approved *Brown* v. *Davies* [1958] 1 QB 117, CA.
[45] This argument actually succeeded in *Taylor* v. *Webb* [1937] 2 KB 283, but the case was overruled in *Regis Property Co* v. *Dudley* [1959] AC 370, HL.
[46] [1928] 2 KB 45, approved in the *Regis* case *supra*.

This principle severely limits the scope of the fair wear and tear exception. Nonetheless, any other view would deprive a tenant's repairing covenant qualified by the exception of all sensible meaning in the case of liability for consequential losses. For his reason, presumably, Lord Denning said[47] that the fair wear and tear exception exempts a tenant from liability for decorative repairs and from remedying parts that wear out or come adrift in the course of reasonable use, but from nothing else.

This in turn means that if further damage is likely to flow from a matter originally caused by fair wear and tear, the tenant must in reality do the repairs necessary to prevent that further damage from occurring, so that in the example of the slipped slate or tile given earlier, whose slipping led ultimately to water penetration into the interior of the premises, while strictly fair wear and tear means that the tenant is not liable to replace the fallen slate or tile, he ought to put in another one to prevent further damage occurring.

VI. COVENANT TO PAINT AND DECORATE

Many leases will contain not only a covenant by the tenant to repair but also quite possibly a separate covenant by the tenant to paint. The covenant may be very severe: it may cover external and structural work, plus interior redecoration. In the case of a lease of flats or office-blocks, it may be that the landlord will undertake the responsibility for exterior and structural repainting, and the tenant will be liable for interior redecoration only. Covenants to paint and decorate will refer to specific intervals at which the work has to be done. If no specific covenant to paint and decorate is imposed by the lease, then to some extent the tenant may be liable, under his general covenant to repair, to carry out painting and decoration. If the lease contains no general covenant to repair, then the question of how far, if at all, a tenant will be obliged to carry out repainting is a matter of implication. Reference should be made in this connection to the principles outlined in Chapter 3.

---

[47] *Regis Property Co Ltd* v. *Dudley* [1959] AC 370, HL at p. 410.

A. *Examples of Covenants to Paint*

Obviously the form of a covenant to paint will vary depending on the precise requirements of each lease, and the following are merely examples.

Long Leases[48]

"Once in every three years of the said term and in the last year thereof (whether determined by effluxion of time or in any other way) to paint in a proper and workmanlike manner all the outside wood iron and stucco or cement work and other parts of the demised premises heretobefore or usually painted with two coats of good paint of the respective kinds and colours as may be approved by the Landlord."

"Once in every five years of the said term and in the last year thereof... to paint in a proper and workmanlike manner all the inside wood and iron work usually painted of the demised premises with two coats of good paint and so that such internal painting in the last year of the term shall be of a tint or colour to be approved by the Landlord and also with every such internal painting to whitewash colour wash distemper grain varnish paper or otherwise decorate in a proper and workmanlike manner all such internal parts of the demised premises as have been or ought properly to be so treated..."

Short Leases[49]

"... in the last year [of the lease] to redecorate the whole of [the] interior [of the demised premises] ... in materials and colours first approved by the Landlord..."

It will be seen from the extracts above that, as one would expect, much the most onerous obligations to paint will tend to be imposed in a long lease. In both instances however, there were obligations to paint in specific years, whether at intervals, as in the case where the tenant undertook to repaint the exterior every three years, or in the last year of the term.

---

[48] These extracts are taken from *Precedents for the Conveyancer* Vol I, 5–3 Cl 4(6), permission to reproduce which is gratefully acknowledged to Sweet & Maxwell Ltd.

[49] This extract is taken from *Precedents for the Conveyancer* 5–3 Cl 4(7), permission to reproduce which is gratefully acknowledged to Sweet & Maxwell Ltd.

Where, therefore, there is an obligation to paint during a specific year then the obligation to perform the covenant commences as soon as that year starts. In *Kirklinton v. Wood*[50] therefore, where the lease in question contained an obligation to execute outside painting in 1916 and the lease was determined only in March of that year, it was held that since the liability to repaint was fixed on 1 January 1916 the tenant (or rather in this case his executors) were liable to carry out the work. On the other hand, in *Dickinson v. St Aubyn*[51] a flat was let for a seven year term, with an option in the tenant to determine it by notice at the end of the fifth year. The lease contained a tenants' covenant to paint in the "last quarter of the said term" and it was held that if the tenant determined the lease at the end of year five, he would be under no liability to paint under this covenant since the obligation to paint under it arose only in the last quarter of year seven. Note that in this case the covenant to paint was distinct from the general covenant to repair, whereunder liability would arise when the term was determined for whatever reason, whether at the end of year five or year seven. To avoid these complications, it will be necessary to impose the obligation to paint in, for example, the last year of the term whether this arises by effluxion of time or in any other way, as is achieved in the precedent quoted under long leases.

B. *Relief*

No doubt the painting of the outside paintwork and ironwork of demised premises is deemed essential to preserve those parts from decay, but a specific covenant to repaint the interior of the premises (say) every seven years or at other comparatively frequent regular intervals may be both oppressive and unnecessary in the circumstances of a given case. As a result of this the tenant may obtain relief under section 147 of the *Law of Property Act* 1925. Where section 147 applies, if the court is satisfied that the landlord's notice relating to internal decorative repairs is unreasonable, it may by order wholly or partly relieve the tenant from liability for such repairs.[52]

[50] [1917] 1 KB 332.
[51] [1944] 1 All ER 370.
[52] See further Chapter 11.

No order is, it seems, appropriate during the last year of the term, where a covenant to deliver up the premises in a specified state of repair is normal.[53]

C. *Painting under a General Covenant to Repair*

It may be that the lease in question contains no specific covenants to paint and decorate, but does contain a general covenant to repair by the tenant, for example, he covenants to keep the interior (and perhaps also the structure and exterior) of the premises in good tenantable repair. A general covenant to repair will oblige the tenant to carry out a certain amount of painting. This is clear from *Proudfoot* v. *Hart.*[54] The Court of Appeal was dealing with a tenant under an obligation to keep and leave the premises, a dwelling-house, in good tenantable repair, which they stated to involve liability to do such repairs as would be required by a reasonably-minded incoming tenant of the class likely to take the premises. In the context of painting and decoration this meant that the tenant is bound to repaper, whitewash, paint and so on, if the condition of the premises is such that, if the work is not done, no reasonably-minded incoming tenant would be likely to take the house. Therefore, for example, if the paint is in such a state that the woodwork must decay unless it is repainted, the tenant must repaint it. The standard of the painting and decoration required will, it was held, be governed by the nature of the premises, their age and locality, bearing in mind the requirements of reasonable incoming tenants. For instance, as was there pointed out, a person taking a new tenancy of a house in Spitalfields could not possibly require a decorative standard appropriate to a much better locality such as Grosvenor Square; if a tenant quitting a house in Grosvenor Square left it painted and decorated to a standard appropriate to Spitalfields[55] or any other low-class area, that would not be sufficient for the purposes of the general covenant. Extravagent work of decoration (not there before) cannot be required, for in *Proudfoot* v. *Hart* Lord Esher MR thought that no tenant taking a house in Grosvenor Square

---

[53] *Wolstenholme and Cherry's Conveyancing Statutes*, 13th Edn (JT Farrand) Vol 1 p. 274.
[54] (1890) 25 QBD 42, CA.
[55] The examples of high and low class locations given by the court.

would require the provision of an ornamental gilded ceiling. If the general covenant to repair is stronger than to keep in good tenantable repair, as with a covenant to "substantially repair uphold and maintain" a house, the tenant's obligation may be correspondingly heavier than the standard imposed by *Proudfoot* v. *Hart*, and it was held, where these words were used, that such a covenant obliged the tenant to keep up the painting of inside doors and shutters.[56]

Two final points should be made which illustrate that the precise ambit of the extent to which a general covenant to repair will oblige the tenant to carry out painting may be a little uncertain. In the first place it was held in *Scales* v. *Lawrence*,[57] where the tenant was under a general covenant to repaint as part of a general covenant to repair, that, where he had in fact repainted on entering and a reasonable time before leaving, he was not bound on leaving to repaint but only to clean up the existing paint. Secondly, there is authority[58] holding that where a tenant undertook an obligation to keep the interior of the demised premises in tenantable repair, and had done no painting or papering for seventeen years, he was bound to paint and paper only so far as was necessary to prevent the house in question from falling into decay. The case has been said by a leading text to attach insufficient weight to the word "tenantable".[59]

VII. LIABILITY TO REPAIR OR TO ERECT ADDITIONAL BUILDINGS AND FIXTURES

A. *General Rules*

The position may be summarised as follows.

1. A general covenant to repair (and a covenant to leave in repair) generally extends to all buildings erected by the tenant during the lease.[60] Nonetheless, there is no fixed rule and every case, as one would expect, depends on the words used in every particular covenant.[61] For example, in *Doe*

---

[56] *Monk* v. *Noyes* (1824) 1 C & P 265.
[57] (1860) 2 F & F 289.
[58] *Crawford* v. *Newton* (1886) 36 WR 54, CA.
[59] *Woodfall* 1–1447.
[60] Bac Abr Covenant (f); *Dowse* v. *Earle* (1690) 3 Lev 264; *Hudson* v. *Williams* (1878) 39 LT 632.
[61] *Cornish* v. *Cleife* (1864) 3 H & C 446.

d *Worcester School Trustees* v. *Rowlands*[62] the tenant of land with buildings on it covenanted to repair the "buildings demised" and to rebuild them if necessary. It was held that this did not oblige the tenant to keep in repair additional buildings erected on other parts of the land. In other words the term "buildings demised" was taken to refer only to the particular buildings specified and no more.

2. A covenant to leave premises demised in repair is generally taken to extend not just to the original premises but also to all landlords' fixtures attached by the tenant during the term. Moreover, if the tenant is under a general covenant to repair and he erects trade fixtures on the demised premises and then takes a new lease of the same premises, it is assumed in the absence of strong language to the contrary that the tenant's covenant will extend to the fixtures.[63]

3. If the landlord wishes to make sure that any general covenant to repair is to extend to all buildings, both those currently on the land and those to be erected thereon, some care must be taken with the wording of the appropriate covenants. If the covenant is too specific there is a risk that it will be held not to cover the building in question, as in *Smith* v. *Mills*,[64] where a lease provided for the erection on the demised land of a certain number of specified buildings. In addition to these, the tenant put up a factory during the term. The question arose whether he was bound, under a general covenant to repair the buildings erected on the land, to repair the factory and it was held that he was not liable, because the covenant referred to specific buildings only. What was not settled in this case was whether, in any event at the end of the lease, the tenant could have been held liable for the condition of the factory, if then it was out of repair, on a covenant to leave the premises in repair. It may be suggested that if the lease contains a general covenant to repair which refers only to certain specified buildings to be erected during the term, the covenant to leave in repair on expiry of the term should be no wider that the general covenant to repair.

[62] (1841) 9 C & P 734.
[63] *Thresher* v. *East London Waterworks Co* (1824) 2 B & C 608.
[64] (1899) 16 TLR 59.

B. *New Buildings*

The question of the liability of the tenant to repair new houses or other buildings depends on the facts of each case, as with the liability to repair additional buildings. In *Dowse* v. *Earle*[65] for example, the tenant covenanted to pull down three houses demised to him and to build three others and then to repair the "said premises and houses thereon to be erected." He pulled down the three houses and then built five to replace them. It was held that the tenant must, as things now stood, deliver up all five houses in repair, since the covenant to repair was general and not expressly confined to the three houses required to be built. Contrast *Smith* v. *Mills* above, where the covenant to repair new buildings was narrowly confined to the buildings specified in the covenant itself. On the other hand in *Field* v. *Curnick*[66] the lessee of a long lease of land covenanted to build two houses and to keep in repair "the said premises" (ie the covenant to repair was general and not specifically confined to the two houses). The lessee built six houses and these were finished at the same date. It was held that the covenant to repair extended to all six houses in view of its generality, particularly because it was not in terms confined to the two houses. Sankey J summarised the law in this helpful way:[67]

"If... the lessor demised a piece of land, and there is an express covenant by the lessee to repair any house subsequently erected thereon... the lessee is bound by it. Further, a general covenant to repair includes not merely buildings existing when the demise is made, but all those which may be erected during the term. If, however, the covenant to repair is one to keep in repair the demised premises, it applies to those existing at the date of the lease only, unless the new buildings are made part of the old ones."

In other words, if there is a general and non-specific covenant to repair, this is taken to refer, in principle, both to buildings erected at the date of the lease and subsequently; if there is a covenant to repair specifically and in terms con-

---

[65] (1690) 3 Lev 264.
[66] [1926] 2 KB 374.
[67] *Ibid* at p. 379.

fined to particular buildings, it will extend only to those particular buildings.[68]

C. Breaches of Covenant to Build

The lease may contain a covenant to erect certain buildings
by a specified date and then a covenant to repair, uphold
and maintain those buildings (for questions of the extent of
this term see the above discussion). There are two possibilities
at least, the first being that, at the date of the demise, the
premises as demised actually include the buildings, whether
completed or not. This was the position in *Bennett* v. *Her-
ring*[69] where the premises were two houses partly built at
the date of the demise: the lessee was supposed to complete
building the houses within a given time but never did so.
It was held that the landlord's assignee could bring a forfeiture, since the buildings were dilapidated.

The second possibility is that there is nothing for the covenant to repair any buildings erected to operate on. Thus, in
Stephens v. *Junior Army and Navy Stores*[70] where the lessees
of a 99 year lease of land covenanted to erect certain buildings
on the land by a given date in 1911 and then to repair, uphold
and maintain the buildings so erected. In fact the date passed
and no buildings had been erected. The landlords were, in
fact, held to have waived their right to bring a forfeiture for
the tenant's admitted breach of the covenant to build by a
certain date. (This breach, unlike a breach of the covenant
to repair, is a once-and-for-all breach of covenant so that
a single acceptance of rent, with knowledge by the landlord
or his agent of the basic facts which in law entitle him to
a forfeiture, will waive the breach irrevocably.) In any event,
the Court of Appeal held that the covenant to repair did not
imply in the landlord's favour a covenant to build and then
to repair, since there was nothing that the covenant to repair
could operate on, no buildings having been put up. All that
the landlord was able in the circumstances to do was to claim
damages. This case serves as an ominous warning to landlords: if there is a given date for the erection of buildings

[68]   *Smith* v. *Mills* (1899) 16 TLR 59.
[69]   (1857) 3 CB(NS) 370.
[70]   [1914] 2 Ch 516, CA.

and forfeiture is desired for breach of such covenant, all tenders of rent due after that date should be sedulously refused by the landlord or his agent or his agent's servants.

VIII. COVENANTS AGAINST ALTERATIONS TO THE PREMISES

A covenant against the making of alterations may commonly be inserted in a lease and it may take one of many forms. It may be an absolute prohibition against the making of any alterations, or it may be qualified (such that no alterations may be made without the landlord's prior licence or consent), or fully qualified (prohibiting alterations without the landlord's prior licence or consent but providing that such consent is not unreasonably to be withheld).

Whatever the form of the covenant, the first problem is to decide whether what is done constitutes an alteration. It appears that "alteration" is to be limited to anything which alters the form and construction of the building, and hence, a large clock erected outside a watchmaker's shop and supported on iron stays bolted to the framework was held to be no breach of a covenant against making alterations to the premises.[71] Similarly, the erection of an electric lighting advertisement was held not to be a breach of a covenant not to permit any alteration in the building.[72] On the other hand where a large electric sign was attached to the front of a building by T-irons and iron brackets cemented into holes cut into the stonework, this was held to breach a covenant not to cut or maim any of the principal walls or timbers.[73] Likewise, a covenant not to make any alteration to the external appearance of a building was broken by letting a wall for bill-posting.[74]

Where there is a covenant against the making of alterations in whatever form, statute has, as will be seen, intervened in the case of alterations which amount to the making of improvements (which covers most alterations, provided the tenant can prove that the alteration he intends to carry out will be an improvement from his point of view). The effect of the

[71] *Bickmore* v. *Dimmer* [1903] 1 Ch 158.
[72] *Joseph* v. *London County Council* (1914) 111 LT 276.
[73] *London County Council* v. *Hutter* [1925] Ch 626.
[74] *Heard* v. *Stuart* (1907) 24 TLR 104.

statute is to provide for some judicial relief and it does not re-write the covenant itself, save to a limited extent. Where the various statutory relieving rules do not apply, as with the case notably of an absolute prohibition on the making of alterations, two specific statutory reliefs are given. These are first considered, followed by the general statutory relieving rule.[75]

A. *Housing Act 1985 section 610*

The object of section 610 of the *Housing Act* 1985 is to facilitate the conversion of a large house held on a long lease into smaller units of accommodation where the lease prohibits or restricts such conversions, or where they are prohibited by a restrictive covenant, or otherwise. Provided that one of two conditions apply, the local housing authority (ie a local district council, a London borough council, the Common Council of the City of London) or any person interested in the house (such as the leaseholder) may apply to the county court (s 610(1)). The county court may then vary the terms of the lease or other instrument imposing the prohibition or restriction, subject to such terms and conditions as the court thinks fit. The court must (s 610(2)) give any person interested an opportunity of being heard before making any order. The two conditions for section 610 to apply are:

either (a) that owing to changes in the character of the neighbourhood of the house, it cannot readily be let as a single tenement but could readily be let for occupation if converted into two or more tenements;

or (b) that planning permission has been granted for the use of the house as converted into two or more separate dwellings as opposed to a single dwelling.

To come within this provision, the conversion proposed need not necessarily involve any structural alterations at all and the court has power to permit a conversion which amounts to a change of user.[76] Moreover, "house" apparently may include a block of offices suitable for conversion into dwelling-houses.[77] On the other hand the word "char-

---

[75] For special rules in the case of protected and statutory tenants see *Housing Act* 1980 ss 81–83.

[76] *Stack* v. *Church Comissioners for England* [1952] 1 All ER 1352, CA.

[77] *Johnstone* v. *Maconochie* [1921] 1 KB 239, CA.

acter" has been narrowly interpreted. It was held in *Alliance Economic Investment Co Ltd* v. *Berton*[78] that though a neighbourhood might change from one consisting of large houses in single family occupation to one consisting of large houses mainly converted into flats, if the flats were as high-class as the houses had been, then there would still be no change in the "character" of the neighbourhood within section 610(1)(a), and the provision does not apply to such a case.

A further limit on section 610 is that it was held in *Josephine Trust* v. *Champagne*[79] that it did not apply to a scheme for the division of adjoining terraced houses into flats, even though the flats would extend to the full width of the former houses.

B. *Law of Property Act 1925 section 84*

This applies to leaseholds where the original term of the lease was for a term of over 40 years, of which at least 25 years have expired (s 84(12)). If this is so, any person interested in the land may apply to the Lands Tribunal for the discharge or modification of the restrictions affecting the land. There are four sets of grounds on any one of which the Lands Tribunal may discharge or modify the covenant (s 84(1)). The first is that by reason of changes in the character of the property or the neighbourhood or otherwise the restriction is obsolete. The second is that the continuation of the restriction would impede some reasonable user of the land for public or private purposes. The third is that the persons entitled to the benefit of the restriction have agreed, expressly or impliedly, to the discharge or modification of the restriction. The fourth ground is that the proposed discharge or modification will not injure the persons entitled to oppose it. In certain cases compensation may be awarded for the loss of the restriction.

C. *Landlord and Tenant Act 1927 section 19(2)*

Section 19(2) of the *Landlord and Tenant Act* 1927 provides, firstly, that all qualified and fully qualified covenants

---

[78] (1923) 92 LJ KB 750.
[79] [1963] 2 QB 160, CA.

in leases against the making of improvements without the licence or consent of the landlord are deemed (notwithstanding any express provision to the contrary) to be subject to a proviso that such licence or consent is not to be unreasonably withheld. This provision accordingly applies to a covenant under which the tenant is prohibited from making alterations without the landlord's consent, such consent not unreasonably to be withheld.[80] By definition, it has no application to a covenant which is an absolute prohibition on the making of any alterations to the demised premises.

Secondly, however, the landlord may, as a condition of giving his consent, require the payment of a reasonable sum "in respect of any damage to or diminution in the value of the premises or any neighbouring premises" of his; and he may require also the payment of his legal and other expenses incurred in connection with the consent (such as, for example, the cost of obtaining references). Thirdly, in the case of an improvement which does not add to the letting value of the holding, the landlord may require, as a condition of his licence or consent, an undertaking by the tenant to reinstate the premises to their pre-improvement condition.

Section 19(2) applies to alterations which are, from the tenant's point of view, improvements—as will appear.

If the tenant wishes to make improvements where the lease contains a qualified or fully qualified covenant against alterations, he should first apply to the landlord for his consent. If it is unreasonably withheld then the tenant may ask the county court for a declaration to that effect.[81] If the tenant is advised that the landlord's refusal of consent is unreasonable, he may, as an alternative to applying for a declaration, carry out the alterations without further ado on the basis that the landlord will be unable, if the advice is correct, to bring a forfeiture or obtain any other relief, such as an injunction, in such a case.[82]

On the construction of the word "improvements" in section

---

[80] Also where there is a prohibition on the tenant making alterations without the landlord's consent.

[81] *Landlord and Tenant Act 1954* s 53.

[82] See *Commissioner for Railways* v. *Avrom Investments Proprietary Ltd* [1959] 1 WLR 389, JCPC.

19(2), it was held in *Balls Bros Ltd* v. *Sinclair*[83] that the land-lord cannot unreasonably withhold consent to the making of an alteration or addition which constitutes an improvement. In this case the alteration (unreasonably) objected to consisted of moving the position of a staircase in the demised premises to facilitate the business of a sub-tenant. In *Lilley & Skinner Ltd* v. *Crump*[84] it was held that the landlord was not entitled to refuse consent to the tenant's alterations, ie the proposed making of an aperture in the main wall in two places between the demised premises and neighbouring premises, to connect them. In both these cases the improvements were to the advantage of the tenants. In *Balls Bros Ltd* v. *Sinclair* Luxmoore J relied greatly on the fact that the landlord has the statutory right to require a reinstatement undertaking as a condition of granting consent, in support of the rule that the question whether a particular alteration is an improvement or not is to be considered from the tenant's point of view alone. This approach has been accepted by a majority in the Court of Appeal.[85] A trap from the landlord's point of view is that if he refuses consent, but fails to ask for money compensation or a reinstatement condition where appropriate, he will lose his right to both if his refusal of consent is held unreasonable.

As was seen, the question of whether a proposed alteration consititues an improvement is to be judged from the tenant's point of view alone. In *FW Woolworth & Co* v. *Lambert*[86] which is the leading case in point, the tenant of a shop on a long lease which contained a fully qualified covenant against making structural alterations or additions, wished to enlarge the shop by pulling down a wall at the back of the demised premises and connecting the shop with adjoining land held from another person, building one large shop covering both the demised premises and the other land. It was held that the proposed alterations were "improvements" within section 19(2). The question of whether a proposed alteration was an improvement was to be judged from the point of view

---

[83] [1931] 2 Ch 325.
[84] (1929) 73 SJ 366.
[85] *Lambert* v. *FW Woolworth & Co (No 2)* [1938] Ch 883, CA.
[86] [1937] Ch 37, CA.

of the tenant. In this, the fact that the work will not improve the letting value of the premises from the landlord's point of view is not material. The test, said Romer LJ[87] was whether the alterations would render the tenant's occupation of the demised premises more convenient and comfortable to him. An example of this would be the making of an entrance or passageway, he said, from adjoining land of the tenant's to the demised premises. In any event, the work in this case was plainly an improvement from the tenant's viewpoint. The Court of Appeal also held however, that the onus of proving that a refusal of consent was unreasonable was on the tenant and he had not discharged it on the particular facts.

In the case just discussed the landlords had demanded the payment of £7,000 as a condition of any consent they might give. The tenants had offered reinstatement undertakings, but refused to pay the sums demanded. The litigation continued in *Lambert* v. *FW Woolworth & Co (No 2)*[88] where the landlord completely refused consent and did not ask for reinstatement or for compensation. It was held that the proposed alterations would be improvements within section 19(2) and that the consent of the landlord to them had been unreasonably withheld. Slesser LJ considered[89] that in some cases (such as this) complete reconstruction of demised buildings and premises might be permitted. On the other hand it is not clear on the present state of the authorities whether if the tenant were proposing completely to destroy the identity of the demised premises, as by demolition of the whole of the buildings comprising or including them, the landlord could refuse his consent reasonably to such a proposal as that. It is thought that he ought to be able to do so.

As to the grounds on which a landlord may reasonably withhold his consent, these were canvassed in *Lambert* v. *FW Woolworth & Co (No 2)*.[90] It seems that if the landlord gives no reason for his refusal then this puts on him the duty of showing that his action was reasonable even though the initial onus of proving the consent was unreasonably withheld

---

[87] [1937] Ch 37 at p. 56.
[88] [1938] Ch 883, CA.
[89] [1938] Ch 883, at p. 901.
[90] [1938] Ch 883, CA.

is on the tenant. On what grounds may be advanced as reasonable by the landlord, Slesser LJ said[91] that many considerations, "aesthetic, historic or even personal, may be relied on..." To take Slesser LJ's example, if the tenant proposed to replace a beautiful casement and substitute for it a garish window or false marble facade, the landlord could, on this view, reasonably refuse his consent. But it must be stressed that if the alteration proposed is, from the tenant's point of view, an improvement, the fact that it will produce a diminution in the letting value or damage to the landlord's reversion is immaterial. In the *Woolworth* litigation just examined, much reliance was placed by the courts on the landlord's twin rights under section 19(2) to require reinstatement in cases of this sort and, where appropriate, to require money compensation from the tenant. The harsh truth in this matter is that if the landlord wishes to play safe, he may wish to exact a total prohibition against the making of alterations or additions to the demised premises.

D. *Effect of Tenants' Improvements on Rent Review*

For the sake of completeness, a brief resume of the effect of tenants' improvements on rent reviews seems appropriate. The question of whether an alteration which constitutes an improvement must be taken into account in a rent review clause depends on a number of factors which may be summarised as follows.

1. *No Express Provision.* The rent review clause may contain no express provision about tenants' improvements. The question of whether tenants' improvements carried out by the tenant or his predecessor must be taken into account on a rent review is one of construction of the particular clause. If it is objective, as where it refers to an open market or reasonable rent for the demised premises, then the improvements will be taken into account on a rent review, because they form part of the demised premises.[92] If the clause is subjective, as where it refers to a rent to be agreed between the parties, the reviewed rent will depend on subjective assessment of what a fair rent for the parties to agree on must be: if the

---

[91] *Ibid* at p. 907.
[92] *Ponsford* v. *HMS Aerosols Ltd* [1979] AC 63; (1978) 247 EG 1171, HL.

tenant or his assign (as the case may be) proves that he paid for, or contributed to, the cost of the improvement, to that extent the effect of the improvement on new rent will be ignored.[93]

2. *Disregard Clause.* The rent review clause may contain a clause in various forms that the effect of tenants' improvements carried out at defined times (say during the currency of the term) by defined persons (say the tenant or his predecessors in title) to the demised premises, should be disregarded on a rent review. Some clauses may incorporate section 34 of the *Landlord and Tenant Act* 1954, for example, and may refer either to the originally-enacted provision or as amended. This should be specified to avoid doubt.[94] The clause should define what it means by the "tenant" and the "demised premises" for these purposes.

3. *Failure in Disregard Clause to Define Terms.* The court will be left to construe each clause if terms are not fully defined. For example, in *Hambros Bank Executor & Trustee Co Ltd* v. *Superdrug Stores Ltd*[95] the "tenant" was held to refer to persons who were, or who would soon become, tenants—so the disregard clause was held to extend to improvements carried out by prospective tenants prior to the granting of the lease. On the other hand, in *Euston Centre Properties Ltd* v. *H & J Wilson Ltd*[96] where the prospective tenants carried out improvements under licence, and where no lease was intended to be granted unless and until the relevant works were completed to plans and specifications approved by the landlord, it was held that a disregard clause incorporating section 34 of the 1954 Act did not apply to the pre-lease improvements.

4. *Protection of Landlord.* Tenants' improvements are clearly related to the consent provisions discussed earlier. It has been suggested that the landlord should see to it, if possible, that any disregard of improvements clause is limited expressly to improvements carried out with the landlord's consent.[97] If the landlord reasonably refuses his consent, and

---

[93] *Lear* v. *Blizzard* [1983] 3 All ER 662; (1983) 268 EG 115.
[94] See *Brett* v. *Brett Essex Golf Club Ltd* (1986) 278 EG 1476, [1986] 1 EGLR 154, CA.
[95] (1985) 274 EG 590.
[96] (1982) 262 EG 1079.
[97] Tromans (1987) 84 LS Gazette 716.

the tenant carries out the improvement concerned, a rent review disregard clause will be itself ignored and the effect of the improvements concerned will be fully taken into account on a rent review.[98]

5. *Reinstatement Obligation.* If the tenant is under an obligation to reinstate alterations he carried out during the term, the question whether this must be taken into account in a review of rent is one of construction, but in *Pleasurama Properties Ltd* v. *Leisure Investments (West End) Ltd*[99] it was held that where a sub-lessee carried out improvements under licence with an obligation to re-instate the premises at the end of the sub-lease, he should not have both the benefit of the licence and of a reduction of rent on rent review. Express words could reverse this result.

[98] *Hamish Cathie Travel England Ltd* v. *Insight International Tours Ltd* [1986] 1 EGLR 244.
[99] (1986) 278 EG 732, CA.

Chapter 6
SCOPE AND STANDARD OF TENANT'S COVENANT TO REPAIR

I. INTRODUCTION
A. *Outline of Subject-Matter of this Chapter*

In this Chapter attention is focused on two main topics, of which the first is by far the most difficult. These are, first, the scope of the tenant's general covenant to repair. Secondly, the question of the standard of repair required by certain well-known terms in the tenant's covenant to repair.

Reference may be made to examples of the standard form tenant's covenants to repair in Chapter 5, where some of these are set out. In what follows, on the scope of the tenant's covenant to repair, attention is given first to the question of how far repair includes renewal, and secondly, whether a general covenant to repair by the tenant ever includes any obligation to carry out improvements to the demised premises. The third and most vexed problem to be dealt with here is the question of liability as between the parties to a lease for inherent defects in the demised premises. There is some discussion of the differing standards which may be imposed on tenants of long and short leases.

On the further question of the tenant's liability to repair the premises in the event of their being destroyed by accident or negligence, a tenant under a general covenant to repair during the term is in the absence of express contrary provision bound to rebuild the premises, if they are wholly or partially destroyed or damaged by fire, storm, earthquake or other act of God unless excused from having to do so by the covenant itself.[1]

Before going into these matters, some preliminary remarks are made.

---

[1] *Bullock* v. *Dommitt* (1796) 2 Chit 608; 6 TR 650; *Redmond* v. *Dainton* [1920] 2 KB 256. See further Chapter 10.

B. *Operative Date of Covenant to Repair*

A covenant to repair is construed as referring to the condition of the premises at the time when the covenant begins
to operate.[2] If, therefore, the tenant has covenanted to keep
a newly let building in good structural repair and condition
and it falls out of condition in the first few years of the term,
unless he shows that the work of repair is so extensive that
it amounts to complete or near complete renewal of the
premises, or unless the damage is due to a design fault for
which the tenant is exempted from liability under the lease,
he will, in principle, be liable to carry out necessary repairs.[3]

Another consequence of the rule that a covenant to repair
operates only from the commencement of the term to which
it relates, is that if the tenant sub-lets and imposes a covenant
to repair on the sub-tenant in identical language to the covenant to repair in his own lease, the sub-tenant may be under
a less onerous duty than the tenant. The court will qualify
his obligation by reference to the age of the premises at the
date of the sub-lease, not the earlier date when the head lease
commenced.[4]

If the tenant covenants to keep premises in repair, and where
he covenants to put them in repair, if the premises are, at
the commencement of the lease, in a dilapidated state, the
tenant, to comply with his covenant, must first put the
premises into the state of repair that is necessary to enable
him to occupy the premises for the purposes of the demise,
and thereafter keep them in suitable repair.[5]

C. *Outline of Scope of Covenant to Repair*

As will be seen in the next section of this Chapter, one
of the most difficult and uncertain aspects of the subject is
how far a tenant's general covenant to repair may properly
require him to carry out (or in default, pay for) the cost of
works of renewal. It is worth indicating at this point the
general approach which the courts will adopt in interpreting
repairing covenants.

[2] *Walker* v. *Hatton* (1842) 10 M & W 249; *Brew Bros* v. *Snax (Ross) Ltd* [1970] 1 QB
612; *Smedley* v. *Chumley & Hawke Ltd* (1982) 261 EG 775, CA.
[3] Cf *Smedley* v. *Chumley & Hawke Ltd. supra.*
[4] See *Ebbetts* v. *Conquest* [1895] 2 Ch 377, CA.
[5] See Chapter 5 and *Belcher* v. *McIntosh* (1839) 2 M & R 186.

In *Lurcott* v. *Wakely and Wheeler*[6] Fletcher Moulton LJ said that when the word "repair" was applied to a complex matter like a house, "I have no doubt that the repair includes the replacement of parts. Of course, if a house had tumbled down or was down the word 'repair' could not be used to cover rebuilding." In other words, there is a difference of principle between subordinate renewal of part of the demised premises necessitated by its disrepair, and total renewal of the whole subject-matter demised, which is required by its state of dilapidation. One would not normally expect a tenant under a general covenant to repair to carry out works of total renewal of the whole premises—unless clear language such as to repair and rebuild appears.[7] On the other hand it was pointed out by Buckley LJ in *Lurcott* v. *Wakely and Wheeler*[8] that "repair and renew are not words expressive of clear contrast. Repair always involves renewal; renewal of a part; of a subordinate part. ... Repair is restoration by renewal or replacement of subsidiary parts of the whole. Renewal as distinguished from repair, is reconstruction of the entirety, meaning by the entirety, not necessarily the whole, but substantially the whole subject-matter under discussion." In other words, as will be seen, a tenant's general covenant to repair may require him to undertake substantial and onerous liabilities in relation to the preservation and maintenance of the demised premises. However, the tenant is not, save in so far as necessary to effectuate repairs, bound to improve the demised premises, so that if, at the date of the lease they did not have a damp-proof course, the tenant cannot, under a general covenant to repair, be forced to pay for the installation of one.[9]

If what the tenant is being asked to do is to replace some subordinate part of the premises (assuming the part is in a condition of disrepair), the fact that this may to a limited extent improve the premises is, of itself, no defence to liability under the tenant's general covenant to repair (provided that he is not being asked to renew the whole premises). This

---

[6] [1911] 1 KB 905, at p. 918.
[7] See *Norwich Union Life Insurance Society* v. *British Railways Board* (1987) 283 EG 846.
[8] *Ibid* at p. 923.
[9] Cf *Pembery* v. *Lamdin* [1940] 2 All ER 434, CA; *Quick* v. *Taff-Ely Borough Council* (1985) 276 EG 452, CA.

is so even if in the course of the work of repair an inherent design fault is cured.[10] That is because if the work is replacement of a part of the premises out of repair using modern materials, leaving the subject as nearly as possible as though undamaged[11] and subordinate renewal only is involved, this method is the only sensible way of carrying out the work. The question of whether, in the case of repairs, an item in disrepair must, to comply with a tenant's general covenant to repair, be merely patched up, or completely replaced, is one of fact and degree—but if the only sensible way of curing the disrepair and consequent damage is to replace the whole of the damaged item by a new one, this latter course of action will be required as a repair.[12]

In the end the question of liability to carry out particular work is one of degree, depending on the terms of the covenant, the cost of the work, the surrounding circumstances, whether the premises are old or new, the state of the premises at the date of the lease, and the contemplation of the parties when the lease was entered into.[13] (Obviously a full survey of the condition of the premises at the commencement of the lease or at the date of assignment is essential for any intending tenant or assignee of a lease.)[14]

D. *Repairing Covenant Operative only if Disrepair Exists*

The tenant will be liable to repair under a general covenant only if the premises or items thereon in question are out of repair. In *Quick* v. *Taff-Ely Borough Council*[15] a local authority landlord (the same rule applies to tenants) was held not liable under section 11 of the *Landlord and Tenant Act 1985* (considered in Chapter 11) to insulate certain lintels and to replace metal-frame windows in the house in question. These items were in good condition in themselves. The house suffered from very severe condensation.

---

[10] See *Ravenseft Properties Ltd* v. *Davstone (Holdings) Ltd* [1980] QB 12; (1978) 249 EG 51, [1979] Conv 429 (P. F. Smith).

[11] See *Calthorpe* v. *McOscar* [1924] 1 KB 716.

[12] *Stent* v. *Monmouth District Council* (1987) 282 EG 705, CA.

[13] See Sachs LJ in *Brew Bros* v. *Snax (Ross) Ltd* [1970] 1 QB 612, at p. 640.

[14] Otherwise a very heavy bill for dilapidations may await the tenant/assign at the end of the term, as dramatically shown by *Elite Investments Ltd* v. *TI Bainbridge Silencers Ltd* (1986) 280 EG 1001, below.

[15] (1985) 276 EG 452; [1985] 1 QB 809, CA.

Dillon LJ said that: "Disrepair is related to the physical condition of whatever has to be repaired and not to questions of lack of amenity or inefficiency ... [the] covenant will only come into operation where there has been damage to the structure and exterior which requires to be made good."

This principle was applied to tenants of commercial premises held under a long lease in *Post Office* v. *Aquarius Properties Ltd.*[16] There, the tenant of a 1960s office building who was subject to a general covenant to repair, was held not liable to pay for the cost of installing an asphalt tanking scheme in the basement, which had for a five-year period been flooded with water. The basement was dry at the date of the action. The reason for the entry of water was a structural design fault. It was held that on the unusual facts of this case, there had been no proof of physical damage; therefore there was no condition of disrepair. This meant that the tenants were not liable under their covenant to pay for remedial work to cure the structural design fault in the basement. (Neither were the landlords liable.)

The issue of liability for inherent defects is discussed in section IV of this Chapter. Suffice it here to note that if there are unsuspected design faults, as in the *Ravenseft* case, which produce or contribute to a state of disrepair, then the tenant under a general covenant will be liable to execute remedial work, if it is repair, though in the process he cures the design fault. If a design fault produces work so extensive that it is beyond repair, the tenant will not be liable for it. If the fault has so far caused no disrepair, the same result follows.

II. HOW FAR REPAIR INCLUDES RENEWAL

A *General Principles*

It was seen from the statement in the previous section that repair necessarily involves some degree of subordinate renewal and that there is no fixed test which will automatically decide whether, in a given case, the work which the tenant is being asked to do is properly subordinate renewal, in which case he will be liable for it, or total or near total renewal, in which case he will not be liable. The two general tests

---

[16] (1987) 281 EG 798; [1987] 1 All ER 1055, CA.

mentioned above apply: especially the dicta of Sachs LJ in
Brew Bros v. *Snax (Ross) Ltd.*[17]

The principal approach is to be found in *Ravenseft Properties Ltd* v. *Davstone (Holdings) Ltd.*[18]

Forbes J. in *Ravenseft*, said "The true test is ... that it
is always a question of degree whether that which the tenant
is being asked to do can properly be described as repair, or
whether on the contrary it would involve giving back to the
landlord a wholly different thing from that which he
demised". In deciding this question, Forbes J indicated that
the proportion which the cost of the disputed work bore to
the value or cost of the whole premises might sometimes be
a helpful guide. This must be read subject to the qualification
that cost (ie rebuilding cost) rather than value must be stressed
if they are seriously divergent.[19]

A second more general pointer is that there may be some
difference in the end result depending on whether the premises
in question are old, especially where they may have reached
the end or near the end of their life expectancy, and where
they are new or fairly new.

Several important cases illustrate the contrast between total
or near total renewal on the one hand, which lies outside
the scope of the tenant's covenant to repair, and repair (which
may be very extensive) involving subordinate renewal, which
falls within it.

B. *Total or Near Total Renewal*

In *Lister* v. *Lane and Nesham*[20] the leading case, the facts
were that the tenants held a seven year lease of a 100 year
old house in Lambeth. They were under a general covenant
to "repair, uphold, sustain (and maintain)" the premises and
to deliver them up at the end of the term in that condition.
Just before the lease expired, a survey showed that a front
wall of part of the premises was bulging; the matter was not
remedied by the tenants and the house had to be demolished.
It was rebuilt and the landlords unsuccessfully sought the

[17] [1970] 1 QB 612, at p. 640, CA. See Chapter 5.
[18] [1980] QB 12 at p. 21; (1978) 249 EG 51. Approved in *Quick* v. *Taff-Ely Borough Council
supra*. CA and *Post Office* v. *Aquarius Properties Ltd supra*, CA.
[19] *Elite Investments Ltd* v. *TI Bainbridge Silencers Ltd* (1986) 280 EG 1001.
[20] [1893] 2 QB 212, CA.

cost of demolition and rebuilding from the tenants. It emerged that the foundations of the old house were defective, having consisted of a mud-sill (ie logs of timber resting on muddy soil). The timber had become rotten. To have saved the house would have involved underpinning through several feet of muddy ground to solid soil. The Court of Appeal had no difficulty in holding the tenants not liable for the costs claimed. They held that no covenant to repair, however widely cast, could ever force the tenant to give back to the landlord at the end of the lease a new and different thing from the house demised (ie a house with defectively built foundations). The tenant was not bound to underpin the walls, which had sunk and bulged owing to the premises' own inherently defective condition. Lord Esher MR said[21] that if a tenant took a house "which is of such a kind that by its own inherent nature it will in the course of time fall into a particular condition, the effects of that result are not within the tenant's covenant to repair. . . He (the tenant) has to repair the thing which he took: he is not obliged to make a new and different thing."

The crux of the matter is in the remark of Lord Esher MR that what had happened in this case was due to the nature and condition of the house itself. It, in short, had to be demolished due to its having reached the end of its life and the tenant having covenanted to repair the house as originally built, was not bound to replace it with a new house. An identical result was, therefore, reached in this case to that arrived at in the case of the landlord's covenant to repair.

Further Illustrations

A further two examples of this principle may be given. In *Sotheby* v. *Grundy*[22] the tenant was held not liable to pay for the costs demolishing a house which had earlier been condemned as unsafe, its walls having bulged, fractured and overhung. The foundations had been built by an illegal method and so the effective possible life of the house had been shortened. Lynskey J held that the general covenant to repair imposed on the tenant did not oblige him to rebuild the house with proper foundations. He distinguished between

---

[21] [1893] 2 QB 212, at pp. 216–217.
[22] [1947] 2 All ER 761.

a partial collapse, which the tenant would have to put right even if it came about due to inherent design faults, and a total collapse, which he did not have to rectify though it came about for the same reason.

This was a case of total collapse the results of which, in principle, lie outside the scope of a tenant's general covenant to repair and so the only relevance of the design fault was that it accelerated that collapse. A more modern example of near total renewal was *Brew Bros* v. *Snax (Ross) Ltd.*[23] There, a 14-year lease contained a general covenant to repair by the tenant. The flank wall of the demised premises began to tilt towards the plaintiff's premises, this being caused by a shift in the foundations due in part to defective drains. On the question of whether the tenants were liable to pay for the cost of rebuilding the wall, it was found that to carry out this work would entail putting in new foundations and other work, costing virtually the same as a new building. The work was held on the renewal side of the line and the tenants were held not liable for it. Therefore the owners, who in fact ultimately carried out remedial work on the wall on a smaller scale than they originally pressed for, could not recover any of the cost as damages from the tenants.

Appraisal of decisions

Some comments may be made:

(1) The cost of the work in all these cases was very high, being admittedly equal in the last two to rebuilding virtually the whole subject-matter demised.

(2) The disrepair in all three cases came about because, due partly to the way the foundations were originally built, the premises or part out of repair had reached the end of their effective life.

(3) The premises in all cases were not newly-built; none of the leases expressly dealt with the question of inherent defects; and in all cases the court refused to hold the tenant liable to rebuild the foundations of the premises.

Where the landlord undertakes reponsibility for repairs and also in his covenant guarantees the structural soundness of

---

[23] [1970] 1 QB 612, CA.

the premises (at any rate where they are newly built) he may be liable to carry out even very extensive and costly work of renewal.[24] There is some doubt whether in such a case, even a tenant under a strong general covenant to repair could be liable to carry out such work and the view of the present author is that he would not, on the *Lister* v. *Lane and Nesham* principle. In any case, it is not likely that the tenant will wish to guarantee the structural soundness of the landlord's building.

By contrast, the cases show that if the work is in fact merely extensive work of subordinate renewal, then the tenant cannot escape liability merely because he has to replace part of an old property with a newly built part constructed according to the latest methods. As was pointed out above, that is the only sensible way of doing the necessary work—assuming a condition of disrepair exists. If the design of the premises may be to a subordinate extent improved, this is no defence to the tenant.

C. *Subordinate Renewal*

An important case on the extent of subordinate renewal required under an admittedly strong tenant's general covenant to repair is *Lurcott* v. *Wakely and Wheeler*.[25] The tenants of an old house held on a 28 year lease covenanted "well and substantially (to) repair and keep in thorough repair and good condition" the demised premises. Shortly before expiry of the lease, the local authority required by a dangerous structure notice that an external wall be taken down. The landlords complied with the notice and rebuilt this wall with concrete foundations and a new damp course (in other words they used the latest design methods at the time). They successfully recovered the cost of this work from the tenants. The Court of Appeal held that the work, being subordinate renewal, was clearly contemplated by the covenant the tenants had entered into, and the tenants were liable accordingly. Cozens-Hardy MR said[26] that if a subordinate part of the premises collapsed due to old age (as here) the tenant was not excused

---

[24] See *Smedley* v. *Chumley & Hawke Ltd*(1982) 261 EG 775, CA.
[25] [1911] 1 KB 905, CA.
[26] *Ibid* at p. 914.

from liability under his covenant. He distinguished *Lister* v.
Lane and Nesham on the ground that there, a change in circumstances outside the contemplation of the parties had taken
place. The test was whether the work was something which
went to the whole, or substantially the whole, or whether
it went to a subsidiary portion of the demised property.

Fletcher Moulton LJ went further and, despite their context,
these dicta are of importance in interpreting the scope of a
tenant's general covenant to repair in relation to old and new
buildings alike. He said[27] that it was held in *Lister* that the
tenant was held not liable to pay for the cost of foundations
which did not exist in the premises he gave up. (That, it is
suggested, is the key to the matter.) Fletcher Moulton LJ said
that nothing in *Lister's* case relieved the tenant from his covenant even if, to a certain extent, it might require him to rebuild
the premises.

"While the age and nature of a building can qualify the
meaning of the covenant, they can never relieve the lessee
from his obligation. If he chooses to undertake to keep in
good condition an old house, he is bound to do so whatever
the means necessary. ... He can never say: 'The house was
so old that it relieved me from my covenant to keep it in
good condition.' If it was so old that to keep it in good condition would require replacement of part after part until the
whole was replaced—if that was necessary—then, by entering
into a covenant that he would do it, he took on his own
back the burden of doing it. ...''

Comments and Further Authorities

Some further comments may be made about *Lurcott*. In
the first place, the only way of complying with the covenant
to repair which satisfied the building regulations was to carry
out the rebuilding with concrete foundations and a damp
course, even though these features, being new, improved the
property to a subordinate extent. In other words, even if the
result of complying with a general repairing covenant which
has no express exclusion of inherent defects liability, is to

[27] *Ibid* at pp. 921–922.

give back to the landlord premises with the defect cured, provided that the work is subordinate not total or near total renewal and is required to cure a proved condition of disrepair, this result is no defence to liability under the covenant. (See also the discussion in Section I D above.)

This principle that it is assumed that repairing work will be done to the latest standards required by regulations may assist the tenant. In *Wright* v. *Lawson*[28] for instance, the tenant was under a general covenant to repair. A first floor window developed cracks and had to be taken down after a dangerous structure notice was served. It was impossible to rebuild the window exactly as before without contravening building regulations; a new window was built by the tenant set back in the main wall of the demised house. The landlord failed in an attempt to get the tenant to rebuild the bay window with extra design features to conform to building regulations. It was found that substantial extra supporting work would have been required for the proposed bay window (a feature not part of the old, demolished, window). The work required by the landlord would have required the tenant to make a new bay window of a totally different character to the old bay window.

A second comment on *Lurcott* v. *Wakely and Wheeler* is that the tenant's repairing covenant there was very strong and the work was clearly subordinate renewal. It was not a marginal case. It has been seen that if the court finds that the work is equal or near equal in cost to rebuilding the whole premises, the tenant may be excused liability, as also where the work falls outside the contemplation of the parties. This will depend on the facts of each case, and the terms of each covenant, as well as the age of the premises.

A good example of these principles is furnished by *Halliard Property Co Ltd* v. *Nicholas Clarke Investments Ltd*[29] where the tenants under a 14 year lease of premises built in 1910 were under a general covenant to repair both the exterior and interior of the premises. There was a jerry-built structure at the rear of the premises (a utility room) which was defectively built (its walls being inadequate and in danger of collapse

---

[28] (1903) 19 TLR 510, CA.
[29] (1984) 269 EG 1257.

at the date of the demise). The structure eventually collapsed and French J held that the tenants were not obliged to replace it under their covenant to repair, rebuilding costs being found to be about one-third of the cost of rebuilding the whole premises. It should be noted that rebuilding would of necessity have given the landlords a different edifice (a properly-built room) from the defectively-built room which fell down because its life ended.

The basis of the *Halliard* case is that the utility room was regarded as a separate part of the demised premises, needing, as such, total renewal. By contrast, in *Elite Investments Ltd* v. *TI Bainbridge Silencers Ltd*[30] the tenants by assignment of the residue of a short term of an old industrial unit were held liable to pay for the cost of replacing the roof of the unit. The roof was deteriorating at the date of the assignment. The cost of the work was £84,364 and the value of the whole building as repaired was between £140,000 and £150,000. However, in this case, the new roof would not be significantly different from the old roof (though made of modern materials). Nothing better illustrates the heavy liabilities which may await a tenant holding a short lease of old premises or an assignee of the residue of a term of old premises.

Defence based on No Disrepair

At the risk of repetition it should again be stressed that it is assumed in the above discussion that a proved condition of disrepair exists requiring remedying. If not, then the tenant cannot in any event be liable.

Distinction between Covenant to Repair and to Rebuild

It is perfectly possible for the tenant, especially where he has a long term, expressly to undertake liability not merely to repair but also to rebuild any buildings forming part of the demised premises, during the the term, by use of the words, following a general covenant to repair "when necessary to rebuild or reconstruct or replace" any buildings. Clear words are required to impose this onerous obligation, as was seen. In relation to a regular rent review on a 150-year term with

[30] (1986) 280 EG 1001.

a covenant to rebuild the entire premises, it was held that an arbitrator could justifiably reduce the open market rental by 27.5 per cent due to the onerous nature of the covenant.[31] In the case of a general covenant to repair *simpliciter*, however, no such reduction would appear justifiable.

Now we deal with the distinction between improvements and repairs, before turning to inherent defects.

III IMPROVEMENTS AND REPAIRS

A covenant to repair does not involve a duty to improve the property by the introduction of something different in kind from that which was demised. Accordingly, as was seen in Chapter 4, the landlord is not liable under a general covenant to repair to insert a new damp course into old demised premises where there was none before.[32] The landlord of a dwelling-house to which section 11 of the *Landlord and Tenant Act* 1985 applies, is not liable to cure rising damp by inserting a new damp course where the house has none.[33] The same rule applies to tenants.

If the work required to be done is a repair, then the fact that there is a limited improvement of the property—as where a design fault is, in the process of executing the repair, cured as the only sensible way of doing the work—this fact will not of itself prevent the tenant being held liable to carry out the work. In *Quick* v. *Taff-Ely Borough Council*[34] a landlord (similar rules apply to tenants) was held not liable to replace metal-frame windows or to insulate lintels which were not themselves out of repair, even though it was claimed that replacing these items would at least alleviate condensation problems in the house, caused by lack of insulation around the lintels and sweating from the windows: the windows and lintels were not out of repair. The house was built in the early 1970s in accordance with building regulations then in force.

The Court of Appeal held however, that if the only sensible way to repair an item in disrepair, is by in the process curing

---

[31] *Norwich Union Life Insurance Society* v. *British Railways Board* (1987) 283 EG 846.
[32] *Pembery* v. *Lamdin* [1940] 2 All ER 434, CA.
[33] *Wainwright* v. *Leeds City Council* (1984) 270 EG 1289, CA.
[34] (1985) 276 EG 452, CA.

a design fault (and thus to improve to a limited extent the premises without wholly renewing them) the landlord (or tenant) cannot avoid liability. If therefore, the tenant is able to show that the work required to cure a design fault was so extensive as to amount to renewal or near renewal of the whole premises, then he is not liable for that work.[35] (See further later in this Chapter.) An extreme example was *Collins* v. *Flynn*[36] where an old house settled due to its defective foundations causing subsidence of the supports for part of the rear end wall of the house and part of a side wall. To remedy this state of affairs would have required rebuilding the foundations of the wall and its supports, and the official referee held this outside the scope of the tenant's covenant to repair.

If the basis of this decision is that the foundations had to be replaced, constituting an improvement to the premises, then assuming that improvement was to the whole premises, no objection can be taken to it; if it goes further than that, then it is not good authority, for reasons which will appear.

Improvements in Design as Opposed to Repair

The tenant is not liable to pay for nor to carry out work which will improve the basic design of the premises. So, if the landlord replaces windows (or other items) with windows of a different design (say metal frame windows for the old wooden-frame ones) but the old windows could have been repaired, then he will not be able to charge the tenant with the cost of the work (under service charges provisions in the lease) because this is an improvement.[37] Nor presumably may the tenant be required to pay for the cost of replacing unrepairable wooden-frame windows with windows of a different, more expensive, design. On the other hand, if the work is replacement of a defective item (say a failed damp course) with a new, properly-constructed item (eg a proper damp course) which does not involve the reconstruction of the whole or nearly the whole premises, then the tenant will have to

[35] See *Ravenseft Properties Ltd* v. *Davstone (Holdings) Ltd* [1980] QB 12; (1978) 249 EG 51.
[36] [1963] 2 All ER 1068.
[37] *Mullaney* v. *Maybourne Grange (Croydon) Management Co Ltd* (1986) 277 EG 1350.

pay for that work as a repair.[38] The dividing line is difficult to draw in advance and would be largely a question of fact and degree: see sections II and IV of this Chapter.

IV. THE PROBLEM OF INHERENT DEFECTS

In this section the issue discussed is, how far, if at all, a tenant may be obliged by a general covenant to repair to carry out remedial work which, wholly or partly, is necessitated by the inherent nature of the demised premises. It is most convenient if the question is first discussed in relation to old, then new, buildings.

A. *Old Buildings*

In *Lister* v. *Lane and Nesham*[39] Lord Esher MR said that the tenant under a general covenant to repair an old building (in that case an old house) is bound to repair the thing he took and is not bound to make a new and different thing; and the result of the nature and condition of the house itself, the result of time upon that state of things, is not a breach of the covenant to repair. In other words if a building is so old that it reaches the end of its life and is in a state of total collapse, the tenant is not, under a general covenant to repair, bound to replace the building with a new one. The tenant must carry out any repairs, in the sense explained above, which are required to keep the existing building maintained but he is not bound to try to alleviate the effects of time and the elements on the building, which will have a finite life.[40] If, therefore, there is an inherent defect or design fault in the building which causes it to collapse totally, at an earlier date than a comparable but soundly-constructed building would have collapsed, then the tenant will not be liable to pay for the cost of putting up a new building nor even of demolishing the old one.[41] This is due to the fact that total renewal, as was seen, lies outside the scope of any tenant's covenant to repair. The sole relevance of an inherent defect to this question is that it may, as pointed out earlier, accelerate

---

[38] *Elmcroft Developments Ltd* v. *Tankersley-Sawyer* (1984) 270 EG 140, CA.

[39] [1893] 2 QB 212, at pp. 216–217.

[40] *Gutteridge* v. *Munyard* (1834) 1 M & R 334.

[41] See eg *Sotheby* v. *Grundy* [1947] 2 All ER 761.

the ultimate end of the building's life. The tenant is therefore not, in principle, liable under a general covenant to repair to prolong the life of the building demised taken as a whole.

It was also seen from the discussion in section II above that the mere fact that a building is old will not of itself relieve the tenant from his obligation to repair but it may qualify that obligation. If part of the (old) building collapses due to its disrepair, then that part will have to be replaced at the tenant's cost under a tenant's general covenant to repair—using, as was seen, the latest methods of design. If those methods to a limited extent rectify inherent design defects in the original article out of repair, then this fact by itself is no defence to an action against the tenant on his repairing covenant, as was seen. Note that in *Lurcott* v. *Wakely and Wheeler*,[42] for example, the new wall was built in accordance with the then building regulations and included a new damp course. Since the overall effect of the work was subordinate renewal, the fact that minor design improvements resulted was treated as of no significance.

It has been suggested that it may be advisable for a tenant taking a lease of an old building to agree with the landlord on the production of an agreed schedule of the condition of the building.[43] This is relevant to fixing the standard of repairs under a covenant, for example, to keep the building in good tenantable repair, if that is what the tenant agrees to, for reasons given in Chapter 5. It might also be prudent to endeavour to agree that the landlord will be responsible for putting right major structural design faults, given that minor inherent defects will of necessity be the tenant's responsibility if he is under a general covenant to repair.

B. *New Buildings*

Cases have arisen in relation to buildings put up in the 1960s and 1970s, where the tenant may well be under a widely drawn unqualified general covenant to repair the structure, exterior and possibly all other parts of the building; or where he covenants to pay service charges for structural and exterior

---

[42] [1911] 1 KB 905, CA.
[43] *Murray J Ross*, Chapter 8, p. 143.

repairs carried out by the landlord to a multi-occupied office building or block of residential flats, for example.

Several problems arise where a design defect manifests itself occasioning remedial work and the question of the tenant's liability to carry out the work or pay for it arises.

State of Disrepair must Exist

This matter was discussed in section I D of this Chapter but its importance justifies repetition. In *Quick* v. *Taff-Ely Borough Council*[44] Dillon LJ said that a covenant to repair will only come into operation where there has been damage which requires to be made good. If there is such damage caused by an unsuspected inherent defect, "it may be necessary to cure the defect, and thus to some extent improve without wholly renewing the property as the only practicable way of making good the damage to the subject-matter of the repairing covenant."

Before any question of whether the tenant is liable to remedy an inherent defect under an unqualified general covenant to repair arises, proof, where required, of a state of disrepair by the landlords must be adduced.

In *Post Office* v. *Aquarius Properties Ltd*[45] the landlord failed to prove damage to the building in question and the tenant escaped liability. The facts of this case are fully set out in section I D above, to which reference may be made. The Court of Appeal stressed that the facts of that case were highly unusual. Ralph Gibson LJ did state that: "Neither a landlord nor a tenant [under] a covenant to repair in ordinary form, thereby undertakes to do work to improve the premises in any way." This was implicit in the *Quick* case, but the principles there stated were extended in the instant case because in *Quick*, as was seen, the house was accepted to have been built in accordance with design standards then in force.

If the tenant expressly covenants in clear terms to put the premises into a particular state or condition and to keep them in that condition, then if for any reason the premises fall

---

[44] (1985) 276 EG 452; [1985] 2 EGLR 50, CA.
[45] (1987) 281 EG 798, CA; [1987] Conv 224 (P. F. Smith).

out of that defined condition, the tenant will be liable to execute or pay for remedial work to bring them back into the defined condition—this was accepted in the *Post Office* case.

Exclusion Clauses

A clause in the tenant's general covenant to repair will be required expressly to limit or exclude the tenant's possible liability to cure inherent defects which produce damage to the premises. An example of such a clause is given in Chapter 5 Section II.

Another possibility would be expressly to limit the tenant's liability to any defect not discoverable after a reasonable survey or inspection of the premises.

Position where No Exclusion Clause and Inherent Defect Produces Damage to Premises

The question of the tenant's liability to rectify inherent design defects under a general, unqualified covenant to repair, was extensively considered in *Ravenseft Properties Ltd* v. *Davstone (Holdings) Ltd*.[46] In this case there was proved to be a condition of disrepair—an essential condition precedent to liability.

The facts in *Ravenseft* were that the underlessees of a block of maisonettes built at round 1960 were under a very wide general covenant to repair, "well and sufficiently to repair renew rebuild uphold support sustain maintain ... and keep the premises". The building had a reinforced concrete frame with external stone cladding. In error, expansion joints were omitted from the structure when it was built. The stones were not properly tied to the building.

These design faults caused structural damage. The stones bowed away from the concrete frame of the building. The landlords, due to the urgency of the matter, themselves (pursuant to a right in the lease entitling them to do so) remedied the damage. The stones were taken off and re-tied, and in the process the design fault was rectified, new expansion joints being inserted at a cost of £5,000. The whole work cost

---

[46] [1980] QB 12; (1978) 249 EG 51. Approved in *Quick* v. *Taff-Ely Borough Council, supra.*

£55,000 and this the landlords claimed under the lease from the tenants. They succeeded. (It was found that the cost of rebuilding at the time the work was carried out was some £3 million.)

The sole issue was whether the tenants were liable to pay under their covenant for the remedial work to cure the disrepair. Forbes J held them liable, on the short ground that the work, as a matter of fact and degree, was a repair not total or near total renewal. While the insertion of the expansion joints amounted to adding a new design feature not there before, they formed a trivial part only of the whole building and the cost of their insertion compared to the value of the whole building was trifling. The remedying of an inherent defect may be the only sensible way of doing a repair. If so the work will be classified as a repair.

The basic tests of liability to cure an inherent design defect under a general and unqualified covenant to repair may accordingly be summarised as follows.

Basic tests of Liability: Summary

1. It is a question of fact and degree whether work which the tenant is asked to execute or pay for is a repair or is the giving back to the landlord of a wholly different thing from that demised. This classification is carried out on the same general principles as apply to decide whether work is repair (including subordinate renewal) or total or near total renewal.

2. There is no absolute rule that, if there is an inherent design defect in the premises, this will by itself exempt the tenant from liability under a general and unqualified covenant to repair. The question depends on:

(a) What is the answer to issue 1 above?

(b) If the answer to that issue is that the work (in view of its nature, and cost, comparing the cost of the work with the cost of rebuilding the whole premises at the date of the action and so on) is total renewal or near total renewal, then the tenant will not be liable to carry out the remedial work. The fact that the remedial work (if it is of repair) will cure the design fault as a necessary consequence, does not affect the tenant's liability.

3. In deciding whether remedial work falls within a general covenant to repair, regard is had to the factors set out, for example, by Sachs LJ in *Brew Bros* v. *Snax (Ross) Ltd*[47]— these are listed in Chapter 4.

4. A relevant factor in deciding whether remedial work, in the process of which an inherent design defect may be cured, is repair or renewal or near total renewal, is to find the cost or estimated cost of the work. Then one must find the proportion this bears to the value or cost of the demised premises as a whole. In *Ravenseft*, for instance, the cost of the repairs, in total, was £55,000 and this compared with total rebuilding costs of some £3 million. So gross a disparity failed in any way to assist the tenants. In *Elite Investments Ltd* v. *TI Bainbridge Silencers Ltd*[48] where the tenants were held liable to pay for the cost of replacing the roof of an industrial unit, the figures were £84,364 for the work and £140,000–£150,000 for the value of the building as repaired (there was no evidence as to the rebuilding costs). Judge Paul Baker QC there said that cost rather than value must be stressed if seriously divergent.

5. The cost comparison basis, used in isolation, will only apparently free the tenant from liability if the cost is very near total replacement cost of the building. This was so in *Brew Bros* v. *Snax (Ross) Ltd*[49] and was the case in *Halliard Property Co* v. *Nicholas Clarke Investments Ltd*.[50] The court there had regard to the fact that the part of the premises in question (a utility room) would have to be totally rebuilt at a cost of one-third the total cost of rebuilding the whole premises. That part of the premises was a separate section of them: and the case may partly depend on this particular factor. It must be remembered that the cost comparison is only a useful guide, and one of a number of other relevant matters to be taken into account.

6. The length of the tenant's lease might conceivably be a factor, in a marginal case. This remains to be seen. The possibility that this matter might be relevant was accepted

---

[47] [1970] 1 QB 612, at p. 640, CA.
[48] (1986) 280 EG 1001.
[49] *Supra.*
[50] (1984) 269 EG 1257.

in the *Post Office* v. *Aquarius Properties Ltd*[51] but was dismissed as a factor of little weight there.

Applicability of Principles to Landlords

The question of landlord's liability under a general covenant to repair to remedy inherent design faults in new buildings (and also old buildings) is discussed in Chapter 4.

Similar rules as was seen, apply to those applicable to tenants under an unqualified general covenant to repair. Much depends on the type of building in issue, the words of covenant, and the surrounding circumstances. For example in *Smedley* v. *Chumley & Hawke Ltd*[52] the landlord's covenant amounted virtually to a guarantee to the tenant of the structural design soundness of the (new) demised building so that the landlord was held liable for the expense of virtually rebuilding it when it suffered serious damage due to its inherently faulty design.

Whether a tenant could ever be held liable for work on so extensive a scale on a general covenant to repair (as opposed to a covenant to rebuild) is very doubtful.

V. STANDARD OF REPAIR IN SHORT AND LONG LEASES

In this section there are considered first, the significance of any qualifications of the word "repair"; then the standard of repair required of a tenant holding a short lease or tenancy by the words "good tenantable repair" or some comparable expression; finally, the standard of repair required by a tenant's general covenant to repair on a long lease.

A. *Qualifications of the word "Repair"*

The tenant's covenant to repair in a particular lease may be qualified by additional words such as "good", "habitable", "sufficient" or "substantial". However, if the basic term "repair" is used, these additional words are strictly surplusage: the particular form of words in a covenant to repair was not of special significance. The effect is the same "whatever words the parties used provided that they plainly expressed the intention that the premises are to be repaired,

---

[51] *Supra.*
[52] (1982) 261 EG 775, CA.

kept in repair and yielded up in repair."[53] While the words used by the parties must be given proper significance, the overriding aspect required is an obligation to repair.

In deciding what standard is to be required of a tenant under his covenant to repair, the length of the term and all the other circumstances of the lease and the premises will affect the standard required so that, in principle, a higher standard of repair will be required by the same basic formulation (such as an obligation to keep the demised premises in "good tenantable repair") in the case of a long lease (say for 7 years and above) of business or residential premises of a high-class nature, than would be required of a short residential tenant in a lower-class district. This is borne out by *Firstcross Ltd* v. *Teasdale*[54] where in the case of short leases of residential flats (protected by the *Rent Act* 1977), it was held that an obligation imposed on the tenants in their leases to keep the interior of the demised flats in "good and tenantable condition" did not import an obligation to keep or put the premises into repair, but merely imported the (light) obligation to use the premises in a tenant-like manner (as to which see Chapter 2).

B. *Standard of Repair in Short Leases and Tenancies*

It is usual to find in the case of a short lease or tenancy that the tenant is only under an express obligation to keep the premises in "good tenantable repair," or some similar expression. As to the position where there is no such covenant, see Chapter 2: the sole duty of the tenant in such a case is to use the premises in a tenant-like manner or at least not to commit waste. If the lease is for less than seven years and is of a dwelling-house or flat, the tenant cannot be made liable to carry out structural or exterior repairs.[55]

It has been seen (Chapter 5) that if the tenant is under an obligation to keep the premises in good tenantable repair, he is impliedly bound first to do whatever work may be required to put them into that state of repair and thereafter

---

[53] *Calthorpe* v. *McOscar* [1924] 1 KB 716, at 722 (Bankes LJ) CA.
[54] (1983) 265 EG 305.
[55] *Landlord and Tenant Act* 1985 s 11(4) (which invalidates to this extent both express covenants and covenants to pay service charges).

to keep them in that state and to deliver them up at the end of the tenancy in good tenantable repair.[56] This principle is confined to any premises whose condition has deteriorated from a former better condition. It does not compel a tenant under an ordinary covenant to repair to carry out work to improve the premises so as to remove a defect present since the building was constructed (assuming that the defect has not yet produced actionable damage)—see above.

If the premises are out of repair in any respect at the end of or during the tenancy, then the onus of proving that there had been a breach falls on the party alleging it and proper evidence must be produced.[57] If, therefore, the premises are not in a state of disrepair the tenant is not liable.

In the case of short leases or tenancies, the main case on the standard of repair is in *Proudfoot* v. *Hart*.[58] The decision gives general guidelines only and so, if the context of the short lease or tenancy requires it, the principles there laid down will not necessarily apply (as shown by *Firstcross Ltd* v. *Teasdale*, discussed above). Moreover, as will be seen, it does not apply to long leases.

General Standard of Repair in Short Leases or Tenancies

Proudfoot v. *Hart*[59] concerned a three-year tenancy of a house in Kentish town, London. The tenant was under a covenant to keep the house in good tenantable repair and to leave it in that condition at the end of the tenancy. This is the usual standard in this class of case.

The landlord claimed damages for disrepair at the end of the tenancy and was awarded various items, for example the cost of repapering the walls of rooms where the paper on them at the start of the tenancy had worn out, repainting the internal woodwork, where the paint on the woodwork at the commencement of the tenancy had worn off, whitewashing and cleaning the staircases and ceilings and replacement of the kitchen floor. It was conceded that at the commencement of the tenancy, the house was not in good

---

[56] *Proudfoot v. Hart* (1890) 25 QBD 42, CA.
[57] See eg *Foster* v. *Day* (1968) 208 EG 495.
[58] (1890) 25 QBD 42, CA.
[59] *Supra.*

tenantable repair. The official referee awarded the cost of the items claimed to the landlord and the tenant successfully appealed to the Court of Appeal which ordered a retrial.

It held that the obligation of the tenant under the covenant to keep the premises in good tenantable repair was, first to put the premises into good tenantable repair and then to keep them in such repair, and secondly, that the standard required was to put and keep them in such repair as, having regard to the age, character and locality of the house, would make it reasonably fit for the occupation of a tenant of the class who would be likely to take it.

Lord Esher MR said:[60] "The age of the house must be taken into account, because nobody could reasonably expect that a house 200 years old should be in the same condition of repair as a house lately built; the character of the house must be taken into account, because the same class of repairs as would be necessary to a palace would be wholly unnecessary to a cottage; and the locality of the house must be taken into account, because the state of repair necessary for a house in Grosvenor Square would be wholly different from the state of repair necessary for a house in Spitalfields."

That is to say that the court judges the standard of repair required by a tenant's covenant to keep the premises in good tenantable repair by a subjective measure varying with the age, character and locality of the premises. If, therefore, during the tenancy the standard of the locality declines or rises, then the amount of repairs required of the tenant will be lower or higher at the end of the tenancy than at its commencement. In the case of short tenancies these variations are not, except in special circumstances, very likely to have much overall impact. (Such variations will, of course, be potentially significant in the case of long leases which is no doubt why the courts apply a much higher standard of repair thereto.) However, there is uncertainty as to whether, even if the locality is proved to have gone downhill somewhat during a short tenancy, the standard of repairs required of the outgoing tenant will be significantly reduced thereby, for there are dicta in *Calthorpe* v. *McOscar*[61] that the requirements

---

[60] *Ibid*, at p. 52.
[61] [1924] 1 KB 716, at p. 733 (Atkin LJ).

of an incoming tenant are assumed to remain the same throughout the term. In that case the outgoing tenant would have to adhere to the same standard of repair at the end of the tenancy as bound him at its commencement.

Lord Esher MR in *Proudfoot* v. *Hart* analysed[62] various kinds of work which a tenant under an obligation to keep the premises in good tenantable repair might have to do. For example, a tenant was not bound to repaper simply because the old paper had worn out, but in some circumstances he might have to repaper. In the case of a house in Grosvenor Square, for example, if the paper was at the end of the tenancy merely worse than it was when the tenant went in then this alone would not oblige him to repaper; if damp caused the paper to peel off the walls and it lay on the floor, the outgoing tenant was bound to put up new paper. In both instances the repairs required would be judged by what a reasonably-minded incoming tenant of the class likely to take the house would require. Lord Esher MR applied the same rule to painting. If the paint was in such a state that the woodwork would decay unless it was repainted, the tenant would have to repaint. The amount of decoration would be governed by the locality of the house, for "if a tenant leaves a house in Grosvenor Square with painting only good enough for a house in Spitalfields, he has not discharged his obligation." Likewise with the new floor claimed by the landlord: Lord Esher MR said that if the floor was totally rotten then the tenant must put down a new floor; if he could make good the existing floor then he was not bound to replace the existing floor.

The above standard of repair applies to the landlord where he is under the statute-implied obligation to keep in repair the structure and exterior of a dwelling-house imposed by section 11 of the *Landlord and Tenant Act 1985*.[63]

C. *Standard of Repair in Long Leases*

In the case of long leases it was held in *Calthorpe* v. *McOscar*[64] that the principles laid down in *Proudfoot* v. *Hart* have

---

[62] (1890) 25 QBD 42, at pp. 52–55.
[63] *Jaquin* v. *Holland* [1960] 1 All ER 402, CA.
[64] [1924] 1 KB 716, CA.

no application. The standard of repair in the case of long leases is, accordingly, that required to put the premises in such a condition as they would have been in had they been managed by a reasonably-minded owner having full regard to the age of the buildings, their locality, the class of tenant likely to occupy them, and the maintenance of the property in such a way that only an average amount of annual repair would be necessary in the future.

Calthorpe v. *McOscar* was concerned with very different circumstances to those applying in *Proudfoot* v. *Hart*. The facts were that in a 95 year lease of three houses in London, the tenant covenanted "well and sufficiently to repair and keep in repair" the demised premises. At the start of the lease the neighbourhood had been a high-class district; but by the end of the lease the district had changed in character so that the only type of tenants who would be likely to occupy the houses would be tenants holding on short periodic tenancies. This class of tenant would not, by definition, accept any significant form of repairing obligations and would require only a modest standard of repair. The question of dilapidations at the end of the lease was referred to the Official Referee and the Court of Appeal had to decide which of two different standards of repair, one higher and one lower, applied (the result affected the amount of damages awarded to the landlord). The Court of Appeal applied the higher standard. (The lower standard unsuccessfully contended for by the tenant was that he was only liable to carry out all repairs required by reasonably-minded tenants of the class now likely to take the premises, which would exclude a number of structural repairs.)

Bankes LJ said[65] that *Proudfoot* v. *Hart* did not lay down a general rule. It provides guidance as to the standard of repair on short tenancies only.

In the case of a long lease, it was held that in assessing the required standard of repairs, regard is to be had to the words of the covenant, the subject-matter of the lease, the age of the premises and their locality. Changes in the neighbourhood or surrounding premises could not affect the stan-

---

[65] [1924] 1 KB 716, at p. 726.

dard of repair required of the tenant in an action for damages for breach of his covenant to repair at the end of the lease.

This point is illustrated by *Morgan* v. *Hardy*[66] where there was a 50 year lease of premises including a house, the tenants being under covenant to keep and leave the premises in repair at the end of the term. Owing to changes in the surrounding property, the house would still be lettable if some of the repairs required under the literal interpretation of the covenant were omitted or carried out more cheaply. Denman J held that the fact that there had been changes in the neighbouring property did not affect the measure of damages payable by the original tenant to the landlord at the end of the term for breaches of the tenant's covenant to repair. All repairs literally required by the covenant had to be carried out under the covenant, and damages awarded on the appropriate basis.

---

[66] (1886) 17 QBD 770.

Chapter 7
LANDLORD'S CLAIM FOR DAMAGES

In this Chapter, the question of the landlord's claim for damages is considered. The subject is complex and of great importance. Before going through the various rules, partly statutory and partly common law, which govern, and in some cases limit or restrict, landlords' claims to damages from the tenant either during or at the end of the term, it is essential briefly to outline the general question of enforcement of claims for dilapidations during and at the end of a lease. This is because the landlord may wish to enforce a claim to damages (or as discussed in the next Chapter, to forfeiture of the lease) both against the person presently entitled to possession of the land (or last entitled to it) and also the person to whom the lease was first granted, as well as against guarantors of the lessee. These general rules are accordingly outlined and these apply *both* to damages and forfeiture claims. After this, the impact of the *Leasehold Property (Repairs) Act* 1938 on damages claims made during the lease is discussed. Next, the rules in section 18(1) of the *Landlord and Tenant Act* 1927 are considered: these fix a maximum ceiling on the amount of damages which the landlord may claim against the tenant for breaches of the covenant to repair. Special rules are then outlined, as where the premises are requisitioned and in various other cases. Finally, the question of landlords' re-entry to do repairs is discussed in this Chapter although it has nothing to do with damages, for the sake of convenience.

I. GENERAL PRINCIPLES OF ENFORCEMENT OF LESSEES' COVENANTS BY LESSOR AND ASSIGNS OF THE REVERSION

A. *Position of Original Tenant*

It appears convenient to here include an outline of the main difficulties which a landlord or assign of the reversion may face in enforcing a claim to damages whether during or after the end of the lease.[1] If the original landlord wishes to enforce a covenant to repair (either claiming damages or forfeiture or both) against the original tenant, then under privity of contract, the original tenant is liable to the original landlord throughout the term and this, even though the lease may have been later assigned. This is illustrated by *Thames Manufacturing Co v. Perrotts (Nichol & Peyton)*.[2] The case concerned an underlease of business premises under which the defendants were sureties. The tenants were under an obligation to repair the premises and in due course they assigned their interest to a third party. The landlords obtained summary judgment[3] against the original tenant and his sureties for damages for breaches by the assign of the covenant to repair in the underlease on the simple basis that the liability of the tenant (and the sureties) lasted throughout the whole term. The only way this could have been avoided was by a release of the original tenant from liability by the landlord at the date of the assignment.

In a case such as this, the tenant is being held liable, though, as he is out of possession, he is no longer able to see to it that the covenant is complied with. The result is rather harsh on him, though he may well try to limit the danger to himself by means of express indemnity covenants from the assignee. If this is not done, then if the original lessee is held liable to the landlord he has an implied right of indemnity from the immediate assignee.[4] In this it should be noted that the liability of the original tenant ends with the expiry of a term (which has been assigned) at common law.

But it is not clear whether the original tenant's liability is continued into any continuation of the term under Part II of the *Landlord and Tenant Act* 1954 in the case of business tenancies. Since old tenancy is continued by section 24(1) of the 1954 Act, it is assumed that the original tenant's liability will be extended into any continuation, because the original term (and estate) is automatically extended.[5] However, if

---

[1] See *Woodfall* 1–1095–1–1115; *Adkin* Chap 4; *Evans* Chap 5; *Yates & Hawkins*, Chap 7.
[2] (1984) 271 EG 284. Also *Baynton v. Morgan* (1888) 22 QBD 74, CA.
[3] Under RSC Ord 14.
[4] See Sandi Murdoch (1984) 272 EG 732 and 857 to which the author is indebted.
[5] *Woodfall* 2–0659.

a new lease is agreed on or ordered to be granted by the court, then at that point the original tenant's liability under the contractual term as continued is extinguished.

At common law a surety guaranteeing performance of the original tenant's covenants will not be liable once the common-law term ends in the absence of express stipulation.[6] If the existing term is extended, then the liability of the original tenant for breaches of the covenant to repair will also be extended.[7] In the event of the bankruptcy of an assignee, the landlord may still be able to enforce the covenant to repair in the lease against the original tenant even though the lease itself is disclaimed by the assignee's trustee in bankruptcy.[8]

On the question of whether the original tenant could reduce, or avoid altogether, his contractual liability if he could show that the landlord's own neglect to sue the assignee promptly caused the premises to fall into a greater state of disrepair than they might otherwise be in, there are two views. One is that as the landlord can choose whether to sue the assignee or the original tenant, it may be difficult to show that the liability has in fact been increased. The other is that if the landlord could be shown to be guilty of unreasonable delay, he should not be able to visit the consequences of that on the tenant.[9]

B. *Position of Assignee of Lease*

An assignee of a lease is liable for any breaches of the covenant to repair which occur during the period that he holds the lease and in principle he is not liable for pre- or post-assignment breaches.[10] If the landlord wishes to increase the liability of an assignee, which is based on privity of estate, then he should require each successive assignee to covenant direct with him to observe the covenants in the lease for the remainder of the term.[11]

[6] *Junction Estates Ltd* v. *Cope* (1974) 27 P & CR 482; *Plesser (A) & Co Ltd* v. *Davis* (1983) 267 EG 1039. His liability will presumably extend into any continuation tenancy under s 24 of Part II of the *Landlord and Tenant Act* 1954.
[7] *Baker* v. *Merckel* [1960] 1 QB 657.
[8] *Warnford Investments Ltd* v. *Duckworth* [1978] 2 All ER 517 (original lessee remained liable for rent for remainder of lease since disclaimer does not destroy lease).
[9] *Tucker* v. *Linger* (1882) 21 Ch D 18 (landlord's breach).
[10] *Woodfall* 1–1095.
[11] As in *Lyons & Co* v. *Knowles* [1943] KB 366, CA.

Where this is not done, then the assignee of a lease may still be liable for a breach of the tenant's covenant to repair which continues after the date of the assignment to him. In *Middlegate Properties Ltd* v. *Bilbao*[12] it was accordingly held that, where at the date of the relevant assignment premises were, in breach of the tenant's covenant to repair, out of repair, an assignee of the lease was liable to indemnify the tenant against his liability in damages to the landlord, the basis of this being that the assignee accepted the liability to undertake repairs by taking an assignment of premises out of repair.

If the landlord fails, for some reason, to recover damages from the assignee then he may, as indicated above, claim damages from the original tenant. In that event, the tenant has an implied right of indemnity[13] against the person to whom he assigned the lease.[14] Alternatively the tenant may have an express right of indemnity from that assignee. The original tenant may also claim reimbursement from the current tenant in possession if different.[15] Likewise an assignee who has been held liable for the breach by a person to whom he in turn assigned, he having covenanted direct with the landlord as above, will have an implied or (express) right of indemnity against the assignee in possession.

C. *Enforcement by Assignee of Reversion*

As far as enforcement by an assignee by deed of the freehold reversion is concerned, the position, as far as the covenant to repair is concerned, depends on whether the assignee of the reversion is taking action to enforce the covenant against the original tenant or an assign of the lease.

---

[12] (1972) 24 P & CR 329.

[13] Under *Law of Property Act* 1925 s 77 and Schedule 2 Parts IX and X.

[14] This implied right may be invoked by the tenant against his assignee even where the lease is later re-assigned by the assignee, and this, no matter whether the consideration for the original tenant is for a nominal sum or not: *Johnsey Estates Ltd* v. *Lewis and Manley (Engineering) Ltd* (1987) 284 EG 1240, CA (rent arrears, but plainly applicable to breaches of repairing covenants).

[15] *Moule* v. *Garrett* (1872) LR 7 Ex 101.

Assignees of the Lease

The main principles are as follows. Where the assignee of the reversion seeks to enforce a claim for damages or forfeiture against an assignee of the lease, provided the assignment of the reversion is by deed, he will be able to rely on section 141(1) of the *Law of Property Act* 1925. This annexes the benefit of the covenant to repair to the reversionary estate. In other words, an assignment by deed of the freehold reversion or of a severed part of the reversion, means that the assignee is able to sue the present tenant (original or by assignment) for damages for all breaches of the covenant to repair, whether these took place before or after the assignment of the reversion.[16]

Original Tenant

It has been held that where the freehold reversion was assigned (and before this the tenant had assigned his lease), the assignee of the reversion was entitled to recover rent arrears from the original tenant even though the arrears arose before the assignment: no doubt this principle would apply with equal force to claims for damages for pre-assignment breaches of the tenant's covenant to repair.[17]

Some Problems

It would appear that, provided that the assignment of the reversion is by deed, an assignee of the reversion may enforce a covenant to repair in the lease under section 141 of the 1925 Act, if the lease is not by deed, but is oral or written.[18]

If the performance of the tenant's covenants is guaranteed by a surety or sureties, it has been held that the benefit of these guarantees will pass automatically to any assignee by deed of the landlord's reversion—there is no need for a separate assignment of the benefit of these covenants.[19] Hence, if the covenant of guarantee extends to the performance of

---

[16] *Re King* [1963] Ch 459, CA.
[17] *Arlesford Trading Co Ltd* v. *Servansingh* [1971] 3 All ER 113, CA.
[18] *Law of Property Act* 1925 s 154 (oral tenancies); *Cole* v. *Kelly* [1920] 2 KB 106 (written tenancies.)
[19] *Kumar* v. *Dunning* (1987) 283 EG 59; [1987] 2 All ER 801, CA. (Original tenant/assignor of sub-lease entitled to benefit of covenant of guarantee in subrogation to assignees of reversion as against sureties though covenant of guarantee not separately assigned to assignee of reversion).

the tenant's covenant to repair, this result will be beneficial to any assignee by deed of the original landlord's reversion.

D. *Further Questions*

Two further general questions deserve mention.

Limit on Damages claims

If the landlord is claiming damages for breach of the covenant to repair, and is at the same time bringing a forfeiture of the lease, damages for breach of the tenant's covenant to repair will only be capable of being claimed down to the date of notional re-entry, ie the date when the landlord serves a writ claiming forfeiture. This results from *Associated Deliveries Ltd* v. *Harrison*[20] where the landlords issued a writ on a given date and thereafter, the premises already at that date being out of repair, they fell into a much worse state of repair. Nonetheless, it was held that the date of service of the writ claiming forfeiture marked the date down to which damages for breaches by the tenant of his covenant to repair fell to be assessed. The remedy of the landlord during the "twilight period" which follows the service of the writ to the date when the court orders possession (or grants relief from forfeiture) appears to lie in tort for wrongful occupation of the land, but such a claim must be separately made. Otherwise it may go by default, as in the *Associated Deliveries* case.

Estoppel against Asserting Landlord's Want of Title

If the tenant is in occupation of the demised premises throughout the term and he then leaves and the premises are, in breach of covenant, out of repair, it has been held that, vis-à-vis the landlord, it is no defence to a claim for damages that the landlord did not have a valid title to the legal estate at the time the lease was granted. So, where the lessees took a lease with full repairing covenants from a landlord who was not in fact entitled to the legal freehold at the date of the grant, it was held that this want of title in the landlord did not, after the end of the lease, give any defence to the ex-tenants against a damages claim for breaches of their

[20] (1984) 272 EG 321, CA.

covenant to repair—they being estopped from asserting the landlord's want of title.[21]

II. IMPACT OF LEASEHOLD PROPERTY (REPAIRS) ACT 1938 ON DAMAGES CLAIMS

A. *General Rules*

By section 1(2) of the *Leasehold Property (Repairs) Act 1938*, a right to damages for breach of a tenant's covenant to keep or put in repair which is commenced by action at any time when three years or more of the lease remain unexpired is unenforceable unless the landlord serves on the tenant not less than one month before commencing the action a notice under section 146(1) of the *Law of Property Act 1925*. Where such a notice is accordingly served, then the tenant has the right to serve, within 28 days of the service of the section 146(1) notice, a counter-notice claiming the benefit of the 1938 Act. The full details of the 1938 Act procedure and the effect of a counter-notice are discussed in Chapter 8. Suffice it here to mention, generally, certain points specially relevant to damages claims.

Firstly, the effect of a counter-notice, if served by the tenant, will be that all proceedings in the action will be stayed and the landlord will then have to apply under section 1(5) for the leave of the High Court or county court to proceed with the claim to damages. As will be seen from Chapter 8, leave to proceed may be given to the landlord on one of five grounds. Secondly, a notice required to be served under section 1(2) must comply with certain formalities: by section 1(4) it must contain a statement, in characters not less conspicuous[22] than those used in any other part of the notice, to the effect that the tenant is entitled under the 1938 Act to serve a counter-notice on the lessor and a statement in the like characters specifying the time within which, and the manner in which, under the Act a counter-notice may be served and specifying the name and address for service on the landlord. It will be

---

[21] *Industrial Properties (Barton Hill) Ltd* v. *Associated Electrical Industries Ltd* [1977] 2 All ER 293, CA.
[22] Ie no less easily readable: *Middlegate Properties Ltd* v. *Messimeris* [1973] 1 WLR 168, CA.

sufficient for the purposes of the 1938 Act if there is a letter
containing all the required information and referring to an
earlier section 146 notice (where the landlord is also claiming
forfeiture).[23] Thirdly, if the landlord is taking proceedings
for forfeiture as well as for damages, then the landlord should
protect himself—because the proceedings will amount to a
pending land action they should be registered in the appropriate register.[24]

It is provided in section 1(2) that the 1938 Act does not
apply to any claim for damages for breaches of the tenant's
covenant to repair which arise during the last three years of
the lease. Nor, by definition, does the 1938 Act apply to any
claims by the landlord made against the tenant for damages
after the lease comes to an end. If, however, the landlord
brings a forfeiture during the lease at a time when it has over
three years to run, then the 1938 Act will apply to the forfeiture and to any damages claim made by the landlord.

B. *Application of 1938 Act to Damages Claims*

The 1938 Act in its application to claims for damages by
landlords has caused serious problems because unless great
care is taken, the landlord runs the risk of losing his right
to claim damages in any case where there is urgency and
he carries out the necessary repairs and then seeks to charge
the tenant with their cost on the basis that the lease imposes
liability for repairs on the tenant. The position as discussed
in what follows is, however, a little uncertain because to date
there has been no pronouncement by the Court of Appeal.[25]

The impact of the 1938 Act on claims for damages depends
on whether what the landlord is claiming is in substance
damages, in which case non-compliance with the requirements
of section 1(2) before the claim is sought to be enforced will
be fatal to his claim; or whether what is in substance being
claimed is a contract debt under a term in the lease which
is so drafted that it enables the landlord:

(a) to carry out the repairs in the event of the tenant's
having been called on to repair and failing to do so; and

---

[23] See *Sidnell* v. *Wilson* [1966] 2 QB 67, CA.
[24] *Selim Ltd* v. *Bickenhall Engineering Ltd* [1981] 3 All ER 210.
[25] See PF Smith [1986] Conv. 85.

(b) to charge the tenant with the cost of the repairs so carried out on demand.

In this latter case the costs may be regarded as a contract debt and not damages so that section 1(2) of the 1938 Act will not apply to them but this view is not uncontested.

Damages Properly so called

The main case is *SEDAC Investments Ltd* v. *Tanner*,[26] where certain premises were held by the tenants on a 14 year term and the tenants were under a full repairing covenant. The landlords discovered that some of the stonework on the front wall of the demised premises was loose and that fragments of the front wall at first-floor level were in danger of falling into the pavement below. The landlords carried out the necessary work (being apparently entitled to do so under the lease). After this they purported to serve on the tenant a notice under section 146 of the *Law of Property Act* 1925 claiming the cost of the repairs and incidental expenses as damages, a sum of about £3,000, and failed.

The reason was that before any remedy of the disrepair took place, section 1(2) of the 1938 Act rendered it essential, since the landlords were claiming damages, that they *first* serve a section 146 notice on the tenants. In fact they had remedied the breach. Therefore they could not, having not before making their claim, served a section 146 notice on the tenants, recover any damages. The assumption is, that at the time the section 146 notice required by section 1(2) of the 1938 Act is served, the breach in question is unremedied and then the tenant will be given a reasonable time to remedy the breach. The landlords lost their right to damages because they had acted too promptly.

One way around this is to invoke a default covenant (ie a covenant of the kind outlined above). If however there is none in the lease (as in *SEDAC*) then it is not easy to see what can be done, if urgent repairs have to be executed and the landlord wishes to be able to recover their cost. He will then have to comply with the 1938 Act, so possibly he could give a very short time in the requisite section 146(1) notice

---

[26] [1982] 3 All ER 646.

to the tenant in which to remedy the breach and hope that
the court will take the view that, if the repairs are urgent,
a short time (even a few days) is reasonable in the circumstances.[27] Even then, the tenant can delay matters by serving
a 1938 Act counter-notice on the landlord which will stay
proceedings unless the landlord obtains leave to proceed. This
very unsatisfactory situation is far removed from the mischief
of the 1938 Act, this allegedly being to prevent oppressive
forfeitures.[28]

Default Covenants

The position where there is proved disrepair of a serious
kind, but the lease contains a default covenant, is almost certainly different from the above. By default covenant is meant
a covenant that if the tenant fails after notice to execute repairs
for which he is liable under the lease, the landlord has the
express right to enter the premises, to carry out the work
and to charge the tenant with its cost (see above).

There have, in fact, been two different approaches to this
matter.

1. The presence of a default covenant makes no difference
and the sum claimed under it as costs, is damages in disguise:
therefore if the 1938 Act requirements are not complied with
before the damages (on this view) are claimed, the landlord
loses his claim. This was the approach in *Swallow Securities
Ltd* v. *Brand*[29] where the landlords under a default covenant
carried out certain repairs and then sought to recover the
cost from the tenants without, before carrying out the work,
first going through the 1938 Act procedure. McNeill J held
that the landlord's action for damages should be struck out
since they were claiming damages and the default covenant
was a device attempting to remove from the tenant the choice
given to her by the lease to carry out the repairs at her own
expense with contractors of her choice.

2. The reverse approach of Vinelott J in *Hamilton* v. *Mar-
tell Securities Ltd*[30] where the landlord, who had a default

[27] See *Murray J Ross*, Chapter 8, p. 157.
[28] *National Real Estate and Finance Co Ltd* v. *Hassan* [1939] 2 KB 61, at p. 68.
[29] (1981) 260 EG 63.
[30] [1984] 1 All ER 665.

covenant, tried to get the tenant to comply with his repairing covenants and then finally carried out the repairs himself and successfully charged the tenant with the cost, even though the landlord had not gone through the 1938 Act procedure before carrying out the work. Vinelott J held that no leave to enforce the covenant was required since the landlord was seeking recovery under an express covenant in the lease, ie recovery of a contract debt rather than damages. This approach was by analogy with section 146(3) of the *Law of Property Act* 1925, which allows the landlord to recover reasonable costs and expenses of employing a solicitor and surveyor or valuer as a contract debt.

Summary

The position is uncertain at present, and although in two subsequent first-instance cases[31] the approach in *Hamilton* was followed, it is possible that a future Court of Appeal might prefer the *Swallow Securities* case. Any other view, after all, leads to differences in result depending on narrow wording in particular leases. The best that may be said is that the 1938 Act is a significant headache to landlords who wish to claim urgent repairing costs before the start of the last three years of the lease but who do not necessarily wish to bring a forfeiture.

III. SECTION 18(1) OF THE LANDLORD AND TENANT ACT 1927

The rule until the passing of section 18(1) of the *Landlord and Tenant Act* 1927 was that the measure of damages for breaches of the tenant's covenant to repair was the amount by which the landlord's reversion had depreciated in market-able value due to the disrepair.[32] An upper limit is placed by section 18(1) of the 1927 Act on the amount of damages recoverable by the landlord and the implications of this form the subject-matter of the present section of this Chapter. By the material part of section 18(1):

"Damages for a breach of a covenant or agreement to keep or put premises in repair during the currency of a lease, or

---

[31] *Colchester Estates (Cardiff)* v. *Carlton Industries plc* [1984] 3 WLR 693; *Elite Investments Ltd* v. *TI Bainbridge Silencers Ltd* (1986) 280 EG 1001, at p. 1012.
[32] *Woodfall* 1–1493.

to leave or put premises in repair at the termination of a lease, whether such covenant or agreement is express or implied, and whether general or specific, shall in no case exceed the amount (if any) by which the value of the reversion (whether immediate or not) in the premises is diminished owing to the breach of such covenant or agreement ..."

If the landlord brings an action claiming damages at any time before the commencement of the last three years of the term, he should bear in mind the requirements where applicable, as mentioned above, of the *Leasehold Property (Repairs) Act* 1938 as well as the effect of section 18(1) of the 1927 Act. If the action is brought during the last three years or at or after the end of the term then section 18(1) alone is relevant.

A. *General Principles*

Section 18(1) refers to the landlord's "reversion" and this is apt literally to cover any sort of reversion, whether immediately expectant on the current lease or not. However a narrow view is taken and it has been held that "reversion" means in this context the immediate reversion expectant on the lease.[33] To anticipate, if the value of the immediate landlord's reversion is very small or nil, then no substantial damages for breaches of covenant by the tenant will be recoverable.[34] The impact of section 18(1) has been limited by *Hanson* v. *Newman*.[35] This concerned a lease which was forfeited for breach by the tenant of his covenant to repair, damages being assessed down to the date of (notional) re-entry by service of the writ claiming forfeiture.[36] The tenant argued that he could set off against the drop in the value of the landlord's reversion the difference between the value of the reversion as at the date of repossession and as it would have been had the lease not been forfeited. The argument was rejected. Luxmoore J held that under section 18(1) there must be compared the value of the property in its unrepaired state as at the date of re-entry (ie service of the writ claiming forfeiture)

---

[33] *Terroni* v. *Corsini* [1931] 1 Ch 515.

[34] *Espir* v. *Basil Street Hotel* [1936] 3 All ER 91, CA.

[35] [1934] Ch 298, CA, affirming Luxmoore J.

[36] After this date no damages are recoverable: *Associated Deliveries Ltd* v. *Harrison* (1984) 272 EG 321, CA.

and the value of the property had the tenant complied with his obligations. Section 18(1) meant that the amount of damages awarded should not exceed the amount by which the value of the property as repaired exceeded the value of the property as unrepaired. In other words, section 18(1) fixes a maximum ceiling on the amount of damages recoverable but does not alter the manner in which they are to be calculated. In the next part of this section the general principles on which damages are calculated are discussed, bearing in mind this ceiling.

B. *Basis of Assessment of Damages*

Much depends, when damages come to be assessed, on whether the landlord intends first to carry out the repairs required, or whether, at any rate where the action is brought at or after the expiry of the lease by forfeiture or otherwise, he is able to re-let or sell the premises without first carrying out repairs thereto.

Repairs to Re-Let Premises

If the landlord carries out repairs to the premises with a view to re-letting them then it was held in *Jones* v. *Herxheimer*[37] that the cost of any reasonably necessary repairs is *prima facie* (though not conclusive) evidence of the damage to the landlord's reversion within section 18(1). In this case the landlord let rooms in a house on a short residential tenancy, the tenant being responsible for interior decorations. The tenant quit, leaving the interior out of repair. The landlord obtained an award of damages based on the cost to him of redecorating. The Court of Appeal made it clear that the rule in *Hanson* v. *Newman*—which involves comparing the value of the premises in and out of repair—was not inflexible and in a simple case where merely necessary repairs to enable re-letting were done, the cost of these should be the starting-point of any award. There was, in this case, no evidence of the capital value of the house and of the part let to the tenant but such evidence was not required as the rooms would not be sold off apart from the house itself.[38] If the landlord re-lets

---

[37] [1950] 2 KB 106, CA.
[38] See also *Maddox Properties Ltd* v. *Davis* (1950) 155 EG 155, CA.

the premises out of repair to new tenants and they undertake responsibility to carry out the repairs in question, in return for reimbursement by the landlord out of any sum he might recover from the ex-tenant, the fact that the premises have been re-let will not prevent the landlord from recovering the cost of such repairs from the ex-tenant.[39] This is because if the landlord pays the new tenants compensation for their carrying out repairs, or reduces their rent on that account, this is the equivalent of the landlord doing the repairs. In *Drummond* v. *S & U Stores Ltd*[40] it was pointed out (in the case of commercial premises) that while the measure of damages was the diminution in the value of the reversion, evidence of values of comparable properties would relate to premises in repair (or presumed so to be) so that evidence of the value of comparables out of repair might be difficult to obtain. That being so, and there being no capital values evidence in the case, the basis of assessment was taken to be the cost of putting the property into repair. Where the premises, though out of repair, were re-let to a new tenant (having simply been made presentable for re-letting at very small cost) at the same rent as the last tenant paid, it was held in *Jacquin* v. *Holland*[41] that the fact that there was a scarcity in demand for the premises (a house) in the area was an extraneous factor: damages would be assessed subject to section 18(1) of the 1927 Act, without regard to the "scarcity factor".

Special Factors

Complications may arise, however, if there are special factors. Two in particular may arise. The first is that the premises may be held by business tenants or sub-tenants protected by Part II of the *Landlord and Tenant Act* 1954 and entitled to court-ordered new tenancies thereunder. Section 34 of the 1954 Act postulates that the landlord is entitled to the open market rent of the premises. The fact that the premises may be out of repair due to the tenant's breach of covenant is

---

[39] *Haviland* v. *Long* [1952] 2 QB 80, CA.
[40] (1980) 258 EG 1293.
[41] [1960] 1 All ER 402, CA.

to be ignored. Therefore, in *Family Management* v. *Gray*[42] the premises were occupied by business sub-lessees whom the court assumed would apply for new tenancies under the 1954 Act Part II, but where repairs costing over £6,000 were required to comply with the lessee's covenant to repair. It was held that, since the sub-lessees would have to pay an open market rent and could not plead their default in complying with their obligations to repair to reduce that rent, the landlord suffered no damage to his reversion.

The second factor arises where the premises cannot be re-let for the same purposes as they were let for under the lease just ended, the premises being out of repair. For example, it might be that the premises had originally been let for residential purposes, with a high standard of repair, but that at the date of the action they cannot, because of planning restrictions or for some other reason, be re-let for those purposes but only for commercial purposes, with possibly a lower standard of internal repair at all events. In this sort of case, section 18(1) may have a significant impact. In *Portman* v. *Latta*[43] a house was let on a 19 year lease and at the end of the lease it was left out of repair (in breach of covenant) by the tenant. It was found as a fact that the house could not be re-let for residential purposes and could only be let for other purposes. Damages were awarded to the landlord but these were far less than the amount he claimed as the cost of repairs necessary literally to comply with the covenant to repair. In other words if it can be shown that at the end of the lease, a literal compliance with the covenant to repair is unnecessary, section 18(1) will preclude the landlord from claiming the full cost of complying with the tenant's repairing covenants.

A like limitation on the landlord's damages applies thanks to section 18(1) where it can be shown by the outgoing tenant that the capital value as realised on a sale of the premises is unaffected by the want of repair. If the full capital value of the premises is, after expiry of the lease, realised by the landlord on sale then he may get no damages at all even though there is disrepair of the premises. Two cases illustrate this.

---

[42] (1979) 253 EG 369, CA.
[43] [1942] WN 97.

In *Landeau* v. *Marchbank*[44] the premises in question, though out of repair, sold for a good price for conversion into two flats and two maisonettes. It was held that, on the facts, the landlord could not show that the value of his reversion had been diminished by the breach and that he was entitled to nominal damages only. (In this case it should be assumed that the dilapidations were not enough in themselves to affect the sale price of the premises.) In *Espir* v. *Basil Street Hotel*[45] the tenant of part of certain premises sub-let that part for the remainder of his own term less 15 days. The sub-tenant later obtained a long lease of the whole premises subject to the tenant's nominal reversion in part of the premises. In an action against the sub-tenant for alleged breaches of his covenant to repair, it was held that no diminution to the value of the tenant's nominal reversion had been suffered and he was not entitled to claim as damages the cost of restoring the premises (which had been converted into an hotel). Slesser LJ emphasised that the length of the landlord's reversion was a material factor in deciding on whether the value of the reversion had been diminished by the breach in question.[46] Since the claimants had only a nominal reversion in part of the premises, they were entitled only to nominal damages.

Lastly, *James* v. *Hutton*[47] is relevant: if the breach is of a covenant against alterations or of a covenant to restore the premises to their condition before the alterations were made, the measure of damages will simply be the usual contractual measure (unaffected by section 18(1)) namely, the amount of the loss suffered by the landlord.

Conclusions

1. If the landlord intends to re-let the premises then the cost of proper and necessary repairs to render the premises suitable for re-letting is a *prima facie* measure of the loss to the landlord's reversion; but if sale on the open market takes place at market values or if some other special factors

[44] [1949] 2 All ER 172.
[45] [1936] 3 All ER 91, CA.
[46] *Ibid*, at p. 95.
[47] [1950] 1 KB 9, CA.

are present, such as the landlord not having more than a nominal reversion, or the fact that the premises cannot be re-let for the same purposes as under the old lease, then section 18(1) may reduce or eliminate any damages he might otherwise obtain and the cost of repairs is not the proper measure of the diminution in the value of the reversion.

2. If the landlord wishes to realise the reversion on premises out of repair, and the price paid by a notional assign is reduced by the effect of the disrepair of the premises, the difference is presumably evidence of diminution in the value of the reversion.[48] Where demised premises became the subject of a compulsory purchase order and were then acquired at an agreed price (this being, in principle, the market value) then, as the premises would have been taken off the market by the compulsory purchase proceedings, no depreciation in the value of the reversion was shown and the landlord recovered nothing, even though the tenant under a lease which had expired before the making of the compulsory purchase order was in breach of his covenant to repair, it not having been shown that the price paid for the premises reflected their disrepair.[49] On the other hand, presumably if it could be shown that the price paid for the landlord's reversion on a compulsory purchase (the land then being subject to a subsisting lease) was reduced by the state of disrepair of the premises, the landlord could recover damages based on the difference between the price a willing purchaser would have paid for the premises out of repair, immediately before the compulsory acquisition, and their price with the repairing covenants performed.[50]

C. *Covenants Outside section 18(1)*

It has been held that section 18(1) does not apply to a covenant either to spend a stated sum on repairs and decorations or to pay the landlord the difference between the stated sum and the amount actually expended, because such amounts are not classified as "damages".[51]

---

[48] See dicta of Buckley J in *Re King* [1962] 1 WLR 632 at p. 647.
[49] *London County Freehold and Leasehold Properties* v. *Wallis-Whiddett* [1950] WN 180.
[50] Cf *Re King* [1963] Ch 459, CA.
[51] *Moss Empires Ltd* v. *Olympia (Liverpool) Ltd* [1939] AC 544. Cf *Hua Chiao Commercial Bank* v. *Chiaphua Industries Ltd* [1987] 1 All ER 1110.

Section 18(1) applies only to covenants to repair and does not affect the measure of damages recoverable where there is a covenant by the tenant not to alter the demised premises or their internal planning. Then, the measure of damages is at large but will not necessarily be the cost of re-instatement of the premises. In *Eyre* v. *Rea*[52] the assignee of a lease under a covenant not to alter the internal planning of the premises sub-let parts of the premises and the sub-tenants, by arrangement, converted the premises into five separate flats. It was held that section 18(1) of the 1927 Act did not apply as the covenant was not to repair and that in this case the landlord was entitled to the cost of re-instatement as damages, and this, though the premises as flats were more valuable financially than they were as a single dwelling-house.[53] In *James* v. *Hutton*[54] a landlord, who claimed damages for breach of a covenant to restore shop premises to the same state they were in before the relevant alteration, was held entitled to no damages because there was no evidence that he had suffered any loss to the sale value of the premises.

D. *Special Rules*

In five circumstances the application of section 18(1) gives rise to special problems. These are: where the premises are requisitioned, protected tenancies, building leases, sub-leases and impossibility of compliance with the covenant to repair.

Requisitioned Premises

Where the demised premises are requisitioned, the relevant date for the assessment of damages is the date when the lease terminates, even though the premises, at that date, remain requisitioned with the result that the landlord is not in a position to resume possession himself. The measure of damages is the difference in the value of the reversion at the termination of the lease, between the premises in their then state of disrepair and in the state which they would have been in had the covenants been fulfilled. If, however, the requisitioning authority has made alterations to the premises prior to the

---

[52] [1947] KB 567.
[53] But cf *Duke of Westminster* v. *Swinton* [1948] 1 KB 524.
[54] [1950] 1 KB 9, CA.

termination of the lease which render any repairs covenanted for valueless, then the tenant is not liable in damages to that extent; if the authority prior to the date of termination of the lease makes good any disrepair, the tenant is entitled to the benefit of that work.[55] In the case of requisitioning, therefore, the relevant date for the assessment of damages is the actual termination date of the lease and not the date of actual or notional re-entry by the landlord.

Under section 1 of the *Landlord and Tenant (Requisitioned Land) Act* 1944, dilapidations accruing while the premises are requisitioned are not the responsibility of the tenant. If there is a want of repair prior to the requisition, then the tenant is liable in damages for that, to the extent that it continues into the requisition.

Protected Tenancies

A special rule applies where the premises are held on a protected (or presumably, statutory) tenancy under the *Rent Act* 1977. In *Jeffs* v. *West London Property Corporation*[56] it was held that where a house at the end of a long lease was occupied by a protected tenant and was badly out of repair, the measure of damages was not the agreed cost of putting the hosue into the state of repair required by the lease, but the difference in price if the house was sold, subject to the protected tenancy, in and out of repair. Apparently, if the landlord proved that he had carried out, or intended to carry out, repairs necessary to comply with housing legislation, he could recover these costs as damages.[57]

Building Leases

In the case of a building lease, it has been accepted that the measure of damages for non-compliance with a tenant's covenant to build is the difference between the freehold value of the vacant site as at the latest date for compliance with the tenant's obligation and the value, as at that date, of the

---

[55] *Smiley* v. *Townshend* [1950] 2 KB 311, CA.
[56] [1954] CLY 1807.
[57] *Woodfall* 1–1406. Query whether the tenant should be burdened with costs of such possible magnitude.

site and buildings which ought to have been created—as in *Lansdowne Rodway Estates Ltd* v. *Potown Ltd.*[58] There, the tenants under a 126-year building lease failed to comply with their covenant to erect buildings on the land by a certain date. The court took the freehold value of the reversion assuming the tenant had performed his covenants by the certain date and made a deduction based on the anticipated remunerative rate for the buildings, taking into account (1) the design and quality of the buildings (2) their location (3) the security of capital and income and (4) the pattern of income and the prospects of an increase.

Sub-Leases

In the case of a sub-lease the same basic rule as to damages applies as to head leases: the measure of damages is the diminution in value of the sub-lessor's reversion. Moreover, if the sub-lessee has notice that there is a superior landlord, with whom the sub-lessor is under a covenant to repair, the sub-lessor's own potential liability to the superior landlord must be taken into account in assessing damages due from the sub-lessee, and the cost of putting the property into repair at the end of the term may be the appropriate measure of damages where the premises are sub-let but the sub-lease expires shortly before the expiry of the head lease.[59] On the other hand, if the sub-lessee has no notice that his interest in the premises is a sub-lease, then damages for breaches by him of his covenant to repair will have to be assessed independently of any damages payable by his sub-lessor to the superior landlord.[60] It may be that the court considers that the diminution in value to the sub-lessor's reversion is the amount he, in fact, has expended on necessary repairs (assuming these fall within the sub-lessee's covenants) in which case, the fact that the sub-lessee has no notice of the superior title will be of no practical effect.

Whether the sub-lessee has notice of the existence of a superior landlord or not, it will be appreciated that breaches by him of his covenant to repair may convert the sub-lessor's

[58] (1984) 272 EG 561.
[59] *Ebbetts* v. *Conquest* [1895] 2 Ch 377, CA.
[60] *Lloyds Bank Ltd* v. *Lake* [1961] 1 WLR 884.

reversion into an onerous burden, as where, for example, his reversion in the premises is merely nominal, determining at the same time or very soon after (say a few days) the termination of the sub-lease. It appears that, in principle, the amount of the diminution in value of the sub-lessor's (or mesne landlord's) reversion is the minus value of the reversion, namely, the amount the mesne landlord must pay a notional third party to take over the fag-end of the head lease incumbered with the sub-lessee's breach of covenant.[61] Where it cannot be shown that the mesne landlord would suffer any loss by the sub-lessee's breach of covenant, then his reversion will be deemed to have suffered no damage. That was the position in *Espir* v. *Basil Street Hotel*[62] where the mesne landlord had a nominal reversion in part of the premises of 15 days and where the sub-lessee (in breach of a covenant against alterations) had acquired the freehold reversion in the whole premises. There was no damage to this nominal reversion because the sub-lessee/head landlord would not wish to reconvert the premises back to their original state.

It may be that the covenants in the sub-lease are different to those in the head lease, in which case the amount of damages recoverable by the mesne landlord from the sub-lessee will not necessarily be the same as the cost of carrying out repairs. Moreover, the amount of repairs required may be less for a sub-lessee than for a head lessee if the sub-lease is at a later date than the head-lease for the sub-lessee's covenant only begins to run from the date of the sub-lease.[63]

Impossibility of Performance

If the tenant has covenanted to carry out repairs and then finds that, due to building regulations (such as were imposed during the Second World War for example), he cannot fully make good the disrepair because the cost exceeds allowable amounts in the regulations, this will afford no defence and

---

[61] *Ibid.*

[62] [1936] 3 All ER 91, CA.

[63] See *Walker* v. *Hatton* (1842) 11 LJ Ex 361 and *Williams* v. *Williams* (1874) LR 9 CP 659 (sub-lessee not liable for cost of repairs because they had not received a proper notice to repair as provided for in sub-lease). Also *Colley* v. *Streeton* (1823) 2 B & C 273, where the sub-lessee was held liable to pay for the cost of repairs because he received proper notice from his lessor.

the landlord will recover damages for the amount of the diminution in the value of his reversion, as, for example, where
he intends re-letting, the full cost of necessary repairs.[64] If
the tenant alleges that he has carried out all repairs necessary
to comply with his covenant and that further compliance is
simply impossible, the onus (a heavy one) is on him to show
this and rarely will such a defence succeed.[65] In *Sturcke* v.
SW Edwards[66] such a defence partially succeeded. Assignees
of a lease covenanted to carry out and complete repairs to
factory premises by a given date, at a time when they knew
that planning permission would have to be obtained for the
work since the old premises had been destroyed. In fact planning permission was refused. While the assignees were held
liable in damages on this covenant (the failure to get planning
permission not being enough to discharge them from either
performing their covenant or paying damages), they were not
liable under a covenant to rebuild in the landlord's licence
to assign, since at that time the fact that the premises had
been destroyed was known.

E. *Demolition or Alteration of Demised Premises*

Until the passing of the 1927 Act, the damages payable
by a tenant for breach of his covenant to repair at the end
of the term were unaffected by the fact that the buildings
were to be demolished as soon as the lease ended.[67] Moreover,
such damages were payable even if the repairs would be nulli-
fied by structural alterations which were in contemplation
at the end of the lease.[68] These rules explain the second
limb of section 18(1) of the *Landlord and Tenant Act* 1927
which provides:

"... no damage shall be recovered for a breach of any such
covenant to leave or put premises in repair at the termination
of a lease, if it is shown that the premises, in whatever state
of repair they might be, would at or shortly after the termination of the tenancy have been or be pulled down, or such

[64] See *Maud* v. *Sandars* (1943) 60 TLR 81; *Eyre* v. *Johnson* [1946] KB 481.
[65] See *Regal Property Trust* v. *Muldoon* (1947) 149 EG 428.
[66] (1971) 23 P & CR 185.
[67] *Rawlings* v. *Morgan* (1865) 18 CB(NS) 776.
[68] *Inderwick* v. *Leach* (1884) 1 Cab & E 412.

structural alterations made therein as would render valueless the repairs covered by the covenant or agreement."

Relevant Date

In *Salisbury* v. *Gilmore*[69] it was held that the relevant date for intended demolition or structural alterations is the date of the termination of the lease. This may either be the date when the lease ends by effluxion of time, or the date when the landlord notionally re-enters by serving a writ claiming forfeiture (this will usually precede the date of recovery of possession), or the date of peaceable re-entry, where applicable.

In *Salisbury* v. *Gilmore* it was also held that the onus of proving the intended fate of the building in question is on the tenant. In this case it appeared that the landlord, at the date of termination, intended to demolish the building in question. Not very long after the end of the lease he changed his mind owing to the War. It was held nonetheless that the tenant was not liable in damages since at the date the lease ended, the landlord had been shown to have had the requisite intention.

It may be that the landlord has plans for demolition or structural alterations at the end of the lease but these are provisional. In *Cunliffe* v. *Goodman*[70] it was held that the landlord must be shown definitely to have made up his mind at the relevant date: if there is a sufficiently formidable succession of fences to be surmounted before his intention can be realised then the landlord does not "intend" the project and the tenant has no defence based on the second limb of section 18(1). In *Cunliffe* the landlord had a project for redevelopment of the site in question but had yet, at the date of termination of the lease, to obtain planning permission, a building licence and to determine the financial viability of the project. It was held that the tenant could not escape liability in damages under section 18(1) as the landlord's project was too provisional to be definite. As Asquith LJ said, neither project moved out of the zone of contemplation—out of the sphere of the

---

[69] [1942] 2 KB 38; [1942] 1 All ER 457, CA.
[70] [1950] 2 KB 237, CA. Cf *Capocci* v. *Goble* (1987) 284 EG 230, CA (business tenancies where the landlord's plans were far advanced).

tentative, the provisional and the exploratory—into the valley of decision.

Section 18(1) affords a defence to the tenant if the project of the landlord is definite "at or shortly after the termination of the lease". This date means either the expiry date of the lease at common law (whether that resulting from effluxion of time or from forfeiture) or the date at which, having held over, the tenant quits.

The requisite onus of proof was successfully discharged by the tenant in *Keats* v. *Graham*,[71] a case showing how relevant planning enforcement may be to the question of intention of the landlord. Planning permission to erect and use premises for industrial purposes was limited to a certain date. After that date, the tenants having been told that no further planning permission would be granted, they elected to quit the premises, which the local planning authority was then insisting should be demolished. After this the premises were re-let and the authority changed its mind. Nonetheless, it was held that the tenants had a complete defence under section 18(1): events subsequent to the ending of the lease were not relevant. It had to be assumed at the date the lease ended that the authority would require the buildings to be demolished. Both this case and *Salisbury* v. *Gilmore* above show that the tenant is not to take the risk of changes of mind by the landlord or a planning authority in the period after termination of the lease, if the relevant intention is present at that date, because it is at the date of termination of the lease that the covenant to repair is to be performed.

Local Authority Compulsorily Acquires Reversion

If a local authority is the tenant and it compulsorily acquires the landlord's reversion, it cannot use section 18(1) to reduce damages otherwise payable. This results from *Hibernian Property Co* v. *Liverpool Corporation*[72] where a local authority tenant was in breach of its covenant to repair—then held over. Eventually the house in question was certified by one of its officers as unfit. It was then included in a slum clearance area and was compulsorily purchased by the authority:

[71] [1959] 3 All ER 919, CA.
[72] [1973] 2 All ER 1117.

if it had been fit, it would either have been excluded or compensation would have been computed on a higher base than site value only. It was held that the landlords were entitled to damages for the breach of covenant by the authority, assessed at the difference between the value of the reversion if the repairing covenant had been complied with on the date of notice of entry less the site value payable on the compulsory purchase. Caulfield J said, on the relevant part of section 18(1), that it could not be construed as enabling a local authority by its own failure to comply with a repairing covenant, so that the house had to be demolished, to claim relief in an action for damages for breach of covenant. If it were otherwise, they would be rewarding themselves for their breach of their own obligation.

IV. SUMMARY AND CONCLUSIONS ON SECTION 18(1)

The following summary and conclusions are offered as a general set of pointers in view of the rather complex position.

1. Section 18(1) of the *Landlord and Tenant Act* 1927 does not alter the measure of damages recoverable for breaches of the tenant's covenant to repair whether the action is brought during, or at the end of the term: but it fixes an upper limit on the amount of such damages.

2. There appear to be two main methods of calculation of the amount of damages.

(a) If the landlord intends to sell the reversion then there is an inquiry as to the price a willing purchaser in the open market might be expected to give for the landlord's interest, with the premises in their dilapidated state and for the premises if the tenant had complied with his covenant to repair. If there is a difference between the two figures then this is the diminution in the value of the reversion and forms the basis of the award of damages.

(b) If, on the other hand, the landlord intends to re-let the premises for the same purpose as they were held under the previous lease then *prima facie* the cost of any repairs which are necessary to the premises in the interests of good estate management, bearing in mind the requirements of reasonably-minded incoming tenants, is the diminution in the value of the landlord's reversion and the measure of damages payable. The fact that there may be a strong demand in the locality for the premises for the purpose for which it is intended that they should be re-let, is an extraneous factor and cannot of itself affect the quantum of any award.

3. If, however, it appears that the landlord cannot re-let the premises for the purposes for which they were used under the previous lease, then the cost of repairs necessary to bring the premises up to the standard required for the former use (where higher than for the present use) is not the proper measure of damages, and so, in this case, section 18(1) will directly reduce the amount of damages recoverable, for the old rule, which section 18(1) has superceded, was that the measure of damages was, where the action was brought at the end of the term, the amount of repairs necessary to put the premises into the state of repair originally contemplated by the tenant's covenant to repair.[73] For example, if for some reason the premises, having been let as high-class residential premises, may only now be let for commercial purposes, section 18(1) will limit the amount of damages the landlord may recover to whatever repairs are reasonably required to put the premises into a state of repair suitable for commercial letting.

4. The relevant date for the purposes of section 18(1) is the date of re-entry by the landlord, in most cases either the termination date of the lease by effluxion of time or the date of (notional) re-entry by service of a writ claiming forfeiture on the tenant.

5. The fact that there may be an acceleration of the reversion by forfeiture is ignored. If the reversion is postponed by, for example, requisitioning or the existence of a reversionary lease then the relevant date remains the date when the lease in question ends.

6. The tenant has a complete defence under section 18(1) if he is able to show that at, or shortly after, the date the lease terminates the premises will be demolished or structurally altered so as to render the repairs valueless. For this to apply, the tenant must show that at that date the landlord has a definite and not merely a provisional intention to carry

---

[73] *Whitham* v. *Kershaw* (1886) 16 QBD 613; *Joyner* v. *Weeks* [1891] 2 QB 31.

out those works. If, however, this is shown then the fact that the landlord later changes his mind, will make no difference and he will be able to recover no damages. If there are structural alterations which merely reduce the value of the repairs but do not eliminate them, then damages will simply be reduced.[74]

---

[74] *Fairclough (TM) & Sons* v. *Berliner* [1931] 1 Ch 60.

Chapter 8

FORFEITURE FOR BREACH OF COVENANT TO REPAIR

I. GENERAL

A. *When Right to Forfeit Arises*

If the tenant is in breach of his covenant to repair, then, provided the lease expressly reserves the landlord a proviso for re-entry for such breach, the landlord may either bring an action for possession or, if the premises are unoccupied, peaceably re-enter the premises. The tenant's breach of covenant causes a forfeiture to take place and provided that the landlord does not expressly, or impliedly, affirm the breach, a process known as "waiver", he may regain possession of the demised premises. As will be seen, the court has power to grant the landlord an order for possession over a physically separate part of the demised premises and may grant the tenant, or other applicant, relief against forfeiture in respect of another part of the same premises, if it is unaffected by the breach of covenant to repair. For example, relief might be granted in respect of a ground-floor flat or office, physically separate from other parts of the same building, in favour of a tenant or sub-tenant of that part of the premises, the landlord obtaining possession of the rest of the building.

B. *Relevant Courts*

Forfeiture may generally only be enforced by an action for possession, unless the tenant is prepared to leave the premises voluntarily. (It is unlawful, by section 2 of the *Protection from Eviction Act* 1977, to enforce a right of re-entry or forfeiture, otherwise than by proceedings in court, while any person is lawfully residing on the premises or any part of them.)

The landlord's action for possession will follow service of a writ on the tenant claiming forfeiture: this, as will be seen, is the equivalent of a conclusive and final determination by the landlord to end the lease. Such action may be brought in the High Court, or, by section 21 of the *County Courts Act* 1984, if the net annual value for rating of the land in question does not exceed £1,000, in the county court. (The parties may jointly agree to the county court having jurisdiction where the £1,000 limit is exceeded as a result of section 18 of the 1984 Act.)

C. *Re-Entry and Outline of Notice Requirements*

Once there has been a breach of a covenant to repair on the part of the tenant then a forfeiture is incurred, but the landlord has no automatic right to take possession of the land as a result of that. In the first place, as will be seen in the next section of this Chapter, he may, knowingly or not, expressly or impliedly affirm or waive the breach, since the breach merely renders the lease voidable at his option.

Prior to the service of a writ claiming possession, and to seeking to enforce the forfeiture incurred by the breach, certain steps must be taken by the landlord as regards notices and service of notices. If these steps are not taken, then the forfeiture cannot be enforced by any proceedings or in any other way (section 146(1) of the *Law of Property Act* 1925). The requirements relevant to the covenant to repair are set out in section III of this Chapter but some general points may here be summarised.

1. Prior to serving any writ claiming possession, the landlord must serve on the tenant a notice which complies with sections 146(1) and 196 of the *Law of Property Act* 1925, in particular, the notice must be in writing, it must specify the breach, or breaches, in question and must require the tenant to remedy them. In the case of alleged breaches of the covenant to repair, the section 146 notice must refer to, and have annexed to it, a detailed schedule of dilapidations.

2. If, at the date of service of the section 146 notice, the lease has three years or more to run (and was originally granted for seven years or more) then, except in the case of agricultural tenancies, the section 146 notice must comply with the requirements of the *Leasehold Property (Repairs) Act* 1938, as to which see below. If the notice fails to do

this it will be invalid; and the effect of the 1938 Act, if claimed by a tenant's counter-notice, is that the landlord's action will only proceed if the leave of the court is obtained on one of five statutory grounds. These are designed so as to preclude forfeiture for trivial breaches of the tenant's covenant to repair.

3. The landlord must prove, by section 18(2) of the *Landlord and Tenant Act* 1927, that the fact of service of a section 146 notice was known either to the lessee or to certain other persons with a substantial interest in the premises. Otherwise the forfeiture will be unenforceable.

D. *Re-Entry by Writ*

While in most cases the landlord may only obtain actual re-entry as the result of an action for possession relying on the tenant's breach of his covenant to repair for certain purposes, the lease terminates notionally at the date of the service or issue (it matters not which) of the writ claiming possession by the landlord.[1] This is because the issue of the writ to recover possession is regarded as an unequivocal decision by the landlord to put an end to the lease. The consequences of this none too rational position, given that actual re-entry will only take place as a rule after the delay entailed in possibly lengthy court proceedings, are these:

1. Once the writ claiming possession is issued or served, the tenant's covenant to repair ceases to operate. As a result, no damages for a tenant's breaches of his covenant to repair may be recovered by the landlord for any period after the date of notional re-entry, by issue of a writ claiming forfeiture. The remedy of the landlord during the twilight period, between issue of the writ and re-possession, is specifically to claim damages for wrongful occupation. This does not mean that during the twilight period the tenant retains no interest at all in the premises: he may, for example, apply for relief against forfeiture once the writ is served.[2]

---

[1] *Associated Deliveries Ltd* v. *Harrison* (1984) 272 EG 321, CA.
[2] *Associated Deliveries Ltd* v. *Harrison, supra; Liverpool Properties Ltd* v. *Oldbridge Investments Ltd* (1985) 276 EG 1352; [1985] 2 EGLR 111, CA.

2. After the issue of a writ claiming forfeiture, no equitable remedies, such as a mandatory injunction, are available to enforce any of the other covenants in the lease.[3]

3. The position of any sub-lessees in the premises, once a writ claiming forfeiture has been issued by the landlord, is complex but it would appear that for some purposes the sub-leases remain in force unless and until the landlord actually re-enters following a re-possession order, there having been no relief granted to the tenant or sub-lessees. In *Peninsular Maritime Ltd* v. *Padseal Ltd*[4] a tenant was ordered to comply with his covenant with sub-lessees to put a lift in good working order even though he himself was threatened with a landlord's forfeiture, the latter having served the tenant with a writ claiming forfeiture. The decision was based on the fact that, for the purposes of remedies as between tenant and sub-lessees, the sub-leases continued to subsist during the twilight period.

4. However, only if and when the landlord finally regains possession by actual re-entry usually after a court order (if not by peaceable re-entry) is the lease finally determined. (Under section 6 of the *Criminal Law Act* 1977 forcible entry is a criminal offence.) Any acts done by the landlord after the court orders possession are valid unless and until the order is reversed on appeal.[5] At any time up to actual re-entry by the landlord the tenant may, in the landlord's action, or in a separate action brought by him, claim relief against forfeiture under section 146(2) of the *Law of Property Act* 1925. If granted, an order for relief re-instates the lease as if there had been no forfeiture. (See section III of this Chapter.) Sub-lessees and mortgagees may, under section 146(4) of the *Law of Property Act* 1925, claim relief in the form of a vesting order.

5. Once the landlord actually re-enters following an order for possession, then the lease and also any sub-leases derived out of it are destroyed (see further below). This ends all possibility of further relief, but subject to the fact that there may be an inherent jurisdiction to grant relief to a lessee or sub-lessee or mortgagee outside the statutory provisions.

[3] *Wheeler* v. *Keeble (1914) Ltd* [1920] 1 Ch 57.
[4] (1981) 259 EG 860, CA.
[5] *Hillgate House Ltd* v. *Expert Clothing Service and Sales Ltd* (1987) 282 EG 715, CA.

6. If, for some reason such as the tenant not being in occupation of the premises, the landlord is able to re-enter peaceably, then the lease determines from that moment. But if in the process the landlord accepts a sub-lease as subsisting he affirms the existence of the head-lease and peaceable re-entry will not take place.[6]

II. DOCTRINE OF WAIVER

A. *General Principles*

The landlord does not have any automatic right to enforce a forfeiture incurred by the tenant's breach of his covenant to repair. Until he is in a position to issue a writ claiming forfeiture (this is a final and conclusive determination to bring a forfeiture) the landlord must take great care, if he wishes to regain possession, not to affirm the lease by express waiver of the breach (this would be by deed) or by implied waiver. Waiver means the relinquishment by the landlord of his right to re-enter the premises because of the breach.[7]

When Implied Waiver Arises

For an implied waiver to take place, the landlord must be shown to have a sufficient degree of knowledge to be put on his election whether to affirm the lease or to enforce his right to re-entry. The requisite degree of knowledge is that of the basic facts which in law constitute the breach of covenant entitling the landlord to forfeit the lease.[8] The knowledge may be that of the landlord personally. Since waiver is judged objectively, the knowledge may be that of the landlord's agent, which will be imputed to the landlord, or of the landlord's servant, and again this will be imputed to the landlord if the servant is under a duty in the course of his employment to pass on the information in question to the landlord. For example, in *Metropolitan Properties Co Ltd v. Cordery*[9] the landlord's porters were found to have been fully aware of the breaches in question for some time; their knowledge,

---

[6] *Ashton v. Sobelman* (1987) 281 EG 303; [1987] 1 All ER 755.
[7] *Banning v. Wright* [1972] 1 WLR 972 at p. 990 (Lord Simon).
[8] *David Blackstone Ltd v. Burnetts (West End) Ltd* [1973] 3 All ER 782.
[9] (1979) 251 EG 567.

which came to them in the course of their employment, was imputed to the landlords who, having accepted rent, with imputed knowledge of the breaches from the tenant, due in a post-breach period, were held to have waived the breach though they intended forfeiture all along.

B. *What Acts Constitute Waiver*

General

Waiver is judged objectively. Common acts relied on as amounting to (implied) waiver are: an unequivocal demand for future rent, or an acceptance of rent due in a post-breach period, by the landlord or his agent, where the landlord or the agent has sufficient knowledge of the breach. The fact that the demand or acceptance is made "without prejudice" to the landlord's right to forfeit will not prevent waiver of the breach in question from taking place.[10] Waiver was held to arise automatically where the landlord's agent's servant demanded and accepted rent in advance from the tenant, for a period after the breach took place, even though the landlord stated that he intended to re-enter: this is because the landlord's actions (ie those of his agent's servants, which were imputed to the landlord) spoke louder than his words.[11] However, if the landlord, on the basis of information given him by the tenant, proceeds on the basis that what the tenant says is true then (unless presumably no reasonable landlord would have believed the tenant) it cannot be said that the landlord has a sufficient degree of knowledge, if later it turns out that the tenant was in breach of covenant.[12]

Special Rules

This severe rule does not apply with equal force where the tenant has statutory protection, for example under the *Rent Acts* as protected or statutory tenant, because until such time, if any, as the landlord is able, as the result of special proceedings, to end the tenancy, he has no choice but to continue

---

[10] *Segal Securities Ltd* v. *Thoseby* [1963] 1 QB 887.
[11] *Central Estates (Belgravia)* v. *Woolgar (No 2)* [1972] 1 WLR 1048, CA.
[12] See *Chrisdell Ltd* v. *Ticker* (1987) 283 EG 1553, CA.

to accept rent tendered by the tenant, and in that case the demand for future rent, or an acceptance of such rent is an equivocal act and waiver cannot be inferred from that act alone.[13]

Other Examples of Waiver

Another clear example of implied waiver is where the landlord distrains on the premises for rent—the effect of that is to waive all breaches up to the day of the distress.[14] Other acts may be relied on, but according to *Expert Clothing Service & Sales Ltd* v. *Hillgate House Ltd*[15] in such cases, all the circumstances will be looked at fairly and objectively. The act relied on must be unequivocal and a clear affirmation of the lease, and in that case it was held that the sending of a letter by the landlords' ex-solicitors to the tenant, plus a draft variation of the tenant's lease (after service on the tenant of a statutory forfeiture notice but not a writ) was not an unequivocal enough act to amount to waiver.

Limits on Waiver

Some acts cannot, as a matter of law, amount to waiver, such as a demand for rent arrears due before the breach took place.[16] The service of a notice under section 146 of the *Law of Property Act* 1925 was held in *Church Commissioners for England* v. *Nodjoumi*[17] not to be waiver: it was not an unequivocal affirmation of the lease; a statutory notice must be served as an essential pre-requisite of forfeiture and, as Hirst J said: "... it cannot ... be said ... that the service of that notice destroyed the very right it was served for the purpose of achieving." An assignee of the freehold reversion will not waive a tenant's breach of covenant merely by taking an assignment of the reversion subject to the lease in question.[18]

---

[13] *Trustees of Henry Smith's Charity* v. *Willson* [1983] QB 316, CA; also *Chrisdell Ltd* v. *Ticker* (1987) 283 EG 1553, CA.

[14] *Ward* v. *Day* (1863–64) 4 B & S 337.

[15] (1985) 275 EG 1011; [1985] 3 WLR 359, CA.

[16] *Price* v. *Worwood* (1859) 4 H & N 512.

[17] (1985) 51 P & CR 155.

[18] *London & County (A&D) Ltd* v. *Wilfred Sportsman Ltd* [1971] Ch 764, CA.

C. *Impact of Waiver on Repairing Covenants*

In the case of a breach of a covenant of a once and for all nature (such as a covenant against assignment or under-letting without consent) the effect of waiver is to totally destroy the landlord's ability to forfeit the lease for that particular breach. A breach of the covenant to repair is regarded as a continuing one for each day the premises are out of repair. If the covenant is not to alter the structure of the premises or against improvements, for example, or if the covenant is a tenant's covenant to put up buildings by a certain date and then to keep them in repair, waiver may have disastrous consequences for the landlord. If he waives a breach of such covenants, he waives the right to forfeit in relation to the breach in question for ever; if in the case of a covenant to erect buildings there is, as part of that covenant, a covenant to repair when the buildings are put up, waiver of the breach of the covenant to build includes waiver of the latter covenant.[19]

In the case of a tenant's covenant to repair however, the main effect of waiver is that the landlord will, if he waives a particular breach, lose his right to enforce a forfeiture as at the date of waiver. Since the breach of covenant is a continuing one, a fresh cause of action will automatically arise as from the next day after waiver took place. In other words, waiver operates backwards for the particular breach only and if the breach continues after the waiver, the landlord is once again put on his election whether to enforce his right to a forfeiture.[20] Accordingly, in *Penton* v. *Barnett*[21] a lease contained both a general covenant to repair and a covenant to repair within three months after notice. The premises were out of repair and the landlord gave the tenant a statutory forfeiture notice to repair within three months. He then claimed rent for the quarter falling within the three months but it was held that he did not thereby waive the breach of covenant, as it was a continuing one: the landlord's right to re-enter was intact as regards the period after the rent was due, the premises being then out of repair; moreover, no further statutory notice was held to be required to enforce

---

[19] *Stephens* v. *Junior Army and Navy Stores Ltd* [1914] 2 Ch 516, CA.
[20] *Cooper* v. *Henderson* (1982) 263 EG 592, CA.
[21] [1898] 1 QB 276.

the forfeiture.[22] Similarly, in *New River Co* v. *Crumpton*[23] the landlord accepted rent due for a period after the expiry of a statutory forfeiture notice but the breach of covenant to repair continued after the date when rent was due; it was held that the landlord could bring a forfeiture in view of the continuing nature of the breaches, without, as above, his having first to serve a fresh notice: and this, even though the tenant had partially (but not totally) remedied the breaches complained of.

D. *Conclusion*

In relation to breaches of the covenant to repair, waiver is an affirmation by the landlord of the lease up to, but not beyond, the date of waiver: if the breaches continue after that date the landlord has a fresh right of action. This is simply the application of general principles of waiver as they relate to all breaches of covenant, for, as was said by Sachs J in *Segal Securities Ltd* v. *Thoseby*,[24] "... the acceptance of rent in advance can at highest only waive breaches that are at the time of the demand known to be continuing, and to waive them for such period as it is definitely known that they will continue."

If the breach is of a covenant which can only be broken once, such as a covenant to erect buildings then keep them in repair, or of a covenant against structural alterations and improvements, the effect of waiver is to disable the landlord from bringing an action for possession in respect of such breach. If the breach is of a covenant of a continuing nature, such as that to repair, the effect of waiver is to waive all breaches up to the date of the waiver but not beyond that.

In any case, the effect of waiver is limited by section 148(1) of the *Law of Property Act* 1925, which provides that where waiver by the lessor is proved to have taken place "... in any particular instance, such waiver shall not be deemed to extend to any instance, or to any breach of covenant ... save that to which waiver specially relates, nor operate as a general waiver of the benefit of such covenant." In other words, just

---

[22] Accepted in *Farimani* v. *Gates* (1984) 271 EG 887, CA.
[23] [1917] 1 KB 762.
[24] [1963] 1 QB 887 at p. 901.

because the landlord may have waived a particular breach, the tenant does not obtain leave and licence to continue to leave the premises out of repair for the rest of the term.

III. STATUTORY NOTICE REQUIREMENTS

A. *Requirement of Notice under section 146(1) of the Law of Property Act 1925*

Section 146(1) of the *Law of Property Act* 1925, with a view to enabling the tenant to have some warning of the landlord's intention to bring forfeiture proceedings for breaches (in this context) of the tenant's covenant to repair, provides as follows:

"(1) A right of re-entry or forfeiture under any proviso or stipulation in a lease for a breach of any covenant or condition in the lease shall not be enforceable, by action or otherwise, unless and until the lessor serves on the lessee a notice—
  (a) specifying the particular breach complained of; and
  (b) if the breach is capable of remedy, requiring the lessee to remedy the breach; and
  (c) in any case, requiring the lessee to make compensation in money for the breach;
and the lessee fails, within a reasonable time thereafter, to remedy the breach, if it is capable of remedy, and to make reasonable compensation in money, to the satisfaction of the lessor, for the breach."

Some general points as to the construction of this provision as it affects tenants' covenants to repair may be made, followed by some analysis of any formal defects which may invalidate a notice.

General Construction of section 146(1)

It was said in *Church Commissioners for England* v. *Nodjoumi*[25] that a section 146 notice: "... is by statute a necessary preliminary to forfeiture where the breach is remediable, its whole purpose and effect is to operate as a preliminary to actual forfeiture." The aim of requiring a section 146 notice is, therefore, to afford what Lord Russell described in *Old*

---

[25] (1985) 51 P & CR 155 at p. 159 (Hirst J).

Grovebury Manor Farm Ltd v. *W Seymour Plant Sales and Hire Ltd* (No. 2)[26] as "a cooling off period during which the person at risk of forfeiture can consider his position and see what offer he can make to avoid forfeiture".

As will be seen, therefore, a section 146 notice will be invalid (or "bad") if it is insufficiently precise as to what exact work of repair it is that the tenant is being asked to execute; it will also be invalid, unless special exceptions apply, if it fails to comply with the formal requirements of the *Leasehold Property (Repairs) Act* 1938. The landlord will in any event be unable to proceed to enforce any forfeiture if, having served a section 146 notice on the tenant, he fails to allow the tenant (in the notice or otherwise) a reasonable time to remedy the breach before proceeding to issue a writ claiming possession.

The tenant may, by remedying all the breaches of the covenant to repair within the reasonable time allowed, prevent the landlord from forfeiting the lease. If action is heard, the tenant may still in that action or in a separate action, apply for and possibly obtain relief against forfeiture, as may sub-lessees or mortgagees, and the effect of relief is, as far as tenants are concerned, that the tenant is re-instated as if no forfeiture took place; as far as sub-lessees and mortgagees are concerned, they will hold a new lease from the date of the court's order.

Contents of a Good section 146 Notice

In the context of alleged breaches of the tenant's covenant to repair, the general rule, as stated by the House of Lords in *Fox* v. *Jolly*,[27] is that a section 146 notice, to be valid, must sufficiently specify the landlord's complaints; it must give the tenant adequate notice of what he is required to do; and it must provide full and sufficient information upon which he can decide which course of remedial action to adopt. However, since the notice will be addressed to the person who knows, or at least who ought to know, of the nature and condition of the premises of which he is tenant, as Lord Atkinson pointed out,[28] "a statement might be sufficient to draw his attention to the things of which the landlord complains,

---

[26] [1979] 3 All ER 504, at pp. 506–507, CA.
[27] [1916] 1 AC 1.
[28] *Ibid*, at p. 18.

which might be insufficient in the case of a stranger who had
never seen ... the premises". An example of an insufficient
notice is *Fletcher* v. *Nokes*[29] where the notice simply stated
that the tenant was in breach of his covenants to repair (it
recited the covenants but was no more specific than that).
This notice was held bad and no forfeiture action could be
based on it. By contrast, in *Fox* v. *Jolly*, a statutory forfeiture
notice was served in relation to six houses: it stated that the
covenants to repair were broken, the breaches being listed
in a schedule of dilapidations. The schedule indicated, under
general headings, repairs required to be done in all the houses
and, in a few instances, specified repairs to be done in particular houses. This schedule was held to be sufficiently precise,
for the statutory notice to which it is appended is not required
by the 1925 Act to inform the tenant of anything apart from
particulars of the breaches of covenants complained of—not
for instance as to the means of remedying them.[30] Clearly,
however, it would be advisable to give fairly precise details
of each alleged breach (for if a breach is not specified in this
way then it cannot later be relied on as a ground of forfeiture).
If the notice is insufficiently precise as regards alleged breaches
of the covenant to repair, even if it is upheld as regards other
breaches, it will certainly fail as regards the alleged disrepair.[31]

Potential Trap for Landlords

A potential trap for landlords is that if the notice is at
variance with the terms of the particular covenant to repair
in the lease, either generally or in some particular respect,
then apparently this will invalidate the notice: no severance
into good and bad parts is possible.[32] If, however, the notice
refers to an alleged breach of a covenant which does not exist,
it may be severed and treated as good as regards other alleged
breaches of covenants which do exist.[33] The tenant, equally,
cannot claim that a notice is invalid merely because the notice
relates both to alleged breaches of the covenant to repair and

---

[29] [1897] 1 Ch 271.
[30] [1916] 1 AC 1; also *Pigott* v. *Middlesex County Council* [1909] 1 Ch 134.
[31] *Re Serle* [1898] 1 Ch 652.
[32] *Guillemard* v. *Silverthorne* (1908) 99 LT 584.
[33] *Silverster* v. *Ostrowska* [1959] 1 WLR 1060.

to repaint, and he has succeeded in disproving a breach of the covenant to paint: the rest of the notice will apparently be good nonetheless.[34]

Money Compensation

The fact that a section 146 notice fails to ask for money compensation for the breach of covenant will not invalidate the notice. In *Lock* v. *Pearce*,[35] where there were very serious breaches of the tenant's covenant to repair, the landlord's statutory notice did not, in its terms, allow a reasonable time to remedy the breaches (proceedings were begun three months from the service of the notice), nor did it require the tenant to pay compensation for the breach. The notice was upheld.

A statutory notice need not accordingly, expressly allow the tenant time to remedy the breach, though, as will be seen, if the landlord brings proceedings (by issuing a writ) too soon after the service of the notice, the proceedings will fail. As far as compensation is concerned, the lessor need not, if he does not want compensation, ask for it.[36] The effect of not asking for compensation is that if the landlord in due course obtains actual re-entry and possession, or if the tenant is required, as a condition of relief, to remedy the breaches in question, the landlord cannot subsequently ask for compensation. He must decide on the matter once and for all when he is about to serve the statutory notice.

Effect of Remedied Breaches

Strictly speaking, as just noted, the landlord need not state in his statutory notice a time within which the alleged breach or breaches complained of must be remedied (after which reasonable time, he will issue a writ claiming possession). Section 146(1) of the 1925 Act simply envisages that a forfeiture claim may only be enforced if, a statutory notice having been served, "the lessee fails, within a reasonable time ... to remedy the breach."

No specific guidance is possible as to what this reasonable time, which must elapse between service of the section 146

[34] *Pannell* v. *City of London Brewery* Co [1900] 1 Ch 496.
[35] [1893] 2 Ch 271, CA.
[36] *Rugby School Governors* v. *Tannahill* [1935] 1 KB 87, CA.

notice and issue of a writ, is to be. It has been held that
this period of suspension will vary in every particular case
and, if the notice simply states that the breach must be remedied within a reasonable time, then such time must elapse
before the writ is issued and reasonable time must be allowed
for a remedy of *all* breaches.[37] The reasonable time runs
from the time when the lessee has knowledge of the fact of
service of the statutory notice (as a result of section 18(2)
of the *Landlord and Tenant Act* 1927 discussed below). If
the breach or breaches are in fact remedied within the reasonable time[s] then the landlord cannot proceed any further.
In other words, a remedied breach destroys the landlord's
right to enforce a forfeiture for breach of the tenant's covenant
to repair, as illustrated drastically by *SEDAC Investments
Ltd* v. *Tanner*.[38] There, the landlord's action for damages
failed because they had, prior to serving a statutory notice,
themselves entered the premises, executed the repairs in question, and thus remedied the breach of covenant. As the tenant
was not served with a statutory notice, which would have
given him the opportunity of remedying the breach, the landlord's claim failed.

In *Expert Clothing Sales and Service Ltd* v. *Hillgate House
Ltd*,[39] a landlord's section 146 notice failed to require a
remedy of a tenant's covenant and was held bad. The case
concerned a lease for 25 years with a covenant by the tenant
to demolish the interior and roof of the demised premises
and then to reconstruct them by a certain date; that date
passed with no work done. One month after the date passed,
the landlord served a section 146 notice on the tenants, which
alleged that the breaches of covenant were incapable of
remedy. The action failed, because the notice wrongly failed
to require the tenants to remedy the breach. The Court of
Appeal took the view that the breach in question was capable
of remedy, by the tenants doing the work within a reasonable
time after the stated date, even though the actual breach of
covenant in this case was not continuous.

[37] *Hopley* v. *Tarvin Parish Council* (1910) 74 JP 209; also *Horsey Estate Co* v. *Steiger*
[1899] 2 QB 79.
[38] [1982] 3 All ER 646.
[39] (1985) 275 EG 1011; [1985] 3 WLR 359, CA.

It was pointed out in that case, that the statutory notice procedure is aimed at giving the tenant two opportunities before the landlord proceeds to enforce his right to re-entry: first, to remedy the breach within a reasonable time of the notice, secondly, the opportunity to apply for relief. If the breach is remedied or relief obtained, the landlord (obviously) will not regain possession.

Further Comments

Firstly, the landlord will have the onus of predicting accurately just how much time it will be reasonably necessary to allow the tenant to remedy the breach, either expressly in the statutory notice, or impliedly by not issuing a writ before a reasonable time after the fact of service is known to the tenant. By the breach is to be understood *all* the tenant's breaches of covenant to repair. If the landlord fails to allow a correct reasonable time for remedy of *all* breaches, then the whole notice will be bad and no action can be based on it.

Secondly, no matter what the merits of the case, a remedied breach (before issue of the writ) cannot be the basis of any forfeiture action. Thirdly, no matter whether the nature of the breach is continuous, or once and for all, if the covenant in question is positive, be it to repair or to build or construct by a certain date, it appears to be remediable by the tenant. The question apparently is "whether the harm that has been done to the landlord by the relevant breach is for practical purposes capable of being remedied".[40]

Severance of Notices

It will be appreciated that a given statutory notice may well contain allegations of breaches (additionally to those to do with repairs) which have nothing to do with the covenant to repair. If this is so, a question might then arise as to whether, for example, if the notice was bad in so far as it related to some other covenant in the lease, it would still be capable of being valid as regards alleged breaches of the covenant

---

[40] *Expert Clothing Service & Sales Ltd* v. *Hillgate House Ltd* (1985) 275 EG 1011, at p 1016 (Slade LJ), CA.

to repair. No final answer may be given to this, but in *Starro-kate Ltd* v. *Burry*[41] May LJ stated that severance might be possible, so that a notice relating partly to repairs and partly to other alleged breaches of covenant could be severed and proceedings allowed in relation to the other breaches of covenant. Presumably, this could apply in reverse.

Concluding Remarks

Section 196(1) of the *Law of Property Act* 1925, which applies to section 146 notices, requires that such notices be in writing. So what must be achieved, is a notice which complies fully with section 146 of the 1925 Act.

1. The *Leasehold Property (Repairs) Act* 1938 may apply to the lease in question. If it does, then the tenant must, in the notice, be told that he is entitled to serve a counter-notice under the 1938 Act, claiming the benefit of the Act. The notice must in all other ways comply with the 1938 Act, so that it must contain the required statements and so on. See section J of this Chapter.

2. The notice must, in any event, whether or not the 1938 Act applies, set out *verbatim* the covenants to repair, it must allege that these have been broken, state that the particular breaches are as set out in a schedule of dilapidations appended to the notice, and require that all alleged breaches be remedied. There should also be a statement that in the event of failure by the tenant within so many calendar months to comply with the notice, it is the landlord's intention to re-enter. A precedent of a section 146 notice is given in the Appendix to this book.

3. As to the person on whom the statutory notice is to be served, the general principle is that it is the person for the time being holding a subsisting lease who is entitled to be served with a statutory notice. See further section D below. If the lease has been assigned, then the notice must be served on the assignee currently entitled to and in possession, and not on the original lessee—even though, of course, the original lessee is under a continuing liability to fulfil the covenant

---

[41] (1982) 265 EG 871 at p. 872, CA.

to repair: but he has no longer an estate in the land.[42] It would appear that, if the lease is held by two or more joint lessees, all of them must be served with a section 146 notice.[43]

B. *Attempts to avoid Necessity for Statutory Notice*

It has been held that attempts to circumvent the necessity for a section 146 notice are in principle invalid. For example, where the landlord obtained an undated deed of surrender from the tenant, the date to be filled in if a condition in the lease was not complied with by a certain date, the deed of surrender (with the date later filled in) could not be relied on in the landlord's action for possession as it was a disguised forfeiture, and the only way to enforce a forfeiture was to serve a statutory notice.[44] Similarly, a provision in a lease under which the landlord could terminate the lease by means of a three months' notice for breaches of certain tenants' covenants was treated as a disguised forfeiture clause.[45] If these devices were allowed to succeed, not only would tenants lose the benefit of section 146 warning notices, but they might be deprived of their right to apply to the court for relief against forfeiture.

C. *Requirement of Compliance with Leasehold Property (Repairs) Act 1938*

Where the *Leasehold Property (Repairs) Act* 1938 applies to the section 146 notice, the latter will be invalid unless it fully complies with the 1938 Act. See section J below.

D. *Service of section 146 Notice*

Proof of Service

By section 18(2) of the *Landlord and Tenant Act* 1927, a right of re-entry or forfeiture for breach of a covenant or agreement to repair is unenforceable by action or otherwise unless the lessor proves that the fact of service of a section 146 notice on the lessee was known to the lessee or to certain

---

[42] *Old Grovebury Manor Farm Ltd* v. *W Seymour Plant Sales and Hire Ltd (No 2)* [1979] 3 All ER 504, CA.
[43] *Blewett* v. *Blewett* [1936] 2 All ER 188.
[44] *Plymouth Corporation* v. *Harvey* [1971] 1 WLR 549.
[45] *Richard Clarke & Co Ltd* v. *Widnall* [1976] 3 All ER 301, CA.

other persons. These are: an underlessee of an underlease reserving a nominal reversion only to the lessee, and the person last paying rent under the lease on his own behalf or as agent.

The lessor must also prove that a time reasonably sufficient to enable the repairs to be executed has elapsed since the time when the fact of such notice came to the knowledge of the lessee or other person. This point is discussed above.

The severity of the rule that actual knowledge by the lessee or other persons must be proved by the landlord is mitigated by section 18(2) of the 1927 Act. This provides that where a section 146 notice has been sent by registered post addressed to a person at his last-known place of abode in the UK, that person, unless the contrary is proved, is deemed to have knowledge of the fact of service as from the time at which the letter would have been delivered in the ordinary course of the post. Posting by recorded delivery has the same effect as sending the notice by registered post.[46]

Form and Service of Notices

Section 196(1) of the *Law of Property Act* 1925 provides that a section 146 notice is to be in writing. By section 196(2), such a notice is sufficient if addressed to the lessee by designation. A notice may, by section 196(3), be left at the lessee's last-known place of abode or business, or affixed, or left for him, on the land or any house or building comprised in the lease. Or, section 196(4) enables the notice to be sent by post in a registered letter, the effect of which is mentioned above.[47]

Lastly, it is important to note that once a landlord serves a section 146 notice, the tenant may thereafter apply for relief against forfeiture.[48]

E. *Relief Against Forfeiture*

The tenant may apply for relief against forfeiture under the statutory rules either in the landlord's action, or in a separate action of his own. The application must be made before the landlord actually re-enters.[49] The statutory jurisdiction

---

[46] *Recorded Delivery Act* 1962 s 1(1) and Schedule.

[47] See *Re 88 Berkeley Road* [1971] 1 All ER 254.

[48] *Pakwood Transport Ltd* v. *15 Beauchamp Place* (1978) 36 P & CR 112, CA.

[49] *Rogers* v. *Rice* [1892] 2 Ch 170; *Smith* v. *Metropolitan City Properties Ltd* (1986) 277 EG 753; [1986] 1 EGLR 52.

as to relief is conferred by section 146(2) of the *Law of Property Act* 1925 which provides as follows:

"(2) Where a lessor is proceeding, by action or otherwise, to enforce such a right of re-entry or forfeiture, the lessee may, in the lessor's action, if any, or in any action brought by himself, apply to the court for relief; and the court may grant or refuse relief, as the court, having regard to the proceedings and conduct of the parties ... and to all the other circumstances, thinks fit; and in case of relief may grant it on such terms, if any, as to costs, expenses, damages, compensation, penalty, or otherwise, including the granting of an injunction to restrain any like breach in the future, as the court, in the circumstances of each case, thinks fit."

Various aspects of this important provision must now be dealt with.

Principles on which Relief is Granted

The general principles on which relief is granted were summarised in the following way by Lord Wilberforce in *Shiloh Spinners* v. *Harding*:[50] "... we should re-affirm the right of courts of equity in appropriate and limited cases to relieve against forfeiture ... where the primary object of the bargain is to secure a stated result which can effectively be obtained when the matter comes before the court, and where the forfeiture provision is added by way of security ... The word 'appropriate' involves consideration of the conduct of the applicant for relief, in particular whether his default was wilful, the gravity of the breaches, and of the disparity between the value of the property of which forfeiture is claimed compared with the damage caused by the breach."

Therefore, a wide discretion is conferred on the court in applications by the tenant for relief from forfeiture for breach of his covenant to repair.[51] Some general guidelines may be given.

General Guidelines as to Relief

1. To obtain relief the tenant must, as far as possible, remedy the breaches alleged in the notice, and pay reasonable

---

[50] [1973] AC 691 at pp. 723–724.
[51] *Hyman* v. *Rose* [1912] AC 623; HL.

compensation to the landlord for any unremedied breaches. The tenant may have to give an undertaking not to commit further breaches of the covenant to repair.[52] Under section 146(2), the court has a very wide discretion to impose any terms it thinks fit, as part of the granting of relief, such as imposing a time-limit within which remedial work is to be done (though this time-limit may be extended on the tenant's application[53]).

2. If, by the date of the hearing (though not at the date of issue of the writ), the tenant has fully complied with his covenant to repair he will, in the court's discretion, ordinarily get relief, unless there are exceptional circumstances which would render such a course of action inappropriate as, for example, where the breaches have been gross or wilful, or where it appears that the tenant is not likely to comply with his obligations in the future. The mere fact that the tenant has been slow to comply with his obligations is not, in itself, a ground for refusing relief if he has remedied all the breaches by the date of the hearing, or is willing and able to do so within a reasonable time thereafter.[54]

3. In relief applications it would appear that the value of the tenant's interest in the premises is a relevant question to the granting or refusing of relief: if it appears that the tenant is able and willing to remedy the breaches at a cost which is small compared to the value of his interest, he strengthens the case for relief. If, on the other hand, there are wilful breaches, and the tenant only offers to put matters right as late as the hearing, forfeiture may be enforced and relief refused.[55]

4. The effect of relief, if granted, is that the tenant is re-instated to his interest in the premises as though no forfeiture had ever been incurred.[56] The court has power to grant relief over a physically separate part of the premises, such as one flat in a block, where that part is unaffected by the breach.[57]

---

[52] See *Rose* v. *Hyman* [1911] 2 KB 234 at p. 241.
[53] See *Chandless-Chandless* v. *Nicholson* [1942] 2 KB 321, CA.
[54] *Cremin* v. *Barjack Properties Ltd* (1985) 273 EG 299, CA.
[55] See *Tulapam Properties Ltd* v. *De Almeida* (1981) 260 EG 919.
[56] *Dendy* v. *Evans* [1910] 1 KB 263; *Liverpool Properties Ltd* v. *Oldbridge Investments Ltd* (1985) 276 EG 1352, CA.
[57] *GMS Syndicate Ltd* v. *Gary Elliott Ltd* [1982] Ch 1.

However, relief cannot be granted to only one of two or more joint tenants.[58]

F. *Relief to Underlessees and Mortgagees: section 146(4) of the Law of Property Act 1925*

Where a head landlord is proceeding to forfeit a lease, the court has power, on the application of any underlessee or mortgagee, to grant them relief. This is by section 146(4) of the *Law of Property Act* 1925, the material parts of which provide as follows:

"(4) Where a lessor is proceeding ... to enforce a right of re-entry or forfeiture ... the court may, on application by any person claiming as under-lessee[59] any estate or interest in the property comprised in the lease or any part thereof, either in the lessor's action (if any) or in any action brought by such person ... make an order vesting, for the whole term of the lease or any less term, the property comprised in the lease or any part thereof in any person interested as under-lessee to any estate or interest in such property upon such conditions ... as the court in the circumstances of each case may think fit, but in no case shall any such under-lessee be entitled to require a lease to be granted to him for any longer term than he had under his original sub-lease."

Certain aspects of this provision as they affect the covenant to repair must be considered.

Principles on which Relief is Granted or Refused

The granting or refusing of relief under section 146(4) of the 1925 Act is a matter for the discretion of the court. The court will usually insist, as a condition precedent to granting relief, that the sub-lessee or mortgagee pays off all rent arrears, and remedies any outstanding breaches of covenant to repair, and also pays off all the landlord's costs.[60] For example, in *Official Custodian for Charities* v. *Mackey (No 2)*[61] relief

---

[58] *TM Fairclough & Sons Ltd* v. *Berliner* [1931] 1 Ch 60.
[59] This has been held to include a legal mortgagee or chargee: see *Grand Junction Co* v. *Bates* [1954] 2 QB 160.
[60] *Belgravia Insurance Co* v. *Meah* [1964] 1 QB 436, CA.
[61] [1985] 2 All ER 1016, at p. 1023.

was granted under section 146(4), the lessee's interest having been forfeited, on a mortgagee's application, subject to his giving an undertaking to pay the costs of the landlord so far as he failed to recover these in his forfeiture action against the lessees, and to use his best endeavours to carry out works of repair to the demised premises within 15 months of the hearing, the premises being, in breach of lessees' covenant, out of repair. The case applies the principle that, under section 146(4) applications, the court aims to put the landlord back in the same position as he was in before the forfeiture took place.[62]

As the *Mackey* case shows, the court will generally insist, as a condition precedent to making an order under section 146(4), that any breaches of the head tenant's covenant to repair are remedied by the applicant for relief, as respects the premises which are the subject-matter of the application. These may be the whole or any part of the premises.

In addition, it will generally be a condition of a vesting order, that the mortgagee or sub-lessee must undertake the same, or at least as stringent, repairing obligations as those in the (forfeited) head lease.[63] In accordance with these principles, relief was refused in discretion, under section 146(4), to the sub-tenant of a basement, part of the premises demised to a head tenant whose lease was forfeited. Relief was refused because, firstly, the applicant refused to pay for repairs, which were required to put the basement into good repair, at a cost of £10,000 to £15,000. Secondly, the applicant was not prepared to undertake the same onerous repairing obligations as those in the head lease, under a mere monthly tenancy, which was all that he was held entitled to obtain.[64]

Section 146(4) is essential to guard sub-lessees against the fact that if the head lease is finally forfeited and the landlord actually re-enters the premises, all sub-leases are *ipso facto* brought down with the destruction of the head-lease.[65] In

---

[62] This principle applies even where the sub-lessee's or mortgagee's interest is in part only of the demised premises: *Chatham Empire Theatre (1955) Ltd* v. *Ultrans Ltd* [1961] 1 WLR 817.

[63] *Creery* v. *Summersell* [1949] Ch 751 at 767.

[64] *Hill* v. *Griffin* (1987) 282 EG 85, CA.

[65] See *Chelsea Estates Investment Trust Co Ltd* v. *Marche* [1955] Ch 328 at p. 339; also *Moore Properties (Ilford) Ltd* v. *McKeon* [1977] 1 All ER 262.

the case of a mortgagee of a lease (or sub-lease for that matter) the destruction of his security may well turn out to be a greater catastrophe financially than his having to preserve the security as a saleable asset, at the cost of complying with the court's terms as to relief, which may involve some little expense.

Nature of Relief under section 146(4)

If a sub-lessee or mortgagee obtains relief under section 146(4), it will take the form of a new lease which is vested by the court's order in the applicant; the term vested, by section 146(4), cannot exceed the term held under the original sub-lease.[66] The new lease vested in the applicant takes effect as from the date of the court's order, and it is not retrospective so that if the landlord had at some earlier time re-entered, and at a later date a vesting order is made by the court in favour of, for example, a mortgagee, the order will have no effect on acts done by the landlord between his actual re-entry and the date of the vesting order.[67]

Obligation to Notify Mortgagee or Underlessee

Where the landlord requires possession of land or premises, he is required to indorse his writ with a statement showing the name and address of any underlessee or mortgagee, where he knows of any such person—as they are entitled to claim relief under section 146(4) of the 1925 Act. Where particulars are given as above on the landlord's writ, he must then send a copy of the writ to the underlessee or mortgagee named.[68] A mortgagee or sub-lessee notified under these rules has 14 days after service to acknowledge service of the writ; if he fails to do so then he will be bound by any order made as if he were a party.[69]

---

[66] This will include any continued term under Part II of the *Landlord and Tenant Act* 1954: *Cadogan* v. *Dimovic* (1984) 270 EG 37, CA.

[67] *Official Custodian for Charities* v. *Mackey (No 2)* [1985] 2 All ER 1016.

[68] Rules of Supreme Court (Amendment No 2) Order SI 1986/1187 in force from 1 October 1986. For similar rules applicable in the county court, see County Court (Amendment No 2) Rules SI 1986/1189, in force from 1 October 1986. On service of the writ, in this latter case, the landlord must file a copy of particulars of the claim with the court for service on the person named.

[69] RSC Ord 15 r 13A.

These rules are designed, no doubt, to improve the position of mortgagees and sub-lessees, and should reduce the significance of the inherent jurisdiction which is next mentioned. However, the rules do not appear to require any inquiry by the landlord into the existence of any mortgagees or sublessees, though in many cases leases will expressly require the tenant to notify the landlord of any mortgages or subleases. Nor do the rules provide for a sanction in the event of the landlord failing to comply with them. In that case presumably the mortgagee or sub-lessee can apply to the court to have the proceedings stayed or set aside. If the proceedings are only found out about too late, where a possession order is made due to a landlord's failure to notify a mortgagee or underlessee in accordance with these rules, this might still be a case for an application under the court's inherent equity jurisdiction, if the failure to notify was deliberate or due to a lack of proper care.

Inherent Jurisdiction to Grant Relief outside 1925 Act

Once an order for possession is made in favour of the landlord then section 146(4) ceases to apply: no relief applications may thereafter be entertained.

If any mortgagee or underlessee is properly notified in accordance with the above rules of court, then the matter should adequately be covered. No late applications by either ought then to be possible.

If no notification or proper notification in accordance with the rules takes place, potential disaster will follow for mortgagees or underlessees. The effect of an order for possession is that the lease and any sub-leases derived out of it will be destroyed. This may cause the mortgagee or sub-lessee serious financial loss. In circumstances where the non-notification of these parties has been due to some sharp practice, or possibly deliberate or negligent failure to notify by the landlord, in accordance with the rules of court, then there might still be a case for granting relief outside the statute. This took place in *Abbey National Building Society* v. *Maybeech Ltd*,[70] for example. The landlord had repossessed a flat for relatively

---

[70] (1984) 271 EG 995; [1985] Ch 190.

small amounts of rent arrears and the mortgagees were not notified by the landlord. Their security was worth £17,600 and they only came to know of the forfeiture when informed of its effect by the Land Registry. Not surprisingly, relief was granted to them in the inherent equity jurisdiction of the court.

G. *Inherent Equity Jurisdiction in the Case of Relief Applications Outside section 146(2) of 1925 Act*

If the tenant fails to apply to the court for relief against forfeiture under section 146(2) of the 1925 Act, before the making of an order for possession, then apparently the court cannot entertain any application for relief outside the terms of the statute. In *Smith* v. *Metropolitan City Properties Ltd*[71] the landlord re-entered for breaches of the tenant's repairing covenants and Walton J held that the court had no power to grant relief.

That case lacked any merits in the applicant; but Walton J based his decision on the wider ground that no inherent equity jurisdiction to grant relief against forfeiture existed in any case, apparently no matter what the circumstances or the merits. This is consistent with the view that if Parliament has legislated in a particular area, then any wider equitable jurisdiction is excluded.[72]

The view just expressed was in a different context. *Smith* gives a simple solution for tenants, perhaps an over-simple one, as there might be cases of fraud or surprise. In such instances, exceptionally, an inherent jurisdiction seems appropriate.

H. *Recovery of Landlords' Costs*

Certain landlords' costs incurred in forfeiture proceedings are recoverable. By section 146(3) of the *Law of Property Act* 1925:

"(3) A lessor shall be entitled to recover as a debt due to him from a lessee, and in addition to damages (if any),

---

[71] (1986) 277 EG 753; [1986] 1 EGLR 52.
[72] *Official Custodian for Charities* v. *Parway Estates Developments Ltd* [1985] 1 Ch 151 at p. 155 (Dillon LJ)—a case on LPA 1925 s 149(10).

all reasonable costs and expenses properly incurred by the lessor in the employment of a solicitor and surveyor or valuer, or otherwise, in reference to any breach giving rise to a right of re-entry or forfeiture which, at the request of the lessee, is waived by the lessor, or from which the lessee is relieved, under the provisions of this Act."

There are limits on the scope of this provision:

1. It applies only if the tenant obtains relief against forfeiture, or where he persuades the landlord to waive the breach in question.

2. It was held in *Nind* v. *Nineteenth Century Building Society*[73] not to apply where the tenant, sub-lessee or mortgagee in question remedied the breach, and thus avoided further proceedings, by actually complying with the statutory forfeiture notice.

3. It is also thought that, if a forfeiture actually takes place and the landlord in fact re-enters, then section 146(3) will not apply.

The way around these limits is to insert in the lease an express covenant by the tenant to pay all expenses, including solicitors' costs and surveyors' or valuers' fees, incurred by the landlord, incidental to the preparation and service of a section 146 notice, notwithstanding that forfeiture is avoided otherwise than by relief granted by the court.

In the case of repairs, if the tenant serves a counter-notice claiming the benefit of the *Leasehold Property (Repairs) Act 1938*, then the landlord's claim to his costs may only be exercised if he obtains leave to proceed (due to section 2 of the 1938 Act). However, this provision is limited to damages claims under section 146(3) of the 1925 Act itself, and there is a way around it, namely, to insert in the lease an express covenant by the tenant to pay solicitors', surveyors' or valuers' costs, in which case the 1938 Act will not apply. This is because the claim will be classed as a claim for a simple contract debt; the 1938 Act will be excluded; no leave under it will be required.[74]

[73] [1894] 2 QB 226, CA.
[74] *Bader Properties Ltd* v. *Linley Property Investments Ltd* (1968) 19 P & CR 620; approved in *Middlegate Properties Ltd* v. *Gidlow-Jackson* (1977) 34 P & CR 4, CA.

I. *Special Relief for Decorative Repairs*

The tenant may have covenanted expressly to carry out both external and internal decorative repairs at regular intervals (say in the case of external work, once every three years and for interior work once every seven years).

Plainly, a breach of covenant in relation to external decorative repairs may be a serious matter as injury to the structure and exterior of the premises can rapidly result from non-observance of this covenant; rigidly to insist, on pain of forfeiture, that the tenant comply with his covenant as regards interior decoration is concerned might, in some circumstances, be totally unreasonable where no actual damage to the premises could be shown from the breach.

Accordingly, by section 147(1) of the *Law of Property Act* 1925, after a notice is served on a lessee relating to internal decorative repairs to a house or other building, the lessee may apply to the court for relief and if, having regard to all the circumstances (including in particular the length of the lessee's term of interest remaining unexpired), the court is satisfied that the notice is unreasonable it may wholly or partly, relieve the lessee from liability for such repairs.

Unlike relief from forfeiture, any repairs not executed will, as a rule, have to be carried out by the tenant as a precondition of his obtaining relief, under section 147(1) the court has a discretion to relieve the tenant from the need to do any internal decorative repairs at all, and the tenant may, on receipt of the notice, immediately apply to the court for relief. Section 147(1) extends in appropriate cases to under-lessees.

Section 147 is excluded in four cases by section 147(2):

(i) where the liability arises under an express covenant or agreement to put the property in a decorative state of repair and the covenant or agreement has never been performed.

(ii) to any matter necessary or proper—

    (a) for putting or keeping the property in a sanitary condition, or

    (b) for the maintenance or preservation of the structure.

(iii) to any statutory liability to keep a house in all respects reasonably fit for human habitation.

(iv) to any covenant or stipulation to yield up the house or other building in a specified state of repair at the end of the term.

Finally by section 147(4) the above povisions have effect notwithstanding any stipulation (say in the lease) to the contrary.

J. *Leasehold Property (Repairs) Act 1938*

The effect of the *Leasehold Property (Repairs) Act* 1938 on a landlord's forfeiture action is profound. Essentially, where the 1938 Act is claimed by the tenant, all further proceedings are stayed and the landlord will only be able to proceed to enforce a forfeiture if he obtains the leave of the court on at least one of five statutory grounds.[75]

Application of 1938 Act

The 1938 Act applies to all leases except two types. First, by section 7(1) of the 1938 Act, it does not apply to a lease of an agricultural holding (within the meaning of the *Agricultural Holdings Act* 1986). Secondly, by sections 1(1) and 7(1), the lease in question must be for a term (when originally granted) of seven years or more and also at the date of the service of the landlord's forfeiture notice, three years or more of the term must remain unexpired. The 1938 Act applies, therefore, to residential and business tenancies alike, no matter what the rateable value of the premises. It extends to head leases and sub-leases, subject to the rules as to duration just mentioned (see s 7(1)).

The 1938 Act applies to a notice served under section 146(1) of the *Law of Property Act* 1925 that, by section 1(1) of the 1938 Act, "relates to a breach of a covenant or agreement to keep or put in repair during the currency of the lease all or any of the property comprised in the lease." However, the 1938 Act does not apply, as a matter of construction, where the tenant covenants merely to leave the property in repair at the end of the lease. Also, by section 3 of the 1938

[75] See PF Smith [1986] Conv 85.

Act, there is an express exclusion: the 1938 Act does not apply to a breach of covenant by a lessee to put in repair which is performable upon his taking possession or within a reasonable time thereafter. This means that an obligation to put in repair premises which are dilapidated at the commencement of the lease is excluded from the 1938 Act procedures. Finally, the 1938 Act has no application to breaches of the tenant's covenant to carry out internal decorative repairs: in this case, however, there is a special form of relief under section 147 of the *Law of Property Act* 1925 discussed above.

Policy and Effect of the 1938 Act

The policy of the 1938 Act is to prevent oppressive forfeitures being brought by landlord during the currency of the lease for relatively trivial breaches of a tenant's covenant to repair. In *National Real Estate and Finance Co Ltd* v. *Hassan*[76] Goddard LJ said: "The mischief (the 1938 Act) was designed to remedy was speculators buying up small property in an indifferent state of repair, and then serving a schedule of dilapidations upon the tenants, which the tenants cannot comply with." However, as Harman LJ remarked in *Sidnell* v. *Wilson*[77] "Like most remedial Acts ... it catches the virtuous in the net which is laid for the sinner."

A clear example of the potentially oppressive effect of the 1938 Act, which, as discussed in Chapter 7 of this book, applies not only to forfeiture but also to damages claims, is that no damages may be recovered for remedied breaches where the remedy precedes service of a section 146 notice as required by the Act.[78]

Moreover, the 1938 Act applies to all forfeiture claims for disrepair, no matter how serious the alleged breaches of covenant, and no matter what the rateable value of the premises and no matter what their user, be it commercial or residential. While the Act is not expressly limited to inhibiting forfeiture

---

[76] [1939] 2 KB 61 at p. 78, CA.
[77] [1966] 2 QB 67 at p. 79, CA.
[78] *SEDAC Investments Ltd* v. *Tanner* [1982] 3 All ER 646.

for trivial breaches of tenants' repairing covenants, it is judicially recognised that the 1938 Act is not supposed seriously
to inhibit forfeitures for serious breaches.[79]

There are, however, many opportunities for tenants to use
the 1938 Act's procedural requirements as a technical delaying
device. At the same time, the 1938 Act provides essential protection to the tenants.[80] In particular, the statutory requirement that the landlord, if a tenant's counter-notice is served
on him, must obtain leave to proceed, casts on the landlord
the onus of justifying continuing with his action, and he will
only obtain leave for good reason.

Requirements of section 146 Notice where 1938 Act applies

By section 1(4) of the 1938 Act, a section 146(1) notice
(under the *Law of Property Act* 1925), which relates to a
breach of a covenant or agreement to keep or put in repair
during the currency of the lease all or any of the property
comprised in the lease, will be invalid unless it contains a
statement, in characters not less conspicuous than those used
in any other part of the notice, to the effect that the lessee
is entitled under the 1938 Act to serve on the lessor a counter-
notice claiming the benefit of the 1938 Act and a statement,
in the like characters, specifying the time within which, and
the manner in which under the Act, a counter-notice may
be served and specifying the name and address for service
of the lessor.

Section 196 of the *Law of Property Act* 1925 applies, by
section 7(2) of the 1938 Act, to notices or counter-notices
required or authorised by the 1938 Act. As a result, these
notices must be in writing. (See further the discussion under
section 146 notices, above.)

The requirements of section 1(4) must be strictly complied
with in the relevant section 146 notice, and the effect of section
1(4) of the 1938 Act must be set out *verbatim*. It was accepted
in *Sidnell* v. *Wilson*[81] that a landlord who served a section
146 notice, which failed to comply with section 1(4) of the

---

[79] See *Re Metropolitan Film Studios Ltd's Application* [1962] 1 WLR 1315 at p. 1323.
[80] The Law Commission Report on Forfeiture (No 142 1985 HC 279) wished to preserve
intact the present rules, with modifications, on forfeiture for breaches of the tenants' repairing
covenants. See paras 8. 33 ff.
[81] [1966] 2 QB 67, CA.

1938 Act, could later rely on the combined effect of this defective notice and a subsequent letter which did fully comply with these requirements.

Moreover, the words "not less conspicuous" in section 1(4) have been limited to meaning "equally readable" or "equally sufficient": if the statement is no less easily readable than the rest of the notice, the whole notice will be valid even though the parts of it required to be included by the 1938 Act (say in blank spaces in a section 146 notice) are in a larger, or smaller, type face from other parts of the notice; and if a notice sets out one of a number of different methods of service of a tenant's counter-notice, it will be valid and the notice does not necessarily have to set out all the different methods of service on the landlord.[82]

Tenant's Counter Notice

By section 1(1) of the 1938 Act, the lessee may, where he has received a section 146 notice relating to breaches of his covenant to repair, within 28 days of the service of the lessor's notice, serve a counter-notice on the lessor to the effect that he claims the benefit of the 1938 Act.

The effect of a counter-notice is stated in section 1(3) of the 1938 Act: no proceedings, by action or otherwise, may be taken by the lessor for the enforcement of any right of re-entry or forfeiture under any proviso or stipulation in the lease for breach of the covenant or agreement in question, or for damages for breach thereof, otherwise than with the leave of the court.[83] As will be seen, leave may only be given if the lessor can establish one or more of five statutory grounds (s 1(5) of the 1938 Act).

Moreover, by section 2 of the 1938 Act, a lessor on whom a tenant's counter-notice has been served is not entitled to the benefit of section 146(3) of the *Law of Property Act* 1925, in so far as the costs relate to the breach of the covenant to repair in question, unless he applies for and obtains the leave of the court to take proceedings: on such leave application the court has the power to direct whether, and to what extent, the lessor is entitled to such costs.

---

[82] *Middlegate Properties Ltd* v. *Messimeris* [1973] 1 WLR 168, CA.
[83] Ie by s 6(1) of the 1938 Act, generally, the county court.

The provisions of section 196 of the *Law of Property Act 1925* apply, by section 7(2) of the 1938 Act, to the tenants' counter-notice. Moreover, the tenant, by section 51(4) of the *Landlord and Tenant Act 1954*, may serve the counter-notice on the person to whom he has been paying rent.

Limits on Tenant's Ability to serve a Counter-Notice

If the tenant fails, within the statutory period of 28 days, to serve a counter-notice then the benefit of the 1938 Act cannot be claimed. It appears that, if a tenant fails to serve a counter-notice, no one else can do so. Hence it was held that a legal or equitable mortgagee cannot independently of the tenant, serve a counter-notice claiming the benefit of the 1938 Act.[84] The basis of this is that mortgagees are not expressly included within the scope of the 1938 Act.

On the other hand, it has been held that an assignee of the lease who is currently in possession is entitled to have a section 146 notice, which complies with section 1(4) of the 1938 Act, served on him, and hence he may serve a counter-notice, where forfeiture is sought for breaches of the tenant's covenant to repair.[85] If the assignee has, by the date of service of a section 146 notice, re-assigned his lease out and out then, as he will be out of possession with no estate or interest in the land, he is not entitled to claim the benefit of the 1938 Act.[86] This distinction appears reasonable: if an assignee is in possession holding a substantial interest and thus in privity of estate with the landlord, he has a substantial interest in the ultimate outcome of proceedings and stands in the shoes of the original tenant. Not so if he is no longer interested in the land after re-assignment. Yet it could be argued that a mortgagee of the current lessee who is not in possession has similarly a substantial interest in the outcome of proceedings as forfeiture will annihilate his security. However he may presumably resort to section 146(4) of the 1925 Act to protect his interest.

---

[84] *Church Commissioners for England* v. *Vi-Ri-Best Manufacturing Co Ltd* [1957] 1 QB 238.

[85] *Kanda* v. *Church Commissioners for England* [1958] 1 QB 332.

[86] *Cusack-Smith* v. *Gold* [1958] 1 WLR 611.

Finally, if the person in present occupation of the premises has no substantial interest therein, as is the case with a contractual licensee or squatter, the benefit of the 1938 Act cannot be claimed.[87]

Defective Notices

A section 146 notice which contains the statements required by section 1(4) of the 1938 Act will be valid, even if it refers to breaches of covenant which do not exist.[88] If a section 146 notice refers both to breaches of the covenant to repair and to the non-existent breaches and is held bad as regards the other breaches but fully complies with the 1938 Act as regards the covenant to repair, it might be severable and enforced as regards the covenant to repair.[89]

Requirement of Leave to Proceed

If the tenant serves a counter-notice, within the time allowed, on the landlord then the forfeiture action cannot proceed without the leave of, generally, the county court (section 6).

What is said here as to leave gateways applies both to forfeiture actions and to damages claims.

The landlord must prove at least one of five grounds to obtain leave to proceed and they are separate and alternative.[90] A leave application under section 1(3) of the 1938 Act is regarded as a preliminary stage in forfeiture proceedings relating to land and is a pending land action registrable under section 5(1) of the *Land Charges Act* 1972.[91]

The standard of proof required by the landlord to obtain leave to proceed is not as high as in the full hearing. In *Sidnell* v. *Wilson*,[92] it was held that the landlord did not have to satisfy the court that a breach of covenant by the lessee had taken place, but only that a *prima facie* case existed that a breach had occurred, in other words, a case which, if believed, would establish the relevant ground. The landlord only has

---

[87] *Cusack-Smith* v. *Gold, supra; Tickner* v. *Buzzacott* [1965] Ch 426.
[88] *Silvester* v. *Ostrowska* [1959] 1 WLR 1060.
[89] *Starrokate Ltd* v. *Burry* (1982) 265 EG 871 at p. 872 (May LJ), CA.
[90] *Phillips* v. *Price* [1959] Ch 181.
[91] *Selim Ltd* v. *Bickenhall Engineering Ltd* [1981] 3 All ER 210.
[92] [1966] 2 QB 67, CA.

to make out an arguable case that at least one of the paragraphs of section 1(5) applies: the court will not at this stage evaluate the evidence in rebuttal, if any, put forward by the tenant.[93] The landlord must however adduce some evidence.[94]

Leave Grounds: section 1(5)

Section 1(5) of the 1938 Act provides that leave to proceed shall not be given unless the landlord proves that one, or more, of the following five grounds applies. These are:

(a) that the immediate remedying of the breach in question is requisite for preventing substantial diminution in the value of his reversion, or that the value thereof has been substantially diminished by the breach;

(b) that the immediate remedying of the breach is required for giving effect in relation to the premises to the purposes of any enactment, or of any byelaw or other provision having effect under an enactment, or for giving effect to any order of a court or requirement of any authority under any enactment or any such byelaw or other provision as aforesaid;

(c) in a case in which the lessee is not in occupation of the whole of the premises as respects which the covenant or agreement is proposed to be enforced, that the immediate remedying of the breach is required in the interests of the occupier of those premises or of part thereof;

(d) that the breach can be immediately remedied at an expense that is relatively small in comparison with the much greater expense that would probably be occasioned by postponement of the necessary work; or

(e) special circumstances which, in the opinion of the court, render it just and equitable that leave should be given.

The court has a discretion to refuse leave even though the landlord proves that the case falls within one or more of the above paragraphs. A fairly generous interpretation of this aspect of section 1(5) was taken in *Re Metropolitan Film Studios Ltd's Application*.[95] The landlord applied for leave to proceed where the premises were in a very bad state of

---

[93] *Land Securities plc* v. *Receiver for Metropolitan Police District* [1983] 1 WLR 439.
[94] *Charles A Pilgrim* v. *Jackson* (1979) 29 P & CR 328, CA.
[95] [1962] 1 WLR 1315.

repair and no steps were taken by the tenants to comply with the landlord's notice until the issue of a summons for leave to proceed. Ungoed-Thomas J held that while the court had an overriding discretion to refuse leave to proceed, even though the landlord proved compliance with one (or more) of the above paragraphs, the discretion was not to be exercised unless the court was clearly convinced that in these circumstances the leave application should be refused. Leave was granted in the case on grounds (a) and (d) and the discretion exercised in the landlord's favour.

It is possible that the discretion to refuse leave is not quite that narrow. In *Land Securities plc* v. *Receiver for Metropolitan Police District*[96] Megarry VC said that the discretion of the court was not so narrow as to suggest that unless the court was clearly convinced that leave should be refused, it should be given, for other factors (in his view) entered the picture, apart from whether the landlord is within one or more of the leave gateways. In this particular case leave to proceed was refused because the best way of dealing with the case on the facts was, it was said, to allow a concurrent tenant's action to proceed and for the landlords to defend that, rather than being allowed to run a concurrent forfeiture and damages claim.

The fact is, however, that much depends on the view taken of the 1938 Act procedure: is it truly a preliminary hurdle, with the main forfeiture action to follow, or is it an isolated procedure all by itself to make forfeitures more difficult for landlord? The two cases just discussed show that the courts have not finally resolved this matter, but this is probably of little significance.

Conclusion: What the 1938 Act does not apply to

1. The 1938 Act does not apply to any covenant which is not a covenant to repair, and so in *Starrokate Ltd* v. *Burry*[97] it was held not to apply to a breach of a covenant to cleanse the premises—though misdescribed as a covenant to repair them.

---

[96] [1983] 1 WLR 439.
[97] (1982) 265 EG 871, CA.

2. If the term of the lease in question is, at the date of commencement of the relevant proceedings, for less than three years, then no counter-notice can be served by the tenant and the Act is (impliedly) excluded.[98]

3. Leases of agricultural holdings and for terms granted initially of less than seven years are outside the 1938 Act by reason of sections 1(1) and 7(1).

4. While the 1938 Act applies both to forfeiture and to damages claims, it has no effect on equitable remedies, and so it has been suggested[99] that one way of mitigating the Act's requirements in an urgent case would be for the landlord to seek a mandatory injunction to force the tenant to execute remedial works.

---

[98] *Baker* v. *Sims* [1959] 1 QB 114, CA.
[99] J Martin [1982] Conv 71.

Chapter 9

TENANT'S REMEDIES FOR BREACH BY LANDLORD OF COVENANT TO REPAIR

I. INTRODUCTION

In this Chapter, various remedies of a tenant whose landlord is in breach of his covenant to repair are discussed. These are damages, set-off, specific performance, and the right to apply to the court for the appointment of a receiver in the case of residential flats. In addition, the controls, both at common law and under statute, of service charges on tenants of commercial premises and flats are outlined.

Some preliminary points may be made. First, in all cases the landlord is not in breach of his covenant to repair unless and until he is given notice of the want of repair by the tenant, or a third party, and a reasonable time from notice has elapsed to enable the landlord to execute the repairs (see Chapter 4 and also Chapter 11). A second point is that while a landlord may in certain circumstances, discussed in Chapter 8, forfeit a lease for breach of his tenant's covenant to repair, the fact that a landlord may be in breach of his covenant to repair does not entitle the tenant to repudiate his lease and to quit the premises: in principle, he is under a continuing liability, notwithstanding the landlord's breach, to pay rent.[1]

Continuing Liability of Landlord Despite Assignment of Reversion

On general principles, once the landlord assigns his reversion by deed, he might expect to cease, after the date of the assignment, to be under any liability to the tenant or his assigns. Under section 142(1) of the *Law of Property Act 1925*, the burden of the landlord's covenants runs with the reversion and is annexed to the reversion. It might be thought by analogy with section 141(1) of the 1925 Act that, once

---

[1] *Surplice* v. *Farnsworth* (1844) 13 LJ CP 215.

the lease is assigned by the original tenant, the only person who can bring any action for pre- or post-assignment breaches of the covenant to repair is the landlord by assignment—ie the current tenant. This is, apparently, not so.

In *City and Metropolitan Properties Ltd* v. *Greycroft Ltd*,[2] it was held that the original tenant who had assigned the lease to another person could nonetheless maintain an action in damages against the landlord for landlords' breaches of covenant to repair committed during the period of the original tenant's occupation. John Mowbray QC said that, if the original tenant remains liable (under privity of contract) for all post-assignment breaches to the landlord and his assigns, there was no reason why the liability of the landlord to the original tenant should not survive an assignment of the residue of the latter's term. If this case is followed, then the original tenant could presumably maintain an action for damages against any assignee of the landlord's reversion, notwithstanding that it has been held that, where the reversion is assigned, the original landlord cannot enforce any post-assignment breaches nor any pre-assignment breaches which continue into the post-assignment period.[3]

It has also been held that, where the reversion has been assigned, the new landlord is only liable in damages, under section 142(1) of the 1925 Act to the tenant, for post-assignment breaches of the covenant to repair, and is under no liability for pre-assignment breaches by his predecessor in title.[4]

Duty of Landlord of Residential Premises to Notify Tenant of Assignments

Section 3(1) of the *Landlord and Tenant Act* 1985 obliges the new landlord by assignment of premises consisting of or including a dwelling, to give written notice of his name and address to the tenant, not later than the next day on which rent is payable, or within two months of the date of the assignment if that date is earlier. This requirement does not apply where the tenancy is one to which Part II of the *Landlord*

[2] (1987) 283 EG 199.
[3] *Re King* [1963] Ch 459, CA.
[4] *Pettiward Estates* v. *Shephard* [1986] CLY 1861 (Cty Ct).

and Tenant Act 1954 applies, and it does not apply to assured tenancies (s 32); but it does apply to statutory tenancies.

Until written notice of the assignment, and of the new landlord's name and address, is given to the tenant by the new landlord or the old landlord (whichever happens first), then by section 3(3A)[5] the old landlord remains liable for all breaches of the landlord's covenant until such notification; where the liability relates to a post-assignment period, the liability of the old landlord is joint and several with the new landlord.

II. DAMAGES FOR BREACH OF LANDLORD'S COVENANT TO REPAIR

The ceiling placed by section 18(1) of the *Landlord and Tenant Act* 1927 on the maximum amount of damages recoverable by landlords from tenants, does not apply to the assessment of tenants' damages for breaches by landlords of their covenant to repair. Assuming that the landlord is in breach of covenant, the general principle applied is this: the object of any award of damages is to put the tenant, so far as money is able to, in the same position as he would have been in, but for the landlord's breach of covenant.[6]

Position where Tenant is in Occupation

Let us consider the position if the tenant intends to, and does, use the premises personally, for his own occupation. The principles discussed have arisen in relation to residential premises, but, no doubt, are of general application. The tenant may recover his costs reasonably incurred in renting alternative accommodation, if necessitated by the want of repair of the demised premises, during the period the breach of covenant continues. This particular head of damage may not be recovered if a move into alternative accommodation is not essential to enable repairs to be done, and is occasioned merely for reasons of personal convenience.[7] However, this is modified to the extent that if, to facilitate the work of repair,

---

[5] Added by *Landlord and Tenant Act* 1987 s 50 (which commences on a day to be appointed).
[6] *Calabar Properties Ltd* v. *Stitcher* (1983) 268 EG 697; [1983] 3 All ER 759, CA.
[7] *Green* v. *Eales* (1841) 2 QB 225, as explained by Griffiths LJ in *Calabar Properties Ltd* v. *Stitcher, supra.*

the tenant moves into alternative accommodation and puts his furniture into store, the reasonable expenses of doing this will be recoverable from the landlord. If, however, the tenant stays in the premises, the landlord will have to pay for the extra costs of carrying on the work, with the tenant in occupation.[8]

If it is not essential to allow the landlord access to all parts of the demised premises to do the repairs, the cost to the tenant of alternative accommodation is not recoverable, but if the tenant does the work of repair, he apparently can elect, provided it is reasonable to do so, to move out into alternative accommodation during the repairs, or to stay on the premises, paying the contractors more, and then recovering either set of costs from the landlord.[9]

The tenant is also entitled to recover damages to compensate him for the cost of making good any interior decorations consequent on the execution of repairs necessitated by the landlord's breach of covenant.[10] Also, he may claim for the inconvenience of having to live in an undecorated house pending repairs.[11] The tenant is entitled to damages for loss of personal comfort and injury to his personal health caused by the disrepair—even if the premises are only used by him to sleep in.[12]

Position Where Tenant Intends Sale or Sub-Letting

Where the tenant intends using the premises as an investment for sale, he will be able to recover, as damages, the difference between the sale price in fact realised with the premises out of repair, and the price which he would have been able to realise, had the premises been kept in proper repair by the landlord. If the tenant intends to sub-let the premises—to the landlord's knowledge—and fails to do so because of their disrepair, caused by the landlord's breach of his covenant to repair, the tenant may claim his loss of potential rental income as damages.[13]

---

[8] See *McGreal* v. *Wake* (1984) 269 EG 1254, CA.
[9] *McGreal* v. *Wake, supra.*
[10] *Bradley* v. *Chorley Borough Council* (1985) 275 EG 801; [1985] 2 EGLR 49, CA.
[11] *McGreal* v. *Wake, supra.*
[12] *McCoy & Co* v. *Clark* (1982) 13 HLR 89, CA.
[13] *Calabar Properties Ltd* v. *Stitcher* (1983) 268 EG 697, CA.

If the tenancy is totally incapable of sale on the open market, as is the case with, for example, a statutory tenancy under the *Rent Act* 1977, then the measure of damages is the cost to the tenant of carrying out necessary repairs (assuming the landlord refuses to do them) plus substantial damages for inconvenience and discomfort.[14]

If the landlord attempts, within a reasonable time of notice of the want of repairs, to do the repairs himself, and is prevented from doing so by the tenant refusing him entry onto the premises, no damages claim may be sustained by the tenant, so long as he continues to refuse the landlord entry as he is not in breach of covenant.[15]

Finally, outgoings on the premises out of repair are not recoverable from the landlord—the money would have been spent on these anyhow.[16]

III. SET-OFF

A tenant whose landlord is in breach of his covenant to repair may himself carry out the necessary work, and then set off the actual cost of repairs against his liability for future rent, and may also set off the estimated cost of repairs, as unliquidated damages, against this liability to arrears of rent.

Carrying out Work

If a landlord claims future rent but is himself in breach of his covenant to repair, having failed to repair after a reasonable time after the giving of notice, the tenant, or any lawful occupier of the premises, may, having first spent a definite and ascertainable sum on repairs within the landlord's covenant, recoup himself out of future rent for that sum.[17]

Set-Off

Where rent arrears are claimed by a landlord, and he is in breach of his covenant to repair, the tenant has the right in equity to set off, against the amount claimed as rent arrears, any sums claimed in respect of the breaches of covenant to

---

[14] *Hewitt* v. *Rowlands* [1924] WN 135, CA.
[15] *Granada Theatres Ltd* v. *Freehold Investments (Leytonstone) Ltd supra* per Jenkins LJ at p 184.
[16] *Calabar Properties Ltd* v. *Stitcher supra.*
[17] *Lee-Parker* v. *Izzet* [1971] 3 All ER 1099.

repair, as unliquidated damages—ie not a fixed sum quantified in advance. This is because the claim for damages goes to the foundation of the landlord's claim for rent arrears.[18] A claim to a set-off against rent arrears may be made, though the tenant has spent no money on repairs. Therefore, in *Melville* v. *Grape Lodge Developments Ltd*,[19] where rent arrears and other sums were claimed by the landlord, the tenants counter-claimed successfully, for a set-off for damages, in respect of various items of disrepair to the roof and to other parts of the premises, and the fact that the tenant had not spent any money on these repairs, did not affect his claim. It is, however, assumed that the equitable right of set-off depends on the tenant having given notice to the landlord of the want of repair, and that the landlord has failed after a reasonable time has elapsed, to do the repairs in question.

IV. SPECIFIC PERFORMANCE

General Equitable Jurisdiction

Curiously, a landlord cannot obtain an order for specific performance of his tenant's covenant to repair.[20] There is, however, no reason why he should not be able, in a sufficiently serious case, to obtain a mandatory injunction to compel the tenant to comply with his covenant to repair.

This contrasts completely with the position of the tenant, both in equity, and under statute. In *Jeune* v. *Queen's Cross Properties Ltd*,[21] a landlord was ordered by specific performance to re-instate a balcony forming part of the structure of the property in question, which he had expressly covenanted to repair. In *Gordon* v. *Selico Co Ltd*,[22] landlords of a block of flats seriously neglected their obligations to repair and maintain the premises, which were known to them to be seriously out of repair, there being damp in the outside walls, leaking gutters and other dilapidations. While the leases contained a clear scheme for the management and maintenance of the premises, no steps had been taken to run the

---

[18] *British Anzani (Felixstowe) Ltd* v. *International Marine Management (UK) Ltd* [1979] 3 WLR 451.

[19] (1980) 254 EG 1193. See also *Asco Developments Ltd* v. *Gordon* (1978) 248 EG 683.

[20] *Hill* v. *Barclay* (1810) 16 Ves Jun 402.

[21] [1974] Ch 97.

[22] (1986) 278 EG 53, CA.

scheme in such a way that necessary work was carried out. In due course, the tenants were forced to quit the premises on account of their state. The Court of Appeal affirmed the judge's order of specific performance, under the statutory jurisdiction, of the landlord's repairing and maintenance covenants. The orders required the landlords within a definite time to put the relevant premises into a reasonable condition and made consequential provisions.

The equitable jurisdiction to grant an order of specific performance is not confined to particular types of repair and an order was even granted against an insolvent landlord in *Francis* v. *Cowcliffe*[23] ordering him to ensure that lifts he covenanted to provide and maintain, actually worked.

The usual discretionary bars to relief will apply, such as unreasonable delay by the tenant in seeking to enforce his rights, or where it can be shown that an award of damages will be an adequate remedy. It has been said that the jurisdiction to award specific performance of landlords' repairing covenants is one to be carefully exercised, but also that in a proper case, where there has been a plain breach of covenant and it is clear what specific work will be required of the landlord, an order will be granted.[24]

Statutory Jurisdiction

There is a statutory jurisdiction to award specific performance under section 17 of the *Landlord and Tenant Act* 1985, but it is narrower than the equity jurisdiction, in that it applies to tenants of dwellings. This term is defined by section 38 of the 1985 Act in such a way as to include flats and also any yard, garden, outhouses and appurtenances belonging to it or usually enjoyed with it. Section 17(1) gives the court a discretionary jurisdiction to order specific performance of the landlord's repairing covenant to repair relating to any part of the demised premises, whether imposed on him by statute or at common law. The court has power to make an order for specific performance, whether or not the breach relates to a part let to the tenant. Presumably, the landlord

[23] (1977) 33 P & CR 369. See also *Peninsular Maritime* v. *Padseal Ltd* (1981) 259 EG 860.
[24] *Jeune* v. *Queen's Cross Properties* [1974] Ch 97.

could be compelled to execute roofing repairs, even if the complainant tenant held a lease of a ground-floor flat or a top-floor flat where the roof was not demised to him.

Moreover, the court expressly has jurisdiction notwithstanding any equitable rule restricting the scope of the remedy, whether on the basis of a lack of mutuality or otherwise. Section 17(2)(d) defines "repairing covenant" so as to mean a covenant to repair, maintain, renew, construct or replace any property.

It was said, of this provision, by Goulding J[25] that the court is given a statutory power to make an order for specific performance of a repairing covenant as an isolated obligation, and on a particular occasion. So it is not to be regarded as a semi-automatic means of enforcement.

V. APPOINTMENT OF A RECEIVER AND MANAGER

If the landlord of, for example, a purpose-built block of residential flats is a persistent defaulter in complying with his obligations to repair, it is obvious that the value of tenants' interests in the premises will be adversely affected: at the same time, because, presumably, there will be some sort of scheme for the payment to the landlord of service charges (and possibly also into a sinking fund for future repairs) the tenants have the reasonable expectation that, as and where necessary, routine repairs and maintenance will be promptly carried out regularly.

Background

In recent years, some tenants have had recourse to an application to the High Court to appoint a receiver, in its equitable jurisdiction under section 37 of the *Supreme Court Act* 1981. This is of general application; there is also a statutory jurisdiction in the case of certain types of residential flat, which is dealt with immediately after the general jurisdiction.

General Jurisdiction to Appoint a Receiver

Section 37 of the *Supreme Court Act* 1981 enables the High Court to "appoint a receiver in all cases in which it appears to the court to be just and convenient to do so." The receiver

---

[25] *Gordon v. Selico Co Ltd* (1985) 275 EG 899 at p 906; [1985] 2 EGLR 79 at p 84.

is an officer of the court, and will be required to give security as a condition of his appointment. The appointment may be discharged by the High Court, on a further application, by the landlord or the tenant, if the necessity for it has come to an end. The receiver's appointment displaces the landlord from the right to receive rents: this means that the receiver will collect the rental income, and the assumption is, that he will be able to use funds so built up to carry out necessary repairs. The court order will be likely to invest the receiver with managerial powers in relation to the property. In relation to flats to which Part II of the *Landlord and Tenant Act* 1987 applies, the equitable jurisdiction to appoint a receiver is superceded by the statutory jurisdiction (s 21(6) of the 1987 Act). Therefore, the general jurisdiction applies to houses and commercial premises but not, generally, to residential flats.

The first reported exercise of the jurisdiction to appoint a receiver and manager in support of the covenant to repair was in *Hart* v. *Emelkirk Ltd.*[26] There, the landlord neglected for two or three years to collect rent or service charges or to effect insurance, and the condition of the premises (flats) seriously deteriorated. Goulding J appointed a receiver under section 37 of the 1981 Act, with control over the rental income and service charges and managerial powers. Goulding J said that it was "just" within section 37 to appoint a receiver, because it was done to support the repairing covenants. It was "convenient" within the provision because the properties were in a condition that demanded urgent action.

This decision was followed in similar circumstances in *Daiches* v. *Bluelake Investments Ltd*[27] where a block of flats needed repairs estimated at £300,000 (due to the landlord's failure in breach of covenant to execute them). Sufficient funds did not appear to exist to pay for all the requisite work and there was no sinking fund. A receiver was appointed to collect rents with extra financial assistance from the tenants. In both these cases, no application under the general jurisdiction of the court would be possible after the passing of Part II of

[26] [1983] 3 All ER 15.
[27] (1985) 275 EG 462; [1985] 2 EGLR 67. See also *Clayhope Properties Ltd* v. *Evans* (1986) 279 EG 855, [1986] 2 All ER 795, CA, where it was held that an order appointing a receiver was capable of being protected by lodging a caution against the landlord's title under s 54(1) of the *Land Registration Act* 1925.

the *Landlord and Tenant Act* 1987, as both related to blocks of residential flats.

A limit was placed on the general jurisdiction in *Parker v. Camden London Borough Council*[28] where tenants whose local authority landlords were not, in breach of covenant, supplying them with heating and hot water, failed to obtain the appointment of a receiver, on the ground that local authority landlords have independent, statute-based management duties; relief was granted, however, in the form of a mandatory injunction.

A further problem with receivers appointed under the general equity jurisdiction, is that a receiver (and manager) cannot compel the landlord, on an interim application, to meet his expenses, where the assets turn out to be inadequate to do so, and even the expenses of drawing up a specification of repairs were held to be irrecoverable.[29] This particular problem does not apply to managers appointed under Part II of the *Landlord and Tenant Act*.

Appointment by Court[30] *of Manager of Block of Flats under Part II of Landlord and Tenant Act 1987*

Under Part II of the *Landlord and Tenant Act* 1987,[31] the county court (the normal forum for disputes under the 1987 Act) has jurisdiction to appoint a manager over premises consisting of the whole or part of a building, if it contains two or more flats (s 21(1) & (2)). Part II does not in terms apply to dwelling-houses, but, presumably, it would apply where a dwelling-house has been converted into a block of flats.[32] The jurisdiction to appoint a manager under Part II of the 1987 Act excludes the general equitable jurisdiction (s 21(6)), which still applies to houses and commercial premises.

As will be seen, the tenant/applicant must go through a notice procedure, and as a rule, the landlord must have been

---

[28] [1985] 2 All ER 141, CA.

[29] *Evans* v. *Clayhope Properties Ltd* (1987) 282 EG 862 affd (1987) *Times* November 20.

[30] S 52 of the 1987 Act confers jurisdiction on the county court under Part II no matter what the rateable value of the premises may be.

[31] In force on a day or days to be appointed: s 62.

[32] This jurisdiction where it applies excludes the equitable jurisdiction (s 21(6)) but the equitable jurisdiction still applies in the case of houses and commercial premises, for example.

in serious breach of his covenant to repair the premises in question, or guilty of some other management dereliction, such as a failure to collect service charges rent or to keep down insurance on the building.

Part II Excluded

Part II does not apply where the landlord's interest in the block is held by an exempt or resident landlord (s 21(3)).[33] Nor does it apply where the premises are included within the functional land of any charity.[34]

Who May Apply

A Part II application may be made by one flat tenant, or jointly by two or more flat tenants; and an application in relation to two or more blocks of flats may be also made (s 21(4)). Moreover, (s 21(5)) if any tenancy of a flat within Part II is held by joint tenants, an application may be made by one of the joint tenants.

Position of Business Tenants

Part II of the 1987 Act is expressly excluded in the case of business tenants to whom Part II of the *Landlord and Tenant Act* 1954 applies (s 21(7)). Assured tenants of flats (who are governed by Part II although residential tenants) are expressly excluded from Part II of the 1987 Act (s 60(2)). Presumably, however, an assured tenant could apply for a receiver under the general jurisdiction.

Notice Procedures

Section 22 makes any application for a management order conditional on the tenant/applicant complying with a notice procedure. The tenant must serve a notice on the landlord (ie the immediate landlord, s 60). In many ways this procedure resembles the statutory forfeiture procedure under section 146 of the *Law of Property Act* 1925. If it is not complied with by the applicant, then unless the court is disposed to exercise

---

[33] "Exempt landlord" is defined in s 58(1), which lists various public sector landlords. "Resident landlord" is defined by s 58(1) in similar terms to s 12 of the *Rent Act* 1977.
[34] As defined in s 60.

a discretionary dispensation power under section 22(3), no application under Part II by the applicant[s] concerned is possible. The dispensation power is narrow: it arises only if the court is satisfied that it would not be reasonably practicable to serve a section 22 notice on the landlord. The court may then direct that such a notice be served.

Under section 22(2) the notice must comply with a list of formalities:[35] these include:

(1) A statement that the tenant intends to apply for a management order, but if the breach is remediable, he will not do so if the landlord complies with the requirements of the notice (s 22(2)(b)).

(2) A specification of the grounds on which the court will be asked to make a management order and of the matters the tenant will rely on to establish those grounds (s 22(2)(c)).

(3) Where, as in the case of a landlord's covenants to repair, the matters specified are capable of remedy, the landlord must be required to remedy the breach, in steps specified in the notice, within a reasonable period specified in the notice (s 22(2)(d)).

Once the landlord has been served with a section 22 notice, he must serve a copy of it on any mortgagee of his interest (s 22(4)).

After service of a section 22 notice the tenant must allow a reasonable period to expire—to allow the landlord to remedy the breach or breaches (s 23(1)(a)). This does not apply, if the breaches of the landlord are not capable of remedy (s 23(1)(b)) as where, for example, the landlord has allowed an insurance policy over the building to lapse. Moreover, unlike the position with forfeiture notices, the court has a discretion to make a management order even though the tenant's notice failed to specify a reasonable period for the landlord to remedy the breach or breaches concerned; or failed to contained required information under section 22(2) or regulations (s 24(7)).

Appointment of a Manager. The power to make the appointment of a manager is governed by section 24. The

---

[35] Including any prescribed information (s 22(2)(e)) and the name and address of the tenant (s 22(2)(a)) including an address for the service of notices.

order may be interlocutory or final, it may apply to the whole premises the subject-matter of the application, but it may be applied to more, or less, extensive premises than those specified in the application (s 24(3)). Presumably, the court could make an order applicable to all flats in the same block, even if the application related only to a particular tenant's flat. The order appoints a manager to carry out either management functions or receivership functions, or both—as the court thinks fit (s 24(1)). "Management" expressly includes repair, maintenance or insurance of the premises (s 24(11)).

Grounds for Making a Section 24 Order

An order appointing a manager may only be made in one of two alternative circumstances (s 24(2)): *either*—
1. Where the court is satisfied:
    (a) that the landlord is in breach of a tenancy obligation to the tenant which relates to the management of the whole or part of the premises—such as to repair,[36] manage or insure; *and*
    (b) the breach is likely to continue; *and*
    (c) it is just and convenient to make the order in all the circumstances.

or—
2. The court is satisfied that other circumstances exist which make it just and convenient to make the order.

The order may make provision for ancillary matters (s 24(4)) and, by section 24(5), for any rights and liabilities under contracts to become the liabilities of the manager, for the remuneration of the manager, and for the manager's functions to be exercisable for a specified or an unlimited period. Apart from that the court may impose such conditions as it thinks fit and may make a suspended order (s 24(6)). Presumably, the idea of this is to give the landlord further time to comply with his obligations. A Part II order is registrable under the appropriate provisions of the *Land Charges Act*

---

[36] In the case of repairing obligations if it is shown (by the tenant) that no notice was reasonably practicable, then the court may make a management order (s 24(2)(a)(i))—presumably for example where a latent defect suddenly manifests itself.

1972 or the *Land Registration Act* 1925, as a pending land action or by caution as the case may be (s 24(8)).[37]

Variation or Discharge of Management Order

Section 24(9) empowers the court to vary or discharge a section 23 order either conditionally or unconditionally, on the application of any "person interested", such as a new landlord by assignment or a mortgagee. There is no automatic discharge of a section 24 order, once made, by reason only of the fact that the premises covered by it have subsequently ceased to be premises to which Part II applies (s 24(10)).

VI. CONTROL OF SERVICE CHARGES

In the case of purpose-built or converted blocks of residential flats, or in any lease of commercial premises, landlords may well covenant to keep the structure and exterior of the demised building and exterior parts of the individual flats or offices in repair and to provide and pay for attendance (say a porter), maintenance, service and, possibly, insurance cover in return for service charges payable by all the individual tenants. If the covenant reserves the service charges as additional rent then, if these are not paid by the tenant, the landlord can distrain for them or bring a forfeiture for non-payment of rent.

In what follows, common law rules as to ascertainment of the service charges payable, and connected issues are considered. These rules apply to residential and commercial multi-lettings alike. Statutory provisions governing service charges, in the case of residential dwellings, are then dealt with. Those rules do not apply to commercial lettings.

General Rules

The lease in question may provide that the amount of money to be paid, as a contribution by each individual tenant, is to be some proportion of an amount certified as due by a surveyor. If, however, the certificate of the surveyor is stated in the lease to be conclusive, it is still open to being challenged

---

[37] Confirming the pre-1987 Act rule: see *Clayhope Properties Ltd* v. *Evans* [1986] 2 All ER 795; (1986) 279 EG 855, CA.

in the courts, as such provisions do not oust the jurisdiction of the court.[38] Still, such statements may well mislead the tenant into accepting inaccurate certificates, which is deplorable.[39] If the surveyor is not in fact acting independently of the landlord, then there is a far greater risk that any tenant's challenge to a certificate issued by him will succeed, although it has also been held that if the tenant overpays for items not properly chargeable under a mistake of law, he will not be able to recover the sums paid.[40] However, if the lease provides that all differences as to the contributions are to be decided, in a final manner, by the landlord's surveyor, since the latter is not independent, and yet has been given an arbitral function, no binding decision may be made by the landlord's surveyor, and an independent surveyor would presumably have to be appointed for the purpose.[41]

It is implied into any method of calculating service charges, that any costs recoverable from the tenants will be fair and reasonable, and the landlord is not to be given an unfettered discretion by a service charge covenant, to adopt the highest conceivable standard of maintenance, and then to charge that to the tenant.[42] If the circumstances change during the lease, so that one method of calculation becomes fair and reasonable, and an earlier one inappropriate, then the latter method can no longer be adopted. In one case, the basis of calculation for heating charges in the lease was on a floor-area basis, but this, in view of the actual area heated in the particular tenant's flat, was unfair, and it was held that he was entitled to be charged only on the basis of his actual heating use. The terms of the lease, in view of the radical change, were held no longer to apply.[43]

Unless the lease expressly, or by necessary implication, enables the landlords to charge the tenants with interest on money borrowed by the landlords, to enable them to comply

---

[38] *Re Davstone Estates Ltd's Leases* [1969] 2 Ch 378; *Rapid Results College Ltd* v. *Angell* (1986) 277 EG 856, CA.

[39] See Law Com No 162 (May 1987) para 4. 78.

[40] *Concorde Graphics Ltd* v. *Andromeda Investments SA* (1983) 265 EG 386.

[41] See *Concorde Graphics Ltd* v. *Andromeda Investments SA, supra.*

[42] *Finchbourne Ltd* v. *Rodrigues* [1976] 3 All ER 581, CA.

[43] *Pole Properties Ltd* v. *Feinberg* (1982) 43 P & CR 121; cf *Parkside Knightsbridge Ltd* v. *Horwitz* (1983) 268 EG 49, CA.

with their repairing and maintenance obligations, interest cannot be recovered from the tenants.[44] If objective and independent advice has been given to the landlord, by a surveyor, to the effect that comprehensive work of repair is needed, not just short-term patching-up, the tenant will have to pay his share of the long-term work (assuming the conduct of the landlord is reasonable in having it executed and accepting the surveyor's advice) so that a tenant who, in the face of independent advice, disputed the need for long-term roofing repairs, was held liable to contribute his share of the cost.[45] It has also been held that, in some cases, depending on the wording of the covenant in question, the landlord may be able to recover the cost of repairs to installations not actually situated in the particular flat of the tenant disputing the item.[46] However, the landlord cannot recover the cost of improvements to the demised premises under charges for repair and maintenance.[47] Nor, unless very clear language is used, may he recover for work contracted for, but not completed until after the lease ends.[48]

A drawback of service charges covenants is that the sums payable by each tenant are ascertainable only at the end of a particular maintenance year: indeed the liability of the landlord to carry out his repairing and maintenance obligations has been held in one case not to be conditional on the tenant's first paying service charges.[49] This matter can be met possibly by some provision in the lease for the establishment and maintenance of a reserve or sinking fund.

Trusts of Service Charges Contributions

In connection with service charges and repairing costs generally, in *Re Chelsea Cloisters (In Liquidation)*[50] tenants of a block of flats, held under grant from a management company, agreed to pay deposits against any claim by the landlord for dilapidations, the balance to be credited to the tenants

---

[44] *Boldmark Ltd* v. *Cohen* (1985) 277 EG 745, CA.
[45] *Manor House Drive* v. *Shabazian* (1965) 195 EG 283.
[46] *Campden Hill Towers* v. *Marshall* (1965) 196 EG 989.
[47] *Mullaney* v. *Maybourne Grange (Croydon) Management Co Ltd* (1986) 277 EG 1350.
[48] *Capital & Counties Freehold Equity Trust Ltd* v. *BL PLC* (1987) 283 EG 563.
[49] *Yorkbrook Investments Ltd* v. *Batten* (1985) 276 EG 545; [1985] 2 EGLR 100 (another covenant might be differently construed of course).
[50] (1980) 41 P & CR 98, CA.

on termination of their respective tenancies. Later, the management company went into liquidation and its own lease expired, the deposits being held in a separate bank account opened by a supervisor of the management company, and used for that, and no other purpose. In liquidation proceedings, it was held that a trust of the sums due to the tenants on quitting, subject to any claim of the landlords for dilapidations, had been created. The landlord was entitled to them on trust for the tenants, and the moneys did not, therefore, belong to the general creditors of the company. It was significant that the supervisor intended to keep the deposit in a separate account from general moneys. No doubt this principle could, in a suitable case, extend to service charge balances, held in a separate account by landlords' managing agents, which are kept totally separate from any other moneys or funds. In the event of the liquidation of the agents, the tenants' moneys would thus be saved from the general creditors of the management company.[51]

Trust of Service Charge Funds: Dwellings and Flats

In relation to tenants of two or more dwellings (including flats) who are liable to pay service charges to the landlord, a new statutory provision applies, which prevails over any express or, as in the *Chelsea* case, implied trust, except as mentioned below (s 42(9)).

By section 42(2) of the *Landlord and Tenant Act* 1987, any service charges paid to the landlord or any other person to whom the tenants are required by their leases to pay service charges, must, together with all other service charges payments, be held by the payee as a single fund or in two or more separate funds, for each contributing tenant. The fund or funds are to be held on trust to pay for the matters covered by the service charges (s 42(3)(a)) and subject to that, on trust for the contributing tenants for the time being (s 42(3)(b)) in shares proportionate to the liabilities of tenants to pay service charges (s 42(4)). On termination of the lease of a tenant, he is not entitled to any part of the trust fund

---

[51] In *Gordon* v. *Selico Co* (1986) 278 EG 53, CA, it was held that the lease in question required the landlords to open and operate a maintenance account and to act as trustee in respect of its repairing and maintenance obligations.

(s 42(6))—the fund will continue to exist as above. After termination of a lease, if there are no contributing tenants, the trust fund is dissolved as at termination of that lease and the fund is either to vest in the landlord or in the payee (say his agent) if the landlord did not receive the service charges (s 42(7)). The provisions just mentioned are subject to any express terms of the lease, no matter at what date the lease was granted (s 42(8)).

Section 42 of the 1987 Act does not apply, as noted, to business tenancies. Service charges payable by regulated tenants, whose rent is registered under Part IV of the *Rent Act* 1977, are generally excluded from section 42, unless the amount registered is variable.

Reform

Incoming tenants of office premises may apparently be met by a landlord refusing to agree to any changes in the service charge terms, on the ground that all leases must be in the same form and leases of other parts of the property have already been granted.[52] On the other hand, landlords do have the management of the whole block to consider. Nonetheless, short-term incoming tenants may find the service charges provisions of their leases rather oppressive.[53] It must be said, however, that if Parliament had deemed it appropriate to extend the statutory service charges controls and variation of leases powers (to be discussed below) to commercial tenants, nothing would have been easier than for it to have done so.

Statutory Limitations on Residential Service Charges

The relevant rules as to service charges payable by, in particular, tenants of residential dwellings are in sections 18 to 30 of the *Landlord and Tenant Act* 1985.[54] It is however to be noted that, subject to the statutory limitations, advance payments prior to the costs being incurred are allowed to

[52] See Law Commission Report No 162 (1987) para 4. 74.
[53] Especially if they have to pay for remedial work to cure inherent or other design faults or even heavy reconstruction: cf Lord Wilberforce in *O'May* v. *City of London Real Property Co Ltd* [1983] 2 AC 726 at 749.
[54] The rules here summarised are as amended by s 41 and Sched 2 to the *Landlord and Tenant Act* 1987.

be charged on tenants, but in all cases there is a limit of reasonableness.

The rules are very detailed and the following is a brief digest of what appear to be the most important aspects.

1. *Scope.* The rules apply to service charges (ie charges payable as part of or in addition to rent) imposed on tenants of dwellings, which are payable for services, repairs, maintenance, insurance or the landlord's management costs (an example of the latter being the costs of employing managing agents).[55]

2. *Dual Limit.* Section 19(1) of the *Landlord and Tenant Act* places a dual limit on landlords' costs. To be recoverable, first, they must be reasonably incurred, and secondly, where the costs are incurred on works or services, these latter must be provided to a reasonable standard. No amount for costs incurred in excess of such reasonable standard is recoverable. As was noted above, section 19(2) of the 1985 Act allows payments in advance of incurring the costs to be recovered subject to the reasonableness requirement.

3. *Estimates and Other Consultation*

Where the cost of qualifying works exceeds £25 multiplied by the number of dwellings or £500 (whichever is the greater) the excess is disallowed unless section 20(4) or (5) is complied with or dispensed with by the court (s 20(9)). "Qualifying works" are, by section 20(2), works on the building or any other premises to the cost of which the tenant is required to contribute service charges.

The position depends on whether the tenant is represented by a recognised tenants' association or not.[56] These rules supply a powerful incentive for tenants to set up associations if none exist.

If the tenant is not represented by a recognised tenants' association then, under section 20(4), detailed requirements about obtaining estimates and notification apply. They include a requirement of at least two estimates being obtained for the work in question, one of them from a person wholly unconnected with the landlord, plus advance notification to the tenants of impending works, and provision for the giving

[55] *Embassy Court Residents' Association* v. *Lipman* (1984) 271 EG 545.
[56] Defined by *Landlord and Tenant Act* 1985 s 29.

by the tenants and the taking into account by the landlord, of any tenants' observations. The court may, if satisfied that the landlord acted reasonably, dispense with all or any of these requirements (s 20(9)).

If the tenant is represented by a recognised tenants' association, then the secretary of the association must be given a notice with a detailed specification of the works, and giving a reasonable period in which the association may propose to the landlord the names of one or more persons from whom estimates should, in its view, be obtained (s 20(5)(a)). There is a requirement that at least two estimates be obtained—as for individual tenants (s 20(5)(b)).[57] All tenants liable to pay service charges and represented must also receive a notice briefly describing the works, summarising the estimates and complying with certain other requirements (s 20(5)). The landlord is however only bound to "have regard" to any observations of the tenants (s 20(5)(g)). Works which are not urgent cannot be begun before the date for their commencement, which must be specified in the landlord's notice (s 20(5)(g)).

What these provisions appear to amount to, is an improved consultative procedure: ultimately, the landlord will be able to recover the service charges, provided he complies with them, or if he is dispensed from compliance in any proceedings.

By section 19(3), any covenant or agreement by a tenant of a flat providing for the determination of any question of reasonableness of costs or standards is void.[58] This invalidates terms that the certificate of a landlord's surveyor is conclusive.

4. *Information about Costs.* Section 21 of the 1985 Act enables the tenant in writing to require the landlord[59] to supply him with a written summary of costs incurred in the last 12 months ending with the date of the request or, if the accounts are made up for 12 month periods, in the last period ending with the date of the request. In effect, full details of the costs must be provided.

---

[57] A copy of which must go to the secretary of the association (s 20(5)(c)).

[58] This does not apply to an agreement within *Arbitration Act* 1950 s 32.

[59] If the information is provided by the landlord's accountant it must not be provided by someone who is his employee or partner or managing agent or the latter's employee or partner (1985 Act, s 28, as amended by 1987 Act Sched 2 para 9).

5. *Costs Incurred over 18 months before Demand.* Section 20B(1) of the 1985 Act[60] provides that, if the landlord demands as a service charge, or as part of a service charge, the payment of costs incurred over 18 months before the demand was served then the tenant is not liable for those costs. To avoid this, all the landlord has to do, is to notify the tenant within these 18 months that the costs have been incurred and that they will subsequently be demanded from the tenant (s 20B(2)).

6. *Insurance Information Controls for Residential Tenants.* New controls applicable where the cost of insurance forms part of a service charge or service charges rent for dwellings or flats, are imposed by the Schedule to the *Landlord and Tenant Act* 1985. The tenants are given a host of rights. Public sector landlords, such as local authorities, are excluded from the new controls (para 9).

(a) To request from the landlord, or from the landlord's agent or rent collector a written summary, or copy, of the insurance cover in force for the dwelling or flat (para 2(1)).

(b) These details must be supplied to the individual tenant, or, at the landlord's option, provided the tenant consents, to the secretary of a recognised tenant's association if the tenant is represented by it (para 2(2)).

(c) The details are to be supplied within one month of the request. They must include the insured amount[s],[61] the insurer's name; the risks insured (para 2(4)).

(d) Once the tenant, or the secretary of a tenants' association, has a summary or copy of the policy, he has a statutory right, exercisable within six months of obtaining it, to inspect any relevant policy, accounts, receipts and so on and to take copies or extracts (para 3).

(e) If the landlord receiving the request is not the landlord who has effected (wholly or partly) the insurance, he must request his superior landlord to supply the relevant information and the superior landlord must, within a reasonable time, comply with this request (para 4).

---

[60] Added by *Landlord and Tenant Act* 1987, Sched 2, para 4.
[61] This means in the case of a dwelling, the amount of the insurance for it; in the case of a flat, the insurance for the whole building and the individual flat if specified for in the policy (para 2(5)).

Failure to comply without reasonable excuse with these duties by the landlord or superior landlord is a summary criminal offence (para 6).

7. *Other Controls on Residential Insurance Payable as Part of Service Charges.*—

(a) The tenant is given the right, where the insurance policy requires notification of damage to the premises within a specified period,[62] and the tenant pays for the cost of insurance out of service charges, to notify the insurer in writing, in prescribed forms,[63] that it appears to the tenant that damage has been caused, either to the dwelling, or, if a flat, to the flat or to any other part of the block (para 7). The nature of the damage must briefly be described. One of two or more joint tenants may give a notice (para 7(4)).

(b) The tenant has the right, where a tenancy of a dwelling or flat requires the tenant to insure the dwelling with an insurer nominated by the landlord to challenge in court the landlord's choice of insurers (para 8). The tenant must apply to the county court. If it is satisfied that the insurance is unsatisfactory in any respect, or that the premiums paid are excessive, the court may either order the landlord to nominate a specified insurer, or any insurer complying with requirements specified in the order (para 8(2)).

Variation of Service Charges Provisions in Long Leases of Flats

Part IV of the *Landlord and Tenant Act* 1987 enables the court (ie normally, the county court) to vary the service charges provisions of any long lease of a flat where the lease fails to make satisfactory provision with respect to computation of service charges (s 35(1) and (2)). Long lease means generally, a term certain exceeding 21 years, including assured tenancies (ss 59(3) and 35(7)).[64]

A lease fails to make satisfactory provision in this regard, if the aggregate amounts of the total service charges payable

---

[62] By para 7(3), the tenant is given an overriding period of six months from the date of the tenant's notice for notification of claims.

[63] To be prescribed in regulations (para 7).

[64] Also included are a perpetually renewable lease and a lease granted under the right to buy; excluded are leases to which Part II of the *Landlord and Tenant Act* 1954 applies (s 59(3) and 35(7)).

by the tenant and the other tenants liable to pay it, would exceed the whole of the landlord's or superior landlord's actual expenditure (s 35(4)). If one tenant makes an application for variation, other tenants may also apply to the court for corresponding variations of their leases (s 36(1)).[65] A majority of the parties in a block of flats may apply for variation of all leases—either in the same building or more than one building, provided all the leases are long leases and the landlord is the same person: but the leases need not be drafted in identical terms (s 37).[66] If the grounds are made out then the court may make an order varying the lease as specified in the order (s 38(1))[67] but it has power also to make an order directing the parties to vary the lease in a specified manner (s 38(8)). A memorandum of any variation will generally be endorsed on any specified documents—such as the lease or leases themselves (s 38(9)). The court has a discretionary power (s 38(10)) to order the payment of compensation, by the applicant[s] to the landlord or other party prejudiced, any loss or disadvantage he is likely to suffer as a result of the variation. The court is not bound by the terms of the variation application (s 38(4)). If, in relation to any particular lease, the grounds are not made out, then the court cannot make a variation order with regard to that lease (s 38(5)). There is no power to make a variation order where it is shown that an order would be likely substantially to prejudice any respondent, such as the landlord or his mortgagee or a superior landlord, or a person not a party to the application, and that an award of financial compensation would not be adequate (s 38(6)). The court has no power, where an application relates to the insurance provisions of any long residential lease, to make an order which terminates any right of the landlord to nominate an insurer, or as a result of which the landlord is required to nominate a number of insurers from whom

---

[65] Under s 35(5) rules of court are to be made governing service of notice of a Part IV application on any respondent known to be affected thereby, and enabling joinder of such parties.

[66] The majorities are these: if the application relates to less than nine leases, all but one or all parties consent to it; if it relates to more than eight leases, it is not opposed by more than 10% of the total parties concerned and at least 75% of the parties consent (s 37(5)). The tenant of any one lease counts as one party; the landlord counts as one party (s 37(6)).

[67] There are appropriate powers in the case of multiple applications (s 38(2) and (3)). In that case each of the leases specified in the application will be subject to a variation order.

the tenant is entitled to select one, or to vary any term under which the lease requires the tenant to effect insurance with a specified insurer (s 38(7)).

A variation order may be made in relation to dwellings other than flats, by section 40, only in the case of inadequate provision of insurance with regard to the dwelling (including recovery of insurance costs).

Variation orders are binding on the parties and their predecessors in title no matter whether they were given notice of proceedings or not and whether or not they were parties to the application (s 39(1)). In particular, any surety guaranteeing an original obligation is expressly taken to be bound by a varied obligation (s 39(2)), which may benefit or injure him, as the case may be. If a party not served with notice, but who was entitled to be served, suffers loss, then he may bring an action for breach of statutory duty against the person who should have served him with notice and apply to the court for cancellation or modification of the variation (s 39(3)). In this case, a cancellation or modification of the variation order will be ordered, or, alternatively, the payment of compensation (s 39(4)).

Non-Recovery of Service Charges if Certain Information Not Furnished to Tenants

Section 47 of the *Landlord and Tenant Act* 1987, which applies to any tenant of premises consisting of or including a dwelling (s 46(1)), renders irrecoverable until the following information is given, any rent or service charges (or service charges rent) demanded under a written demand unless it contains the name and address of the (immediate) landlord, and if the address is not in England and Wales, an address for the service of notices in England or Wales by the tenant must be given. This provision does not apply if, at any time, there is a receiver and manager in possession of the premises under a court order, whose functions include receiving service charges from the tenant (s 47(3)). It does not apply to any tenancy to which Part II of the *Landlord and Tenant Act* 1954 applies.

Under section 48 of the *Landlord and Tenant Act* 1987, unless the landlord (ie the immediate landlord) of residential premises, by notice furnishes the tenant with a name and address in England and Wales for service of any notices on him by the tenant, any rent or service charges otherwise due from the tenant are not due, until the landlord does comply with his statutory duty. As with section 47, section 48 is excluded in the case of business tenancies and subsisting receiverships.

VII. OUTLINE OF TENANTS' COMPULSORY ACQUISITION OF LANDLORDS' INTEREST IN RESIDENTIAL FLATS

Right to Acquire Landlord's Interest

Under Part III of the *Landlord and Tenant Act* 1987[68] "qualifying tenants" of flats in a residential or predominantly residential block have the right compulsorily to acquire the landlord's interest by applying to the county court for an order that a person (or company) nominated by them shall acquire the landlord's interest. This right applies in one of two cases:

(1) A preliminary notice was served on the landlord by the tenants concerned under section 27 and, where relevant, the "reasonable period" there specified for the execution of repairs has expired, then, an acquisition order must have been applied for to the court under section 28 (s 29(2)). The court must be satisfied that the landlord is in breach of any repairing, maintenance, insurance or management obligations in the lease owed to the tenants, that the landlord's breach is likely to continue, and that the appointment of a manager under Part II of the 1987 Act would not be an appropriate remedy (s 29(2)). So, if the landlord remedies the particular breaches complained of by the tenants, no acquisition order is possible—no matter how bad the landlord's past record may have been.

(2) At the date of the application, and for the whole of the three years immediately preceding the application, an appointment under Part II of the 1987 Act, of a manager in relation to the premises concerned, was in force (s 29(3)). The making of a management order may eventually trigger the acquisition of the landlord's interest, if the tenants are qualifying tenants.

---

[68] To be brought into force on a day to be appointed in regulations (s 62(2)).

Premises to which Part III Applies

Part III applies to qualifying tenants of flats (s 25) provided the landlord's interest is not held by exempt landlords, a term bearing an identical meaning in Part III as in the rest of the 1987 Act.

Qualifying Tenants. In principle, a person is a qualifying tenant if he is tenant of the flat under a long lease. The same definition of "long lease" applies to Part III as to the rest of the 1987 Act.

Exclusion of Certain Tenancies

Tenancies to which Part II of the *Landlord and Tenant Act* 1954 applies are expressly excluded from Part III of the 1987 Act and this exclusion expressly extends (s 60(2)) to assured tenants.

Meaning of Tenancy or Lease

A tenancy or lease includes, where appropriate a sub-lease or sub-tenancy if it is a long tenancy (s 59(1)).

Premises to which Part III applies: Further. Part III applies to premises consisting of the whole of a building, for example, a block of flats, or part of a building, such as flats above commercial premises (s 25(1)) which contain two or more flats held by qualifying tenants.[69] Part III will not apply even though there are flats occupied by residential tenants who might otherwise qualify for the buy-out if (s 25(4)):

(a) any part or parts of the premises are occupied or intended to be occupied otherwise than for residential purposes; *and*

(b) the internal floor area of that part or parts exceeds 50% of the internal floor area of the premises taken as a whole, but disregarding the internal floor area of the common parts (s 25(4)). The 50% figure is variable, by regulations (s 25(6)).

---

[69] They must comply with the "appropriate requirement" (s 25(3)) ie where the premises contain less than four flats, all must be held on long leases; where more than three but less than ten flats, all but one flat must be so held; where ten or more flats, at least 90% of the flats must be so let.

Tenants Eligible to Serve Notice

A section 27 notice may only be served by qualifying tenants (as above) on the landlord—either all of them in the premises to which Part III applies, or the requisite majority at the date of the application, which means over 50% of the available votes of qualifying tenants (s 27(1) and (4)). Generally, no acquisition order may be made unless a section 27 notice is served, but the court has power to dispense with this requirement if it is shown not to have been reasonably practicable (s 27(3)).

Applications under Part III: Some Further Considerations

1. No application may be made after a section 27 notice has been served where the landlord, if appropriate, remedies the breaches specified in the notice within the reasonable time specified (s 28(2)).

2. An application may relate to two or more premises to which Part III applies (s 28(3)) and it is registrable in the appropriate register (s 28(5) and (6)).

3. No application may be maintained if, at the date of service of the section 27 notice, or if, at the date of the application being made to the court, the premises were outside Part III, these dates are the crucial dates.[70] Moreover, the court is not absolutely bound to make an acquisition order, even if either of the required two conditions for making an acquisition order apply. The court must consider whether it is appropriate to make the order (s 29(1)(c)).

4. Where the premises in question are part only of the premises held by the landlord and his interest cannot reasonably be severed under section 29(4)(b), this is an absolute bar to the making of an acquisition order (s 29(5)).

5. As with Part II orders, even if the period for remedying breaches specified in the qualifying tenant's notice was not reasonable, this may be ignored and the court may make an acquisition order (s 29(6)(a)).

6. The *terms of an acquisition order* are that the order will provide for the nominated person, or company, to acquire

---

[70] The fact that since the time of the application to court the landlord's interest is assigned to an exempt or resident landlord or comes to be held within the functional land of a charity will not prevent Part III from applying (s 29(5)).

the landlord's interest in the premises specified in the order (s 30(1)). The terms will be either as agreed between the parties or determined by a rent assessment committee in default (s 30(1)). If the landlord is a mesne landlord, and under a qualified prohibition on assignments, he is bound to secure the consent of his head landlord and, if it is withheld, he is bound to take proceedings for a declaration that consent has been unreasonably withheld (s 30(5)). If, however, after all this, the consent is reasonably withheld, then the acquisition order ceases to have any effect (s 30(6)). The terms of the court's order are at its discretion, and its operation may be suspended (s 30(2))—possibly to give the landlord one last chance to comply with his obligations.[71]

7. The rent assessment committee, to be known for these purposes as a leasehold valuation tribunal (s 13(5)) if application is made to it to determine the price of the landlord's interest is, by s 31(2), to use an open market formula. The formula is: "an amount equal to [that] which ... that interest might be expected to realise if sold on the open market by a willing seller on the appropriate terms[72] on the assumption that none of the tenants ... was buying or seeking to buy that interest." Otherwise, it seems that the terms to be determined by the leasehold valuation tribunal are at large.

8. After the making of the order the landlord may apply (s 34(1)) for its discharge in one of three cases:

(a) the nominated person, or company, has failed within a reasonable time to carry out the acquisition;

(b) the number of qualifying tenants desiring to proceed with the acquisition of the landlord's interest is less than the requisite majority;

(c) the premises have ceased to be premises within Part III.

Similarly, the qualifying tenants have the right, by further notice, to withdraw from the acquisition (s 34(2)). In that case they will have to pay the landlord's costs, down to the date of service of their withdrawal notice.

---

[71] Existing mortgages must be paid off under s 32 unless the parties agree on acquisition subject thereto. The fact that the landlord cannot be found is no bar to a Part III order: see s 33.

[72] Defined, s 31(3).

If before, or after, the acquisition order is made, the nominated person becomes aware that there is no longer a requisite majority of qualifying tenants or the premises have fallen outside Part III, he must serve a withdrawal notice on the landlord (s 34(3)).

However, once the landlord's interest is acquired that is final (s 34(8)).

Chapter 10

LIABILITY FOR DAMAGE BY FIRE, ACCIDENTAL AND OTHER RELATED CAUSES

I. GENERAL POSITION

At common law, in the absence of express covenant, the tenant is not liable to the landlord for accidental fires nor for damage by storm, tempest, flood, earthquake, landslip or other act of God.

This position is confirmed by section 86 of the *Fire Prevention (Metropolis) Act* 1774, (which despite its title applies to the whole of England).[1]

If, however, the tenant deliberately or negligently starts a fire causing damage to the property of his neighbour or negligently allows a fire to spread onto his neighbour's property, then section 86 of the 1774 Act will not protect him from liability.[2]

If there is an express covenant between landlord and tenant then section 86 of the 1774 Act will not apply and the express covenant will regulate the liability of the tenant.

A. *Liability of Tenant to Reinstate if no Clause Excepts Fire Damage*

If the tenant is under a general covenant to repair, without any exception for fire or other accidental damage, then he will be liable to make good all fire damage and liable to reinstate the premises if destroyed by fire, negligence or any other accidental cause such as flood, or tempest.[3] This particular liability applies to any case where the tenant holds over after expiry of his original lease and then becomes a yearly tenant by implication of law.[4]

[1] *Sinnott v. Bowden* [1912] 2 Ch 414.
[2] *Musgrove v. Pandelis* [1919] 2 KB 43.
[3] *Bullock v. Dommitt* (1796) 2 TR 650.
[4] *Digby v. Atkinson* (1815) 4 Camp 275.

B. *Position if Fire Damage is Excepted from Tenant's Repairing Covenant*

In view of the harshness of the above rules, the tenant may have inserted in his covenant to repair, a proviso avoiding his obligation to reinstate in the event of damage by fire or other accidental cause. Moreover, he may have a further clause, to the effect that his liability to pay rent will end for the residue of the term (or for a defined period) in the event of fire rendering the premises uninhabitable or unusuable. (See as to the position where the latter proviso is not inserted Section V of this Chapter.)

If there is an exception to the tenant's covenant to repair in the event of fire or other accidental damage, this means that the landlord will, presumably, take out an insurance policy against these events and expect a contribution of the whole cost of the premiums if the tenant is the sole occupier of the building concerned, and a proportionate part, if he is one of a number of tenants. The lease may then go on to provide that reinstatement by the landlord will take place in the event of fire destroying the relevant building. It may be that the lease will also deal with the ownership and distribution of the policy moneys if for some reason reinstatement is impossible, or if it is mutually agreed not to undertake it.

It should be noted in this connection that, where the tenant's covenant to repair is qualified so as not to oblige him to rebuild in the event of fire, tempest and so on, the landlord is not impliedly liable to rebuild (or to repair damaged buildings) if these are damaged or destroyed by fire, tempest or other excepted cause.[5] The landlord may well expressly covenant to rebuild or repair in the case of any excepted event and then will be liable to do so, if the event materialises.

C. *Position if Tenant's Own Negligence Causes Fire*

It may be that the tenant expressly covenants to pay for the cost of keeping down an insurance policy effected in the landlord's name (or the joint names of the parties: see below)

---

[5] *Weigall* v. *Waters* (1795) 6 TR 488. The fact that the lease contains an express covenant by the landlord makes no difference: *Brown* v. *Quilter* (1764) Ambl 619.

If an insured event, such as fire, materialises, then it appears from *Mark Rowlands Ltd* v. *Berni Inns Ltd*[6] that the tenant has the right to look to the insurance policy to provide an indemnity and for reinstatement, even if it is his own negligence which produced the fire. In most cases, including that case, the tenant will, after all, be paying for the cost of the insurance premiums.

D. *Rights of Tenants of Dwelling-Houses and Flats with Respect to Insurance under Statute*

As a result of the *Landlord and Tenant Act* 1985[7] tenants (including statutory tenants) of dwelling-houses and flats paying service charges to the landlord, or his managing agent, which include an amount payable towards insurance, have a number of rights with respect to the insurance cover. These are fully discussed in Chapter 9 of this book. The controls do not, ultimately, allow the tenant to decide on the choice of insurer if this resides with the landlord under the lease, and they do not resolve one problem, which is that according to the Law Commission, many insurance companies pay commission to agents who introduce customers to them and also to some landlords (as policy-holders). Some landlords make undisclosed profits from the reimbursement by tenants of premiums which they pay.[8]

II. INSURANCE: FURTHER CONSIDERATIONS

A. *Insurance as Contract of Indemnity*

An insurance contract is a contract of indemnity. This means that if the tenant reinstates the premises after a fire or accident, and the insurer pays the landlord more than the amount of the loss, the insurer may recover the excess paid from the landlord.[9] It also means that where, as in *Mark*

---

[6] (1985) 276 EG 191, CA.
[7] Schedule added by *Landlord and Tenant Act* 1987, s 43 (2).
[8] Law Com No 162 (1987) 4. 81, giving as an illustration *Re Castlebeg Investments (Jersey) Ltd's Appeal* [1985] 2 EGLR 209, where the advantage to the landlord of an agency commission clause relating to fire insurance was taken into account by the Lands Tribunal as a factor raising the price payable for the freehold under s 9(1) of the *Leasehold Reform Act* 1967.
[9] *Darrell* v. *Tibbits* (1880) 5 QBD 560.

Rowlands Ltd v. *Berni Inns Ltd*,[10] it was the tenant's own negligence which caused a fire to break out (destroying the whole demised building) and the full cost of rebuilding was paid out by the insurers, the insurers could not sue the tenant to recover these sums.

"The intention of the parties," said Kerr LJ, "[was] that in the event of damage by fire, whether due to accident or negligence, the landlord's loss was to be recouped from the insurance monies and that in that event they were to have no further claim against the tenants..."[11] Nor, therefore, could the insurers make any claim against them.

Where, in breach of his covenant, a landlord failed to keep down an insurance policy, and a fire took place, and the tenant, having spent large sums on repairs, was reimbursed *ex gratia* by the insurance company, it was held that the damages recoverable by the tenant from the landlord for breach of covenant were unaffected by the insurance payment.[12]

B. *Breach of Covenant to Insure*

If the tenant covenants to insure the demised premises against fire and fails to do so, or if he fails to keep down an insurance policy, then these are a continuing breaches of covenant: any acceptance of rent by the landlord will waive previous breaches of covenant only, not subsequent ones, in respect of which a fresh cause of action will arise.[13] It is a breach of covenant to allow the premises to be or to remain uninsured even for a single day, even if no fire or other damage should materialise.[14]

However, it is not possible to sue the landlord for failure to keep down a policy of insurance where he is not under express obligation to do so, nor for failure to renew an insurance policy in such a case. In *Argy Trading Co* v. *Lapid Developments Ltd*[15] the landlords were not under any express covenant to insure, and they failed to renew a policy of block

---

[10] (1985) 276 EG 191, CA.
[11] *Ibid*, at p. 199.
[12] *Naumann* v. *Ford* (1985) 275 EG 542.
[13] *Doe d Muston* v. *Gladwin* (1845) 6 QB 953.
[14] *Penniall* v. *Harborne* (1848) 1 QB 368.
[15] [1977] 1 WLR 444.

insurance. When the premises burnt down, causing the tenants a £70,000 loss, the landlords escaped liability.

III. SCOPE OF INSURANCE

A. *General*

Leases of any premises will frequently contain a covenant by the tenant to insure the demised buildings to the full value or to some proportion of it, or up to a fixed amount, in an insurance office to be approved by the landlord—so that, if the tenant defaults with his premiums, the office can at once notify the landlord. Naturally, the tenant would expressly covenant to pay the premiums under the policy throughout the lease, and a receipt for the premiums will usually have to be produced, on request, to the landlord or his agent. A tenant's covenant to insure will be linked up with an express covenant to reinstate the building if the event materialises; and if the amount received as insurance monies is insufficient to cover rebuilding then the tenant is, in principle, bound personally to make up the difference.[16]

Leases may contain a covenant by the tenant that, if he fails to insure, the landlord may do so himself and then recover the premiums as rent.

In any event, the lease may provide that the tenant will not do or suffer anything to be done on the premises which would increase the premiums or render the policy voidable (such as storing inflammable material on the premises).

B. *Extent of Insurance*

If the landlord effects the insurance (or the tenant) then ideally the insurance should be in the joint names of the parties or, if insurance monies are paid out, both parties will have control over what is to be done with the fund.

If the landlord does not insure in the joint names of landlord and tenant (as where the tenant's interest does not extend to the whole of the insured building) then the tenant's protection is that, apparently, a note of his interest in the policy

---

[16] *Digby v. Atkinson* (1815) 4 Camp. 275.

should be endorsed on it—enabling notice to be given to the tenant if the policy lapses.[17]

As noted above, it is just as desirable for an insurance to be effected in the joint names of landlord and tenant where it is the tenant who is under covenant to insure. Indeed, should the tenant insure in his own name only, then his interest in the policy monies will correspond exactly, but no more, to the extent of his interest in the buildings in question.[18]

C. *Obligation to Spend Monies on Reinstatement*

Either party has the right, before the insurance office settles with the party insuring (but not afterwards), as where the landlord or tenant insures in their sole name, to invoke section 83 of the *Fires Prevention (Metropolis) Act* 1774.[19] This enables any person interested in the "houses or other buildings," such as the landlord, the tenant or a mortgagee, to require the insurer to spend the insurance monies on reinstatement of the premises.

If, after a request, the insurance office refuses to comply it seems that mandamus to force them to will lie. The landlord has no right himself to rebuild and to recover the money due under the policy.[20] Because a mortgagee is a person interested within section 83, he may claim under it where the tenant is under covenant in his mortgage to insure, and does so, and the buildings in question are destroyed or damaged by fire.[21]

If the party in receipt of the insurance monies is under an express covenant to re-build in the case of fire then no recourse to section 83 is necessary. Moreover, it is further limited by the fact that in *Mumford Hotels Ltd* v. *Wheeler*[2] where a landlord covenanted to keep the property insured against comprehensive risks, but not in terms to reinstate it was held that this particular covenant to insure (the tenant paid the premiums) enured for the joint benefit of landlord

---

[17] Murray J Ross, Chapter 10, p. 168.
[18] *Re King* [1963] Ch 459, CA.
[19] Tenant's trade fixtures are outside the scope of s 83: *Goreley, ex p, Re Barker* (186 LJ Bk 1.
[20] *Simpson* v. *Scottish Insurance Company* (1863) 1 H & M 618.
[21] *Sinnott* v. *Bowden* [1912] 2 Ch 414.
[22] [1964] 1 Ch 117.

and tenant. The landlord was, therefore, bound to apply the insurance monies towards reinstatement of the property.

IV. EXTENT OF INSURANCE

A. *Premises Covered*

The tenant's covenant to insure may be with regard to the existing buildings at the date of the covenant; but it may be so drafted that he is required to insure not only these buildings but also any new buildings which may at any future time be erected.[23]

B. *Reinstatement Basis*

As pointed out earlier in this Chapter, it is normal for an insurance policy to be effected on the basis of the cost of full re-instatement of the buildings insured. If the insurance policy is for "full value", then this has been construed as meaning the actual loss suffered by the insured, which may be far less than the cost of total reinstatement of the building in question, as where in one case the actual loss was found to be the market value of the building.[24]

The advantage of insuring for full reinstatement value is that this means the cost of rebuilding as new at the time rebuilding takes place, inflation being taken into account.[25] Accordingly, advice should be taken as to the likely cost of rebuilding the premises in question, plus an estimate of the time this operation will take, and an allowance for inflation.[26]

Cost of Insurance Premiums

Where the landlord effects insurance he may well require the tenant to pay or to contribute to the premiums. In this there is no implied covenant by the landlord that he will so arrange the insurance that it will not place what the tenant regards as an unnecessarily heavy burden on him.[27]

It may be that insurance premiums will be expressly recoverable from the tenant as additional service charges and, if so,

---

[23] *Sims* v. *Castigolione* [1905] WN 112.
[24] *Leppard* v. *Excess Insurance Co Ltd* [1979] 2 All ER 668.
[25] *Glennifer Finance Corporation* v. *Bamar Wood α Products Ltd* [1978] 2 Lloyds Rep 49.
[26] Suggestion of Murray J Ross, Chapter 10, p. 176.
[27] *Bandar Property Holdings* v. *JS Darwen (Successors)* [1968] 2 All ER 305.

they may be distrained for if unpaid. But it is not, in this, possible for a landlord to rely on a clause in the lease enabling him or his surveyor, conclusively to determine what was a proper proportion of the insurance premiums payable by a tenant, who holds part only of a larger building also demised to other tenants.[28]

V. OBLIGATION TO REINSTATE: SOME FURTHER CONSIDERATIONS

A. *General*

It has been pointed out earlier that where a policy is effected in the joint names of the landlord and tenant, and a fire or other insured event takes place, there will be an express covenant (usually) to apply the monies received in re-instatement of the buildings damaged or destroyed.

If full reinstatement is impossible, for example due to a compulsory purchase order, then the position firstly depends on what, if anything, the lease provides. Possibly it might state that the insurance monies in such a case will be retained by the landlord.[29] The tenant will continue to be liable for rent under the lease even after the building, the subject-matter of the lease, has been destroyed by fire or other event.[30] Only if the whole subject-matter of the lease (ie the underlying land) were to be destroyed, would the tenant be under no further liability to pay rent: so great a catastrophe will frustrate the lease.[31] To overcome this particular problem, a proviso in the lease for cesser of the tenant's liability to pay rent if the destruction of the demised building or buildings takes place is required, whether for a limited period or for the residue of the term, as may be agreed between the parties.

B. *Destination of Monies if No Express Covenant in Lease*

If the primary purpose of reinstatement after a fire is impossible, as where planning consent is refused, then if there is

[28] *Glennifer Finance Corporation* v. *Bamar Wood & Products Ltd supra.*
[29] Murray J Ross Chapter 10, p. 179 suggests this.
[30] *Paradine* v. *Jane* (1647) Aleyn 26.
[31] *National Carriers Ltd* v. *Panalpina (Northern) Ltd* [1981] AC 675.

no express provision in the lease, it was held in *Re King*[32] that the tenant was entitled to all the insurance monies. In this case the insurance was in the joint names of the parties.

The above result may be varied by agreement or conduct, as *Beacon Carpets Ltd* v. *Kirby*[33] shows. There was a fire at the premises and the sum required for reinstatement was about double the value of the insurance monies paid out. The landlords were under express covenant to reinstate. By mutual agreement between landlord and tenant the monies were not applied in reinstatement, the tenants releasing half the monies to the landlords and surrendering the lease. It was held that after the release the tenants could no longer claim to enforce the landlord's covenant to reinstate. Moreover, as to the monies, the parties, not having agreed as to their destination, were entitled to a share in them corresponding to their respective interests in the building, valued as at the date of the fire. The case serves solely as an illustration of what is to happen in the absence of express covenant or agreement between the parties where they are taken to treat the insurance monies as replacing the buildings.[34]

VI. BREACHES OF OBLIGATION TO INSURE: REMEDIES

Forfeiture

If the tenant is in breach of a covenant to insure, then this may afford a ground for forfeiture and will require the preliminary service of a section 146(1) notice under the *Law of Property Act* 1925 on the tenant, who may then apply for relief.

A breach of a covenant to insure is a continuing breach of covenant (so that any waiver by acceptance of rent will not necessarily prejudice a right to forfeit for later breaches). On the other hand, if the tenant fails to expend insurance monies in reinstatement of the premises within a reasonable time of receipt, that is a once and for all breach.[35]

---

[32] [1963] Ch 459, CA (impossibility due to compulsory purchase order).

[33] [1984] 2 All ER 726, CA.

[34] The Law Commission (1987, Law Com No 162) 4.80, state that the beneficial ownership insurance proceeds should be reconsidered in relation to the interests both of landlord and tenant and of mortgagees, but are not specific about what changes they would advocate.

[35] *Farimani* v. *Gates* (1984) 271 EG 887, CA.

Damages

The measure of damages for failure to comply with a covenant to insure depends on whether a fire has occurred. All the same, it cannot be assumed that if no fire takes place merely nominal damages will be awarded.[36] If the premises do burn down then the measure of damages is the cost of full re-instatement.

VII. VARIATION OF LEASES

Part IV of the *Landlord and Tenant Act* 1987 enables the county or High Court to vary the insurance provisions of long leases of flats on the application of one or more flat tenants (s 35(2)). The power extends by s 35(2)(b) to the insurance of the flat in question, or the building containing the flat, or any land or building let to the tenant under the lease. The same considerations apply to variation of the insurance provisions in long leases of flats as apply to variation of service charges provisions, and reference should accordingly be made to Chapter 9, where these matters are discussed.

---

[36] *Hey* v. *Wyche* (1842) 2 G & D 569.

Chapter 11

INCIDENCE OF LIABILITY TO
REPAIR UNDER STATUTE

I. INTRODUCTION

In this Chapter, there are considered various statutory provisions which have a material bearing on the covenant to repair on the part of landlords and tenants.

Section II of this Chapter deals with sections 11 to 16 of the *Landlord and Tenant Act* 1985.[1] These provisions apply to short leases of dwelling-houses and impose repairing obligations on the landlord in relation to the structure, exterior and prescribed installations and by section 12(1), they may not, generally, be contracted out of.[2] Many of the principles which have been discussed earlier, in relation to the covenant to repair and remedies, apply to the statute-implied obligations of the landlord and they are not repeated, in detail, in this Chapter.

The landlord is under a duty in tort, imposed by section 4 of the *Defective Premises Act* 1972, to see to it that all persons who might reasonably be expected to be affected by "relevant defects" in the demised premises (dwellings or not) are safe from personal injury: this provision is discussed in Section III.

One difference between section 4 of the 1972 Act and sections 11 to 16 of the *Landlord and Tenant Act* 1985 is that the landlord is not liable under the 1985 Act provisions unless he has notice from the tenant, or another person such as a rent-collector, of the state of disrepair; whereas under section 4 of the 1972 Act, his duties arise as soon as he knows, or ought to have known, of the defect.

There are a number of classes of both residential and

---

[1] These provisions replaced sections 32 and 33 of the *Housing Act* 1961 from 1 April 1986.
[2] Except that section 12(2) of the 1985 Act empowers the county court on the joint application of both parties, to authorise provisions to be included in the lease which exclude or modify the provisions relating to repairing obligations if the court thinks it reasonable to do so.

commercial leases or tenancies to which specific statutory codes apply. These are discussed in Sections IV and V of this Chapter.

If housing becomes so seriously out of repair that it is unfit for human habitation, local authorities have powers conferred by Part VI of the *Housing Act* 1985 to serve a repair notice requiring certain repairs be carried out by the person having control of the house, failing which there are default powers. These powers are considered in Section VI of this Chapter, followed by an outline of the statutory nuisance procedures.

II. DUTY OF LANDLORD TO REPAIR STRUCTURE, EXTERIOR AND PRESCRIBED INSTALLATIONS OF DWELLING-HOUSES

Sections 11 to 16 of the *Landlord and Tenant Act* 1985 impose obligations to repair in the case of leases of dwelling-houses (ie houses and flats) on the landlord.

A. *Application of Statute-Implied Duty*

At common law, the landlord is under no implied duty to carry out any repairs (see Chapter 3). In relation to leases to which section 11 of the *Landlord and Tenant Act* 1985 applies, to the extent of the statute-implied repairing duties, the common law no-liability rule is totally excluded.

General Rule

The general rule is that, by section 13(1) of the 1985 Act, the obligations imposed by section 11 apply to a lease of a dwelling-house granted on or after 24 October 1961, for a term of less than seven years. There are excluded from section 11, certain types of leases, by section 14(4), notably any lease granted on or after 3 October 1980 to a local authority, a new town corporation, the Development Board for Rural Wales, a registered housing association, a co-operative housing association, and bodies making student lettings to which section 8 of the *Rent Act* 1977 applies. In addition, by section 32(2) of the 1985 Act, section 11 does not extend to assured tenancies. Leases granted to the Crown are excluded by section 14(5). The Crown is not bound by section 11, where it is the landlord.[3]

---

[3] *Department of Transport* v. *Egoroff* (1986) 278 EG 1361, CA.

Definition of "Lease of a dwelling-house"

This is widely defined by section 16(b) of the 1985 Act, as a lease by which a building, or part of a building, is let wholly or mainly as a private residence, and "dwelling-house" means that building or part of a building. This definition includes, accordingly, a head or sub-lease.

To counteract backdating leases as an avoidance device, the term of less than seven years is computed as from the date of the grant of the lease, that is, the date of delivery of the lease, if different from its stated commencement date (s 13(2)(a)).[4] If the landlord obtains a registered rent under Part IV of the *Rent Act* 1977, on the basis that he is under the responsibility for repairs cast on him by section 11 of the 1985 Act, then, even though the term of the lease may exceed seven years, the landlord will be estopped as long as he continues to accept the full registered rent, from denying liability under section 11, though the lease is silent on the matter.[5]

If a lease is determinable at the landlord's option before the expiration of seven years from the commencement of the term, then it falls within the 1985 Act provisions (s 13(2)(b))[6] but, conversely, if the lease gives the tenant an option for renewal which, together with the original term, amounts to seven years or more, section 11 will not apply (s 13(2)(c)).

B. *Scope of Statute-Implied Duty*

This is governed by section 11 of the 1985 Act, which imposes two sets of duties. The first set relates to the structure and exterior of the dwelling-house, and the second to prescribed installations within it.

Structure and Exterior Obligations

Section 11(1)(a) of the *Landlord and Tenant Act* 1985 implies a covenant by the landlord "to keep in repair the

---

[4] See *Brikom Investments Ltd* v. *Seaford,* [1981] 2 All ER 783, CA.
[5] *Brikom Investments Ltd* v. *Seaford supra,* CA.
[6] If there is only an option to determine the lease for a term originally of over 7 years on the death of either party then the 1985 Act s 11 is excluded: *Parker* v. *O'Connor* [1974] 2 All ER 257, CA.

structure and exterior of the dwelling-house (including drains, gutters and external pipes)".

The construction of this provision is considered immediately after the next heading.

Obligations with regard to Installations

Section 11(1)(b) of the 1985 Act implies a covenant by the landlord to "keep in repair and proper working order the installations in the dwelling-house for the supply of water, gas and electricity and for sanitation (including basins, sinks, baths and sanitary conveniences, but not other fixtures, fittings and appliances for making use of the supply of water, gas or electricity)".

Section 11(1)(c) of the 1985 Act implies a covenant by the landlord "to keep in repair and proper working order the installations in the dwelling-house for space heating or heating water".

Meaning of "repair"

The word "repair", in the context of section 11 of the 1985 Act, bears the same meaning in general terms as in any other context, and reference should be made to the discussion in Chapters 4 to 6 of this book.

To take an example specific to section 11, it has been held that the statute-implied obligation on a landlord to repair did not oblige the landlord to put in a new damp course into an old house, which did not have a damp course before.[7] If the house had been built originally with a damp course, then no doubt section 11 would require the landlord to replace it if required.[8]

Structure and Exterior

On the general interpretation of structure and exterior, some aspects are specific to section 11. (General principles are discussed in Chapter 4.)

1. The "structure and exterior" of the "dwelling-house" concerned is taken to mean only the "structure and exterior" within the terms of the actual demise in each case. Any part

---

[7] *Wainwright* v. *Leeds City Council* (1984) 270 EG 1289.
[8] See *Elmcroft Developments Ltd* v. *Tankersley-Sawyer* (1984) 270 EG 140, CA.

of the "structure and exterior" which is expressly retained by the landlord in his control is not covered by section 11 of the 1985 Act, such as a drain or gutter on his land adjacent to or above the tenant's premises.[9]

2. Windows are within the scope of the landlord's statute-implied duty if they are exterior or are structural, an example of the latter being unopenable plate-glass windows.[10] If, however, the relevant windows are themselves in repair, section 11 does not oblige the landlord to replace them with new and differently made windows, in order to cure other problems in the dwelling-house, such as condensation.[11]

3. The "structure and exterior" of the dwelling-house includes a dividing party wall between it and the neighbouring house.[12] Some difficulty has however been experienced in defining the physical extent of the landlord's obligations. Steps and a path (consisting of flagstones) giving access to the front of a house, being a necessary means of access, were held to be part of the "exterior" within the landlord's statute-implied duty.[13] But paving slabs in the rear garden of a house, which were not used for access to the house, were held outside the scope of the landlord's duty.[14]

Special Problems with Individual Flats

Flats are "dwelling-houses" within section 11, and in the case of a lease of one individual flat in a block of flats for a term of less than seven years, it was held in *Campden Hill Towers Ltd* v. *Gardner*[15] that the landlord was not under an unlimited duty under section 11, but that his obligations extended only to the particular flat demised to the particular tenant, as opposed to the whole structure and exterior and installations in the entire block. Therefore, it was said, "anything which, in the ordinary use of words, would be regarded as part of the structure, or of the exterior, of the particular

---

[9] See *Peters* v. *Prince of Wales Theatre (Birmingham)* [1943] KB 73. The only way the landlord may be compelled to repair in such a case is under express covenant: see *Duke of Westminster* v. *Guild* (1983) 267 EG 762; [1984] 3 All ER 144, CA.

[10] *Boswell* v. *Crucible Steel Co of America* [1925] 1 KB 119, CA.

[11] *Quick* v. *Taff-Ely Borough Council* (1985) 276 EG 452; [1985] 2 EGLR 50, CA.

[12] See *Green* v. *Eales* (1841) 2 QB 225.

[13] *Brown* v. *Liverpool Corporation* [1969] 3 All ER 1345, CA.

[14] *Hopwood* v. *Cannock Chase District Council* [1975] 1 WLR 473, CA.

[15] [1977] QB 823, CA.

'dwelling-house' regarded as a separate part of the building, would be within... para (a) [of section 11]". The landlord's statute-implied obligation, in the case of any individual flat in a block of flats would include: "that which... would be regarded as the exterior wall of the flat... [and] that part of the outside wall of the block of flats which constitutes a wall of the flat." So, the landlord's obligation applied to the "outside wall or walls of the flat; the outside of inner party walls of the flat; the outer sides of horizontal divisions between [the] flat and flats above and below; the structural framework and beams directly supporting floors, ceilings and walls of the flat."[16]

Roof of a Flat

On whether, in relation to a top-floor flat, the roof above it is to be part of that flat, in all cases, regardless of whether the roof forms part of the premises demised, the question whether roof repairs fall on the landlord under the statute-implied duty is a question of fact and degree, dependent to some extent on the construction of the building. If the ceiling and roof of a particular top-floor flat form part of one, insepar-able, structural unit then the presumption is that the roof and ceiling are part of the structure and exterior of that flat; but this is not an absolute rule and borderline cases may arise in the case of a void space or uninhabited loft between the flat and roof.[17]

Extent of Duty to Repair: Concluding Points

Section 11(2) contains limits on the extent of the landlord's statute-implied obligation (see C below) and others have been judicially imposed. In *Quick* v. *Taff-Ely Borough Council*,[18] it was held that there must be an element of disrepair before any question arises about whether, in the process of remedial work, it would be reasonable to remedy a design or inherent fault.

If, however, the landlord carries out repairs falling within section 11, he is also obliged to pay for the cost of re-instating

[16] *Ibid*, at p. 834.
[17] *Douglas-Scott* v. *Scorgie* (1984) 269 EG 1164; [1984] 1 All ER 1086, CA.
[18] (1985) 276 EG 452; [1985] 2 EGLR 50.

any decorations which have been consequentially damaged by the work of repair.[19]

"Installations"

Section 11(1)(b) and (c) list the installations which the landlord is, under statute, bound to keep in repair and proper working order. The installations of the prescribed type are confined, however, to those physically within the "dwelling-house" so that in the case of flats, the landlord is bound only to repair those within the physical confines of each individual flat.[20] Accordingly, the landlord is obliged under section 11 to keep a radiator or pipes within a flat or house in repair and proper working order but not a boiler in the basement heating the water supplied to radiators in all the flats. Nor a refrigerator in a flat, where the refrigerator was operated by a central installation under the landlord's control.[21]

It follows from this, that in the case of leases of flats for less than seven years, while section 11(4) and (5) of the 1985 Act will render covenants by the tenant to pay the landlord service charges for the maintenance of any prescribed installations within any individual flat of no effect, the landlord will be able, if he covenants expressly to provide services, validly to charge service charges for installations not within the physical confines of any individual flat, and for maintenance and repair of common user parts (for these latter lie outside the scope of the obligation imposed by section 11).

Repair and Proper Working Order

The landlord's duty to keep installations of the prescribed type in repair and proper working order has been held not to oblige the landlord to lag water pipes.[22] If, due to a design fault, an installation, such as a cistern, floods part of the tenant's premises causing damage, then the landlord is liable in damages,[23] since what is required is that the physical or mechanical condition of the installation in question should be such that it will work properly as an installation.

[19] *Bradley* v. *Chorley Borough Council* (1985) 275 EG 801; [1985] 2 EGLR 49, CA.
[20] *Campden Hill Towers Ltd* v. *Gardner* [1977] QB 823, CA.
[21] *Penn* v. *Gatenex Co Ltd* [1958] 2 QB 210, CA.
[22] *Wycombe Area Health Authority* v. *Barnett* (1982) 264 EG 619, CA.
[23] *Liverpool City Council* v. *Irwin* [1977] AC 239, HL.

Accordingly, a local authority was held liable for damage caused when a discoloured water tank burst—the existence of the defect being known to the landlords some six weeks earlier.[24]

C. *Limits on Landlord's Statutory Duty*

The *Landlord and Tenant Act* 1985 imposes the following express limitations on the landlord's statute-implied duty which may be set out as follows:

1. By section 11(2)(a) the landlord is not liable "to carry out works or repairs for which the lessee is liable by virtue of his duty to use the premises in a tenant-like manner, or would be so liable but for an express covenant on his part."

2. By section 11(2)(b) the landlord's statutory duty does not require him to rebuild or reinstate the premises in the case of destruction or damage by fire, tempest, flood or other inevitable accident.

3. The landlord, by section 11(2)(c), is not, under his statute-implied obligations, bound to keep in repair or to maintain anything which the tenant is entitled to remove from the dwelling-house.

4. The standard of repair required of a landlord under section 11 is not expressly laid down, but section 11(3) provides that:

"In determining the standard of repair... regard shall be had to the age, character and prospective life of the dwelling-house and the locality in which it is situated." This involves the same standard of repair as the required under "good tenantable repair" by *Proudfoot* v. *Hart*.[25]

D. *Prohibition on Contracting-Out*

Section 11(4) of the 1985 Act renders a covenant by the tenant of "no effect" in so far as it purports to apply to the duties imposed on the landlord by section 11(1).

Section 11(5) extends the prohibition on contracting out by catching various indirect methods which might otherwise be relied on. It renders the following covenants by a tenant of no effect in so far as they apply to section 11(1) obligations:

---

[24] *Sheldon* v. *West Bromwich Corporation* (1973) 25 P & CR 361.
[25] (1890) 25 QBD 42, CA: so held in *Jaquin* v. *Holland* [1960] 1 All ER 402, CA.

(a) to put in repair or deliver up in repair;
(b) to point, paint or render;
(c) to pay money in lieu of repairs by the tenant;
(d) to pay service charges (in effect).

Section 13 of the 1985 Act nullifies indirect avoidance of section 11 (see above). Section 12(1) prohibits direct contracting-out, subject to section 12(2) (see above).

E. *Requirement of Notice of Want of Repair*

The landlord has a statute-conferred right, under section 11(6) of the 1985 Act, to enter and inspect the premises to view their condition and state of repair, and this carries with it an implied right to enter and execute the repairs on notice to the tenant.

Despite his right of entry to inspect and implied right to repair, the landlord is not liable to carry out any of the repairs required of him by section 11(1) unless he has actual notice of the want of repair. This means prior notice, and involves the landlord having sufficient notification or information to put him on inquiry as to the nature of the disrepair, and as to the work required. Notice may be given to the landlord by the tenant personally, or by a third party, or as the result of the landlord's or his servant's or agent's own inspections.

Notice was given accordingly, where the landlord carried out an inspection of the premises and discovered a defect,[26] and where the tenant sent a letter to the landlord pointing out, in general terms, a state of disrepair,[27] and where a local authority environmental health inspector observed disrepair in the house concerned, of which the authority was landlord.[28] Notice was also given to the landlord when a local authority repair notice was served on him by a local authority.[29]

After notice is given, the landlord will have to investigate the detailed causes of disrepair. Hence, where a tenant, before agreeing to take a tenancy, notified the landlords' agent of a bulge in the ceiling of the kitchen, the landlords were held

---

[26] As in *Sheldon* v. *West Bromwich Corporation* (1973) 25 P & CR 361.
[27] *Griffin* v. *Pillett* [1926] 1 KB 17. The precise degree of disrepair need not be specified by the tenant.
[28] *Dinefwr Borough Council* v. *Jones* (1987) 284 EG 58.
[29] *McGreal* v. *Wake* (1984) 269 EG 1254, CA.

liable in damages for failing to inspect and repair the ceiling: it fell in some eight months later.[30]

Notice is required to the landlord, no matter whether the defect is patent or latent.[31] It is also required in relation to defects existing at, or before the commencement of the lease.[32] If it is not given, as with a latent defect, and the tenant is personally injured, he is deprived of all remedies.

Once the landlord has notice of the disrepair, then he is bound, as noted earlier, within a reasonable time, and in the case of urgent repairs this is almost forthwith, to investigate the causes, and then to carry out the necessary repairs. If the premises are in a dangerous state then, pending the execution of full repairs, immediate steps must be taken, after notice, to render them temporarily safe if permanent repairs cannot at once be executed.[33] What is a reasonable time is a question of fact: in one case, it was held to be about eight weeks from notice; in other cases, for example where repairs are very pressing, it could be a few days.[34]

F. *Remedies of Tenant*

The tenant is entitled to the same remedies for breach by the landlord of his obligations under section 11 of the 1985 Act, as he is in the case of breaches by the landlord of any contractual duties expressly imposed on him by the lease. The principles on which damages are assessed and those applicable to other tenants' remedies such as specific performance are discussed in Chapter 9.

III. LANDLORD'S DUTY OF CARE UNDER SECTION 4 OF DEFECTIVE PREMISES ACT 1972

Section 4(1) of the *Defective Premises Act* 1972 provides that where premises are let under a tenancy (widely defined by section 6(1)) which puts the landlord under an obligation

[30] *Porter* v. *Jones* (1942) 112 LJ KB 173.
[31] *O'Brien* v. *Robinson* [1973] AC 912, HL.
[32] *Uniproducts (Manchester) Ltd* v. *Rose Furnishers Ltd* [1956] 1 All ER 146.
[33] *Griffin* v. *Pillett* [1926] 1 KB 17. The landlords repaired steps 14 days from notice but having failed temporarily to secure the steps were liable to the tenant in damages for injuries sustained during those 14 days.
[34] *McGreal* v. *Wake, supra.*

to the tenant for the maintenance or repair of the premises,[35] the landlord owes to all persons (including the tenant[36]) who might reasonably be expected to be affected by defects in the state of the premises a duty to take such care as is reasonable in all the circumstances to see that they are reasonably safe from personal injury or from damage to their property caused by a "relevant defect".

By section 4(3) this means a defect in the state of the premises existing on, or after, the material time and arising from, or continuing because of, an act or omission by the landlord which would constitute failure to carry out his obligation to the tenant for maintenance or repair of the premises. "Material time" generally means the commencement date of the tenancy, or the time the tenancy agreement was entered into (s 4(3)).

This duty cannot be contracted out of (s 6(5)). By section 6(2), it is in addition to any duty owed by the landlord under any other rule or enactment, such as section 11 of the *Landlord and Tenant Act* 1985, or in negligence or nuisance. The tenant's rights of action, if any, in these areas, are accordingly preserved.

The duty is owed, by section 4(2), if the landlord knows (whether as the result of being notified by the tenant or otherwise) or if he ought in all the circumstances to have known, of the relevant defect. By section 4(4), where premises are let under a tenancy which, expressly or impliedly, gives the landlord a right to enter and carry out repairs then, as from the time when he first, by notice or otherwise, can put himself in a position to enter and repair, he is under a duty under the 1972 Act. The existence of a statutory right to enter and inspect and repair and the existence of an express contractual right to the same effect will accordingly trigger the landlord's 1972 Act liability as a result of section 4(4). Examples of these rights are rights conferred by section 11(6) of the *Landlord and Tenant Act* 1985 and sections 3(2) and 148 of the *Rent Act* 1977.

---

[35] This may include a patio: *Smith* v. *Bradford Metropolitan Council* (1982) 44 P & CR 171.

[36] *Smith* v. *Bradford Metropolitan Council, supra*; also *McDonagh* v. *Kent Area Health Authority* (1984) 134 NLJ 567.

The landlord is under no liability for defects arising or continuing due to the tenant's failure to carry out his express obligations under the tenancy (s 4(4)).

The duty imposed by section 4 of the 1972 Act is not absolute. The landlord must see to it that the tenant and other persons are *reasonably* safe from injury. It has been claimed[37] that while sometimes the duty could only be complied with by carrying out the repairs, say to a broken glass panel in the house, in other cases suitable warning notices might suffice.

IV. INCIDENCE OF LIABILITY FOR REPAIRS IN PARTICULAR CLASSES OF RESIDENTIAL LEASES

A. *Long Leases to which Part I of the Landlord and Tenant Act 1954 applies*

Part I of the *Landlord and Tenant Act* 1954 confers security of tenure on residential tenants under long leases. Long leases, for this purpose, are terms certain exceeding 21 years at a rent of less than two-thirds of the rateable value of the premises (s 2 of the 1954 Act). The position regarding the incidence of, and payment for, certain repairs is as follows.

1. Assuming that the tenant is entitled, after expiry of the initial term certain, to remain in possession, the landlord may propose a statutory tenancy. Until then, the responsibility for repairs will be governed by the covenants in the original term certain as continued. The effect of a landlord's notice proposing a statutory tenancy, is that the contractual tenancy, as continued, is brought to an end. By section 7(2) of the 1954 Act, the landlord's notice[38] proposing a statutory tenancy must set out his proposals as to the carrying out, and payment for, initial repairs (if any are required), and also deal with responsibility for repairs during the statutory tenancy. The tenant must decide whether he wishes to elect to retain possession and notify the landlord accordingly. The landlord's notice proposing a statutory tenancy may require that if the tenant retains possession as statutory tenant, a record is to be made

---

[37] *Woodfall* 1–1678.
[38] This must be in the form prescribed (Form 1) by Landlord and Tenant (Notices Regulations) 1957 SI 1957 No 1157 as amended.

of the state of repair of the house.[39] If the parties can agree on these matters, then the agreed terms will be embodied in the statutory tenancy.

2. If the parties cannot reach agreement on initial repairs, then the landlord must apply to the court to determine them. In what follows, "court" means the county court (s 63(1) of the 1954 Act).

3. In the event either of agreement or determination by the court, by section 8(1), if the terms include provision for the landlord to carry out specified initial repairs, any of which are required in consequence of the tenant's failure to fulfil his obligations under the former tenancy, the landlord is entitled to compensation. This is a payment for these repairs ("accrued tenant's repairs") equal to the cost reasonably incurred by the landlord in ascertaining what repairs are required and, in the carrying out of such repairs, excluding any sum recoverable by the landlord otherwise than from the tenant or his predecessor in title. Payment for accrued tenant's repairs may be made by instalments or any method agreed, or determined (s 8(2)). If the landlord fails to carry out initial repairs within a reasonable time, the court has power, on the tenant's application, to direct that the rent payable under the statutory tenancy is to be reduced (Sched 2 para 1).

4. The court has no power to compel the tenant to carry out initial repairs except with his consent (s 9(3)) but he may agree to do them. Where, in breach of an agreement to carry out initial repairs, the tenant fails to carry them out within a reasonable time, his failure is treated as a breach of his obligations of the tenancy (Sched 2 para 4).

5. As to repairs during the statutory tenancy, this is to be determined either by agreement, or by the court in default of agreement (s 8(3)).

6. Where the court has to determine the terms of the statutory tenancy as to repairs, section 9(1) provides that the court is not, except with the consent of the landlord and tenant, to require the carrying out of initial repairs in excess of what is required to bring the dwelling-house into good repair, or

---

[39] 1954 Act Sched 2 para 7. If the tenant elects to retain possession he may require a record in his notification to the landlord: para 8.

the carrying out of any repairs not specified by the landlord in his application as repairs which he is willing to carry out. "Good repair" is defined by section 9(2) as good repair in respect to both structure and decoration, having regard to the age, character and locality of the dwelling-house.

7. Section 9(4) restricts the scope of any obligation imposed by the court during the statutory tenancy: it must not require the dwelling-house to be kept in a better state of repair than that subsisting after the initial repairs, if any, have been carried out; or, in the absence of any agreement or determination, in a better state of repair than the state subsisting at the time of the court's determination of what obligations are to be imposed.

8. Once the statutory tenancy commences then, by section 10(1), any liability of the tenant or his predecessors under repairing covenants under the old lease is extinguished.

9. The statutory tenancy will commence either from a date agreed by the parties three months before the termination date specified in the landlord's notice proposing a statutory tenancy, or that determined by the court if later (s 64). Until then, the responsibility for repairs will be governed by the terms of the old lease, as continued by section 3(2), down to the commencement date of the statutory tenancy.

10. A special form of relief is provided by section 16 from forfeiture by the landlord for breaches by the tenant of covenants, including his covenant to repair. Where the term certain has more than seven months to run, any order for possession or damages must be suspended for 14 days, during which time the tenant may give written notice to the immediate landlord, which terminates the term certain. Thereafter, the only way the landlord can enforce the tenant's repairing obligations, is to propose a statutory tenancy (s 16(2)). If the term certain has seven months or less to run then no order for possession or damages can be made by the court (s 16(3)).

11. A limit on repairing obligations under the statutory tenancy, which may be validly imposed on the tenant, is that such obligations must be consistent with Part I of the 1954 Act. Therefore, an obligation to reinstate the premises to their former condition under the term certain could not be

carried into the statutory tenancy, and the 1954 Act simply extinguished this particular liability.[40]

B. *Rent Act Tenancies*

Protected Tenancies

The responsibility for repairs in relation to a protected tenancy under the *Rent Act* 1977 will be governed by common law and statute. If the term is for less than seven years, section 11 of the *Landlord and Tenant Act* 1985 will apply to it. If the tenancy is periodic, the tenant will be governed by the implied duty to use the dwelling-house in a tenant-like manner.

If the landlord is responsible for repairs and services, the registered rent, if any, by section 71(1) of the *Rent Act* 1977, will include sums payable by the tenant for services. The state of repair of the dwelling-house is a matter to be taken into account by the rent officer or rent assessment committee in assessing a fair rent, under section 70(1)(a) of the 1977 Act. The date at which the state of repair is to be taken into account is, apparently, the date of the rent officer's or rent assessment committee's hearing.[41] Disrepair due to a tenant's breach of covenant is to be disregarded (s 70(3)(a)). However, it was held in *Metropolitan Properties Ltd* v. *Wooldridge*,[42] that a landlord's failure to enforce a tenant's covenant to repair could not be taken into account: the premises had to be valued as they were assuming the tenant had complied with his covenants;[43] if a tenant's failure to perform his repairing obligations was due, to any extent, to the landlord's failure to perform his own obligations, this could be taken into account. In *Firstcross Ltd* v. *Teasdale*,[44] where the tenants of furnished flats on short terms were under an obligation to keep them in good and tenantable condition, it was held that the rent assessment committee was entitled to assess a fair rent on

---

[40] *Byrne* v. *Herbert* [1966] 2 QB 121, CA.
[41] Farrand and Arden *Rent Acts and Regulations* (1981), note to s 70.
[42] (1968) 20 P & CR 64.
[43] For a case where it was held that the premises must be valued in their current dilapidated state see *McGee* v. *London Rent Assessment Panel Committee* (1969) 113 SJ 384. If the house is covered by a closing order this is an important factor but does not oblige a nil rent to be registered: *Williams* v. *Khan* (1982) 43 P & CR 1, CA.
[44] (1983) 265 EG 305.

the basis of the state of repair of the flats, having regard to the limited liabilities of the tenants and the landlord's obligations under section 11 of the *Landlord and Tenant Act* 1985.

On the capital costs of equipment (or plant and machinery), such as boilers, lifts, carpets, oil-storage tanks and hot and cold water tanks, provided by the landlord, these must be taken into account, by considering the inclusion of allowances, so as to give the landlord a profit margin for depreciation.[45] The cost of replacement, is to be spread over the equipment's expected lifespan.[46] The calculation is based on the original cost of the equipment and not its likely replacement cost.[47] This basis has been criticised by the Law Commission, who say that inflation means that the case for depreciation based on replacement cost is now stronger than when fair rents were first introduced.[48]

Statutory Tenancies

Section 3(1) of the *Rent Act* 1977 enacts that the liability for repairs under a statutory tenancy is to be the same as under the protected tenancy which it follows, so far as consistent with the provisions of the *Rent Act*. Therefore, if the landlord is liable, under the protected tenancy, for structural and exterior repairs, and for repairs and maintenance of prescribed installations, whether by statute or covenant, this liability will be transmitted to the statutory tenancy. Any duty of the tenant to use the premises in a tenant-like manner will likewise continue. As to fixing of the rent under statutory procedures, see the discussion under protected tenancies, which applies as statutory tenancies are regulated tenancies.

C. *Extended Leases under the Leasehold Reform Act 1967*

Where an extended lease of 50 years' duration is granted under the *Leasehold Reform Act* 1967, its terms, as regards

---

[45] *Perseus Property Co Ltd* v. *Burberry* (1985) 273 EG 405; [1985] 1 EGLR 114.
[46] *Regis Property Co Ltd* v. *Dudley* [1958] 1 QB 346.
[47] *Perseus Property Co Ltd* v. *Burberry, supra*; also *Property Holdings and Investment Trust Ltd* v. *Lewis* (1969) 113 SJ 672.
[48] Law Com No 167 (1987) para 4. 46 and 4. 48.

repairs, will be the same as those of the existing tenancy as at the date of the tenant's notice of desire to have an extended lease, but the terms may be varied by agreement (s 15(1) and (7)). Therefore, the covenants and obligations to repair in the old lease will continue to apply to the extended lease, unless varied by agreement. The landlord and the tenant have the right, under section 15(7), to require the exclusion or modification of any term as to repairs which are unreasonable to include, unchanged, in the extended lease, in view of the date of the original tenancy, and changes since that date which affect the suitability of the provisions of that tenancy: disputes are to be resolved by the county court (s 20). If the new tenancy puts the landlord under obligations to provide services, repair, maintain or insure, there is provision for payment by the tenant of additional rent (s 15(3)). If the old tenancy contains terms about payment of service charges by the tenant, these will be carried into the extension lease unless modified under section 15(7).

D. *Shared Ownership Leases*

A shared ownership lease is essentially one means by which a secure tenant may, in due course, acquire the freehold of the house of which he at present is tenant. The terms of shared ownership leases, as to repairs, are set out in *Housing Act 1985*, Sched 6 Part III.

Landlord's Obligations

In the case only of flats, the landlord is under a statute-implied covenant to keep in repair the structure and exterior and common parts and installations providing services to the tenant and other tenants (para 14). This covenant expressly includes a covenant by the landlord to rebuild or reinstate the premises in the event of fire and other normally insurable risks.

Tenant's Obligations

Unless otherwise agreed, the tenant is under an obligation, in the case of a house, to keep it in good repair, including decorative repair. In the case of a flat, his obligation is limited to keeping the interior in such repair (para 16).

F. *Secure Tenants*

The position regarding repairs in the case of secure tenants (certain types of public sector tenants as defined by section 79 of the *Housing Act* 1985) is this. The obligations of secure tenants, as regards repairs and maintenance, are no different in principle to those of any other residential fixed-term or periodic tenants.

Tenants' Repairs Scheme

Regulations have been made under section 96 of the 1985 Act for a scheme enabling secure tenants to carry out landlord's repairs and then to recover the cost from the landlord.[49] The scheme is as follows. Before the tenant can claim the cost of a given repair, he must serve written notice on the landlord stating the works proposed and the materials which are intended to be used (reg 3). If the notice is validly served the landlord must, in principle, reimburse the tenant for the cost of the repair; but there are a number of limitations on the tenant's rights. For example, the scheme is limited to qualifying repairs and, moreover, repairs costing over £200 or under £20 are totally excluded. The landlord has various grounds to resist the tenant's claim, and has control over the manner of execution of the work and the materials used. Unless all procedures and time-limits are strictly complied with by the tenant, his claim will fail.

F. *Assured Tenancies*

In the case of assured tenancies[50] the incidence of liability for repairs under the contractual term will be entirely a matter for negotiation between the parties. This is so, even if the term certain is for less than seven years, owing to the exclusion of assured tenancies from section 11 of the *Landlord and Tenant Act* (by s 32(2) of that Act). As from the expiry date

---

[49] Secure Tenancies (Right to Repair) Scheme Regulations 1985 SI 1985 No 1493. See Maughan-Pawsey (1986) 136 New Law J 829.

[50] Ie residential tenants holding tenancies from approved body landlords: *Housing Act* 1980, ss 56–58 as amended and eg Assured Tenancies (No 2) Order SI 1987/822.

of the contractual term, it will be, in principle, continued under Part II of the *Landlord and Tenant Act* 1954, which applies, with modifications, to assured tenancies. The principles governing repairs where a new tenancy is agreed or ordered by the court, are presumably the same as for business tenants, as to which see section V of this Chapter.

Extension of Scheme

The assured tenancies scheme was recently extended[51] so that it applies not only, as originally, to buildings, erected on or after 8 August 1980, but also to enable buildings built before, or after 8 August 1986, to be let out on assured tenancies, where qualifying works have been carried out on the building within two years before the grant of first assured tenancy by the landlord.

Qualifying works mean (s 56B(2)) works involving expenditure attributable to the dwelling-house (or flat) of not less than the prescribed amount. In addition, the dwelling-house or flat must be fit for human habitation at the date of the grant of the first assured tenancy (s 56B(1)(b)).[52] The prescribed amounts are:

(a) in the case of a dwelling-house in Greater London: £7,000;

(b) in the case of a dwelling-house elsewhere: £5,000.[53]

These amounts are the minimum that must be spent on the dwelling-house, before it can be let on an assured tenancy.

The qualifying works must be carried out within the two years before the grant of the first assured tenancy. The works must be attributable to the dwelling-house (s 56B(3)), or they may be carried out to other land or buildings let with the dwelling-house, subject to the above financial limits.

If the premises are a flat, works on common parts will count towards the qualifying works limit (s 56B(4)).

---

[51] By *Housing and Planning Act* 1986, s 12 amending *Housing Act* 1980 s 56 from 7 January 1987: Housing and Planning Act (Commencement No 1) Order 1986 SI 1986 No 2262.

[52] The standard for fitness is as laid down by *Housing Act* 1980, s 56D and is similar to that prescribed by *Landlord and Tenant Act* 1985 s 10. Approved body landlords may apply under s 56C for certificates of fitness prior to commencing works: a certificate is conclusive evidence of fitness on the date when given.

[53] Assured Tenancies (Prescribed Amounts) Order 1987 SI 1987 No 122.

V. INCIDENCE OF LIABILITY TO REPAIR AND EFFECT OF
DISREPAIR WHERE PART II OF THE LANDLORD AND TENANT
ACT 1954 APPLIES

General

In the case of business tenants to whom Part II of the *Land-lord and Tenant Act* 1954 applies, the responsibility for repairs during the contractual term is a matter for negotiation between the parties and, if the building is in single occupation, the landlord may well wish to shift all responsibility for repairs and maintenance onto the tenant. If there are several tenants in the building, then while the landlord may undertake such liabilities, the tenant will normally have to pay for their cost, in the form of service charges. The principles on which the covenants to repair in a business lease will be interpreted are discussed in Chapters 4 to 6. It has been pointed out[54] that if the tenant of commercial property is not careful when nego-tiating his lease, he may well find that the burden of upkeep and of repairing unforeseen defects will fall on him, given the fact that landlords will press for "clear leases" where there is a shortage of office accommodation.

Notice to Terminate: Effect of Disrepair by Tenant

If the landlord serves a notice to terminate under section 25 (or where the tenant requests a new tenancy under s 26) and at that date the premises are in disrepair, owing to the tenant's breach of his repairing covenants, the landlord may oppose the grant of a new tenancy under section 30(1)(a) of the 1954 Act. To succeed under this ground, and to obtain possession, the landlord must show a serious breach or breaches, and even then the court has a discretion to refuse to order possession. Moreover, if, between the date of the landlord's notice to terminate and the date of the hearing, the tenant makes good the breaches of covenant, this will be taken into account in the tenant's favour; likewise if the tenant at the hearing undertakes to remedy the breaches, the court may well in its discretion refuse to order possession.[55]

---

[54] Tromans 83 LS Gazette 2642.
[55] *Betty's Cafés Ltd* v. *Phillips Furnishing Stores* [1957] Ch 67, at p. 83 (Birkett LJ).

Interim Rents

Under section 24A of the 1954 Act, the court has a power to determine an interim rent on the landlord's application, following a section 25 notice to terminate, or a section 26 tenant's request for a new tenancy. There is nothing in section 24A concerning the effect of the state of repair of the premises on the interim rent, but in *Fawke* v. *Viscount Chelsea*,[56] it was held that regard must be had to the actual condition and state of the premises at the date for the commencement of the interim rent, and the state of repair or disrepair, will affect the interim rent. The landlord in that case was under a full repairing covenant, and the premises were in a very dilapidated state at the date of the hearing. Since the county court disregarded the state of repair of the premises, a remission was ordered. This particular principle was stated only to apply in cases of serious breaches of a landlord's repairing covenant.

New Tenancies Ordered by the Court

Regarding the incidence of liability for repairs under the new tenancy, if any, granted to the tenant, the first principle is that the matter is to be settled by agreement between the parties, and the incidence of liability for repairs and maintenance may be agreed to be the same as under the contractual lease, or it may be varied by agreement: in either case the result will be embodied in the new lease and it will be binding on both sides.

If the parties cannot agree on responsibility under the new tenancy for repairs, the county court will have to determine it under section 35 of the 1954 Act. This is in the discretion of the court, having regard to the terms of the current tenancy and to all relevant circumstances. It appears from *O'May* v. *City of London Real Property Co Ltd*[57] that the court must consider the question of repairs (if disputed) before dealing with the rent under the new tenancy as the rent will obviously be affected by the incidence of repairs. Moreover, as a result of the *O'May* case, if either party wishes to alter,

---

[56] (1979) 270 EG 855; [1979] 3 All ER 568, CA.
[57] (1982) 261 EG 1185; [1983] 2 AC 726, HL.

without the agreement of the other party, the terms of the current tenancy, with regard to repairs, maintenance, or service charges, or the payment of insurance premiums, he will have an uphill struggle. The onus will be on that party to persuade the court of the necessity of the proposed change. If the proposed change will be to the detriment of the other party, it seems that it cannot be forced on that party by the court if he does not agree to accept it, at least where it is not adequately compensated for. In the O'*May* case, the landlord of an office block wished to shift all repair and maintenance costs to the tenants, in the form of new service charges, for which under the contractual lease the tenants were not responsible, but they did not agree, and they were offered what was found to be inadequate compensation. Lord Wilberforce[58] pointed out that the tenants risked incurring an unpredictable and, in the case of a structural defect, a very great liability.

Rent Payable under New Tenancy

The court has power to determine under section 34 of the 1954 Act a rent increasing by fixed amounts at specified times, where the premises are, due to the landlord's breach of his covenant to repair, very seriously dilapidated. This includes a power to determine that the new rent is not to commence, or will be at a reduced rate, until the landlord carries out the repairs for which he is responsible.[59] The power to award a differential rent will only be exercised where there are very serious dilapidations at the commencement of the new tenancy.

If the premises are at the date of a tenant's application to the court, in disrepair, due to the tenant's own breach of covenant, the tenant cannot set up, in reduction of the rent to be determined for the new tenancy under section 34, any defects in the premises arising from his own breaches of covenant. The same rule applies where the "tenant" holds as sub-lessee.[60]

---

[58] *Ibid*, at pp. 1191 and 749.
[59] *Fawke* v. *Viscount Chelsea, supra*, CA.
[60] *Family Management* v. *Gray* (1979) 253 EG 369, CA.

VI. REPAIR NOTICES

A. *Procedure*

Local authorities have powers under Part VI of the *Housing Act* 1985 to compel repairs to unfit houses or houses seriously out of repair. These enable the local authority concerned to serve a repair notice on the person having control of the house. After a repair notice has been served, either the person in question carries out the work within a reasonable period, allowed in the notice itself, or he appeals against it. An appeal delays the operation of the notice unless confirmed by the county court and either the period for appealing to the Court of Appeal has expired or the notice is confirmed by the Court of Appeal (s 191(4)). If the person in control of the house, who is the person liable to do the repairs, fails to execute them, the authority may themselves enter the house, carry out the work and charge the person with their cost (1985 Act, ss 193 and 194).

Unfit Housing Provision

Section 189 of the 1985 Act deals with repair notices in the case of unfit housing. By section 189(1), where a local authority is satisfied that a house is unfit for human habitation[61] it must serve a repair notice on the person having control of the house (see below) unless it is satisfied that the house is not capable of being rendered fit at reasonable expense. The section 189 unfitness procedure is mandatory on local authorities, once the conditions precedent for its application exist.[62]

A repair notice must, on pain of invalidity, comply with the following formalities by section 189(2):

(a) it must require the person in control of the house, within such reasonable time, not less than 21 days, as may be specified in the notice, to execute the works specified in the notice;

(b) it must state that, in the opinion of the authority, the works will render the house fit for human habitation.

---

[61] As laid down by s 604 of the 1985 Act: this standard is the same as for the landlord's statute-implied duty to keep dwellings at a low rent fit for human habitation.
[62] *R v. Kerrier District Council ex p Guppys* (1976) 32 P & CR 411, CA.

A repair notice, by section 189(4), becomes operative, unless appealed against, on the expiration of 21 days from its date of service and is final and conclusive as to matters which could have been raised on an appeal though an invalidly served notice cannot be cured by this provision.

A copy of the notice may, additionally, be served on any other person having an interest in the house whether as freeholder, mortgagee, lessee or otherwise (s 189(3)).

Repair notices must be served on the person having control of the "house" concerned. "House" is defined by section 207 of the 1985 Act as including any "yard, garden, outhouses and appurtenances belonging to the house or usually enjoyed with it". Section 205 provides that "house" for the purposes of a repair notice includes part of a building used or suitable for use as a dwelling.

Where repair notices were served on a number of individual long leaseholders of a block of flats, requiring repairs to the roof and common parts, the notices were held invalid.[63] The roof and common parts did not form part of the demise to the leaseholders.

However, it was accepted in this case, that a repair notice may validly be served on an individual leaseholder, in respect of repairs to an individual flat demised to that leaseholder. The combined effect of the *Lambeth* decision and a further case[64] may be to make it impossible for a local authority to exercise control, under Part VI of the 1985 Act, over the repair of the external and common parts of a block of self contained flats. However, the Court of Appeal in the *Lambeth* case thought that this gap in the legislation was deliberate, Parliament being assumed to rely on the contractual position between the freeholder and long leaseholders.

Triggering of Repair Notice Procedure by Occupying Tenant

A local authority has a discretion, but it is not obliged to go through the repair notice procedure where, under section 190(1)(b) of the 1985 Act, it is satisfied, on a representation by an occupying tenant, that a house is in such a state of

---

[63] R v. *Lambeth Borough Council, ex parte Clayhope Properties Ltd* (1987) 283 EG 73, CA.

[64] *Pollway Nominees Ltd* v. *Croydon Borough Council* (1986) 280 EG 87, HL.

disrepair that, although it is not unfit for human habitation, its condition is such as to interfere materially with the personal comfort of the occupying tenant. This plugs a gap in the statutory nuisance procedure, outlined in Section VII below, which is only available to enable the curing of a state of affairs prejudicial to the health of occupiers.

Reasonable Standard Repairs

Under section 190(1)(a) of the 1985 Act, a local authority has a discretionary power to go through the repair notice procedure, where it is satisfied that a house is in such a state of disrepair that, although it is not unfit for human habitation, substantial repairs are required to bring it up to a reasonable standard, having regard to its age, character and locality.

In the case both of the above repair notices and those triggered by representations from an occupying tenant, the repairs specified cannot include works of internal decorative repair (s 190(2)) but otherwise the procedures, governed by section 190, are identical to those for section 189 in the case of unfitness.

B. *Specification of Repairs*

A repair notice served either under section 189 or 191 of the 1985 Act must require the person on whom it is served to execute the works "specified in the notice". In *Church of Our Lady of Hal* v. *Camden London Borough Council*,[65] it was held that a repair notice must, on pain of invalidity, contain sufficient information to enable the owner to have the work costed by a reasonably competent builder. If, however, a schedule to a repair notice lists a number of works and, for example, requires the thorough overhaul of the main roof, taking off and renewal of slipped slates and the making good of roof timbers "as necessary", the words "as necessary" are not inherently objectionable, since the owner is left to decide whether the particular works are necessary. As Oliver J said,[66] "Only in very rare cases where the content of the notice is so vague that the owner cannot know what the cost of repairs would be with regard to the major requirements

---

[65] (1980) 79 LGR 103, CA.
[66] *Ibid*, at pp. 109–110.

of the notice, should the court ... quash a notice without evidence."

C. *Meaning of "Person Having Control"*

The significance of the term "person having control" of a house, is that this person is the proper recipient of a repair notice. Section 207 of the *Housing Act* 1985 defines "person having control" as:

"[T]he person who receives the rack-rent of the premises (that is to say, a rent which is not less than two-thirds of the full net annual value of the premises) whether on his own account or as agent or trustee for another person, or who would so receive it if the house were let at a rack-rent."

This means the maximum amount of rent lawfully recoverable by the owner or landlord, as where the rent recoverable is rent-restricted for example, and is less than the full market rent.[67]

However, as a result of the interpretation put on "rack rent" in *Pollway Nominees Ltd* v. *Croydon London Borough Council*,[68] a severe limit has been placed on the power of a local authority to enforce repair notices, where the freeholder has granted long leases of a block of flats to individual tenants. It was held that, where a freeholder granted long leases of 99 years at ground rents, being responsible for repairs, but entitled to be paid service charges by the tenants, the freeholder was not the person having control of the house as he was not competent to receive the rack-rent. That person was the occupying tenant of each flat, as the flats were sub-let at rack rents. Therefore, since it was the tenants taken together who were the persons having control of the house, ie the block, the freehold reversioner could ignore a repair notice served on him, as was done in this case. Moreover, the fact that the time for an appeal had been allowed to expire, made no difference, as the notice had no statutory force or effect at all.

In other words, the freeholder is not a person having control

---

[67] *Rawlance* v. *Croydon Corporation* [1952] 2 QB 803; *Newman* v. *Dorrington Development Ltd* [1975] 1 WLR 1642.
[68] (1986) 280 EG 87; [1986] 3 WLR 277, HL.

of the house, to quote from Lord Bridge[69] "not only where [he] has let the entire premises under a single lease at less than a rack-rent, but equally where he has granted separate leases of all the separate units capable of occupation comprised within the building at rents which in the aggregate are less than the rack-rent of the building and thus retains only a reversionary interest which confers no right of occupation which he can either enjoy for himself or let to anyone else." Any possible inconvenience this narrow view might cause local authorities, was dismissed: "I imagine that normally the contractual rights of the owners of long leasehold interests in flats to enforce repairing obligations against their lessors will provide an adequate solution of the problem."

D. *Defence of Reasonable Expense*

Under section 189(1) of the 1985 Act, the local authority is not bound to serve a repair notice in relation to an unfit house, if satisfied that it is not capable of being rendered fit at reasonable expense, and the person having control of the house may also challenge a repair notice on this latter ground. The condition of reasonable expense is not expressly imposed by section 190 but it has been judicially read into the provision.[70]

Unfit Houses

Under section 206 of the 1985 Act, in determining whether premises can be rendered fit for human habitation, regard is to be had to the estimated cost of the works necessary to render them fit and to the estimated value of the house when the works are completed. Detailed items of expenditure need not necessarily be before the local authority.[71]

The courts adopt a realistic approach to the question of value, namely, the value of the house as a saleable asset in the owner's hands.[72] Accordingly, the principal value to be taken into account is the value of the house on the open market if sold with vacant possession when the repairs are completed,

---

[69] (1986) 280 EG 87 at p. 91.
[70] *Hillbank Properties Ltd* v. *London Borough of Hackney* (1978) 247 EG 807; [1978] All ER 343, CA.
[71] *Bacon* v. *Grimsby Corporation* [1949] 2 All ER 875, CA.
[72] *Phillips* v. *Newham London Borough Council* (1982) 43 P & CR 54, CA.

compared to its present value.[73] That being so, any other method of comparison between the house in and out of repair is not allowed, as where a local authority sought to adduce, without success, rental values from lettings for the remaining life of the house, as opposed to its market value on sale. Letting values were suggested because the repairs were agreed to cost almost as much as the value, when repaired, of the house on the open market.[74]

It would appear that, if there are sitting tenants, and there is evidence that the tenancies have no prospect of coming to an end in the near future, as where the tenants are protected by the *Rent Act* 1977, then the effect of the tenants' occupation on the market value of the house may be taken into account.[75]

Moreover, the county court, when hearing an appeal from a repair notice, may take any relevant factor into account such as the financial means of the owner, the repairs required and the increase in value of the premises which will result therefrom. Where, therefore, repairs would cost over £4,000 raising the value of the house by £1,250, these respective costs and values were held sufficient to enable the court to quash a repair notice.[76]

Conclusion

The effect of these principles is that, if there is a serious disparity between the cost of repairs and the open market value of the house, and sitting tenants with no prospect of their leaving will serve to increase this disparity, a repair notice may well be quashed, though there is no absolute rule.[7] If, due to rent restrictions, it is shown that the landlord will get no return on the capital he would otherwise have to borrow to pay for the cost of repairs under a repair notice, then it seems that the house will not be capable of being rendered

---

[73] *Hillbank Properties Ltd* v. *London Borough of Hackney* (1978) 247 EG 807, CA; v. *Ealing London Borough, ex parte Richardson* (1983) 265 EG 691, CA.

[74] *Inworth Property Co* v. *Southwark London Borough Council* (1977) 34 P & CR 18 CA.

[75] *Hillbank Properties Ltd* v. *London Borough of Hackney, supra; FFF Estates Ltd* v. *Hackney London Borough Council* [1980] 3 WLR 909, CA.

[76] *Phillips* v. *Newham London Borough Council, supra.*

[77] *Dudlow Estates Ltd* v. *Sefton Metropolitan Borough Council* (1978) 249 EG 1271.

fit at reasonable expense and any repair notice, if served, will
be quashed.[78]

E. *Houses in Disrepair but Not Unfit*

Where a repair notice requires a state of disrepair not
amounting to unfitness to be cured under section 190 of the
1985 Act, similar principles apply to the question of whether
the house can be brought up to a reasonable standard as
apply to unfitness (see the discussion above).

The aim of section 190 is, apparently, to deter a landlord
with a sitting tenant from allowing the house in question to
fall into a state of total unfitness so bad that it cannot be
saved under the section 189 procedure, leaving demolition
as the only remaining possibility. Where, therefore, very
extensive repairs were required, costing between £14,000 and
£15,000, to a residential building with a sitting tenant, which,
if carried out, would raise the value of the building by just
over half the cost of the repairs, a repair notice was not
quashed since the repairs, it was held, must be carried out,
to save the house from sinking into a totally unfit state, and
section 190 was designed to prevent that result; the figures
were not the sole relevant factor, and there was no evidence
of financial hardship to the owner.[79]

F. *Enforcement and Recovery of Expenses*

After the expiry of 21 days from the date of service on
the owner, the time for making an appeal to the county court
expires. Thereafter, assuming it is valid or if the repair notice,
on appeal, is confirmed with or without variation, then section
193 empowers the authority itself to do the work on expiry
of the time for completion of the work, normally the period
stated in the repair notice.[80] It may serve on the person having
control of the house and certain other owners (s 207) a notice
of intention to execute the work under section 194 and it
has, under sections 193(3) and Schedule 10 to the 1985 Act,
powers of entry to the house to execute the work and to
recover its expenses from the person on whom the notice

---

[78] *Ellis Copp & Co v. Richmond-upon-Thames London Borough* (1976) 245 EG 931.
[79] *Kenny v. Kingston-upon-Thames Royal London Borough Council* (1985) 274 EG 395;
[1985] 1 EGLR 26, CA.
[80] See *Elliott v. Brighton District Council* (1980) 258 EG 441, CA.

was served. Unrecovered expenses become a charge on the house, in priority to all other interests, enforceable by sale (1985 Act, Sched 10, para 7).

G. *Position if House Incapable of being Rendered Fit at Reasonable Expense*

If the house is not capable of being rendered fit at reasonable expense in the authority's view, it must, under section 264 of the *Housing Act* 1985, serve on the person having control of the house, on owners, and so far as practicable, on mortgagees, a notice. This must give a time, not less than 21 days after service of the notice, and place, at which the condition of the house, and any offer with respect to carrying out works, or the future user of the house will be considered by the local authority. It may accept an undertaking by an owner or mortgagee to carry out works to render the house fit, or that it will not be used for human habitation, or that it will not be so used until the authority is satisfied that it has been rendered fit. Any contravention of these undertakings is a criminal offence. If no undertaking is given or accepted, or the house is at any time used in contravention of an undertaking, then section 265 requires the authority, with some exceptions, notably in the case of a listed building, which must be the subject of a closing order, to make a demolition order or a closing order under section 266. If the authority considers the house to be capable of providing temporary accommodation, it may elect to purchase it (s 300).

VII. OUTLINE OF STATUTORY NUISANCE CONTROL

Section 92 of the *Public Health Act* 1936 enables a local authority to serve a nuisance abatement order on the person responsible for the nuisance, or, if such person cannot be found, on the owner or occupier of the premises concerned. The notice will require the person in question to abate the nuisance. It is a condition precedent to the service of an abatement order that the premises must be in a state prejudicial to health, or a nuisance.

The 1936 Act procedure is limited to the control of nuisances in the common law sense, and cannot be resorted to unless there is a state of affairs which is prejudicial to the health of some person, such as an occupying tenant. In *NCB v. Thorne*[81] it was ruled that nuisance in the 1936 Act procedure meant the same thing as a public or private nuisance at common law, and no statutory nuisance existed if the *only* person affected was the occupier of the premises in question. If the whole of a building is occupied by a tenant, the nuisance procedure will not apply; if he occupies part only the view has been expressed that it will.[82]

If the person on whom an abatement notice is served, fails to comply with it, or if the nuisance is likely to recur, under section 94 of the 1936 Act the authority may apply to a magistrates' court for a nuisance order, ie an order to comply with the abatement notice. After issue of a nuisance order, the penalty for knowing contravention or for failing without reasonable excuse to comply with it, is a fine of £400 and a further fine of £50 for each day on which the offence continues after conviction.[83]

The discretion of the magistrates to make a nuisance order is very wide, so that in one case an order requiring a landlord to effect improvements, not just repairs, was upheld.[84] If the reason for the damage is the fault of the tenant or occupier (eg his use or misuse of something on the premises), then his landlord cannot have a nuisance order made against him.[85] Mere proof that the owner obtained vacant possession of the injurious premises is not a sufficient compliance with a nuisance order.[86]

In the case of a block of flats, if the condition of individual flats is prejudicial to the health of an individual flat tenants but no more, a nuisance order cannot be made against the owner in respect of the whole block. If the state of the block as a whole, as designed, is prejudicial to the health of all the tenants, a comprehensive nuisance order might have to be made.[87]

---

[81] [1976] 1 WLR 543.
[82] Yates & Hawkins, p. 262.
[83] *Public Health Act* 1936 s 95.
[84] *Birmingham District Council* v. *Kelly* (1985) 17 HLR 573.
[85] *Dover District Council* v. *Farrar* (1982) 2 HLR 32.
[86] *Lambeth London Borough* v. *Stubbs* (1980) 78 LGR 650, CA.
[87] *Birmingham City Council* v. *McMahon* (1987) *Times* 25 June.

Chapter 12
PARTY WALLS AND DANGEROUS STRUCTURES[1]

I. INTRODUCTION

This Chapter deals with the rights and liabilities of owners of party walls and briefly with the control by local authorities of dangerous and neglected structures.

In the case both of party walls and dangerous structures, there is a set of rules which applies to Inner London and another set of rules which affect the rest of England and Wales. These are, therefore, considered separately.

The rules which apply in Inner London to party walls are regulated by the *London Building Acts* 1930–1982, of which the principal Act, for present purposes, is the *London Building Acts (Amendment) Act* 1939. Power exists under the *Building Act* 1984 Sched 3 Part I[2] to modify or repeal the 1939 Act by regulations. To an extent, this power has been exercised, so as to bring Inner London building regulations into conformity with those applicable to the rest of England and Wales.[3] All references in this Chapter to the 1939 Act are to it as amended by these regulations.

Party walls outside Inner London are regulated by the common law as modified by section 38 of the *Law of Property Act* 1925 in particular.

Dangerous and neglected structures in Inner London are subject to Part VII of the *London Building Acts (Amendment) Act* 1939. Dangerous and neglected structures outside Inner London are governed by sections 77–79 of the *Building Act* 1984.

---

[1] See generally Aldridge, *Boundaries, Walls and Fences,* 6th Edn 1986; Powell-Smith, *Boundaries and Fences,* 2nd Ed 1975; Anstey, *Trouble with the Neighbours,* 1983.
[2] Paras 3,4.
[3] Building (Inner London) Regulations 1985 SI 1985/1936, in force on 6 January 1986 and Building (Inner London) Regulations 1987 SI 1987/798, in force on 1 July 1987.

A. *Definition of Party Wall*

A party wall is commonly thought of as a wall dividing or separating two adjoining buildings, but it may also be a wall separating open yards. Party walls have been defined as:

"Walls which are divided down the long axis on a plan into two strips, each strip belonging to the owner of the land on which it stands."[4]

At common law, a party wall is a generic term comprising four different categories, which are derived from *Watson* v. *Gray*.[5] These are:

1. A wall of which the two adjoining owners are tenants in common.

2. A wall divided vertically into two portions, one portion belonging to each adjoining owner.

3. A wall belonging entirely to one of the adjoining owners, but subject to an easement in the other owner to have it maintained as a dividing wall.

4. A wall divided longitudinally into two halves, each half being subject to cross easements in favour of the owner of the other half.

B. *Special Types of Party Wall*

First Type of Party Wall

The first type of party wall listed above is obsolete. That type of party wall was, after 1 January 1926, deemed to be a party wall of the fourth type listed above.[6] This provision was essential owing to the abolition by the 1925 Act of legal tenancies in common. The result is that the owner of each part of the party wall (which is treated as severed vertically) is given the same rights of support and user as are conferred on owners of a type four party wall.

Second Type of Party Wall

Walls of the second type within *Watson* v. *Gray* are rare and no details as to the rights of each owner are given. In

---

[4] Powell-Smith, p. 143.
[5] (1880) 14 Ch D 192.
[6] *Law of Property Act* 1925 Sched 1 Part V, para 1.

outline, the rights of support and user will depend on express agreement. If one owner has rights of support then, as with any right of support, demolition without provision of support for the relevant half of the party wall will constitute an actionable interference with the adjoining owner's right of support—and give a cause of action in nuisance for withdrawal of support, as discussed in section II of this Chapter.

It should be noted here, though these principles are of general application, that if a right of support for the portion of the party wall exists then it is no defence to the demolishing owner that the wall was very old and unstable: he must at least provide support for the portion in question.[7] Moreover, if a right of support exists then the demolishing owner cannot avoid liability to his neighbour by employing an independent contractor.[8]

On the other hand, if there is no right of support for the portion in question, the adjoining owner is entitled to demolish his portion without any prior notice to the other and without having to shore up the other's portion of the wall.[9] This situation would be unusual. Even where no rights of support and user exist in relation to the portion of the party wall, the demolishing owner must do the work in a proper and careful manner and he will be liable in negligence to the other if he fails to do so, but he is not bound to do more than that—such as by shoring up the adjoining wall.[10]

Third Type of Party Wall

In the absence of express or prescriptive rights of support in favour of the owner of the adjoining land, he has no right by implication of law to force a wall-owner of the third type of party wall to repair or maintain it. So, if the wall-owner wishes to demolish it, he may do so if he pleases.[11] This has no application if the wall is subject to a right of support and user in favour of the owner of the land adjoining it;

---

[7] *Hoare v. McAlpine* [1923] 1 Ch 167.
[8] *Bower v. Peate* (1876) 1 QBD 321.
[9] *Chadwick v. Trower* (1939) 6 Bing NC 1.
[10] *Southwark and Vauxhall Water Co v. Wandsworth District Board of Works* [1898] 2 Ch 603.
[11] *Wiltshire v. Sidford* (1827) 1 Man & Ry 404.

but even then the owner of the wall may deal with it as he likes provided he maintains it as a party wall. These principles are dealt with later in relation to party walls within category four in *Watson* v. *Gray*. It goes without saying that if the owner of the adjoining land puts up a building against the wall in question, he will in due course acquire an easement of support and user through long uninterrupted user (for example, for 20 or 40 years under the *Prescription Act* 1832).

Fourth Type of Party Wall

This as was seen, is a party wall divided longitudinally into two halves, each half being subject to cross easements in favour of the owner of the other half. This type of party wall is the commonest type. The rules about to be discussed apply to these, but they have no application to Inner London.

II. PARTY WALLS SUBJECT TO RECIPROCAL CROSS EASEMENTS NOT SITUATED IN INNER LONDON

A. *Law of Property Act 1925*

The general effect of section 38 and Schedule I Part I of the *Law of Property Act* 1925 is to convert party walls of the first type listed above into party walls of the fourth type.

Section 38 applies to dispositions after 1 January 1926 and provides as follows:

"(1) Where under a disposition ... which, if a holding in undivided shares had been permissible, would have created a tenancy in common, a wall or other structure is or is expressed to be made a party wall or structure, that structure shall be and remain severed vertically as between the respective owners, and the owner of each part shall have such rights to support and user over the rest of the structure as may be requisite for conferring rights corresponding to those which would have subsisted if a valid tenancy in common had been created."

Under section 38(2) any person interested has the right to apply to the court for an order declaring the rights and interests under section 38 of persons interested in any party structure and the court may make such order as it thinks fit.

In relation to party walls or other party structures created before 1 January 1926, the 1925 Act[12] provides that:

"... the ownership [of the party wall or structure] shall be deemed to be severed vertically as between the respective owners, and the owner of each part shall have such rights of support and of user over the rest of the structure as may be requisite for conferring rights to those corresponding to those subsisting at the commencement of this Act."[13]

What these provisions amount to, apart from converting category one party walls into category four party walls, is that any rights of support and user as between the adjoining owners are preserved as though legal tenancies in common had not been abolished; but they do not provide what these rights are and for that, one has to make reference to the appropriate parts of the general law of easements, some of them ante-dating the 1925 legislation.

B. *General Rights of Support and User for Vertically Severed Party Walls*

While section 38 (and where appropriate Schedule I Part V) of the 1925 Act allows for rights of support and user in favour of each adjoining owner of a party wall, each owner of the vertically severed part of the wall is absolute owner of that part.

However, assuming for the moment that a right of support exists in favour of each adjoining owner over the other's part of the wall, each owner, being absolute owner of his part, may place any amount of weight on his part of the wall provided its stability is not endangered.[14]

The common law governs the general nature of the rights of support and user of each owner over the other's part of the party wall. The law implies the grant and reservation in favour of each owner such easements as may be necessary to carry out the common intention of the parties as to the user of the wall—the nature of the easements will vary with the circumstances of the case.[15] Neither owner may so deal

---

[12] Sched 1 Part V, para 1.
[13] The court has the same power to make orders on the application of any person interested as under s 38(2), by *Law of Property Act* 1925, Sched I Part V para 3.
[14] *Sheffield Improved Industrial and Provident Society* v. *Jarvis* [1871] WN 208.
[15] *Jones* v. *Pritchard* [1908] 1 Ch 630.

with his part of the party wall as to render the easements
implied in favour of the adjoining owner, either incapable
of being enjoyed, or more difficult to enjoy. If, for example,
a flue runs through the party wall, then the flue must not
be stopped by the adjoining owner. An owner is not entitled
to demolish the whole party wall, but he may demolish his
vertically severed part and rebuild it to a greater height, but
in so doing he must provide adequate support for the other
half of the wall. If he fails to do so, he will be liable in damages
to the adjoining owner, subject to the fact that for an action
in nuisance for withdrawal of support to succeed, actual
damage must always be proved.[16] It makes no difference to liability that the actual demolition is carried out by
a local authority under statutory powers.[17] Because each
owner of a party wall is absolute owner of his part, he is
entitled to recover from a third party for damage caused to
his half of the wall only.[18]

C. *No Implied Duty to Repair Party Walls*

No Implied Duty to Execute Repairs

If the owner of a party wall is under express covenant with
the adjoining owner to repair it, then he will be bound to
execute any necessary repairs—as also where any local custom
applies.

Apart from these instances, the owner of a party wall is
not bound to execute any repairs necessary to ensure the
enjoyment by the adjoining owner of his implied easements
of support and user.[19] Therefore, if, as in *Sack* v. *Jones*,[20]
it is alleged that owing to a want of repair, the neighbouring
owner's premises are subsiding, dragging over the party wall
there will be no cause of action at that stage in the absence
of express covenant to repair by the neighbour. If, however
the neighbour demolished his house, leaving the party wall
unprotected, different considerations would arise, as to which
see the next following part of this section.

[16] *Sack* v. *Jones* [1925] Ch 235.
[17] *Bond* v. *Nottingham Corporation* [1939] 2 All ER 610.
[18] *Apostal* v. *Simons* [1936] 1 All ER 207.
[19] *Jones* v. *Pritchard* [1908] 1 Ch 630.
[20] [1925] Ch 235.

Rights of Entry

As part of the implied grant of the reciprocal easements over a party wall, each adjoining owner may enter the premises of the other and there execute repairs on that other's half of the party wall so far as necessary for the enjoyment of any of the implied easements.[21]

Neglect causing Demolition of Adjoining Premises

Where negligence or nuisance, by withdrawal of support by the adjoining owner, is proved against him, he will be liable for the consequences, as where his neglect is so bad that his premises are demolished, causing interference to the implied rights of support and user of the party wall. In *Bradburn* v. *Lindsay*,[22] a wall between two houses was a party wall to which section 38 of the 1925 Act applied. So badly had the defendant neglected her house that it was demolished by the local authority under a demolition order. The party wall between the two houses was then left unsupported. The plaintiff succeeded in nuisance and negligence on the ground that the damage to his house (dry rot penetration) was caused by the exposure of the party wall. It was held that the defendant ought to have appreciated the danger caused by the fact that her premises were so badly out of repair and owed the plaintiff a duty to take reasonable steps to deal with that danger. The damage was required to be made good by suitable supports for the party wall and the curing of the dry rot. The fact that the plaintiff had a right of entry to repair made no difference to the result.

D. *Withdrawal of Support and Repairs: Further Considerations*

1. Party walls to which section 38 of the 1925 Act applies, that is, almost all party walls, enjoy rights of support. But, if no implied express or prescriptive right of support exists then the neighbouring owner has the right with total impunity to demolish his property.[23]

---

[21] *Jones* v. *Pritchard, supra; Sack* v. *Jones, supra.*
[22] [1983] 2 All ER 408.
[23] *Smith* v. *Thackerah* (1866) LR 1 CP 564.

2. Where a right of support for a party wall exists, threatened and imminent withdrawal of support can be stopped by injunction: no action can, however, be maintained until actual damage is occasioned.[24] If the wall falls down due to want of repair, not withdrawal of support, only if the defendant could reasonably have foreseen damage being occasioned to the plaintiff's premises due to the collapse will he be liable to the plaintiff—he must be shown to be at fault. Where no fault is shown, the injured party has a right to enter the premises of the adjoining owner to execute repairs, but he will have to foot the bill and has no right of contribution from the adjoining owner.[25] One possible way round this is to take a covenant of mutual contribution and indemnity from each adjoining owner (say when a new estate is being put up) and to try to enforce it, against the original owners and their successors in title, under the principle of mutual benefit and burden.[26] It is no good merely to take a covenant to contribute to the cost of party wall repairs by an adjoining freehold owner, as the burden of a positive covenant, will not run with his land, and will only bind the adjoining owner and his estate after his death, not his successors in title.[27]

3. As between landlord and tenant, the tenant to a long lease at all events would normally be expected to covenant expressly to contribute to the cost of maintaining party walls.[28]

4. If a tenant occupies the whole of a building, the rights of support for party walls conferred by section 38 of the Law of Property Act 1925, where applicable, will pass to him automatically under section 62 of that Act, provided the lease is by deed, rather than in writing or oral. If the landlord occupies adjoining premises he is, however, under no implied duty to keep a party wall between his and the tenant's premises in repair.[29]

[24] *Smith* v. *Giddy* [1904] 2 KB 448 (overhanging trees).
[25] Nance (1950) 14 Conv NS 380.
[26] *Halsall* v. *Brizell* [1957] Ch 169 (maintenance contributions from purchasers of plots and their successors in relation to private roads held enforceable against original owners and successors in title).
[27] *Austerberry* v. *Oldham Corporation* (1885) 29 Ch D 750, CA.
[28] For a precedent see *Precedents for the Conveyancer* (Sweet & Maxwell) 5–3 p. 2513.
[29] *Colebeck* v. *Girdlers Co* (1876) 1 QBD 234.

5. On the question of withdrawal of support from a party wall between two adjoining properties there are significant cases. The first is *Upjohn* v. *Seymour Estates Ltd.*[30] Two houses were separated by a party wall and the defendants demolished their house and put up shores against the party wall; due to this disturbance the defendant's half of the party wall fell down, exposing two apertures into the plaintiffs' adjoining shop. These apertures then admitted dust and debris, damaging their stock, and they recovered damages for withdrawal of support from their half of the wall. Goddard J held that the right of support included a right of user over the defendant's half of the wall, which until its demolition had protected the apertures. However, in *Phipps* v. *Pears*[31] the Court of Appeal reached a result at first sight inconsistent with these principles. They decided that the owner of a house who demolished it was not impliedly bound under section 62 of the *Law of Property Act* 1925 to weatherproof the exposed, unrendered, flank wall of the adjoining house. In that case there was no party wall between the houses and their walls were not even bonded together. Lord Denning MR claimed without any qualification that "every man is entitled to pull down his house if he likes. If it exposes your house to the weather, that is your misfortune."

However, the principle in *Phipps* v. *Pears* may well not apply to party walls. It was distinguished for that very reason in *Bradburn* v. *Lindsay*.[32] Moreover, in *Brace* v. *South East London Regional Housing Association Ltd*,[33] it was held that if a right of support for a party wall is interfered with by a building owner he will be liable in nuisance (or negligence if proved: it was not in that case) for any resulting damage to the injured party. The owners of an end of terrace house (No 20), next to the plaintiff's house (No 19), demolished No 20, the houses being divided by a party wall. The demolition was carried out under an agreement which supposedly provided strengthening, repairing and underpinning to the plaintiff's wall but in fact, due to drying out of the clay soil after

---

[30] [1938] 1 All ER 614.
[31] [1965] 1 QB 76, CA.
[32] [1983] 2 All ER 408 at p. 414. See above.
[33] (1984) 270 EG 1286, CA.

the demolition of No 20, No 19 subsided and the plaintiff recovered damages. *Phipps* v. *Pears* was distinguished on the grounds first that there was no right of support against the adjoining house in that case; secondly, on the ground that all it did was to reject the existence of an independent right of weatherproofing from mere proximity to the defendant's premises.

In short, if there is an established right of support for a party wall, and actual or imminent withdrawal of support takes place, an action may be taken in nuisance, and *Phipps* v. *Pears* has no relevance to the issue.

6. As to the position where there are party walls between flats and maisonettes, the first question is the nature of the tenure. If it is leasehold, then mutual rights of support will be presumably inserted expressly into all the leases, and these will be enforceable between the different lessees, on ordinary principles of enforcement of leasehold covenants, since positive covenants run with leasehold land. In the case of freehold flats and maisonettes, the position is more obscure. It has been argued that *Phipps* v. *Pears* (if applied in this area) will render it impossible to enforce mutual rights of support and user as between different flat or maisonette owners.[34] The best thing is to avoid conveyances of freehold flats and maisonettes, and to grant long leases of the premises, in which case the rules just mentioned will apply. The next best thing is to hope that, under the doctrine of mutual benefit and burden, rights of mutual support and user between different flat or maisonette owners will be enforceable.[35] This latter suggestion might be a dangerous plank to rely on, in view of doubts about its scope.

III. REGULATION OF RIGHTS OF PARTY WALL OWNERS IN INNER LONDON

A. *Application of Special Rules*

The owners of party walls in Inner London are subject to special rules, which for present purposes are in Part VI of

---

[34] Powell-Smith *loc cit* pp. 154–155.
[35] Under *Halsall* v. *Brizell* [1957] Ch 169.

the *London Building Acts (Amendment) Act* 1939.[36] The parts of London to which the special rules apply are:[37] the City of London, and the Boroughs of Westminster, Paddington and St Marylebone, Hampstead, Holborn and St Pancras, Finsbury and Islington, Hackney, Shoreditch and Stoke Newington, Bethnal Green, Poplar and Stepney, Greenwich, Woolwich, Deptford and Lewisham, Bermondsey, Camberwell and Southwark, Lambeth, Wandsworth, Battersea, Fulham and Hammersmith and Chelsea and Kensington.

Special Definitions in 1939 Act

There are special definitions for the purposes of party walls in Inner London.

For the purposes of Part VI of the 1939 Act, "party wall" is defined by section 44 as:

"(i) a wall which forms part of a building and stands on lands of different owners to a greater extent than the projection of any artificially formed support on which the wall rests; and

(ii) so much of a wall not being a wall referred to in the foregoing paragraph (i) as separates buildings belonging to different owners."

The rules in Part VI of the 1939 Act apply also to party fence walls and party structures and these are defined in section 4 as follows:

"Party fence wall" means "a wall (not being part of a building) which stands on lands of different owners and is used or constructed to be used for separating such adjoining lands but does not include a wall constructed on the land of one owner the artificially formed support of which projects into the land of another owner."

"Party structure" means "a party wall and also a floor partition or other structure separating buildings or parts of buildings approached solely by separate staircases or separate entrances from without."

---

[36] As amended by Building (Inner London) Regulations 1985 SI 1985/1936 from 6 January 1986 as amended SI 1987/798 from 1 July 1987. The text given of the 1939 Act Part VI, is as amended by the 1985 regulations.
[37] *London Government Act* 1963, s 1 and Sched 1.

Effect of Part VI

1. It is vital to note that the rules in Part VI of the 1939 Act, by section 54, do not authorise any interference with any easement of light or other easement in or relating to a party wall, nor do they prejudicially affect the right of any person to preserve any right in, or in connection with, a party wall which is demolished or rebuilt and to take any necessary steps for that purpose.[38] An award may, therefore, be signed by surveyors under Part VI and it will have no effect on these rights.

2. The rules in Part VI of the 1939 Act do not affect the legal title to a party wall or party structure. They limit the building rights of owners for the general benefit of the public.[39] So whether a wall is a party wall or not depends on its user as such and it may be a party wall for part of its height and above that simply an external wall—that latter part being wholly the property of the relevant owner.[40]

Definitions of Owner and Building Owner

The terms "owner" and "building owner" are employed throughout Part VI and are defined as follows by section 5 of the *London Building Act* 1930. "Owner" includes every person in receipt of the whole or part of rents or profits from the land, but not a tenant from year to year or for any less term or at will. "Building owner" means such one of the owners of adjoining land as is desirous of building; or such one of the owners of buildings, storeys or rooms separated from one another by a party wall or party structure as does or is desirous of doing work affecting that party wall or party structure.

Therefore, a tenant in possession of part of a house under a lease for a greater term than as tenant from year to year is an "owner" within Part VI of the 1939 Act and so is entitled to receive service of a copy of any statutory notices.[41] Likewise, a long leaseholder who has sub-let the land but receives

[38] See *Frederick Betts Ltd* v. *Pickfords Ltd* [1906] 2 Ch 87.
[39] *Knight* v. *Pursell* (1879) 11 Ch D 412.
[40] *London, Gloucestershire and North Hants Dairy Co* v. *Morley and Lanceley* [1911] 2 KB 257.
[41] *Fillingham* v. *Wood* [1891] 1 Ch 51.

rents: he is entitled to service of notices and bound to contribute costs to the building owner.[42]

The building owner, his servants, agents and workmen are given by section 53 of the 1939 Act a wide power of entry to premises to execute work under Part VI.[43]

The main impact of the 1939 Act rules is on existing party structures.

B. *Existing Party Structures*

Introduction and Scope of Rights of Building Owner

Under section 46 of the 1939 Act, a building owner has a statutory right to interfere with the proprietary rights of the adjoining owner without his consent. The building owner might wish to resort to his rights under section 46, for example, by rectifying defects, want of repair, renewal before repair becomes necessary, or rebuilding with more durable materials.

Section 46 is limited in scope. It was held in *Gyle-Thompson* v. *Wall Street (Properties) Ltd*,[44] that it does not confer on a building owner the right to demolish a party fence wall and rebuild it to a reduced height. The right of the building owner to "demolish and rebuild" in section 46 is limited to a right to reconstruct the wall to the same height. Were it otherwise, it was held, section 46 would have given the building owner the right to expropriate his neighbour's property.

Notice Procedures

None of the rights (listed below) given to a building owner by section 46 are exercisable at all until he has complied fully with the notice procedure laid down in section 47.[45]

Party Structure Notice

By section 47(1) the building owner must serve on the adjoining owner a party structure notice, stating the nature and particulars of the proposed work, and the time at which it will be begun. If the building owner proposes to construct

---

[42] *Hunt* v. *Harris* (1859) 19 CB NS 13.
[43] If accompanied by a police officer then, subject to certain conditions force may be used to break into the premises for the purpose: s 53(2) and (3).
[44] [1974] 1 All ER 295.
[45] By section 121 all notices must be in writing and for method of service see section 124 (pre-paid post). Forms of notice are published by RIBA, 66 Portland Place, London.

special foundations his particulars must include plans sections and details of the construction of these with reasonable particulars of the loads to be carried. "Special foundations" mean, by section 44, foundations in which an assemblage of steel beams or rods is employed for the purpose of distributing any load.

By section 47(2), service of a party structure notice must be as follows:

(a) in respect of a party fence wall or special foundations, at least one month before the date stated as that on which the work is to begin;

(b) for a party structure, at least two months as above.

Unless, within six months after service of a party structure notice, the work to which it relates is begun and prosecuted with due diligence, by section 47(3), the notice ceases to have effect.

Counter-Notice

Section 48 gives the adjoining owner the right to serve a counter-notice, in writing, on the building owner: this notice must generally be within one month of the service of the party structure notice (s 48(3)). With special foundations, however, the period is 21 days. Under section 48(2), the counter-notice may require the building owner to build, in or on the party fence wall or party structure, such chimney copings, breasts, jambs or flues or such piers, recesses or other like works, as may reasonably be required for the convenience of the adjoining owner, and may also require better special foundations. The importance of a counter-notice is that section 48(4) obliges the building owner to comply with it, unless the execution of the works would be injurious to him or would cause unnecessary inconvenience or unnecessary delay.

If there is more than one adjoining owner, all of them are entitled to receive a notice under section 47.[46]

If, within 14 days of service of a party structure notice or counter-notice on him, an owner fails to express his written consent to it, by section 49, a difference is automatically deemed to exist between the parties. Silence equals dissent.

[46] *Crosby v. Alhambra Co Ltd* [1907] 1 Ch 295.

An actual or deemed difference triggers the section 55 procedure for the settlement of the dispute by surveyors.

All these notice procedures must be diligently complied with—see later.

When Local Authority Consent is Required

Certain types of work require the consent of the local authority of the borough in which the party fence wall or structure is situated before they can be executed. First, consent is required for openings in a party wall (s 4). Secondly, under section 21, consent is required for openings made in any party wall separating divisions of a building of the warehouse class, or a building used for trade or manufacture and, where such divisions or buildings, if taken together, would extend to more than 7,100 cubic metres. There are certain exceptions to this rule—in particular, consent is not required if the width of any opening in the wall is not over half the length of the wall. There are penalties for non-compliance with these provisions.

Rights of Building Owner under section 46

These are as follows:

(a) A right to make good underpin thicken or repair or demolish and rebuild a party structure or party fence wall where the work is necessary on account of a defect or want of repair;

(b) A right to demolish a timber or other partition separating buildings belonging to different owners which does not conform to the *London Building Acts or the Building Regulations* 1985 and to rebuild them to conform thereto;

(c) A right, in relation to a building with rooms or storeys belonging to different owners intermixed, to demolish such of the rooms or storeys or any part thereof which do not conform to the *London Building Acts or the Building Regulations* 1985 and to rebuild them to conform thereto;

(d) A right where buildings are connected by arches or structures over public ways or over passages belonging to other persons, to demolish such of the buildings arches or structures as do not conform to the *Acts or Regulations* in (b) and (c) above, and to rebuild them as above;

(e) A right to underpin, thicken or raise any party structure or party fence wall permitted by the 1939 Act to be underpinned, thickened or raised or any external wall built against such a party structure or party fence wall subject to:

(i) making good all damage to the adjoining premises, including internal finishings and decorations;

(ii) carrying up all flues and chimney stacks belonging to the adjoining owner on or against the party structure or external wall, up to an agreed height and with agreed materials: disputes are to be resolved by section 55 arbitrations.

(f) A right to demolish a party structure of insufficient strength or height for the purposes of any intended building of the building owner and to rebuild it of sufficient strength or height for these purposes, subject to identical conditions as in (e) above;

(g) A right to cut into a party structure—subject to identical conditions as apply to paragraph (e)(i) above;

(h) A right to cut away any footing or any projecting chimney breast, jamb or flue or other projection on or over the land of the building owner from a party wall, party fence wall, external wall, or boundary wall, in order to erect, raise, or underpin an external wall against such wall, or for any other purpose, subject to making good all damage to the adjoining premises, or to its internal finishings and decorations;

(i) A right to cut away or demolish such parts of any wall or building of an adjoining owner overhanging the land of the building owner, as may be necessary to enable a vertical wall to be erected against that wall or building, subject to making good all damage to the wall or building, or to the internal finishings and decorations of the adjoining premises;

(j) A right to execute any other necessary works incidental to the connection of a party structure with the premises adjoining it;

(k) A right to raise a party fence wall and use as a party wall, a party fence wall, or to demolish a party fence wall and rebuild it as a party fence wall, or a party wall.

As to the notice procedures which must be followed by the building owner before he is entitled to exercise any of these rights, see above.

Execution of Works

Section 51(1) requires a building owner in executing any works to do so in such a matter and time as not to cause unnecessary inconvenience to the adjoining owner or occupier. Moreover, under section 51(2), where a building owner lays open any part of the adjoining land or building he must take all necessary steps (by erecting hoardings and so on) to protect the adjoining land or building and the security of the adjoining occupier.

The 1939 Act rights are exercisable without prejudice to any right of the adjoining owner to make a claim in negligence, because it does not authorise negligence.

Expenses of Works

These are dealt with by section 56 of the 1939 Act. As a rule, all expenses are defrayed by each owner in proportion. The building owner has a right of contribution from the adjoining owner for any repairs carried out for the mutual benefit of himself and the adjoining owner; but the building owner bears the whole cost of any works carried out for his sole benefit.[47]

C. *New Party Structures*

Where the building owner wishes to build a new party wall on the boundary between the two properties and there is none in existence—not a very likely situation in Inner London—then section 45 of the 1939 Act applies.

Written notice is required from the building owner to the adjoining owner, describing the intended wall. If the written consent of the adjoining owner is given, the wall will be built half on the land of each owner—or in such other position as may be agreed. Expenses of building are shared out between the owners, in proportion to the use made by each of them of the wall.

If the adjoining owner does not consent, the wall must be built by the building owner at his expense, wholly on his own land. He may at any time, between one and six months

---

[47] Sections 57–59 deal with security for expenses, accounts and recovery of adjoining owner's contributions.

from service of his notice, place projecting footings and foundations on the land of the adjoining owner, below the level of the land, paying appropriate compensation to the adjoining owner. At least one month's notice, and not less than six months' notice, of intention be given (s 45(1)(c)). If the building owner wishes to place special foundations on the adjoining owner's land, written consent is required (s 45(3)). Section 45 does not authorise the obstruction of ancient lights.[48] Any disputes between the owners are to be dealt with under the section 55 procedures.

D. *Resolution of Disputes*

Section 49 presumes a difference to exist between the parties if, after a party structure notice (s 47), or counter-notice (s 48), has been served, the recipient does not consent to the proposal within 14 days of receipt. The difference must be settled under section 55, by surveyors.

The parties may concur in the appointment of one surveyor—the agreed surveyor. Or each party must appoint one surveyor and they must select a third surveyor (s 55(a)).

Until a dispute exists, or is deemed to exist, no surveyors may be appointed, and a separate appointment is required for each dispute. A letter of appointment suffices for section 55 purposes—all appointments having to be in writing, by section 55(h).

If an agreed surveyor refuses for ten days after a written request from either party to act, or before the difference is settled he dies, or becomes incapable of acting, all proceedings to settle the dispute must begin anew and a new surveyor must be appointed (s 55(b)). If either party refuses to appoint a surveyor, or for ten days after a written request from the other party neglects to do so then the other may make the appointment (s 55(c)). Once a surveyor is appointed under the Act, his appointment is not terminable by the party who appointed him. The reason is this: once appointed, surveyors must decide everything that is to be done to the party wall and settle it in their award. If a party could discharge his surveyor early, he could prevent any award being made.[49]

---

[48] *Crofts* v. *Haldane* (1867) LR 2 QB 194.
[49] Anstey, p. 14.

Under section 55(e), if a surveyor refuses to act or for ten days after a written request from either party neglects to act, the surveyor of the other may proceed *ex parte*. In other words, he is then able to draft and make an award by himself.[50]

Usually, the two agreed surveyors will make their award under section 55(i). Failing this, under section 55(j), the third surveyor is bound to make the award within 14 days of being called upon to do so—and may award by signing one of the two agreed surveyors' awards.[51] The award itself will make provision for payment of costs of the award by either or both parties (s 50(l)). The award is conclusive (s 50(m)).

Either party has the right within 14 days of delivery of the award to appeal to the county court under section 50(n)[52] and the county court has wide powers to rescind or modify the award. In certain circumstances, the appellant may bring a High Court action and obtain a stay of any county court proceedings.

A surveyor's award is the result of an arbitration: the High Court has power to set it aside or remit it—for example, where there is misconduct or excess of jurisdiction.[53] The award is of vital significance, for only once it is made, may the work begin.

Challenges to Awards

It was held in *Burlington Property Co v. Odeon Cinemas Ltd*,[54] that surveyors, in making an award, have no power to interfere with existing property rights in the party wall of an adjoining owner. If the award does this, it may be challenged outside the statutory time limits for an appeal.

Moreover, since the rights of a building owner under section 46 of the 1939 Act are limited to demolishing and rebuilding a party wall to the same rather than a reduced height, no

---

[50] For the position where either surveyor refuses or neglects to make an appointment of the third surveyor see s 55(f) (local authority to appoint); if the third surveyor refuses or neglects to act or dies or becomes incapable before the making of the award he is to be replaced: section 55(g).

[51] Anstey, p. 15.

[52] Ie from the date when an owner takes up an award after notification of it by letter: *Riley Gowler Ltd* v. *National Heart Hospital Ltd* [1969] 3 All ER 1401, CA.

[53] *Re Stone and Hastie's Arbitration* [1903] 2 KB 463, CA.

[54] [1938] 3 All ER 469, CA.

award may validly be made which purports to allow the reduction in height of a party wall.[55]

Where two of the three surveyors, in a dispute arising out of a building owner's plan to reduce the height of a party wall by some nine feet, signed an award allowing for this the award was held invalid.[56] That being so, the aggrieved owner could—and did—challenge the award in the High Court, despite the wording of section 55(m) and (n). An interim injunction was granted to restrain the demolition or reduction of the party wall.

An aggrieved owner may, accordingly, challenge an award which is, or may be, invalid for want or excess of jurisdiction, outside the 14 day period for appeals to the county court.

Scope of Awards

It would seem that, in unusual circumstances, an award may impose a continuing obligation on a building owner to keep a party wall proof against the weather—though more usually this will be done, according to *Marchant* v. *Capital and Counties plc*,[57] by the award prescribing stated works. In this case, an owner was held bound to weatherproof a wall which had, until the execution of works, been an internal party wall, but which, as a result of the works, had been exposed and faced outwards. At first sight this case conflicts with *Phipps* v. *Pears*,[58] but that case has no bearing on party wall awards under section 55. What no award is able to do, it was held in *Marchant*, is to purport to decide future disputes which have not arisen or how the wall is to be dealt with in uncertain future contingencies.

Invalidity of Award for Non-Compliance with Procedures

It was held in *Gyle-Thompson* v. *Wall Street (Properties) Ltd*[59] that a surveyors' award under section 55 may be invalid on procedural grounds alone—for instance, non-service, or service on the wrong persons, of the various notices required in Part VI of the 1939 Act. An example is where a party

---

[55] *Gyle-Thompson* v. *Wall Street (Properties) Ltd* [1974] 1 All ER 295.
[56] *Gyle-Thompson* v. *Wall Street (Properties) Ltd, supra.*
[57] (1983) 267 EG 843, CA.
[58] [1965] 1 QB 76, CA.
[59] *Supra.*

structure notice is served not on the owner concerned, but
on his surveyor (where the latter is not authorised expressly
or impliedly to accept service). Other fatal procedural irregu-
larities include, where agreed surveyors or the third surveyor
are not appointed in writing, as required by section 55, or
a failure to deliver the award before commencement of the
work, under section 46—only *after* the award is delivered,
may the work be commenced. Brightman J said in *Gyle-
Thompson*, that the approach of surveyors to the procedural
requirements of the Act must, therefore, be meticulous.
Waiver or estoppel by the recipient of irregular or invalid
service of notices could, however, entitle the other to rely
on such notice.

IV. DANGEROUS AND NEGLECTED BUILDINGS OR STRUCTURES

A. *Outside Inner London*

The control of dangerous buildings or structures outside
Inner London is governed by sections 77–79 of the *Building
Act* 1984.

General Provision

Under section 77(1) of the 1984 Act, if it appears to a
local authority that a building or structure (or part thereof)
is in a dangerous condition, the authority may apply to a
magistrates' court. The court then has power to order the
owner to carry out any remedial work necessary to obviate
the danger or, at his election, to demolish the building or
structure (or any dangerous part of it). In the event of the
owner failing to comply with a court order then (s 77(2))
the local authority have the power to execute the order and
recover the expenses reasonably incurred by them from the
owner. Moreover, non-compliance with a court order is an
offence.[60] If the building is a listed building (within ss 54
and 55 of the *Town and Country Planning Act* 1971) then
a local authority considering demolishing the building must
first consider whether any alternative course of action is open
to them to prevent demolition taking place. Hence, where

---

[60] The penalty is a fine not exceeding level 1 on the standard scale (ss 75 and 126 of the
Criminal Justice Act 1982).

an authority proposed to demolish listed houses in Stroud, without considering any action under sections 101 and 115 of the 1971 Act, mandamus was obtained against the authority.[61]

Emergency Action

If it appears to the local authority that immediate action should be taken to remove a danger caused by a dangerous building or structure, they have emergency powers under section 78. They must if reasonably practicable to do so, give notice to the owner and occupier (s 78(2)). In principle, the authority have a right to recover expenses they incur but by section 78(5), the court, in any proceedings against the owner to recover expenses, must inquire whether the local authority might reasonably have proceeded under section 77 if it decides that they should have done so, the authority will lose any right to recover expenses.

When Statutory Powers Available

It was held in *London County Council* v. *Jones*[62] that the fact that the local authority temporarily shores up a structure will not prevent it being in a dangerous state, and the owner will still be liable to be proceeded against under section 77 (or, presumably, under s 78). Apprehension of danger to any person, not just to highway users, suffices for the statutory power to be available. Moreover, a court order requiring the owner to carry out remedial work to a dangerous building or structure does not necessarily have to specify the works and may simply refer to such works of repair or restoration as may be required to comply with the order.[63] As to what work is necessary to render the building or structure safe it has been held that it is work of a semi-permanent nature which would make the building or structure reasonably safe in respect of any person who might happen to go into it.[64]

---

[61] R v. *Stroud District Council* [1982] JPL 246.
[62] [1912] 2 KB 504.
[63] R v. *Recorder of Bolton* [1940] 1 KB 290, CA.
[64] *Holme* v. *Crosby Corporation* (1941) (Unrep), cited in *Current Law Statutes* (1984) note to *Building Act* 1984, s 77.

Rights of Adjoining Party Wall Owners

If a local authority causes a dangerous building or structure to be demolished and, on one side of the building there is a wall dividing it from other premises, if the wall is a party wall, the owner of the demolished building will, ultimately, have to pay for the costs of supporting the party wall.[65] Not so, if the buildings merely abut, and there is no easement of support in favour of the adjoining wall.[66]

Building Detrimental to Amenities

Under section 79(1) of the *Building Act* 1984, local authorities have power by notice to require the owner of a ruinous building or structure which, by reason of its dilapidated or dangerous condition, is seriously detrimental to the amenities of the neighbourhood, to carry out works of repair or restoration to it, or, at his election, to demolish it and remove rubbish resulting from the demolition. The authority has default powers and may ask a magistrates' court to impose a fine on the owner. It may also, under section 79(2), by notice, require the owner to remove rubbish or other material lying on the site or other land, where a building or structure has been demolished or has collapsed.

B. *In Inner London*

In Inner London, powers to control dangerous buildings or structures are exercisable by the Inner London Boroughs and the Common Council of the City of London.[67] These powers are in Part VII of the *London Building Acts (Amendment) Act* 1939.[68] Space forbids detailed consideration of these powers, which have similar results to those noted immediately above. It may be noted, however, that under Part VII of the 1939 Act, if the owner of a dangerous structure disputes the necessity of any requisitions in a dangerous structure notice he may require a surveyors' arbitration (s 63 of the 1939 Act).

---

[65] *Bradburn* v. *Lindsay* [1983] 2 All ER 408; *Marchant* v. *Capital and Counties plc* (1983) 67 EG 843, CA.
[66] *Phipps* v. *Pears* [1965] 1 QB 76, CA.
[67] *Local Government Act* 1985 s 16, Sched 8 para 14(1).
[68] Subject to the power in *Building Act* in regulations to repeal or modify Part VII: see above.

Chapter 13

AGRICULTURAL DILAPIDATIONS[1]

I. INTRODUCTION

The subject of agricultural dilapidations merits a separate chapter, because there are a number of special rules which apply only to dilapidations on an agricultural holding. But, it should be borne in mind that the general principles of interpretation of repairing covenants and as to the assessment of damages, discussed earlier in this book, will apply to agricultural holdings, unless modified by special rules to be dealt with.

There are two basic possibilities as far as the apportionment of responsibility for repairs, as between landlord and tenant of an agricultural holding, is concerned. These are outlined in what immediately follows, and then some further details of each topic are given.

A. *Contract of Tenancy Makes Express Provision—An Outline*

The first possibility is that the contract of tenancy will itself contain express provisions dealing with responsibility for repairs. If so then these will be enforceable by and against each party.

Limit on Maximum Amount of Damages

If the tenant is in breach of his tenancy obligations, the landlord may claim compensation for deterioration damage or dilapidations to particular parts of the holding under section 71 of the *Agricultural Holdings Act* 1986. The maximum amount of compensation is limited by section 71(5) to the amount by which the value of the landlord's reversion is diminished by the breach or breaches in question. The measure

See generally RG Williams, *Agricultural Valuations—A Practical Guide*, (1985) Estates Gazette; and Rodgers, *Agricultural Tenancies Law and Practice*, (1985) Butterworths. Also: Muir Watt Chapter XVII, Evans, Chapter 29, Yates and Hawkins, Chapter 26.

of damages is, therefore, the actual cost of making good th⬤
deterioration, damage or dilapidations, subject to the statu
tory ceiling.[2]

Power of Arbitrator to Modify Agreements

Section 8(1) of the *Agricultural Holdings Act* 1986 give⬤
an arbitrator wide powers to modify a written agreemen⬤
which effects substantial modifications in the operation o⬤
the so-called "model clauses"—ie those imposed by regula⬤
tions.

B. *Application of "Model Clauses"*

The "model clauses" will apply, in most cases, to the cor⬤
tract of tenancy in question. They are set out in the Agricultur
(Maintenance Repair and Insurance of Fixed Equipmen⬤
Regulations 1973.[3]

Position if Agreement Inconsistent with Model Clauses

If there is a written contract of tenancy which contair⬤
one or more terms inconsistent with the model clauses, th⬤
terms inconsistent with these clauses will apply, and will ove
ride the model clauses in their own particular area, but th⬤
latter will still govern all other aspects of responsibility und⬤
the tenancy for dilapidations—unless, of course, the contra⬤
tual and inconsistent clauses in the contract of tenancy a⬤
so comprehensive as to be totally inconsistent with the mod⬤
clauses.

Position if Neither Party requests Arbitration

Mention must be made of the right of either landlord ⬤
tenant to require arbitration on any express terms in a contra⬤
of tenancy, so that these may be modified, to make the⬤
consistent with the model clauses. Unless and until a par⬤
avails himself of the right to arbitration, the express ter⬤
or terms of the tenancy will prevail. This is a *vital* poir
It is the result of *Burden* v. *Hannaford*.[4] A written tenan⬤

---

[2] The ceiling was introduced by the *Agricultural Holdings Act* 1984 Sched 3 and is incorpora⬤
into s 71 of the 1986 Act.
[3] SI 1973 No 1473. See Section III of this Chapter.
[4] [1956] 1 QB 142, CA.

greement expressly exempted the tenant from responsibility
or dilapidations to hedges on the farm in question. This term
vas not referred to arbitration and prevailed as a result—even
hough under the model clauses the tenant is responsible for
uch dilapidations (reg 5).

Curiously, if the tenancy had been oral, the result would
ave been different, and the regulations would have applied
o the tenancy in any event. This is because section 7(3) of
he *Agricultural Holdings Act* 1986 incorporates the model
lauses into all contracts of tenancy of agricultural holdings,
xcept in the case of written agreements containing a term
f terms imposing a liability on the other party.

II. POSITION WHERE CONTRACT OF TENANCY EXPRESSLY
PROVIDES FOR RESPONSIBILITY FOR REPAIRS

Where the contract of tenancy makes express provision for
epairing liabilities between landlord and tenant, it suffices
o say here that the general principles discussed in Chapters
to 6 above will apply.

However, there is a difference in agricultural land between
he land itself and any fixed equipment on the land.

A. *Fixed Equipment: Responsibility for Repairs*

"Fixed Equipment" is defined by section 96(1) of the *Agri-
ultural Holdings Act* 1986 as including "any building or
ructure affixed to land and any works on, in, over, or under
nd."

The definition applies to any case regulated by express con-
actual terms and/or the model clauses.

Meaning of "Fixed Equipment"—Further

"Fixed equipment" is a wide term. It includes the farm-
ouse, cottages, and farm outbuildings. It also includes walls
d fences of open and covered yards and garden walls and
nces. It also includes any fittings and fixtures in the farm
r farm premises, and hedges, field walls and fences, stiles,
tes, posts, bridges, culverts and so on.[5]

---

[5] SI 1973/1473, reg 1.

Model Clauses Fix Liability for Repair of Fixed Equipment

The general rules is that it is the model clauses which fix the incidence of liability for repairs to fixed equipment. The terms used in the model clauses such as "repair" "structure" and so on, are to be understood in accordance with the general rules, discussed in earlier parts of this book.

If a particular item or items are expressly the liability of the other party—or excepted from liability—then the interpretation of that party's express covenant to repair in relation to the item (for example, where the landlord is under a duty to keep in repair the structure and exterior of the farmhouse) will be governed by the general law, discussed in Chapters 4 to 6 of this book.

B. *Land: Responsibility for Care and Maintenance*

As might be expected, the care and maintenance of the land in good heart is the responsibility chiefly of the tenant. The position with regard to the land is not governed by the model clauses, for the simple reason that they only apply to fixed equipment. The general rule is that, by section 11 of the *Agriculture Act* 1947, the tenant is under a duty to farm the land in accordance with the rules of good husbandry. This duty and the remedies of the landlord where it is not complied with is discussed later in this Chapter.

III. LIABILITY UNDER THE MODEL CLAUSES[6]

A. *When Model Clauses Apply*

Section 7(3) of the *Agricultural Holdings Act* 1986 provides that the model clauses—ie the whole of the 1973 regulations— "shall be deemed to be incorporated in every contract of tenancy of an agricultural holding". In other words, the model clauses are of *general* application to *all* tenancies of agricultural holdings.

Section 7(3) provides, however, that the model clauses will not apply "in so far as they would impose on one of the

---

[6] Ie Agriculture (Maintenance Repair and Insurance of Fixed Equipment) Regulations 19?? SI 1973 No 1473 hereafter referred to as SI 1973/1473 or 1973 regs.

parties to an agreement in writing a liability which under the agreement is imposed on the other." The effect of this, in the case of a written agreement which contains a term or provision inconsistent with the model clauses, was discussed above. It will be remembered that, under section 8(1) of the 1986 Act, either party has the right to refer an agreement which effects substantial modifications to the model clauses to an arbitrator.

At the risk of repetition, it should be mentioned that if the tenancy agreement is oral, then the model clauses apply to it in full.

B. *The Model Clauses: Landlord's Responsibilties*

The responsibilities of the landlord are set out in great detail in the model clauses.[7]

Para 1: Structural Work to Farmhouse etc

The landlord is under an obligation to execute all repairs and replacements to the following parts of the farmhouse, cottages and farm buildings, namely: roofs, including chimney stacks, chimney pots, eaves-guttering and downpipes, main walls and exterior walls, including walls and fences of open and covered yards and garden walls, together with any interior repair or decoration made necessary as a result of structural defect to such roofs or walls, floors, floor joists, ceiling joists and timbers, exterior and interior staircases and fixed ladders (including banisters or handrails) of the farmhouse and cottages, and doors, windows and skylights, including the frames of such doors, windows and skylight (but excepting glass or glass substitutes, sashcords, locks and fastenings) (para 1(1)).

Right of Landlord to Half Cost of Certain Repairs

In the case of the following repairs, the landlord is able to recover half the reasonable cost from the tenant: repairs and replacements to floorboards, interior staircases and fixed ladders (including banisters or handrails), doors and windows

---

[7] SI 1973/1473 Schedule Part I paras 1–3. All subsequent references to "para" are to paragraphs in this Schedule.

and opening skylights (including frames) eaves-guttering and downpipes (para 1(1)).[8]

In the case of all the other repairs listed, the landlord must bear the full cost.

Other Repairs—Installations, Equipment etc

The landlord is also bound to execute all repairs and replacements to underground water supply pipes, wells, bore-holes and reservoirs and all underground installations connected therewith and to sewage disposal systems, including septic tanks, filtering media and cesspools (but excluding covers and tops) (para 1(2)). The landlord must bear the full cost of these items.

Items Incapable of Repair: Landlord to Replace

The landlord is also bound to replace any item which it is the tenant's responsibility to repair which has worn out or otherwise become incapable of further repair (para 1(3)). This does not apply:

(a) where the item which has become worn out or otherwise incapable of repair, because its condition has been brought about by or is substantially due to the tenant's failure to repair it (para 6(2));

(b) to broken or cracked tiles or slates, which must be renewed by the tenant, and also he, not the landlord, must replace all slipped tiles or slates from time to time as the damage occurs, up to a maximum limit for any one year of the tenancy of £25 (para 8).

Insurance

The landlord must keep the farmhouse, cottages and farm buildings insured to their full value against loss or damage by fire. If such buildings should be destroyed by fire then the landlord is obliged to reinstate the building in question and to apply insurance monies received for that purpose (para 2)).

---

[8] In *Robertson Aikerman* v. *George* (1953) (Unrep) referred to by Williams *loc cit* p 64 it was held that the landlord could only recover half the cost of these repairs if the work was in fact done at the *termination of the tenancy*.

The landlord is to bear the full cost of the reinstatement in all cases, even those where, in the case of repairs, he is entitled to half the reasonable cost from the tenant (para 2(2)).

Decorative Repairs

The landlord is obliged, as often as may be necessary to prevent deterioration, and in any case at intervals of not more than five years, to carry out the following decorative works (para 3(1)). That means, in each of the instances listed, painting with at least two coats of a suitable quality (or as the case may be properly and adequately to gas-tar, creosote or otherwise effectively treat with a preservative material):

—all outside wood and ironwork of the farmhouse, cottages and farm buildings

—the inside wood and ironwork of all external outward opening doors and windows of farm buildings (but not of the farmhouse or cottages)

—the interior structural steelwork of open-sided farm buildings which have been previously painted, gas-tarred, creosoted or otherwise treated with preservative material.[9]

Recovery of Certain Decorative Costs

In respect of decorative work carried out by the landlord the following items, he may, in principle, recover half the reasonable cost from the tenant: ie to doors, windows, eaves-guttering and downpipes (para 3(1)).

If any of the work is completed before the fifth year of the tenancy, the recoverable sum is restricted to an amount equal to the aggregate of one-tenth of the reasonable cost for each year that has elapsed between the commencement of the tenancy and the completion of the work.

If the last year of the tenancy is not a year in which the landlord is liable to execute work, the tenant must pay the landlord, either half of the estimated reasonable cost of the work, or the aggregate of one-tenth of the estimated reasonable cost for each year that has elapsed since the last decorative

"Open-sided" means having the whole or the greater part of at least one side or end permanently open, apart from roof supports, if any: 1973 regs para 3(2).

work falling on the landlord was completed, whichever i
the less (para 11(2)).[10]

Landlord Not Liable in Certain Cases

The landlord is not liable to execute repairs or replacement
to buildings or fixtures which are the property of the tenan
(para 4(1)(a)).

Except in the case of destruction by fire of the farmhouse
cottages and farm buildings (para 2(1)(b)), the landlord i
not liable to execute repairs or replacements rendered necess
ary by the wilful act or negligence of the tenant or any membe
of his household or his employees (para 4(1)(b)).

Position if Landlord Fails to Execute Repairs

If the landlord fails to execute repairs, which are his respon
sibility, within three months of receiving a tenant's writte
notice specifying the necessary repairs and calling on him t
execute them, the tenant may execute the repairs and recove
the reasonable cost from the landlord forthwith—except i
so far as the landlord has to bear their cost (para 12(1)).

Exactly the same provision applies to the tenant, whee
the landlord fails within three months of a tenant's writte
notice, to replace any items it is his responsibility to repla
(para 12(2)). There is a limit on replacements' recovery
the rent of the holding for that year or £500, whichever
the smaller.

Landlord's Right to Contest Liability

The landlord has the right to contest liability to execu
any repairs or replacements specified in a tenant's noti
within one month by written counter-notice denying liabili
and requiring the question of liability to be determined
arbitration under the 1986 Act (para 12(3)(a)).

The effect of a landlord's notice is to suspend the operati
of the tenant's notice, including the running of time und
it, as regards the items specified in the landlord's count
notice, until the termination of the arbitration, ie the d

---

[10] Under 1973 regs, para 11(3), in assessing any compensation payable by the tenan
termination of the tenancy for dilapidation, any accrued liability of the tenant to contri
to the cost of certain repairs under para 11(1) and (2) must be taken into account.

of delivery of the arbitration award to the landlord (paras 12(3)(b) and (c)).

C. *The Model Clauses: Tenant's Responsibilities*

Under the model clauses the tenant's responsibilities are as follows.[11]

General

The tenant is bound to repair and to keep and leave clean and in good tenantable repair, order and condition the farmhouse, cottages and farm buildings together with all fixtures and fittings, boilers, ranges and grates, drains, sewers, gulleys, grease-traps, manholes and inspection chambers, electrical supply systems and fittings, water supply systems and fittings in so far as they are situated above ground, including pipes, tanks, cisterns, sanitary fittings, drinking troughs and pumping equipment, hydraulic rams (whether situated above or below ground), fences, hedges, field walls, stiles, gates and posts, cattle grids, bridges, culverts, ponds, watercourses, sluices, ditches, roads and yards in and upon the holding, or which during the tenancy may be erected or provided thereon (para 5(1)).

Scope of Tenant's Obligation

The obligation imposed by the model clauses is not, according to *Evans* v. *Jones*[12] limited to an obligation on the tenant to leave the items enumerated as clean and as in a good condition as they happened to be in at the beginning of the tenancy. In determining whether the obligation has been complied with, regard must be had to the item's age, character and condition at the beginning of the tenancy itself and to the length of the tenancy.

The tenant must repair or replace all removable covers to manholes, inspection chambers and to sewage disposal systems (para 5(2)).

---

[11] SI 1973/1473 Sched., Part II. For specimen claims see Williams *loc cit* Chapter 10, 5.

[12] [1955] 2 QB 58, CA.

The tenant must keep clean and in good working order all roof valleys, eaves-guttering and downpipes, wells, septic tanks, cesspools and sewage disposal systems (para 5(3)).

Further Obligations of the Tenant

1. *Careful User and Notification of Landlord.*—The tenant must use carefully so as to protect from wilful, reckless or negligent damage, all items for the repair or replacement of which the landlord is responsible. The tenant must report in writing, immediately, to the landlord any damage, however caused, to items for the repair or replacement of which the landlord is responsible (para 5(4)).

2. *Decorative Work etc.*—Subject to the landlord's responsibilities, the tenant is liable for the following work:

(a) *Repairs and Replacements.*—To replace or repair and on replacement or repair, adequately to paint, gas-tar, creosote or otherwise treat with effective preservative material as may be proper, all items of fixed equipment, and to do any work, where such replacement, repair or work is rendered necessary by the wilful act or negligence of the tenant or any members of his household or his employees (para 6(1)).

(b) The tenant must replace items of equipment and keep in repair roof-valleys etc, see above (para 6(2)).

(c) *Decorative Repairs.*—The tenant is obliged as often as may be necessary and in any case at intervals of not more than seven years, properly to clean, colour, whiten, paper, paint, limewash or otherwise treat with materials of suitable quality the inside of the farmhouse, cottages and farm buildings, including the interior of outward opening doors and windows of the farmhouse and cottages, which have been previously so treated and in the last year of the tenancy to limewash the inside of all buildings which previously have been limewashed (para 7). This mirrors the landlord's responsibilities under para 3.

Obligations in the Last Year of the Tenancy

If the last year of the tenancy is not a year in which cleaning, colouring, whitening, papering, painting, limewashing or other treatment is to be carried out, then the tenant must pay the landlord at the end of that year, either the estimated reasonable cost of the work, or the aggregate of one-seventh of the cost of the work in question for each year that has elapsed since the last occasion on which the work was completed, whichever is the less (para 11(1)).

This is important because, under the model clauses, an accrued liability of the tenant for internal and external decorations is, accordingly, recoverable.

Hedges.—The tenant is liable to cut, trim or lay a proper proportion of the hedges in each year of the tenancy so as to maintain them in good and sound condition (para 9).

Ponds.—The tenant is liable to dig out, scour and cleanse all ponds, watercourses, ditches and grips, as may be necessary to maintain them at sufficient width and depth, and to keep clear from obstruction all field drains and their outlets (para 10).

Position if Tenant Fails to Execute Repairs

If the tenant fails to start work on repairs or replacements for which, under the preceding paragraphs, he is liable within two months, or if he fails to complete them within three months, in either case after receiving written notice from the landlord (not being a notice to remedy) specifying the necessary repairs or replacements and calling on him to execute them, then the landlord may enter and execute them and recover the reasonable cost from the tenant (para 4(2)).

Tenant's Right to Contest Liability

The tenant has a right, similar to that of the landlord, to contest his liability to carry out any particular repairs or replacements by means of a counter-notice claiming arbitration (para 4(3)). The effect of this is to suspend the landlord's notice, until the termination of the arbitration.

Uncontested Items

The tenant must still comply with the landlord's notice, in so far as it relates to any uncontested items. If, on an arbitration, the arbitrator finds that the tenant is not liable for a given item, the tenant obviously will not be liable to repair or replace that item.

Landlord's Power to Serve Notice to Remedy as Alternative

An alternative method for the landlord to try to force the tenant to execute repairs, for which the tenant is responsible, is for the landlord to serve on the tenant a Notice to Remedy in the prescribed form.[13] If this is not complied with by the tenant, the landlord may follow up his notice to remedy with an incontestable notice to quit, and eventually this will lead to the termination of the tenancy.

Tenant's Right to Contest Notice to Remedy

The tenant may contest a Notice to Remedy by invoking arbitration[14] and the arbitrator is given wide powers to modify the landlord's Notice to Remedy. The tenant must contest particular items. The arbitrator may modify the landlord's notice under his powers conferred by regulations.[15] He may extend the time allowed by the landlord in his Notice to Remedy for carrying out the work.

Full Compliance

Unless modified by arbitration, a Notice to Remedy must be complied with, or it can be followed up by an incontestable notice to quit.[16] If the only reason for the tenant's failure to comply with the landlord's Notice to Remedy, within the time there stated to remedy the tenant's breaches, is the landlord's failure, in breach of his own covenant, to supply materials, the Notice to Remedy will still stand—which is a curious *lacuna*.[17] On the other hand, the landlord will not be able to enforce a Notice to Remedy which fails to allow the tenant a reasonable time in which to do the work, and this means a reasonable time for each and every single item.[18]

Consent of Agricultural Land Tribunal to Case D Notice

Under section 28 of the *Agricultural Holdings Act* 1986, the tenant may require the consent of the Agricultural Land Tribu-

---

[13] Under *Agricultural Holdings Act* 1986, Sched 3 Part I Case D and SI 1987/711. For a specimen Notice to Remedy see Williams, *loc cit*. Chapter 13 pp 86–92.
[14] For a precedent see Williams *loc cit*. Chapter 13 pp 93–96.
[15] Agricultural Holdings (Arbitration on Notices) Order 1987 SI 1987/710.
[16] *Price* v. *Romilly* [1960] 1 WLR 1360.
[17] *Shepherd* v. *Lomas* [1963] 1 WLR 962, CA.
[18] *Wykes* v. *Davis* [1975] QB 843, CA.

nal to a Case D notice, within one month of the notice or of an arbitration award. The Tribunal must consent to the notice, unless it appears to them that a fair and reasonable landlord would not insist on possession, having regard to three factors laid down in section 28(5):

(a) the extent of the tenant's failure to comply with the Notice to Remedy;

(b) the consequences of his failure to comply;

(c) the circumstances surrounding the tenant's failure.

Certificate of Bad Husbandry

There is a still further course open to the landlord who is trying to force the tenant to comply with his repairing obligations.

This is to ask the Tribunal for a certificate of bad husbandry.[19] If the Tribunal is satisfied that the tenant is not fulfilling his responsibilities, then it must issue a certificate. The landlord has six months from the giving of a certificate to serve a Case C notice on the tenant, which is incontestable by counter-notice.[20]

The grant of a certificate is not automatic. The tribunal must disregard certain practices adopted by the tenant to further certain purposes such as conservation or the preservation of buildings.[21]

D. *Record of Condition of Holding*

General

Under section 22(1) of *Agricultural Holdings Act* 1986, either the landlord or the tenant of an agricultural holding may require a record to be made of the fixed equipment of the holding and of the general condition of the holding, including any parts of the holding not under cultivation. The parties may agree on a third party who is to make the record. It may be made by a person appointed by the President of the RICS, if the parties cannot agree (s 22(2)). The cost of making

---

[19] Under *Agricultural Holdings Act* 1986 Sched 3 Part III para 9.
[20] Under 1986 Act, Sched 3. The Case C notice must state that a certificate has been obtained.
[21] See 1986 Act, Sched 3, para 9.

the record is to be borne equally by both parties, in default
of agreement (s 22(3)).

High Farming

If a claim for compensation for high farming is to be made
under section 70 of the *Agricultural Holdings Act* 1986, then
a record of condition of the holding and of the fixed equipment
on the holding must be requested, and made (s 70(2)(b)).
If it is not, then no compensation under section 70 may be
awarded (s 70(2)). This is the only instance where the making
of a record of condition is mandatory. "High Farming" means
by section 70(1), the continuous adoption of a system of farming more beneficial to the holding than that required by the
contract of tenancy or, if no system is required, than the system
normally practised on comparable agricultural holdings.

Significance of Record (Except for High Farming)

A record, if made at the start of the occupation of a given
tenant, will be evidence of the condition of the fixed equipment
at that time, and of the condition of the holding. This could
be vital, for in *Evans* v. *Jones*[22] it was held that the condition
of the fixed equipment and of the holding will be compared
as at the start of the tenancy, with their respective condition
at the date of the landlord's action for alleged breaches of
covenant to repair by the tenant, and so any record will be
evidence as to any such differences.

The record will not settle liabilities beween the parties: if
the condition of the land is poor, the fact that this is shown
in any record will not exempt a tenant from liability, if he
has covenanted to cultivate the land in a good and husbandlike
manner. Nor will it exempt the tenant from liability for the
maintenance and repair of fixed equipment which is dilapidated, in so far as liability to repair the items concerned
cast on him, whether expressly, by the tenancy, or impliedly
by the model clauses.

If the tenant entered the holding a large number of years
ago and at that time a record was made, it usefulness may

---

[22] [1955] 2 QB 58, CA.

well be limited at the end of the tenancy. At the least, it will have "dated".

F. *Redundant Fixed Equipment*

The model clauses contain detailed provisions about items of redundant fixed equipment.

Notice

If at any time, and from time to time, either party is of opinion that any item of fixed equipment is or, prior to its being damaged or destroyed by fire was, redundant to the farming of the holding, the party concerned may by two month's written notice to the other, require that the question whether the item is (or was) redundant, be determined by agreement or in default of agreement, by arbitration (para 13(1)).

Power of Arbitrator to Award Item of Fixed Equipment Redundant

The arbitrator has power to award that the item of fixed equipment is (or was) redundant (para 13(1)), but this is not unlimited. An item of fixed equipment cannot be determined to be redundant to the farming of the holding, unless the arbitrator is satisfied that the repair or replacement of the item is (or was) not reasonably required, having regard to three matters:

—the landlord's responsibilities to manage the holding in accordance with the rules of good estate management;
—the period for which the holding may reasonably be expected to remain a separate holding;
—the character and situation of the holding and the average requirements of a tenant reasonably skilled in husbandry.

Effect of Award

If the arbitrator awards that the item in question is redundant, the effect of the award is as follows (para 14(1)):

(1) Neither landlord nor tenant is bound to maintain, repair, replace or insure the item in question.

(2) Nor are they bound to execute any work if and so far as the execution of such work is rendered impossible

(except at prohibitive and unreasonable expense), by reason of subsidence of any land or the blocking of outfalls not under the control of the landlord or tenant.

The landlord is entitled to demolish the item in question and to enter the holding for the purpose.

Agreement that Item of Fixed Equipment is Redundant

If the parties have—instead of going to arbitration—agreed that an item of fixed equipment is redundant, then the rules outlined above in relation to an arbitrator's award will apply.

There is one exception to this. While an arbitration award will relieve the parties from liability for antecedent breaches of covenant, this will not be the automatic result of an agreement between the parties unless it expressly so provides (para 13(1)).

Obsolete Fixed Equipment

In the case of obsolete, as opposed to redundant, items of fixed equipment, as these are not covered by Part III of the regulations, the parties' repairing obligations will continue with regard to them, unless and until terminated by agreement.[23]

G. *Powers of Arbitrator to Modify Agreements not Consistent with Model Clauses*

Section 8(1) of the 1986 Act confers on an arbitrator wide powers to modify a written agreement which effects substantial modifications in the operation of the model clauses. There must first be a reference of the terms of the tenancy to the arbitrator concerned by either the landlord or the tenant. A reference may be made, where, following a written request by the referring party to the other, to vary the agreement so as to bring its terms into conformity with the model clauses, no agreement as to this has been reached (s 8(2)).

By section 8(3), the arbitrator is then bound to consider whether the terms in question are justifiable having regard to the circumstances of the holding and of the parties, and

[23] Rodgers, Chapter 4 p 54.

if he determines that they are not justifiable he may vary them in such manner as he thinks reasonable and just.

Once a reference has been made to an arbitrator under section 8, no further reference relating to the tenancy may be made for three years from the coming into effect of the award of an arbitrator on a previous reference (s 8(6)). The arbitrator has power to vary the rent in his award, if he considers it equitable to do so by reason of any provision in the award (s 8(4)).

IV. DUTY OF TENANT TO FARM IN ACCORDANCE WITH RULES OF GOOD HUSBANDRY

A. *Introduction*

At common law, the tenant of an agricultural holding is under certain duties with respect to the cultivation of the land itself. If there are express obligations as to the matter in the tenancy itself then these, so far as applicable, will completely override the implied common law duties.[24]

In fact, the implied common-law duties are largely irrelevant because the duties of the tenant are, in the main, set out in sections 10 and 11 of the *Agriculture Act* 1947. If the tenant fails to comply with these, indirect methods of enforcement are open to the landlord. He may obtain a certificate of bad husbandry from the Tribunal and follow it with a Case C notice: see the previous section of this Chapter. For the sake of completeness, however, an outline of the implied common law duties is given.

B. *Outline of Implied Common Law Obligations*

The relationship of landlord and tenant creates an implied obligation on the tenant to manage and use the farm in a husbandlike manner, according to the custom of the country where the farm is situated.[25] That custom is impliedly incorporated into the tenancy, in the absence of express inconsistent covenants in the contract of tenancy itself.

Provided that the tenant farms the holding properly during the tenancy, he is not impliedly bound to leave the land in

---

[24] *Hutton* v. *Warren* (1836) 1 M & W 466.
[25] *Wedd* v. *Porter* [1916] 2 KB 91, CA.

a clean and good condition on quitting, in so far as that imports a greater obligation than the implied duty. In other words, if the land is impoverished at the commencement of the tenancy, the implied duty does not oblige the tenant to put it into a better condition.[26]

By "custom of the country" is meant the general or prevalent course of husbandry in the relevant neighbourhood, and it is only to that standard that the land is to be kept under the implied obligation.[27]

C. *Statutory Rules: Agriculture Act 1947*

Section 11 of the *Agriculture Act* 1947[28] defines the obligation of the tenant to farm in accordance with the rules of good husbandry, and these apply[29] to tenants of an agricultural holding.

While the section 11 obligations of the tenant cannot directly be enforced, the landlord may indirectly enforce them by way of obtaining a certificate of bad husbandry from the Tribunal, and then following it within six months, with an incontestable Case C notice to quit.

The Duties

By section 11(1) of the 1947 Act, the tenant fulfils his responsibilities to farm in accordance with the rules of good husbandry in so far as the extent to which and the manner in which the holding is being farmed is such that, having regard to its character and situation, the owner's standard of management and other relevant circumstances, the tenant is maintaining a reasonable standard of efficient production as respects both the kind of produce and the quality and quantity thereof, while keeping the unit in a condition to enable such a standard to be maintained in future.

Factors Used in Determining Compliance

Section 11(2) lists factors to be used in determining compliance with this standard and these include:

---

[26] *Williams* v. *Lewis* [1915] 3 KB 493.
[27] *Leigh* v. *Hewitt* (1803) 4 East 154.
[28] Not consolidated into the *Agricultural Holdings Act* 1986.
[29] *Agricultural Holdings Act* 1986 s 96(3).

—the extent to which permanent pasture is being properly mown or grazed and maintained in good condition;

—the manner in which arable land is being cropped such as to maintain the land in a good state of cultivation and fertility and in good condition;

—the extent to which necessary work of maintenance or repair is being carried out.

V. DAMAGES CLAIMS BY LANDLORD DURING AND AT THE END OF THE TENANCY

A. *Claims During the Tenancy*

The landlord may claim damages at common law for breaches of the covenant to repair during the tenancy.[30] Claims at common law are limited to the amount of the diminution in value of the landlord's reversion.[31] It has been pointed out that, if the tenant holds under a long lease, then a claim at common law may produce very limited amounts of damages, as it may be difficult to assess damage to the landlord's reversion.[32] As the tenancy becomes shorter, the amount of damages recoverable presumably increases.

Exception to the Right to Claim Damages During Tenancy

There is one exception to the rule that the landlord may claim for damages during the tenancy: no claim may be made where the tenant exercises his right to freedom of cropping under section 15 of the 1986 Act. If he exercises these rights in such a way as to injure the holding, then section 15(5) limits the landlord to two rights only:

(a) to an injunction;

(b) to claim damages on the tenant's quitting the holding.

B. *Landlord's Claims on Termination of the Tenancy*

These fall into two categories. The first is claims under section 71 of the *Agricultural Holdings Act* 1986, referring to specific dilapidations or deterioration affecting particular

---

[30] *Kent* v. *Conniff* [1953] 1 QB 361, CA. This is in spite of the language of *Agricultural Holdings Act* 1986 s 78.

[31] As are all claims at common law, by *Landlord and Tenant Act* 1927 s 18(1), discussed in Chapter 7. Claims under the 1986 Act are subject to the same rule (*Agricultural Holdings Act* 1986 s 71(5)).

[32] Rodgers, *loc cit.* p. 229.

parts of the holding. The second category is for further, additional, claims under section 72 of the 1986 Act, which are for general dilapidations or damage. If the current tenant obtains a new tenancy of the same holding, the landlord's rights to claim compensation against the tenant on quitting are preserved by section 73 of the 1986 Act.[33] This saving rule will not apply if the holding in question alters, whether by enlargement or contraction, at all events to a significant extent. In that case, any claims on determination must be made as at the date of the alteration of the holding. Otherwise, they will be lost.

If the landlord, of the whole or of a severed part of the reversion, resumes possession under a notice to quit relating to part of the holding, his rights to claim compensation from the tenant, with respect to that part of the holding, are expressly preserved by section 74 of the 1986 Act.

C. *First Category of Claims: Dilapidations or Deterioration of Particular Parts*

General

On the tenant quitting the holding (if he does not quit then no claim under s 71 is possible), either voluntarily or in consequence of a notice to quit, section 71(1) of the 1986 Act entitles the landlord to compensation for any dilapidation or deterioration of, or any damage to, any particular part of the holding or anything on or in the holding, caused by the tenant's breaches of obligation.

"Dilapidation" is to be understood widely. Claims may be made in respect of: disrepair of buidings, neglect of fences and hedges, the repair of bent or broken gates, ditches, drains and culverts (these may have become blocked weedy, filled in, or silted), the repair of and maintenance of bridges, and the fouling of land by weed infestation of one kind or another. Claims for damage to pasture, the ploughing out of pasture and excessive or cross cropping may also be included under this head.[34]

The question of dilapidations, in so far as it relates to buildings

---

[33] *Jenkin R Lewis & Son Ltd* v. *Kerman* [1971] Ch 477.
[34] See Williams *loc cit* Chapter 10 p. 63 for a specimen claim.

and fixed equipment, was discussed earlier in this Chapter.

Measure of Damages: Statutory Limitation

Section 71(2) of the 1986 Act entitles the landlord to recover the cost, as at the date when the tenant quits the holding, of making good the dilapidation, deterioration or damage. But, by section 71(5), *in no case* is the amount of compensation to exceed the amount, if any, of the diminution in value of the landlord's reversion caused by the breach. The reason for this provision is that, until amendments made to the predecessor to this provision in 1984,[35] it was unclear whether the landlord's claim to damages for deterioration of particular parts of the holding was limited to the diminution in the value of his reversion or not. It is now clearly stated that the landlord is limited to the diminution in the value of his reversion, that is, to the actual cost of making good the deterioration or injury, but subject to the statutory ceiling, that this cost must not exceed the diminution in the value of his reversion. The principles applicable are discussed in Chapter 7.

Arbitration if No Agreement

The parties may be able to agree on a figure of compensation, but if they cannot, then the figure should be arbitrated on, under section 83 of the 1986 Act. Crucially, the landlord will lose his right to claim arbitration unless, by section 83(2), before the expiration of two months from the termination of the tenancy, the landlord has given written notice to the tenant of his intention to claim compensation. The landlord's notice must, in addition, specify the nature of the claim if it is to be valid (s 83(3)) but it is sufficient if the notice refers to the statutory provision, custom or term of an agreement under which the claim is made.

Essential to Frame Two Claims as Alternatives

If the landlord wishes to claim under the statute (ie s 71(1)) and also under the contract, which he may elect to do, his notice of intention to claim must frame these two claims as *alternatives*.

---

[35] Ie to *Agricultural Holdings Act* 1948 s 57, by *Agricultural Holdings Act* 1984 Sched 3 para 13 (now both repealed and re-enacted in s 71(5) of the 1986 Act).

Both claims may validly be included in the landlord's notice. One claim may, at the arbitration, be abandoned without prejudicing the other claim. However, the landlord *cannot* make a claim under the contract and under the statute. He may get one or other *but not both*. If the landlord puts forward a claim under the contract and as an alternative, a claim under the statute, he is not disqualified from receiving compensation under either the contract or the statute. But, he must abandon one or other claim before he can get any compensation as he cannot claim twice over.[36]

Time Limit for Settlements by Agreement

Once a notice claiming arbitration is served, the parties have eight months from the date of termination of the tenancy to settle the dispute by agreement. In default, it will be arbitrated on.

Inclusion of Schedule of Dilapidations

With his notice of claim to arbitration, the landlord may validly (and definitely should) include a detailed Schedule of Dilapidations.[37] If the circumstances alter since his claim was first made, the landlord has the right to ask the leave of the arbitrator to modify an existing head or heads of claim.[38]

Factors to be Taken into Account in Arbitration

When an arbitrator considers a landlord's claim under section 71, he must have regard to three things, according to *Barrow Green Estate Co v. Executors of Walker*:[39]

(1) the terms and conditions of the tenancy;
(2) any other contractual agreement between the parties;
(3) the terms of the model clauses.

Election by Landlord to Claim under Contract

The landlord has the option to elect under section 71(3) to claim for a particular item or items, under the contract

---

[36] *Boyd* v. *Wilton* [1957] 1 QB 277, CA.
[37] See for an example Williams, *loc cit.* Chapter 10, pp 67–71.
[38] *ED & AD Cooke Bourne (Farms) Ltd* v. *Mellows* [1982] 2 All ER 208, CA.
[39] [1954] 1 WLR 231, CA.

of tenancy, rather than under the 1986 Act, but *only* where the tenancy is written, as opposed to oral.

If the contract makes different—and more onerous—provisions as to the liability of the tenant for dilapidations than the model clauses, a claim under the contract should be advantageous to the landlord. The possibility of it being made in such a case might supply the tenant with an incentive to ask for an arbitration under section 8.

The landlord's statutory right to elect for claims under the contract is without prejudice to his general right to claim either under the statute or under the contract.[40]

D. *Second Category of Claims: General Deterioration*

General

The landlord may be able to show, over and above losses to him which lead him to make particular claims under section 71, that, on the tenant's quitting the holding on the termination of the tenancy, the value of the holding has been generally reduced, either by dilapidation, deterioration or damage, or otherwise. This would be due to the tenant's breaches of covenant to repair in all aspects discussed earlier, or to farm in accordance with his responsibilities. In this case the landlord may make a claim for general deterioration under section 72 (s 72(1)).

Additional Compensation

Compensation under section 72 is recoverable over and above any compensation recoverable under section 71, but the landlord cannot recover double compensation under section 71 and section 72 for the same item.[41] As with section 71 claims, section 72 claims should be accompanied by a suitably prepared Schedule of Dilapidations.[42]

Amount of Compensation

By section 72(3), the amount of compensation is the decrease in the value of the holding as a holding, occasioned by the breaches of covenant, having regard to the character

---

[40] *Kent* v. *Conniff* [1953] 1 QB 361, CA.
[41] *Evans* v. *Jones* [1955] 2 QB 58, CA.
[42] See Williams *loc cit*. Chapter 14 pp 67–72.

and situation of the holding and the average requirements of tenants reasonably skilled in husbandry.

Notice of Intention to Claim Vital

Very importantly indeed, by section 72(4), no claim may be made by the landlord for general deterioration, unless he gives to the tenant written notice of his intention to make a section 72 claim, at least one month before the termination of the tenancy.

If the landlord fails to give one month's written notice and the tenant quits, the landlord will be totally debarred from making any claim.

The landlord has the right to claim arbitration (as under s 71), if the parties fail to agree on the amount of compensation payable under section 72. If the landlord wishes to preserve any right to claim arbitration, however, he must, as with claims under section 71, serve a written notice under section 83(2) on the tenant, before the expiration of two month from the termination of the tenancy.[43]

Record of Condition

Obviously, in dealing with claims for general deterioration (as well as with claims for deterioration of particular parts a section 22 record of the condition of the holding, made at the commencement of the tenancy, might afford useful assistance to all concerned. But, if the tenancy has run for a very long time, the utility of a record in this respect will be very limited. So the first thing to check, no doubt, is the date of the record of condition.

Basis of Assessment of Compensation

Essentially, this is the difference between the value of the holding as at the date the tenant quit, and the value it would have had if the tenant had complied with his obligation. There is no express upper ceiling on the amount of damage recoverable under a section 72 claim, unlike the position with section 71 claims. Nor is this necessary. It is the general decrease in value which must be calculated. To achieve this

---

[43] *Hallinan (Lady)* v. *Jones* (1984) 272 EG 1081.

it will be necessary to compare the value of the holding, the land and the fixed equipment, at the date the tenant quits, and the value they would have had if the tenant had complied with his tenancy obligations. It may be, therefore, that the specific heads of claim are easier to establish than claims for general deterioration.

E. *Contracting Out of Section 71 or 72 of 1986 Act*

Section 71 claims may be contracted out of, because of the power of the landlord to make an alternative claim under the contract, at the end of the tenancy, if it is written; or during the tenancy, as discussed above.

However, section 78 of the 1986 Act expressly precludes any express contracting out of section 72 claims, but it does not apply to the two methods just mentioned.

As to the preservation of landlords' claims (1) against successive tenancies granted to the same tenant and (2) where the landlord recovers possession of part of the holding, see above.

Chapter 14

LIABILITY OF LANDLORD AND TENANT TO THIRD PARTIES

I. INTRODUCTION

In this Chapter, there are considered the main general principles on which a landlord or tenant may be held liable, in nuisance or negligence, or under statute, to third parties for the consequences of any accident or injury sustained by them as the result of the premises being in a dangerous or dilapidated condition.

For present purposes there are four sources of liability:
—Liability of the landlord and tenant in nuisance.
—Liability of the landlord and tenant in negligence—in particular under the *Occupiers' Liability Act* 1957.
—Liability of the landlord under the *Defective Premises Act* 1972.
—Liability of the landlord under other legislation.

II. LIABILITY OF LANDLORD IN NUISANCE

A. *General Rule*

The general rule is that it is the tenant, *not* the landlord of demised premises, who is liable to third parties for any accident or injury occasioned to or sustained by them, due to the dangerous or defective condition of the premises in question. The general rule applies also to negligence claims.

There are certain exceptions to the general rule, and these are as follows, it being assumed in all instances that the landlord is out of occupation.

1. The landlord is under an express covenant to repair.[1] The principles which apply in this case apply equally to the second exception, and these are dealt with together.

---

[1] *Woodfall* 1–1675.

2. The landlord has reserved expressly, or there is reserved impliedly, by common law or statute, the right to enter and repair the premises.

3. The landlord has licensed the tenant to carry out the acts complained of.

4. Section 4 of the *Defective Premises Act* 1972 applies to the landlord (see Chapter 11).

5. The premises abut the highway.

6. The premises are let with a nuisance.

B. *Reservation of Right to Enter and Repair*

If the landlord is under an express, or statutory covenant with the tenant to repair, he will be liable in nuisance to a third party injured by defects in the premises.

Where the lease expressly reserves a right in the landlord to enter and repair the demised premises, or where such a right is impliedly reserved in the lease as a result of statute, such as under section 11(6) of the *Landlord and Tenant Act* 1985, the landlord will be liable to any third parties for injuries caused by the defective condition of the premises. An example is afforded by *Heap* v. *Inde Coope and Allsopp Ltd*,[2] where the landlords let the premises to yearly tenants, reserving themselves a right to enter, inspect and repair. The plaintiff, a third party, was injured by falling down a light shaft on the premises, whose cover was defective, and the landlords were held liable to the plaintiff direct. This principle was extended to landlords' implied rights of entry, inspection and repair in *Mint* v. *Good*.[3] A third party was injured as a result of the collapse of a defective wall abutting the highway and was held entitled to damages from the landlord rather then the weekly tenant-occupier—the landlord having, as against the tenant, an implied right to enter, inspect and repair.

The mere existence of an express, implied, or statute imposed right of entry in the landlord to enter, inspect and repair suffices to attract a potential liability in the landlord in nuisance for injuries suffered by third parties, due to defect. owing to disrepair of the demised premises. It is not a condition precedent to the landlord's liability that he is unde

[2] [1940] 2 KB 476, CA.
[3] [1951] 1 KB 517, CA.

express, implied or statutorily-imposed repairing covenants vis-à-vis the tenant.[4]

C. *Landlord Licences Tenant to Commit Nuisance*

If the landlord lets premises in a defective condition, he may be liable to third parties damaged or injured by their condition: see section E below.

The landlord may also be liable to third parties injured by the defective or dangerous condition of the demised premises, though he is out of occupation personally, where he licences the tenant to commit the acts complained of, if these amount to a nuisance. For example an owner was held liable on this principle to adjoining owners where he expressly licensed an individual to excavate bricks from his land all day, causing a nuisance to the adjoining owners.[5] This principle is of very narrow ambit, and will seldom be invoked, for unless the act complained of is both shown to be a nuisance and also the inevitable result of the purpose of the letting, the landlord is not liable, though this will not, of itself, exonerate the tenant.[6]

In effect, the terms of the lease must actually give the tenant authority to create the nuisance, but in the context of dilapidated premises it is likely that any action will be based on the letting of the premises in a defective or dangerous state, as recently illustrated by *Sampson* v. *Hodson-Pressinger.*[7] The tenant holding under a long lease of a flat successfully recovered damages in nuisance against the assignee of the freehold reversion where the use of the terrace-roof above his flat by another tenant, caused the plaintiff sufficient inconvenience to amount to a nuisance, due to a defect in the terrace-roof known to the original landlord and his assignee. By taking an assignment of the freehold, the reversioner adopted the nuisance occasioned by the defect, of whose existence he had actual notice.

[4] *Heap* v. *Inde Coope & Allsopp Ltd, supra.*
[5] *White* v. *Jameson* (1874) 18 LR Eq 303.
[6] *Ayers* v. *Hanson* (1912) 56 SJ 735; *Tetley* v. *Chitty* [1986] 1 All ER 663.
[7] (1982) 261 EG 891; [1981] 3 All ER 710, CA.

D. *Premises Abutting the Highway*
General Rule

In the case of a public nuisance caused by the dangerous or defective state of premises abutting the highway, the land lord will be liable in nuisance to any third parties injured by the state of the premises—even if the tenant may also be liable to third parties.

If the defect is caused by a state of disrepair occasioned by the act of a trespasser or by a latent defect, the landlord is liable if he adopts the nuisance, or continues it, as from a time when he knew, or ought to have known, of the state of disrepair.

The landlord will not be able to avoid his special responsibility in the case of dangerous or defective premises adjoining the highway simply by taking a covenant to repair from the tenant.

The landlord's special liability applies where the third party has accidentally deviated from the highway, but not where the third party has deliberately deviated from the highway. The landlord's liability for breach of his special duty in the case of premises abutting the highway is extinguished only by an assignment of the reversion, and this in relation only to post-assignment breaches, not pre-assignment breaches. An action may also be brought against the assignee.[8]

Liability of Owner or Occupier: Basic Rules

The rules may be summarised as follows:

1. If, owing to a want of repair, premises on a highway become dangerous and constitute a nuisance, so that they collapse and cause injury to a passer-by or an adjoining owner's premises, the owner or occupier of the dangerous premises, if he has undertaken a duty to repair them, is liable in nuisance. This applies whether or not he knew or ought to have known of the danger.[9]

2. This special liability in nuisance extends also to any case where, although not under an express duty to repair, the landlord is under an implied duty to do so, and it also applies

---

[8] *Woodfall* 1–1679.
[9] *Wringe* v. *Cohen* [1940] 1 KB 229, CA.

where he has expressly reserved the right to enter and inspect and carry out repairs, or where he has an implied right to enter and inspect, or even where the landlord has been given permission to enter and repair whenever he asked.[10] This principle will apply to almost every case because, even where the tenant is, under the lease, liable for all repairs, most leases will reserve to the landlord the express right to enter and inspect and to execute repairs. Moreover, if statute reserves a right of entry to repair, then the principle will for that reason alone render the landlord liable in nuisance for dangerous or defective premises abutting the highway.

3. The special liability of the landlord in public nuisance for premises abutting the highway cannot be escaped merely by imposing a covenant to repair on the tenant.[11]

4. If the dangerous or defective condition of the premises is caused by a want of repair, then principles 1 to 3 above apply, but they are confined to that cause. If the condition of the premises is caused by the act of a trespasser, or by some cause other than neglect to repair, the landlord will only be liable in nuisance to third parties if he adopts or continues the nuisance.

If the third party wishes to rely on continuation as a ground of liability, he must show that the landlord had actual or presumed knowledge of the nuisance and that he, with that knowledge, failed to put an end to the nuisance. If adoption is sought to be relied on as a ground of liability, the third party must show that the landlord made use of any thing or matter constituting the nuisance.[12]

5. A landlord's failure to abate a nuisance within a reasonable time of actual or presumed knowledge of its existence will be actionable by any third party injured as a result, even when the cause of the nuisance is not a want of repair but some other cause, such as a heavy fall of snow.[13] A landlord was also liable, on this principle, once he had knowledge or presumed knowledge, to an injured third party passer-by,

[10] *Mint* v. *Good* [1951] 1 KB 517, at p. 527, CA.
[11] *Mint* v. *Good, supra.*
[12] *Sedleigh-Denfield* v. *O'Callaghan* [1940] AC 880, HL.
[13] *Slater* v. *Worthington's Cash Stores (1930) Ltd* [1941] 1 KB 488.

where the act of a trespasser caused a slate to fall off the roof of the demised premises, injuring the third party.[14]

Obviously, the landlord has a reasonable time as from knowledge, or means of knowledge, in which to execute the necessary repairs to make the premises safe: what is a reasonable time is a question of fact and only a reasonably short time (say a few days) is generally allowed to elapse between knowledge and the imposition of nuisance liability if no action is taken by the landlord.[15]

6. If the third party at the time of the injury caused by the defect in the demised premises has deliberately deviated from the highway—as opposed to accidentally doing so—then the above special rules have no application.[16]

Requirement of Proof of Negligence

In all the above instances of liability for public nuisance imposed on the landlord of defective premises, a failure by the landlord to repair the premises, or to cure the defect was a condition precedent to liability—as is proof by the third party that the landlord had knowledge, or means of knowledge, of the defect and then failed, within a reasonable time to act. It is the result of *King* v. *Liverpool City Council*[1] that in all these cases, irrespective of whether the third party frames his action in nuisance or negligence, negligence by the landlord must be shown—ie a breach of duty owed to the third party, and this will be harder to prove where the damage to the premises is caused by third parties not under the landlord's control, such as vandals or trespassers. In *King* for example, it was held that the landlord of a council tenant was not under a general duty to the tenant to see to it that a vacant flat of which the landlords were freeholders, and which was directly above the tenant's flat, was not vandalised where the flat was vandalised and water escaped from it in consequence, damaging the tenant's flat, her action in nuisance and alternatively in negligence against the landlord in respect of the damage suffered in consequence, failed. The

[14] *Cushing* v. *Peter Walker (Warrington & Burton) Ltd* [1941] 2 All ER 693.
[15] *Leanse* v. *Egerton* [1943] KB 323.
[16] *Jacobs* v. *LCC* [1950] AC 361, HL.
[17] (1986) 278 EG 516; [1986] 3 All ER 544, CA.

landlords could not take, in the circumstances, effective steps to defeat the actions of the trespassing vandals. The crucial point appears to be that, where there is damage occasioned to neighbouring premises of the landlord by third parties over whom the landlord has no control, great caution in imposing liability on the landlord for their acts is exercised. Perhaps a degree of likelihood amounting to inevitability may be required to be shown, in these cases, before the landlord can be held liable for the acts of the third parties.[18] Similarly, in *Smith* v. *Littlewoods Organisation*,[19] the owners of a cinema were held not liable for fire damage caused to adjoining premises, where the fire in question had been started by vandals entering the cinema as trespassers. While the owners were held to be under a general duty to exercise reasonable care to ensure that the condition of the premises they occupied was not a source of danger to neighbouring property, the extent of that duty varied. Where the events were not reasonably foreseeable, and on the facts they were not, it was held that the owners were not liable for the damage caused by the third parties.

Lord Mackay accordingly said:[20] "Where the only possible source of ... the damage or injury ... is agency of a human being for whom the person against whom the claim is made has no responsibility, it may not be easy to find that as a reasonable person he was bound to anticipate that type of damage as a consequence of his act or omission."

In the *King* case, the landlord did not accept liability to carry out repairs and this was an important factor. It may be different where the landlord accepts responsibility for repairs to the damaged or injured premises—even where the damage is caused by third party vandalisation. This was the result in *Ward* v. *Cannock Chase District Council*[21] where the council landlords, who owned a row of terraced houses, were held liable to the tenant of one of these houses for damage caused to the roof of the plaintiff's house when the rear wall

See also *P Perl (Exporters) Ltd* v. *Camden London Borough Council* [1984] QB 342,

[1987] 1 All ER 710.
Ibid at p. 721.
[1985] 3 All ER 537. The fact that liability for negligence was admitted was regarded in *King* v. *Liverpool City Council*, *supra*, as the crucial difference between the two cases.

of an adjoining house fell down due to vandalisation. The council landlords accepted responsibility to repair the wal but failed to act. Eventually, the condition of the plaintiff' house became so bad that he was rehoused and it was demolished—but not before vandals had, on occasions after the collapse of the walls, entered the house and removed chattels of the tenant. It was held that he was not entitled to recover damages to compensate him for damage or loss of his chattel removed or damaged by the vandals, as this was not a reasonably foreseeable consequence of the council's breach of duty. The council were, however, under a duty to keep the adjoining property in a safe condition and to see to it that it did not cause damage to the plaintiff's adjoining house (ie its fabric not contents). It was also held that the plaintiff was entitled to insist on continuing to live in his house and that, thanks to the council's breach of duty, he was entitled to recover as damages, the cost of rebuilding, if he could obtain planning permission. If not, the plaintiff could recover for the diminution in the value of his original property as an alternative. However, it should be stressed that, after *King* and *Smith* there appears to be no general duty on owners or occupiers of property to see to it that it is proof against vandalism. The damage resulting from the vandalism must be shown to be a reasonably foreseeable consequence of a breach duty by the owner, and the courts appear reluctant to infer this merely from the fact that the premises are vacant and thus vulnerable to attack by vandals or other trespassing third parties. In *Smith* v. *Littlewoods Organisation* Lord Goff said,[22] in justification of this narrow approach, that to impose a general duty on occupiers to take reasonable care to prevent others from entering their property "would impose an unreasonable burden on ordinary householders and an unreasonable curb on the ordinary enjoyment of their property."

F. *Landlord Lets Premises with a Nuisance*

Where the landlord lets premises which are in such a state as to amount to a nuisance, and the landlord created or continued the nuisance, then he is liable to a third party injured

---

[22] [1987] 1 All ER 710 at pp. 735–736.

or whose adjoining premises are damaged, as a result of the condition of the premises.[23]

For example, in *Todd* v. *Flight*[24] the landlord let a building whose chimneys were in a very dilapidated condition. The chimneys, which were, to the landlord's knowledge, insecure at the date of the lease, fell onto and damaged the roof and other parts of the plaintiff's adjoining building, and the landlord was held liable in nuisance.

As indicated, the landlord is only liable in nuisance on these principles if he is shown to have known, or to be presumed to have known, of the dangerous or dilapidated condition of the premises and must be responsible for the continuance of the nuisance resulting from that condition. If the landlord liable for repairs, as against the tenant, this suggests that he has continued the nuisance.[25] If, at the date of the lease, the landlord has no reason to suppose that there is a nuisance and could not, at the date of the letting, have discovered it with the exercise of reasonable care, then he escapes liability. Where part of an old city wall, let to a weekly tenant, fell into and damaged the premises of a third party occupying adjoining premises, since the landlords had no knowledge or means of knowledge of the wall's condition, they were, accordingly, held not liable.[26]

If, at the date of the lease, the landlord is not liable in nuisance for hidden defects, because it cannot be shown that he knew or ought to have known of them at that date, he cannot be made liable for damage occasioned to adjoining premises by reason of the condition of the demised premises. Whether the landlord has sufficient knowledge at the crucial time is essentially a question of fact. In *Brew Bros* v. *Snax (Ross) Ltd*[27] a flank wall—part of premises let to a tenant—tilted towards the plaintiff's adjoining premises. It was found to be in a dangerous condition, due to water seepage, which had caused its foundations to shift. The plaintiff's action against both landlord and tenant in nuisance succeeded.

*   *Metropolitan Properties Ltd* v. *Jones* [1939] 2 All ER 202.
*   (1860) 9 CB (NS) 377.
*   *Pretty* v. *Bickmore* (1873) LR 8 CP 401.
*   *St Anne's Well Brewery Co* v. *Roberts* (1928) 44 TLR 703, CA.
    [1970] 1QB 612, CA.

The landlords were held to be presumed to have known o
the existence of the nuisance at the date of the lease.

If the landlord is liable in nuisance for letting premises i
a defective state, he cannot avoid this liability by taking fron
the tenant a covenant to repair; also, if the landlord is liabl
for repairs and has a right of entry, express, implied, or unde
statute, to inspect and carry out repairs, then he will be liabl
for a nuisance of whose existence he knows or ought to hav
known which existed at the date of the lease and which con
tinues thereafter.[28]

III. LIABILITY OF TENANT IN NUISANCE

A. *General*

Despite the statements above as to the liability in nuisanc
of the landlord, it is the tenant, as occupier, who is generall
and solely liable to third parties in nuisance occasioned b
the defective or dangerous state of the demised premises.
Apart from public nuisance, liability here is based on faul
namely, neglect to repair by the tenant. Where, therefor
a tenant under a full repairing covenant held a lease of
building and the plaintiff was a weekly sub-tenant of par
and a heavy piece of guttering fell through the roof of th
part and injured the plaintiff's wife, he was held entitled
damages from the head tenant, who was under a duty
take care to prevent the guttering from falling—however, tl
action was classed as a negligence claim—neglect to comp
with his duty to repair the gutter by the tenant had to b
and was, shown.[30]

If a tenant is responsible for continuing a nuisance, as whe
he is under a liability to keep premises adjoining the highwა
in repair and neglects to do so, he will be liable to third par
highway users and adjoining owners for damage or inju
caused by defects in the premises in the same way as tl
landlord/owner, provided the tenant has continued or adopte
the nuisance with knowledge or means of knowledge.[31]

---

[28] *Mint* v. *Good* [1951] 1 KB 517, CA.
[29] *Cheetham* v. *Hampson* (1791) 4 TR 318.
[30] *Cunard* v. *Antifyre Ltd* [1933] 1 KB 551. It made no difference to the result that
two tenements were part of the same structure.
[31] *Pemberton* v. *Bright* [1960] 1 WLR 436.

for example, the tenant takes a lease of premises known to be in a dangerous or dilapidated state and fails to repair them then he will be liable in public nuisance to third parties (see the next section). Nor must the tenant allow the premises to fall into such a state that they amount to a nuisance.[32] No doubt, these principles will be mainly relevant to tenants holding long leases, as it will be unlikely that a periodic tenant will have the financial means to pay for any necessary repairs, and in that case the aggrieved third party will have to look to the landlord or mesne landlord for his remedies.

The tenant may be liable to injured third parties who are his lawful visitors under the common duty of care imposed on him as occupier by the *Occupiers' Liability Act 1957*—see below.

B. *Public Nuisance*

The tenant is under a strict duty to any users of the highway see to it that no injury results to them from any defective condition of the demised premises. In *Tarry v. Ashton*,[33] the tenant held a lease of a house, from the front of which a heavy lamp projected over the highway. The lamp fell and injured a passer-by, who recovered in nuisance, without any proof of negligence by the tenant. It was assumed that the tenant would regularly inspect the lamp. Therefore, in the case of public nuisance, a tenant may be held liable to a third party for injuries caused to him by a patent, or a latent, defect without proof by the third party of fault by the tenant.

Moreover, the strict liability of the tenant is co-extensive with any liability of the landlord's. This was established in *Wilchick v. Marks and Silverstone*,[34] where the landlords were liable to a third party for injuries caused by the fall of a defective shutter, on the basis that they reserved a right to enter and repair, even though they were under no obligation to repair; but the tenants, as occupiers, were also held liable. In fact, they had issued third party proceedings against the landlords and failed to recover against them, the tenant being liable in this instance to bear the whole loss.

---

[32] *Cunard* v. *Antifyre Ltd, supra.*
[33] (1876) 1 QBD 314.
[34] [1934] 2 KB 56.

The tenant's liability in public nuisance is strict but not unlimited because, as with the case of the landlord, if the tenant has no knowledge or means of knowledge of the nuisance, which is capable of being discovered by reasonable inspection, or if he does not continue the nuisance with such knowledge, he will not be liable.[35] For instance, if a branch were to fall onto the adjoining highway from a tree on the tenant's land due to a cause incapable of discovery by reasonable inspection, the tenant will escape liability in nuisance.[36] No doubt, regular inspections by the tenant will reduce the risk of liability; and if damage is occasioned by an inexplicable cause, he will be able to escape liability.

If the third party is not a user of the highway at the time of the injury, but instead is a lawful visitor to the premises, then it seems that, if the third party is injured by a defective part of the premises, such as a cornice, falling on him, the tenant will only be liable, first, if the defect was patent as opposed to latent, and, secondly, the third party is able to prove that the tenant knew or ought to have known of the defect.[37] In other words, the strict liability rules do not extend beyond the protection of highway users, under the guise of public nuisance. However, in the case of lawful visitors, liability will be regulated by the *Occupiers' Liability Act* 1957.

IV. LIABILITY OF LANDLORD AND TENANT IN NEGLIGENCE

A. *Position if Landlord is Not Occupier*

If the landlord is not in occupation of any part of the premises the rule is simple, but must be narrowly confined.[3] A landlord not in occupation of any part of the demised premises is not liable to third parties in negligence for injuries caused by the defective or dangerous state of the premises because he is not occupier.[39] In such cases, however, the tenant and his family members injured on the premises will, as against the landlord, be subject to section 4 of the Defective Premises Act, discussed in Chapter 11 of this book.

[35] *Barker* v. *Herbert* [1911] 2 KB 633, CA; *Hudson* v. *Bray* [1917] 1 KB 520.
[36] *Noble* v. *Harrison* [1926] 2 KB 332. On damage by tree-roots to the foundations of adjoining premises see *Russell* v. *London Borough of Barnet* (1984) 271 EG 699.
[37] *Pritchard* v. *Peto* [1917] 2 KB 173.
[38] *Rimmer* v. *Liverpool City Council* (1984) 269 EG 319; [1985] QB 1, CA.
[39] *Cavalier* v. *Pope* [1906] AC 428, HL.

If the landlord is out of occupation of all parts of the demised premises and is under no duty to repair, and has no express, implied, or statutory right to enter inspect and repair, then a third party who is a lawful visitor, and who is injured by a dangerous defect on the premises, will have to seek his remedy under the *Occupiers' Liability Act* 1957.

B. *Position if Landlord is Occupier of Part of the Premises*

Meaning of Occupier

The landlord is an occupier where, though he lets premises to a tenant, he retains control and occupation of certain parts of them, as where, for example, in the case of a letting of a block of flats, he retains control over the common user parts of the premises such as the lifts, stairways or other means of access. Or, where office multi-storey premises are let to various tenants and, again, control is retained over the common parts by the landlord.

Limit on Liability

While the landlord, as occupier, is subject to the common duty of care imposed by section 2 of the *Occupiers' Liability Act* 1957, this applies only to such parts of the premises as are retained under his control. The same limit applies to tenants.

Difficulty may, therefore, be experienced in deciding whether it is the landlord or the tenant who is the occupier, for the purposes of the 1957 Act, of a particular part of the building. The question is one of fact. If control of a particular part is exclusively reserved to one or other party, as where a staircase is excepted from the demise, there should be no problem. In *Wheat* v. *E Lacon & Co Ltd*[40] the landlords (the owners) of a public house were held to be "occupiers", for the purposes of the 1957 Act, of living accommodation used by their manager and paying guests of his, but there the manager was the licensee. The deciding factor as to which of landlord and tenant is occupier is the degree of control exercised by either over the relevant part of the premises,

---

[40] [1966] AC 552, HL.

where they are each in occupation of different parts; but exclusive possession is definitely not necessarily required to be shown as a condition precedent to liability. However if the landlord has let the whole premises to the tenant, it will be the tenant, not the landlord, who is occupier and under the common duty of care.

Common Duty of Care

The *Occupiers' Liability Act* 1957 imposes on an occupier whether landlord or tenant, the common duty of care to any lawful visitor. "Lawful visitor" includes any person lawfully entering the premises, as opposed to a trespasser. "Lawful visitor" also includes, by section 2(6), persons who enter the premises in the exercise of a right conferred by law, whether they have the occupier's permission or not. Trespassers are governed by separate rules outlined later.

The expression "occupier" is very wide and, in *Harris v Birkenhead Corporation*,[41] it was held to include a local authority which had served a notice of entry (as part of compulsory purchase) on the tenant of a terraced house, who quit in consequence. When the house was vandalised, the authority was therefore, held liable to a child injured by a dangerous defect in the house.

The duty of the occupier is to comply with the common duty of care. By section 2(2) of the 1957 Act, this is a duty to take such care as, in all the circumstances of the case, is reasonable to see that the visitor will be reasonably safe in using the premises for the purposes for which he is there. The duty applies to protect the lawful visitor's person and property.

If the visitor is on the premises as the result of a contract much depends on the nature and incidents of the contract. If, under a contract, the occupier is bound to allow third parties to enter and use the premises (such as allowing onto them builder's workmen or the occupier's own sub-contractors), section 3 of the 1957 Act will apply. Section 3(1) states that where the occupier is bound to permit strangers to enter or use the premises, his duty of care cannot be restricted or

---

[41] [1976] 1 All ER 341, CA

excluded by the contract. If the contract imposes a higher duty then the stranger is entitled, by section 3(1), to the benefit of that duty. By section 3(2), unless the contract expressly so provides, the occupier will not be liable to strangers for any injury caused by faulty work other than faulty work done by himself, his servants or agents.

Special Factors in Assessing Standard of Care of Occupier

1. Section 2(5) of the 1957 Act provides that the common duty of care does not impose on the occupier any obligation to a visitor in respect of risks voluntarily accepted by him as visitor.

2. Circumstances relevant to the common duty of care include, by section 2(3), the degree of care, and want of care, which would ordinarily be looked for in a visitor.

3. In particular, section 2(3)(a) provides that an occupier must be prepared for children to be less careful than adults. He might, therefore, have to warn a child of a danger which would be obvious to an adult.[42] Section 2(3)(b) provides that if the visitor is on the premises in the exercise of his calling, he will appreciate and guard against any special risks ordinarily incident to it, in so far as the occupier leaves him free to do so. Where, for example, a clerk of works uses scaffolding to inspect roof repairs, the visitor bears the risks entailed, not the occupier.[43]

Subjectivity of Common Duty of Care

Section 2(4) states that in determining whether the occupier has discharged the common duty of care, regard is to be had to all the circumstances. This imports subjectivity and the relevant factors include the type of premises, their standard of lighting, the purpose of the visitor, the nature of the defect causing the injury and the visitor's state of knowledge. The question of whether any warning of the danger was given by notice, or otherwise, is very material and section 2(4)(a) deals with this aspect. It provides that where damage is caused to a

---

[42] See *Phipps* v. *Rochester Corporation* [1955] 1 QB 450.
[43] *Howett* v. *Alfred Bagnall & Sons* [1967] 2 Lloyds Rep 370.

visitor by a danger of which he had been warned by the occupier, the warning is not, by itself, conclusive to enable the occupier to escape liability, unless it was enough to make the visitor reasonably safe.

If the visitor suffers personal injury or damage to his property from a danger caused by faulty work of an independent contractor, the occupier is, by section 2(4)(b), absolved from all liability if, in all the circumstances, it was reasonable for him to entrust the work to an independent contractor and if he took all reasonable steps to satisfy himself that the contractor was competent and the work properly done.

The scope of the duty of care is illustrated by two cases. In *Irving* v. *London County Council*[44] the plaintiff was a tenant of a flat on the third floor and the landlords retained control of the common staircase in the block of flats. This was lit by their lighting system, controlled by a time-switch. The plaintiff was injured when she fell on the dark staircase: the time-switch on the lighting system had apparently malfunctioned. It was held that the defendants were under no liability to keep the staircase lit at all hours of darkness. They were exonerated from liability. Likewise, in *Shortall* v. *Greater London Council*[45] the landlords' servants removed a smashed glass panel in an entrance door leaving simply the frame, which was not boarded up. A visitor pushed her hand through the open space in the frame and fell through the door. It was held that she could not claim damages for her injuries as the landlords had done all that was reasonable to prevent injury.

These cases show that the common duty of care is certainly not absolute and that its exact application will depend on whether what the occupier has done is reasonable—a very flexible notion. If the landlord in the *Shortall* case had simply left the source of danger, the smashed panel, in place, he could not, it is thought, have escaped liability.

Exclusion of Common Duty of Care

Section 2(1) of the 1957 Act preserves the freedom of the

[44] (1965) 109 SJ 157.
[45] (1969) 210 EG 25.

occupier to restrict, modify or exclude his duty to visitors by agreement or otherwise.

Subject to the *Unfair Contract Terms Act* 1977, the occupier is free to exclude the common duty of care by a notice or contract. This could be achieved by a notice at the entrance of the occupier's land or premises, which makes it clear that visitors enter at their own risk.[46] It makes no difference that the visitor does not see or read the notice: but reasonable efforts must be made to warn the visitor that he enters at his own risk.

However, the *Unfair Contract Terms Act* 1977 severely limits the occupier's power to exclude his common duty of care by notice or otherwise.

Unfair Contract Terms Act 1977

1. Where the landlord, for example, retains part of the demised premises in his control, section 2(1) of the *Unfair Contract Terms Act* 1977 provides that he cannot exclude or restrict his liability for death or personal injury resulting from negligence at all. In relation to other loss or damage, the landlord will only be able to exclude or restrict his liability for negligence if the notice satisfies the statutory requirements of reasonableness (section 2(2)). Identical principles apply where it is the tenant who is the occupier of the premises or part concerned.

2. The 1977 Act applies only to business liability (s 1(3)). A purely domestic occupier, whether landlord or tenant, is still free to restrict, modify or exclude his liability for negligence by contract or notice. It has been argued that, if a domestic occupier allowed part of his house to be occupied by a lodger, the restrictions in the *Unfair Contract Terms Act* 1977 might apply to protect the lodger.[47]

3. Under section 2 of the *Occupiers' Liability Act* 1984, a business occupier who permits access to his premises for recreational or educational purposes is not subject to the restrictions on his power to exclude or limit his liability for death or personal injuries imposed by the 1977 Act. This exemption from the 1977 Act will not apply if the business of the occupier

---

[46] *Ashdown* v. *Samuel Williams Ltd* [1957] 1 QB 409, CA.
[47] Mesher [1979] Conv 58.

is the provision of recreational or educational facilities—such as a school, university or circus, for example. In that case the 1977 Act limitations will apply in full.

Duty of Occupier to Trespassers

The occupier's duty to trespassers differs from that to his lawful visitors. Until the passing of the *Occupiers' Liability Act* 1984 the occupier's duty to trespassers, though a little uncertain, depended on its being shown that the injury to the trespasser was deliberately inflicted. If the trespasser was a child known to frequent or visit the premises, possibly attracted by dangerous things there, different rules applied. The duty towards trespassers was labelled one of common humanity.

Section 1(3) and 1(4) of the 1984 Act appear to have altered the rules, but in any event the new duty to trespassers applies only to personal injuries, not to damage to property.

Section 1(3) and (4) of the 1984 Act

In relation to the risk of personal injuries to trespassers on the premises, section 1(3) of the 1984 Act provides that the occupier owes a duty to a trespasser if:

(a) he is aware of the danger (on the premises) or had reasonable grounds to believe that it exists;

(b) he knows or has reasonable grounds to believe that the other is in the vicinity of the danger or that he may come into its vicinity;

(c) the risk is one against which he may reasonably be expected to offer some protection to the trespasser.

The doctrine of assumption of risk by the trespasser is expressly made a defence to the occupier's liability (s 1(6)).

The duty of the occupier, where it arises, by section 1(4) is to take such care as is reasonable in all the circumstances to see that the trespasser does not suffer injury.

The duty may, by section 1(5), be discharged in appropriate cases by taking such steps as are reasonable in all the circumstances to give warning of the danger or to discourage persons from incurring the risk.

It seems that if a warning notice is put up at the entrance to or boundary of the land or premises, and it is sufficiently prominent and legible to be capable of being read by any trespasser, in many cases the occupier will be able to avoid liability: if a trespasser enters he does so at his own risk.[48] It is thought that warning notices might not suffice to avoid liability in the case of child trespassers.

The view just advanced about the efficacy of warning notices has yet to be tested; and it could be open to dispute on the grounds that a trespasser has no right to enter the premises at all; therefore it could be said to be illogical to impose conditions by notice on him.[49]

In any event, no warning notice to a trespasser could be effective to avoid the occupier's liability in relation to concealed or unusual hazards on the land or premises.

C. *Position if Landlord Lets Whole Premises*

Where the landlord demises the whole of the land or premises to the tenant, he ceases to be the occupier for the purposes of the *Occupiers' Liability Acts* 1957 and 1984. It is the tenant who is the sole occupier.

The same rules governing liability to lawful visitors and trespassers apply to a tenant/occupier as to a landlord/occupier.

Section 4 of the *Defective Premises Act* 1972 imposes liabilities on the landlord for dangerous defects on the premises where he is not the occupier, if he is under a contractual or statutory duty to repair the premises. See Chapter 11 above.

V. LIABILITY OF LANDLORD OR OCCUPIER UNDER OTHER LEGISLATION

A very brief outline is given of the liability of a landlord or occupier under legislation dealing with offices, shops and railway premises and factories.

A. *Offices, Shops and Railway Premises*

Certain duties are imposed by the *Offices, Shops and Railway Premises Act* 1963 on on the employer or landlord, to ensure the health, safety and welfare of employees on the premises.

---

[48] *Ashdown* v. *Samuel Williams Ltd* [1957] 1 QB 409, CA.
[49] See Buckley [1984] Conv 413.

The duties imposed by the 1963 Act are cast on:

(a) the occupier of the office, shop, etc, where the whol building is used as an office shop etc: the occupier is th employer.

(b) the owner (ie the landlord) of the office, or shop wher it is held on a lease at a rack-rent and comprises part onl of a single building. If the lease is at a ground rent then th occupier is the person subject to the statutory responsibilitie:

The duties are imposed by section 42 of the 1963 Act.⁵ They include a duty to secure that every common part c the building is kept in a clean state; to secure and maintai sufficient lighting, artificial or natural, of common parts; t ensure that floors, stairs, passages and gangways in a commo part of the building are of sound construction. They als require it to be ensured that there is no contravention of tl statutory duty to provide suitable sanitary and washing facil ties. There must also be compliance with statutory provisior as to fire precautions and equipment.

Contravention of the requirements of the Act by the occ pier or landlord is a criminal offence punishable with a max mum fine of £2,000⁵¹ on summary conviction or, o indictment, to an unlimited fine.

If the occupier or landlord breaks his statutory duty, th any employee injured or suffering damage as a result has cause of action for breach of statutory duty.

If it is the landlord who is the person responsible for cor pliance with the Act and, if he cannot under the lease ent the premises to execute any necessary work to comply wi the Act because the lease fails to provide for this, then I may apply to the county court and it has power under sectic 73(1) to modify the lease (or agreement) as it thinks just ar equitable. The county court may, on the landlord's applic tion, direct that the tenant contribute, by rent increase otherwise, to the costs of any work required to be done enable the landlord to comply with his statutory duti (s 73(2)).

---

⁵⁰ As amended *Offices, Shops and Railway Premises Act* 1963 (Repeals and Modificatic Regs 1974 SI 1974/1943.
⁵¹ Level 5 of the standard scale of fines imposed by *Criminal Justice Act* 1982 ss 35–46.

B. *Factories Act 1961*[52]

The owner of a tenement factory (by s 175, this broadly means any premises where the mechanical power from any prime mover in the premises is distributed for use in manufacturing processes to different parts of the same premises occupied by different persons in different factories) or of a building, part of which is let as a factory, is responsible for fire precautions and fire fighting, not the occupier.

"Owner" means (s 176(1)) the person for the time being receiving the rack-rent—ie where the premises are leased, except at a ground rent, the landlord.

The owner of a tenement factory (ie in some cases the landlord) is responsible for contravention of various statutory duties such as floor drainage, sanitary conveniences, cleanliness, overcrowding, lighting and so on, also provision of fencing and safety appliances and the maintenance and testing of machinery and plant.

---

[52] Sections 48–52, as amended by *Factories Act (Repeals and Modifications) Regulations* 74 SI 1974/1941.

Chapter 15
MISCELLANEOUS ASPECTS

I. INTRODUCTION

In this Chapter, some aspects of property disrepair and improvements, which cannot usefully be grouped together anywhere else are dealt with. These are: first, consideration of the duty, if any, on an owner to fence off his land; secondly, an outline of the rules governing compensation for tenants' improvements to business premises; thirdly, an outline of the consequences for rent review if the demised premises are in disrepair at the date of review; lastly, consideration of the impact of dilapidations on tenant's options to purchase, to renew and to break the lease.

II. OBLIGATION TO FENCE

A. *General Rule*

There is no obligation at common law on any owner of land to erect and maintain a fence around his land,[1] and any covenant by him to do so will be purely personal to the contracting parties and will not impose an obligation on the covenantor's successors in title.[2] Therefore, a liability to fence an expression referring not just to fences but to hedges, for example) arises in exceptional cases such as under statute, prescription or express grant or by agreement.

However, an occupier of land may be under a duty to fence to comply with his obligations under the *Occupiers' Liability Act* 1957—as to which see Chapter 14. It is possible that a person who is injured by contact with an electrified fence in the countryside may have a cause of action in nuisance or negligence—as also where that person's animals are injured,

---

[1] *Hilton* v. *Ankesson* (1872) 27 LT 519; *Jones* v. *Price* [1965] 2 QB 618, CA.
[2] *Austerberry* v. *Oldham Corporation* (1885) 29 Ch D 750, CA. The fact that occasional pairs are done is not evidence of a contract to repair: *Boyle* v. *Tamlin* (1827) 6 B & C 329.

but fault must be proved.[3] If the fence is installed by a competent contractor and competently managed—as where the current is too low to cause direct injury—then no action can be maintained.[4]

B. *Statutory Obligations to Fence*

Highways

Section 165(1) of the *Highways Act* 1980 imposes a duty on an owner to fence off his land if, in any land adjoining a street there is an unfenced, or inadequately fenced, source of danger to any person using the street.[5] The local authority may by notice to the owner or occupier of land require him within a time specified in the notice, to execute any works of repair, protection, removal or enclosure as will obviate the danger, and the authority has default powers to execute the works, and to recover the cost from the person in default.

Railways

Section 68 of the *Railways Clauses Consolidation Act* 1845 imposes a duty on railways undertakers, who acquired land compulsorily, to erect and maintain fences in perpetuity: this duty devolves on British Rail, for example. The liability is to "erect and maintain sufficient posts, rails, hedges, ditches mounds or other fences, for separating the land taken for the use of the railway from the adjoining lands not taken and protecting such lands from trespass, or the cattle of the owners and occupiers thereof from straying thereout, by reason of the railway."

This liability will not end merely with the closure of the railway itself: and may continue even after the track is removed, and the railway abandoned: the purposes for which fencing must be constructed under section 68 include not only preventing cattle from straying onto the railway, but also the separation of the railway land from adjoining land and the protection of adjoining land from trepass.[6]

---

[3] See Samuels (1968) 112 494.
[4] *Green* v. *Fibreglass* [1958] 2 QB 245.
[5] See *Myers* v. *Harrow Corporation* [1958] 2 QB 442.
[6] *Walker (R) & Sons* v. *British Railways Board* [1984] 2 All ER 249.

The fences must be sufficiently strong to prevent sheep and cattle straying out of adjoining lands.[7] "Cattle" bears a wide meaning and so includes pigs, poultry and other smaller animals, and fences must, therefore, be high and strong enough to keep in animals of a normal disposition and strength in normal circumstances from wandering off onto the railway.[8] Where, therefore, excited cattle (because of a division of the herd by the plaintiff) broke through a railway fence to join the rest of the herd and some were killed by a train, the plaintiff failed to recover.[9]

If there is no cause of action under the statute, an alternative claim may be framed in negligence.[10]

Mines, Quarries and Tips

Section 151 of the *Mines and Quarries Act* 1954 imposes a duty to fence on the owner of every abandoned mine, or mine that has not been worked for 12 months. A fence must be provided sufficient to prevent any person from accidentally falling down the mine-shaft.

In connection with tips associated with mines and quarries, section 1(1) of the *Mines and Quarries (Tips) Act* 1969 requires that tips, defined so as to include an accumulation or deposit of refuse from a mine or quarry which is above ground, must be made and kept secure.

C. *Liability to Fence by Prescription or Grant*

An obligation by the owners and occupiers of a piece of land to maintain a fence for the benefit of the owners and occupiers of adjoining land has been recognised at common law. The right to have a fence maintained is not a true easement because generally the law is reluctant to recognise positive easements.

What is required to be shown is that the fence, which may include a hedge, has been maintained and repaired by the owner or occupier, as a matter of obligation, over a long period, as opposed to the carrying out of repairs over a matter

---

[7] *Bessant* v. *Great Western Rail Co* (1860) 8 CB (NS) 368.
[8] *Child* v. *Hearn* (1874) LR 9 Ex 176.
[9] *Cooper* v. *Railway Executive* [1953] 1 All ER 477.
[10] *Short* v. *British Railways Board* [1974] 3 All ER 28.

of years without more. This was the basis of *Jones* v. *Price*,[11] where the owner of the land in question had, from time to time, repaired gaps in the "fence" (a hedge) to contain her own animals. It was held, on the facts, that there was no evidence of repairs having been carried out over a long period under an obligation to the adjoining landowner. The mere fact that the defendant had constantly carried out repairs to the fence on request was not sufficient to establish an easement of fencing. Moreover, it was held in *Egerton* v. *Harding*[12] that merely to prove that local custom obliges the owner concerned to repair fences on his land will not suffice to establish an easement of fencing. What must be shown, as was seen, is long usage of fencing as a matter of obligation as opposed to carrying out the repairs voluntarily, an example being the habitual fencing on demand.

The nature of the fencing easement was discussed in *Crow* v. *Wood*,[13] where it was held that a fencing easement was capable of lying in grant: in other words, if it is shown to exist, it will pass automatically under section 62 of the *Law of Property Act* 1925 and will burden the land with the duty to fence against not merely the present owner, but also his successors in title. Moreover, it is implicit in this case that a right to have fences repaired may be expressly granted, in a conveyance of adjoining land, by deed. This easement may also be acquired by prescription.

Where an obligation to fence is established, if the neighbour's cattle escape onto the land of the owner liable to fence the land concerned against cattle, causing damage, the servient owner will be unable to complain of cattle trespass.[14] If cattle (and this term is wide enough to include horses) escape from land which should have been fenced in, causing damage to animals on neighbouring land, or any other damage, such as to growing produce on the adjoining land, the servient owner will be liable in damages for breach of his duty to fence.[15]

---

[11] [1965] 2 QB 618, CA.
[12] [1974] 3 All ER 689, CA.
[13] [1971] 1 QB 77, CA.
[14] *Crow* v. *Wood*, *supra*.
[15] *Holgate* v. *Bleazard* [1917] 1 KB 443; *Park* v. *J Jobson & Son* [1945] 1 All ER 222, CA.

D. *Duty to Fence Arising out of Agreement*

It has been noted that liability to fence may arise out of both covenant and agreement, but no contractual obligation to maintain a fence is capable of running with burdened freehold land, and it binds only the original contracting parties.

Freehold Land

In the case of freehold land, no covenant to erect and maintain a fence or to share in the costs thereof runs with the land so as to be enforceable against successors in title to the original parties, whether at law or in equity.[16] This rule may be avoided if a prescriptive right to repair and maintain a fence is proved, see below.

Possibly, the rule is open to evasion in other ways and some of these are noted.

1. Every time the burdened land changes hands, a covenant of indemnity could be taken from the latest new servient owner. Sooner or later, by reason of bankruptcy for example, this chain will be broken and the land will cease to be burdened by the covenant to fence.

2. Reliance might be placed on the doctrine of mutual benefit and burden,[17] in which adjoining fence owners contribute to the costs of repairs and maintenance and enjoy the benefits of the fencing.[18] As to what happens if a given owner refuses to contribute and is willing to allow the fencing to decay at the same time, this is not clear.

3. A long lease of the burdened land might be granted, with an obligation to fence imposed on the tenant; then the lease might be enlarged into a freehold under section 153 of the *Law of Property Act* 1925. This is a device which both untried and rather contrived.

Leasehold Land

In the case of leasehold land, any covenants in the lease by the landlord or tenant to repair and maintain fences on

---

[6] *Austerberry* v. *Oldham Corporation* (1885) 29 Ch D 750; *SE Rail Co* v. *Associated Portland Cement Manufacturers (1910) Ltd* [1910] 1 Ch 12.

[7] This and the following suggestion are those of Powell-Smith, p. 110 ff.

[8] Under *Halsall* v. *Brizell* [1957] Ch 169.

the demised premises are fully enforceable as between the parties on ordinary principles: and tenants may well contribute to the cost of fencing. The benefit and burden of these covenants will pass automatically on an assignment of the reversion and of the lease under general rules discussed earlier Such a covenant, as a covenant to repair, will run with the land.

While a yearly tenant or tenant at will is not liable for permissive waste, this does not, of itself, relieve him of his obligation, if shown to have arisen under long usage, to keep a fence in good repair.[19]

III. OUTLINE OF COMPENSATION FOR BUSINESS TENANTS' IMPROVEMENTS[20]

Compensation for tenants' improvements which the tenant leaves on the premises on quitting is governed by the *Landlord and Tenant Act* 1927 Part I (as amended by the *Landlord and Tenant Act* 1954).

A. *Application and Scope of 1927 Act*

By section 17(1) the compensation provisions apply only to a holding used wholly or partly for trade or business purposes (this includes professional purposes) and tenancies of agricultural holdings, and most service tenancies are excluded If part only of the holding is used for business purposes then by section 17(4) improvements only in relation to that part are within the 1927 Act provisions.

A lease of any length will qualify for 1927 Act compensation, and in relation to improvements carried out after October 1954, improvements carried out during the last three years of the tenancy will qualify as much as those carried out at any earlier time.

B. *Qualifying Improvements*

There is no definition of improvements for the purpose of the 1927 Act, but it is provided in section 1(1) that the

---

[19] *Cheetham* v. *Hampson* (1791) 4 TR 318; *Star* v. *Rookesby* (1710) 1 Salk 335.
[20] See generally Fox-Andrews QC, *Business Tenancies*, Chapter 2.

mprovement[21] must add to the letting value of the holding. Trade or other fixtures, which the tenant is entitled to remove at the termination of the tenancy, do not qualify for compensation (s 1(1)).

The tenant (widely defined in s 25(1) as any person entitled to possession under any contract of tenancy) must make a claim as prescribed under section 1(1) in respect of relevant improvements carried out by him or his predecessors in title.[22] No improvement made before 25 March 1928 qualifies (s 2(1)), nor does an improvement made by the tenant or his predecessor in title under a contractual obligation for valuable consideration, including under a building lease s 2(1)). An improvement begun after 1 October 1954, but not before that date, in pursuance of a statutory obligation, will qualify.[23]

C. *Qualifying Conditions*

1. Before making any improvement the tenant must, under section 3(1) of the 1927 Act, serve a notice of intention to make the improvement on the landlord. The notice must be accompanied by a specification.[24] The tenant's notice does not have to be in any particular form. It must be in writing, as must *all* notices under the 1927 Act (s 23).

2. The landlord then has three months after the service of the tenant's notice to serve a notice of objection (s 3(1)) and if he does not the tenant may proceed—but solely in accordance with the plan and specification (s 3(4)). If the landlord objects, the tenant may then apply (s 63 of the 1954 Act) either to the Chancery Division of the High Court, if the rateable value of the premises is over £5,000, or the county court, if it is £5,000 or less. Applications must be as laid down by rules of court.[25]

---

[1] See *National Electric Theatres* v. *Hudgell* [1939] Ch 553. It is *net* additions to the value the holding which the 1927 Act deals with ie their overall effect.
[2] See *Pelosi* v. *Newcastle Arms Brewery (Nottingham) Ltd* (1982) 43 P & CR 18 (sub-lessees o carried out improvements then assigned to X, who obtained an assignment of the head se held to be predecessors in title of X who was entitled to compensation).
[3] *Landlord and Tenant Act* 1954, s 48.
[4] See *Deerfield Travel Services Ltd* v. *Leathersellers of London* (1983) 46 P & CR 132 ter plus final drawings sent to landlord sufficient specifications).
[5] For forms of application see RSC Ord 97 (Chancery Division of High Court) and CCR 1 Ord 43 and Practice Form N395 (county court).

3. Superior landlords will be entitled to service of copies of the tenant's application.

4. The appropriate court has power to decide whether the improvement is proper and will grant a certificate if it decides that it is.[26] It must be satisfied (by the tenant) that the improvement:

—will add to the letting value of the holding at the termination of the tenancy;

—is reasonable and suitable to the character of the holding (if it is shown by the landlord to be calculated to injure the amenity or convenience of the neighbourhood it will not be);[27]

—will not diminish the value of any other property of the same landlord or of any superior landlord from whom the immediate landlord or tenant hold.

5. The proviso to section 3(1) enables the landlord to offer to execute the improvement himself in consideration for reasonable rent increase, and the court can then only give a certificate to the tenant if the landlord fails to carry out his undertaking.

6. Once the tenant has completed the improvement, he may require the landlord to give him a certificate—if within one month of that request the landlord fails to do so, the court is empowered to give a certificate (s 3(6)). No form of request is prescribed.

D. *Claim for Compensation*

A tenant's claim for compensation must be made in accordance with the rules of court mentioned above, and it must be in writing and contain full particulars. Strict time limits are imposed by section 47 of the *Landlord and Tenant Act 1954* so that, for example, claims must be made:

—within three months of a notice to quit, or to terminate being given;

—not more than six but not less than three months before the termination of a tenancy due to expire by effluxion of time;

---

[26] Under s 3(4) the court has power to modify the tenant's plan etc and time for completion must be agreed or determined by the court.

[27] Fox-Andrews, Chapter 2, p. 300.

—within three months of the effective date of an order for possession in forfeiture proceedings or within three months of peaceable re-entry.

There is no power to extend these strictly-enforced time-limits.[28]

If the tenant remains on the holding, as where he obtains new tenancy from the court under Part II of the 1954 Act r by agreement) no compensation is payable under the 1927 ct—quitting is the condition precedent of obtaining compen-tion.[29]

E. *Amount of Compensation*

In principle, the sum paid as compensation is not to exceed 1(1) of the 1927 Act, proviso):

(a) the net addition to the value of the holding as a whole, hich may be determined to be the direct result of the provement; or

(b) the reasonable cost of carrying out the improvement the termination of the tenancy, subject to a deduction of e cost of putting the works constituting the improvement to a reasonable state of repair, in so far as this is not covered the tenant's repairing covenants.

If it is shown that it is intended to demolish or structurally er the premises or any part or to use them for a different rpose after termination of the tenancy, regard must be had, determining the net addition, to the effect of any of these tters on the improvement (s 1(2)). If the court decides that compensation or reduced compensation is payable, it may ow a further application by the tenant, if effect is not given the intention of the landlord, within a time fixed by the urt (s 1(3)). Compensation will be reduced if the tenant eives any benefit from the landlord in consideration for improvement (s 2(3)).

f the tenant has installed trade fixtures, he cannot claim npensation under the 1927 Act for these, as it is assumed t he will remove them on quitting, and his right to do

---

Donegal Tweed Co v. Stephenson (1929) 98 LJ KB 657.
Cave v. Page [1923] WN 178; Preston v. Norfolk County Council [1947] KB 775.

so survives the continuation of a business tenancy and i[*]
renewal under Part II of the 1954 Act.[30]

IV. EFFECT OF DISREPAIR ON RENT REVIEW[31]

Whether a valuer is entitled to take into account the effe[*]
of a state of disrepair to the demised premises on a rent review
will depend on the exact terms of the rent review clause wit[*]
which he is faced, and the other terms of the lease, includin[*]
the incidence of liability for repairs. In a long commerci[*]
lease, the landlord might be responsible, at least in a mult[*]
occupied building, for structural and exterior repairs and t[*]
tenant for other repairs.

It appears from the decision of Walton J in *Clarke* v. *Find[*]
Developments*[32] that an arbitrator has no jurisdiction [*]
determine a rent under review which varies from time to tim[*]
during the review period according to the state of repair [*]
the premises. In this case, the relevant formula provided f[*]
an open market rent on the supposition that the tenant h[*]
complied with all his repairing covenants.

Rent Review Provisions Silent on Repairs

It seems that the valuer is to discover, if the premises are i[*]
poor state of repair at the review date, whether the other ter[*]
of the lease require them to be valued in some other sta[*]
presumably ignoring the disrepair. This view is backed up [*]
Harmsworth Pension Fund Trustees v. *Charringtons Indu[*]
trial Holdings Ltd*,[33] where a rent review clause said nothi[*]
about the state of repair of the premises and required an asse[*]
ment of the fair market rack-rent. Warner J held that t[*]
effect of tenants' disrepair must be ignored in the valuatic[*]
Otherwise the tenant could take advantage of his own wro[*]

Reasonable Rent

Some rent review formulae are objective—referring t[*]
rent for the demised premises and some are subjective, ref[*]

---

[30] *New Zealand Government Property Corporation* v. *HM&S Ltd* [1982] QB 1145.
[31] See generally Bernstein and Reynolds, *Handbook of Rent Review*, Sweet & Max[*]
4–5 *et seq*, the structural analysis of which is here adopted with the permission of the au[*]
and publisher, which is gratefully acknowledged.
[32] (1984) 270 EG 246.
[33] (1985) 274 EG 588.

ing to a reasonable rent between the parties. The view has been expressed that it cannot be "reasonable"—where the objective formula is used—to require the landlord to receive a lower rent on account of tenant's breaches of his covenant to repair.[34] Whether this is correct or not remains to be seen, in the absence of direct authority—but any other view would confer an unfair windfall benefit on the tenant, rewarding him for his own breaches.

Direction to Valuer to Assume Performance by Tenant of his Covenant to Repair

Possibly, a valuer will, under this assumption, have to examine the tenant's covenant to repair as well as the rent review clause, to see if disputed items fall within it.[35]

In any case, the landlord will have to show a state of disrepair. If it is the landlord who is in breach of covenant, the problem is wide open: apparently, it is for the valuer to assess to what extent the tenant's right to enforce the covenant is reflected in the rent in the open market.

Clause Requires Assumption that All Covenants to Repair Duly Performed

This simply means that the tenant will have to pay the open market rent, if that is what he is required to pay. This may be contrary to the facts, for the landlord may be in breach of structural and exterior repairing obligations—devaluing the premises to a notional incoming tenant, who will expect premises in a state fit for immediate occupation.

RICS/Law Society Model Form (and ISVA Clause)

The model form requires it to be assumed that the tenant's covenants to repair have been performed and that the premises are fit for immediate occupation; or, if damaged or destroyed by fire, that they have been fully restored. Again this requires assumptions to be made which may well conflict with the actual facts and cause harsh results. On the other hand if that is the lease the tenant has agreed to take, so be it.

Bernstein & Reynolds, para 4 – 54.
Bernstein and Reynolds, para 4 – 55.

V. EFFECT ON TENANTS' OPTIONS TO PURCHASE, RENEW AND BREAK LEASE OF BREACHES OF REPAIRING COVENANTS

A. Introduction

A tenant with a substantial term may well be entitled t exerise one or more options to purchase, to renew and t break the lease. The right to exercise any or all of them generally made expressly dependent on compliance by th tenant with two preconditions:

(1) *Notice requirements*—These are formal and migł involve the tenant serving a six months' notice in advanc of the date of purchase, renewal or determination on the lanc lord.

(2) *Covenants*—It will generally be a condition precedeï of any right to purchase, renew or break that the tenant ï the operative date has fully complied with all the covenanï in the lease. The lease will probably define "operative date It might be the date of the tenant's notice, or the determinatic of the term.[36]

B. Position Where Tenant is in Breach of Covenant to Repe

General

If, at the operative date of the option in question, the is a subsisting breach of covenant to repair by the tenaï he will be completely disentitled, as a result, to exercise ï option to purchase, renew or break, provided the option (as usually it will be) expressly conditional on the due perfc mance by the tenant of his covenants. "Subsisting" mea either that the breach must not be spent, or, at any rate th the landlord no longer has a subsisting cause of action respect of it. The same principles apply to all three types option.[37]

On the other hand, if at the operative date there is no su sisting breach by the tenant of his covenant to repair or any other covenant in the lease, such as to pay rent or insure, then the tenant may insist on exercising the opti in question, provided his notice to do so is served witł

[36] *Simons* v. *Associated House Furnishers Ltd* [1931] 1 Ch 379.
[37] *Grey* v. *Friar* (1854) 4 HLC 565; *Bass Holdings Ltd* v. *Morton Music Ltd.* [198 All ER 1001 [1987] 1 EGLR 214, CA.

any time-limits imposed by the lease. The fact that the tenant may have committed past breaches of positive or negative covenants, which are spent at the operative date, will not disentitle him to exercise his option.[38]

If the landlord has waived a breach which was subsisting at the operative date, then he cannot rely on that particular breach to disentitle the tenant to exercise an option. Similarly, conduct amounting to estoppel by the landlord in relation to a subsisting breach at the operative date will preclude the landlord from relying on the breach in question as a ground for refusing to allow the tenant to exercise his rights under an option to purchase, renew or break.[39]

Some Further Detailed Considerations

1. The crucial factor in relation to the entitlement of a tenant to exercise options in the lease, which are conditional on due performance by the tenant of his covenants, is whether any breaches of covenant are "subsisting" at the operative date. In *Bass Holdings Ltd* v. *Morton Music Ltd*[40] Kerr LJ said: "There is no reported case in which any tenant's option has been defeated by a spent breach ..."

If the tenant has, in the past history of the lease, broken his covenant to repair and has fully remedied that breach, as after service of a landlord's forfeiture notice and schedule of dilapidations, the landlord cannot subsequently invoke the breach as a ground for refusing to comply with the tenant's notice under an option. If, at some earlier stage to the service of his option notice, the tenant had, in forfeiture proceedings, obtained relief against forfeiture, and had fully complied with any terms of relief, then again the breach of covenant will be spent, and the tenant's rights under the option will be unprejudiced by it.[41] The same rule would, presumably, apply the tenant, at some past date, had been held liable to pay damages to the landlord for a breach of his covenant to repair.

2. If, at the operative date, the tenant is in breach of his covenant to repair, then no matter how trivial the breach

---

[38] *Bass Holdings Ltd* v. *Morton Music Ltd, supra.*
[39] The silence of the landlord is not estoppel: *West Country Cleaners (Falmouth)* v. *Saly* (1966) 199 EG 563, CA.
[40] *Supra* at p. 1006.
[41] *Kitney* v. *Greater London Properties Ltd* (1984) 272 EG 786.

may be, the tenant will be disentitled to exercise any options to purchase, renew or break. In *Finch* v. *Underwood*,[42] the tenant of a seven year renewable lease was held to be disentitled to exercise a renewal option in standard-form because, at the date of the notice of purported exercise, the premises required an estimated maximum of £40's worth of repairs due to the tenant's breach of his repairing covenant. In *West Country Cleaners (Falmouth) Ltd* v. *Saly*[43] breaches at the date of the tenant's notice to exercise an option to renew, of the tenant's covenant to paint every three years and in the last year of the term, disentitled the tenant to renewal. The premises had been kept in a fair decorative state: the fact that the breaches were trivial did not make any difference.

3. As indicated, full compliance with the tenant's covenant to repair at the operative date is required: this requirement is very strict, assuming the breach of covenant is not spent. It appears that if the tenant complies with most but not all aspects of a schedule of dilapidations, and the court decide that his partial non-compliance amounts to a breach of covenant, if the breach is, in the above sense, subsisting at the operative date, it will disentitle the tenant to exercise the option to purchase, renew or break, as the case may be.[44]

4. In the case of a tenant's option to determine, the reason for a strict rule, in relation to any subsisting breaches at the operative date, was, according to Nicholls LJ in *Bass Holding Ltd* v. *Morton Music Ltd*:[45] "With such a clause the commercial purpose achieved by a condition construed as meaning "no subsisting breach" is readily apparent: before the lease can be ended prematurely all the rent due must have been paid, the property must have been put into a proper state of repair, and the other covenants must have been observed and performed in the sense that all liability in respect of any previous breaches must be at an end ..."

This leads to a further point: if the tenant is fully in compliance with his covenant to repair at the operative date, but not in relation to other covenants, whether positive or nega

---

[42] (1876) 2 Ch D 310.
[43] (1966) 199 EG 563, CA.
[44] *Kitney* v. *Greater London Properties Ltd* (1984) 272 EG 786.
[45] *Supra* at p. 1015, CA.

tive, these breaches, as they are subsisting, will of themselves disentitle the tenant to exercise any options. In the case of rent arrears, for example, as with repairs, spent arrears of rent (ie in relation to which the landlord has no further cause of action as where he has distrained for the arrears or brought forfeiture proceedings and the tenant obtained relief) do not preclude the tenant from exercising his options.[46]

---

[46] *Bassett* v. *Whiteley* (1983) 45 P & CR 87, CA.

Appendix
PRECEDENTS

Contents

 I. *Notice under Section 146 of Law of Property Act 1925 to which Section 1 of the Leasehold Property (Repairs) Act 1938 applies*

"To CD of ... the lessee of the house buildings and premises situate etc. comprised in a lease dated ... and made ... [the reversion on which said lease is now vested in me AB] and to all others whom it may concern.

 I, AB of   HEREBY GIVE YOU NOTICE as follows:

1. By the above-mentioned lease [you the said] lessee covenanted [*set out verbatim the covenants[s] relied on*].

2. The above-mentioned covenant[s] has [have] been broken and the particular breaches which are complained of are committing or allowing the dilapidations mentioned in the Schedule hereto.

3. I require you to remedy all the aforesaid breaches [and to make compensation in money for such breaches].

4. On your failure to comply with this notice within   calendar month[s] it is my intention to [re-enter upon the premises and] claim damages for breach of the said covenant[s].

5. The lessee is entitled under the Leasehold Property (Repairs) Act, 1938, to serve on the lessor a counter-notice claiming the benefit of the said Act.

6. Such counter-notice may be served within twenty-eight days from the date of the service upon the lessee of this notice.

7. Such counter-notice must be in writing ...[6]

8. The name and address for service of the lessor is

Dated   Signed AB., lessor

---

[1] Reproduced from *Woodfall* 1 – 2604 by permission of Sweet & Maxwell Ltd.
[2] Extracts reproduced from *Precedents for the Conveyancer* Vol 1 Precedent 5 – 42 Cl 3(1) p. 2834 by permission of Sweet & Maxwell Ltd.
[3] Reproduced from *Precedents for the Conveyancer* Vol. 15 – 5 Cl 2(3) pp. 2560–2561, by permission of Sweet & Maxwell Ltd.
[4] Reproduced from Ross, Precedent P1, Cl 54, p. 284, by permission of Butterworths.
[5] Reproduced from *Precedents for the Conveyancer*, Vol. 1, 5–42, Cl 4, by permission of Sweet & Maxwell Ltd.
[6] Here the precedent describes the appropriate methods of service.

The SCHEDULE above referred to.

II. *Tenant's Covenant to Repair in Long Lease of a Flat*
"... To put keep and maintain the Flat and every part thereof in good and substantial repair order and condition generally and in particular as respects the structure decorative condition ... to keep and maintain in such state of repair order and condition all floors joists walls pipes drains conduits wires and cables and [all foundations land boundaries and fences] [stairs and staircases] [stairs and staircases roofs and roof rafters] as form part of the Flat ..."

III. *Tenant's Covenant to Repair in Short Lease of a Flat*
"To keep the interior of the premises including the fixtures and fittings thereof in good tenantable repair and condition both as respects fabric and decoration and in such repair and condition to deliver up the same together with all fixtures and fittings at the expiration of the tenancy ..."

IV. *Tenant's Covenant to Repair in a Commercial Lease*
"To repair and keep in repair [and where necessary to rebuild] the Premises (damage caused by an Insured Risk excepted other than where the insurance monies are irrecoverable in consequence of any act or default of the Tenant ...) and to replace from time to time the Landlord's fixtures and appurtenances in the Premises which may be or become beyond repair at any time during or at the expiration of the Term."

V. *Covenant to Pay Landlord's Costs where Landlord Enters and Repairs*
"If at any time ... the Lessee shall fail to observe perform or fulfil any of the covenants to repair on the part of the Lessee herein contained and if the [Lessor] ... shall serve a notice in writing upon the Lessee specifying the failure or failures and requiring them to be made good within a period of not less than two months from the date of service of the notice and the Lessee shall fail to make good such failure or failures in all substantial respects then in any such case and as often as the same shall happen ... it shall be lawful for the [Lessor] ... with or without workmen or others ... (a) to enter upon the [premises] and to execute and do such work or acts ... as may be necessary and proper for repairing the same in accordance with the covenants herein contained and (b) to recover all sums of money reasonably expended ..."

INDEX

A

R